From the
Tricontinental
to the Global South

Anne
Garland
Mahler

FROM THE
TRICONTINENTAL
TO THE GLOBAL SOUTH

Race, Radicalism, and Transnational Solidarity

DUKE UNIVERSITY PRESS *Durham and London* 2018

© 2018 DUKE UNIVERSITY PRESS
All rights reserved
Printed in the United States of America on
acid-free paper ∞
Designed by Matthew Tauch
Typeset in Minion Pro by Westchester Publishing Services

Library of Congress Cataloging-in-Publication Data
Names: Mahler, Anne Garland, [date] author.
Title: From the Tricontinental to the global South : race,
radicalism, and transnational solidarity / Anne Garland Mahler.
Description: Durham : Duke University Press, 2018. | Includes
bibliographical references and index.
Identifiers: LCCN 2017047961 (print)
LCCN 2017052455 (ebook)
ISBN 9780822371717 (ebook)
ISBN 9780822371144 (hardcover : alk. paper)
ISBN 9780822371250 (pbk. : alk. paper)
Subjects: LCSH: OSPAAAL (Organization)—History. | Anti-
globalization movement. | Anti-racism. | Civil rights move-
ments. | Internationalism. | Anti-imperialist movements.
Classification: LCC JZ1318 (ebook) | LCC JZ1318 .M3425 2018
(print) | DDC 303.48/21724—dc23
LC record available at https://lccn.loc.gov/2017047961

Cover art: Alfredo Rostgaard, cover illustration from
Tricontinental 10 (1969). Courtesy of OSPAAAL.

CONTENTS

ACKNOWLEDGMENTS

This book is the product of many relationships, collaborations, and conversations. I am grateful to the activists and artists whose perspectives appear in these pages. I have learned a great deal from their courage and vision, and I hope that this book honors them. I thank my editor, Courtney Berger, who supported this project immediately and who has been a consistent source of encouragement and constructive critique, as well as Sandra Korn, Christi Stanforth, and the rest of the staff at Duke University Press. Special thanks to the generous anonymous readers for engaging so deeply and enthusiastically with the manuscript. An Andrew W. Mellon Fellowship through the University of Virginia College and Graduate School of Arts and Sciences' Global South Initiative allowed me the time to revise the manuscript.

My research was supported by several travel grants through the University of Arizona and Emory University. I especially benefited from the holdings in the Benson Latin American Collection at the University of Texas, Austin, where Celeste Krishna opened her home to me. In Havana, Castillo Luciano was a tremendous colleague both at the Cuban Film Institute and at the International School of Film and Television. Santiago Feliú and Lourdes Cervantes Vásquez were of great assistance at the headquarters of the Organization of Solidarity with the Peoples of Africa, Asia, and Latin America (OSPAAAL).

Thank you to Gloria Rolando and Roberto Zurbano Torres for their kindness, especially to Gloria for vouching for me with the OSPAAAL. Special thanks to Luciano, Martha Dineiro, Clara González Ruiz and Nelson Navarrete Jorrin, Ignacio Granados, and Ileana Sanz for keeping me well fed and entertained.

Collaboration with the members of the executive committee of the Modern Language Association's Global South Forum—Rosemary Jolly, Nirmala Menon, Mary Louise Pratt, Roopika Risam, and especially my frequent collaborator Magalí Armillas-Tiseyra—has been important for thinking through the stakes of this book. It was also enriched through the feedback I received through invited lectures at the Summer School in Global Studies and Critical Theory in Bologna; the History Department of the University of Texas, Austin, through its "Transnational Revolution: Tricontinentalism at Fifty" conference; the University of Illinois at Urbana-Champaign's Department of Spanish, Italian, and Portuguese; the Program in Postcolonial and Global Studies at Emory University; the University of Wisconsin–La Crosse's Institute for Latin American Studies; the Global Modernist Symposium at Ithaca College; and the Confluencenter for Creative Inquiry's Lecture Series at the University of Arizona. Many thanks to Roberto Dainotto and Paolo Capuzzo, Mark Atwood and Joseph Parrott, Glen Goodman and Eduardo Ledesma, Deepika Bahri and Abdul JanMohamed, Omar Granados, Chris Holmes and Jennifer Spitzer, Magalí Armillas-Tiseyra and Jonathan P. Eburne, and Javier Durán for these invitations.

A panel on Tricontinentalism for the 2015 Latin American Studies Association convention in Puerto Rico, organized with Stephen Henighan, Lanie Millar, and Sarah Seidman, came at a crucial moment during the development of this project. An exhibit on Cuban poster art organized with Lincoln Cushing provided a creative way to use this work to reach a broader community. I am especially thankful to Lincoln for providing permissions on poster images and for being a wonderful colleague in general. The opportunity to contribute to Kerry Bystrom and Joseph Slaughter's edited volume, *The Global South Atlantic*, was key in developing the core ideas of the introduction. The anonymous readers for that volume and for articles in *Latin American Research Review*, *Small Axe: A Caribbean Journal of Criticism*, and *The Oxford Bibliographies in Literary and Critical Theory*, provided invaluable references and suggestions for revision that helped shape my thinking. Finally, I have been motivated by the support and collaboration of Magalí, Leigh Anne Duck, the members of the advisory editorial board, and the authors for *Global South Studies: A Collective Publication with The Global South*.

This study began in an early graduate school seminar with my dissertation advisor Dierdra Reber in the Department of Spanish and Portuguese at Emory University. Dierdra greatly influenced this study, and she and my department were overwhelmingly supportive throughout the early phases of my writing. The manuscript was further developed through coursework and meaningful relationships with faculty at Emory University, especially with Valérie Loichot and Mark A. Sanders, as well as with Karen Stolley and Donald Tuten, all of whom continue to be valued mentors. I also benefited from exchanges with Robin Clarke, Leroy Davis, Ricardo Gutiérrez-Mouat, Leslie Harris, Vialla Hartfield-Mendéz, Barbara Ladd, Phil MacLeod, and José Quiroga, among others. My doctoral student colleagues at Emory contributed many ideas that made their way into these pages, especially Nanci Buiza, Ángel Díaz, Ania Kowalik, Fernando Esquivel-Suárez, Omar Granados, Sergio Gutiérrez-Negrón, Christina León, Ricardo López, Ronald Mendoza-de Jesús, Stephanie Pridgeon, Dominick Derell Rolle, and Anastasia Valecce. Yet many of the central questions at the heart of the project began much earlier, through my work as a summer research assistant to George Reid Andrews in the Biblioteca Nacional of Montevideo, as a research fellow with the Center for Latin American Studies in Valparaíso, as a Brackenridge Summer Research Fellow, and in courses taken through the Department of Hispanic Languages and Literatures at the University of Pittsburgh, especially with Joshua K. Lund, Erin Graff Zivin, Jerome Branche, and Aníbal Pérez-Liñán. Many thanks to Pitt's Center for Latin American Studies for the opportunities, to Erin for putting me in touch with her editor, to Reid for the wonderful professional experience, and to Christine Waller Maiz for taking good care of me while in Pittsburgh. Josh especially has done much to encourage my professional advancement over the years and has become a valued collaborator. My friendship with Yvette Miller when I worked as the editorial assistant for the Latin American Literary Review Press was formative during those years.

Colleagues at the University of Arizona rallied around me as I advanced the manuscript. Thanks especially to Bram Acosta, Steph Brown, Maritza Cárdenas, Malcolm Compitello, Ana Cornide, Javier Durán, Alain-Philippe Durand, Marcelo Fajardo-Cárdenas, Isela González-Cook, Faith Harden, Anita Huizar-Hernández, Annette Joseph-Gabriel, Kaitlin Mcnally-Murphy, Judith Nantell, Scott Selisker, Miguel Simonet, and Stephanie Troutman. Marzia Milazzo was also an excellent resource during this time. A graduate seminar on "Black Politics in Cuba" and another on "The Global South Imaginary," which I had the pleasure to teach at the University of Arizona, provided a forum for working through the two final chapters, which were improved due to the energy of the students in these courses. Thanks to the following graduate and undergraduate students with whom I had the joy of working at Arizona: Katherine Anson, Dominique Cruz, Nick Havey, Louisiana Lightsey, Kaelyn Mahar, Regla Miller, María Montenegro, and Jen Piatt. Bob Kee, the people I met at the San Juan Bosco shelter, the NAACP Tucson chapter, and my BBBST "little brother" Jeremy Watson and his mother María Luna provided much light during my time in Tucson.

I joined the University of Virginia's Department of Spanish, Italian, and Portuguese as I began revisions to the book. Thank you to all my colleagues for welcoming me into their community, especially to deans Ian Baucom and Francesca Fiorani, search committee members Allison Bigelow, Ricardo Padrón, Gustavo Pellón, and Charlotte Rogers for their enthusiasm and consistent support, department chair Joel Rini for his kindness and care, Michael Gerli and David Gies for solid advice, Miguel Valladares-Llata for being an incredible resource, and Shawn Harris, Tally Sanford, and Octavia Wells for all they have done to support me. Many colleagues have provided good company throughout the transition: Andrew Anderson, Enrico Cesaretti, María Inés-Lagos, Mary Kuhn, Esther Poveda Moreno, Fernando Operé, Randolph Pope, Pamela Devries Rini, Emily Scida, David Singerman, Paula Sprague, Alison Weber, Omar Velázquez-Mendoza, among others. Mathilda Shepard was a superb graduate research assistant in the final stretch, and the students in my undergraduate course "Afro-Latinidad across the Americas" and the graduate students in my "Global South Imaginary" course inspired and challenged me. I express my deepest gratitude to the Charlottesville activist community and to Heather Heyer, as well as to Eli Carter, Steph Ceraso, and Jalane Schmidt for their unwavering friendship.

There are many scholars, artists, and activists whose work has deeply informed this book: Santiago Álvarez, Walterio Carbonell, Deborah Cohn, Alejandro de la Fuente, Johanna Fernández, Nicolás Guillén-Landrián, Michael Hardt and Antonio Negri, Alfred López, Antonio López, William Luis, David Luis-Brown, Jodi Melamed, Denise Oliver-Velez, Vijay Prashad, Julio Ramos and Dylon Robbins, Besenia Rodriguez, Mark Q. Sawyer, Robert F. Williams, Cynthia A. Young, Robert J. C. Young, Manuel Zayas, and Roberto Zurbano Torres, among many others.

To my family for their love: Dotty, Tanory, Sari, Michael, Mary Lauren, Naeem, Mariam, Eliza, Emmeline, Ed, Ruth, Lou, Phil, Karen, Ken, and Sam. To my chosen family: Emily, Celeste and Shiva, Fran, Lessie and Jim, Mimi,

Neil. And especially to my best friend and life partner, Andrew, and our little dogs, who are each twenty pounds of pure joy. Thank you for carrying me.

Edward Furman Still, my grandfather, passed as I was finishing the book. He was unable to complete his education, but he never missed an opportunity to brag about those who did. Ed (as we all called you), we saw the world very differently, but I am forever indebted to you for your critical mind and tenacity.

This book is especially dedicated to my teachers. Thank you for your patience and belief.

INTRODUCTION

When Barack Obama and Raúl Castro shook hands at the December 2013 memorial service for Nelson Mandela in Johannesburg, South Africa, the press called it "the handshake heard 'round the world."[1] Yet few could have been aware of its furthest reaching implications. The White House claimed that this gesture was unplanned, but in retrospect, it appears to have indicated a thawing of animosity between the two nations, foretelling the leaders' announcement one year later of a prisoner exchange and the restoration of full diplomatic relations. In his televised address on December 17, 2014, Obama would remind viewers that the United States had long ago restored relations with China and Vietnam and that the U.S. strategy of isolating Cuba had unequivocally failed to lead to the collapse of its communist government. It was, he put simply, "time for a new approach."[2]

The decision to renew ties between the neighboring countries was widely characterized as a final curtain call for the end of the Cold War.[3] But just as that pivotal handshake seemed to mark the end of an era, it also pointed to the continued impact of the Cold War on our contemporary moment. It was, in a sense, a recognition on Obama's part of Cuba's historic role in supporting the antiapartheid struggle in South Africa and also perhaps in supporting the very African American civil rights struggle to which Obama owed his presidency.

To not shake hands would have been a disavowal of the fact that what binds Obama and Mandela together is the legacy of a Cold War transnational struggle for racial justice in which Cuba played a central role.

From the Tricontinental to the Global South: Race, Radicalism, and Transnational Solidarity examines precisely that Cold War transnational struggle for racial justice to which the handshake alluded, arguing for its profound relevance for understanding social movements today. The promotion of a contemporary social movement was, Obama claimed, a major impetus for the decision to restore ties with Cuba. As he explained in his December 2014 statement on Cuba policy changes, "We are taking steps to increase travel, commerce, and the flow of information to and from Cuba. This is fundamentally about freedom and openness." He added, "I believe in the free flow of information. Unfortunately, our sanctions on Cuba have denied Cubans access to technology that has empowered individuals around the globe."[4] In other words, he seemed to suggest that greater access to the telecommunications system would enable Cubans to organize and—perhaps like with protests in other places—achieve the destabilization and subsequent democratization of the Cuban government that the more-than-fifty-year U.S. strategy of isolation and blockade had been unable to accomplish.[5]

While the link drawn here between access to technology and democratic freedoms is a weak one, it is apparent that contemporary capitalist globalization has created the conditions for a radical expansion in antisystemic politics. The immediacy of global communication and the increased movement of materials and peoples across geopolitical borders have allowed grassroots movements to forge alliances with struggles all over the world. In recent years, this new era of solidarity politics has taken hold of the American continent with widespread protests against neoliberal policies and economic inequality and a growing movement against state brutality toward racially oppressed peoples.

Yet despite the enthusiasm and media frenzy often generated by these so-called Twitter revolutions, there is a paradox within social movements in the Americas today. On the one hand, protests against deregulation and corporate greed within global capitalism tend to reproduce the rhetoric of multiculturalism, generating silences around racial inequities. On the other, movements organized around racial justice tend to frame violence toward racialized populations within a context that is limited to a critique of the state, sidelining a broader consideration of the intersection between racial violence and global capital flows.

This book historicizes this disjuncture between alter-globalization and racial justice discourses by looking back at a profoundly influential but largely forgotten Cold War movement called the Tricontinental.[6] This movement articulated its critique of global capitalism precisely through a focus on racial violence and inequality. Contemporary progressive social movements, this book argues, are reviving key ideological and aesthetic elements of the Tricontinental while leaving aside its primary contribution to the formation of a global struggle specifically against antiblack racism.

The Tricontinental formed in January 1966 when delegates from the liberation movements of eighty-two nations in Africa, Asia, and the Americas came together in Havana, Cuba, to form an alliance against military and economic imperialism. It marks the extension into the Americas of the well-known Afro-Asian movement begun at the 1955 Bandung Conference, a moment that serves as the political cognate for what would eventually emerge as academic postcolonial theory.[7] Through the artistically innovative and politically radical films, posters, and magazines that the Tricontinental published in English, Spanish, French, and sometimes Arabic, and distributed globally, the Tricontinental quickly became the driving force of international political radicalism and the primary engine of its cultural production around the world. While it was consistently hypocritically silent on racial inequities within Cuba, the Tricontinental played a pivotal role in generating international solidarity with the U.S. civil rights movement as well as with the antiapartheid struggle in South Africa, and its vision of global resistance was shaped by its foundations in black internationalist thought and by the close involvement of African American and Afro-Latinx activists.

From the Tricontinental to the Global South analyzes the expansive cultural production of the Tricontinental and traces the circulation and influence of its discourse in related radical texts from the Americas, including Third Cinema, Cuban revolutionary film, the Nuyorican movement, writings by Black Power and Puerto Rican Young Lords activists, as well as works from contemporary social movements such as the World Social Forum and Black Lives Matter. Through this tracing, this book identifies a set of Tricontinentalist texts, referring to any cultural product that engages explicitly with the aesthetics and especially the discourse of Tricontinentalism, meaning it reflects a deterritorialized vision of imperial power and a recognition of imperialism and racial oppression as interlinked, often using a racial signifier of color to abstractly refer to a broadly conceived transracial political collectivity. Through identifying and analyzing Tricontinentalist texts from the mid-twentieth century to the present day, this book contributes to a transnational reorientation of sites of cultural production whose analysis is often contained within the national and linguistic boundaries that traditionally determine the study of cultural production.

As a political discourse and ideology, Tricontinentalism framed its struggle through a spotlight on the Jim Crow South. In other words, Tricontinentalism portrayed the U.S. South as a microcosm of a deterritorialized empire and presented its global vision of power and resistance through the Jim Crow racial binary of white and color. Significantly, however, the racial binary through which these materials present the Tricontinental struggle is not intended to be racially deterministic such that they sometimes describe phenotypically white people who share the movement's views as "colored." This is what I call the Tricontinental's "metonymic color politics," meaning that in these materials the image of a white policeman metonymically stands in for global empire, and conversely, the image of an African American protestor signifies the Tricontinental's global and transracial resistant subjectivity. In this way, Tricontinentalist texts transform the category of color into an umbrella for a resistant politics that does not necessarily denote the race of the peoples who are included under that umbrella.

Through the destabilization of trait-based or racially essentialist requirements for inclusion within its revolutionary subjectivity, Tricontinentalism laid the groundwork for a theory of power and resistance that is resurfacing in the contemporary political imagination. Alter-globalization movements, as well as horizontalist models of cultural criticism like the Global South that have developed alongside them, are recovering the latent ideological legacy of the Tricontinental through a global concept of power and through devising revolutionary subjectivities that are unmoored from territorial, racial, or linguistic categories. However, our amnesia around the Tricontinental movement has meant that this revival is only partial. Within the alter-globalization movement in the Americas, the Tricontinental's nonracially deterministic political signifier of color has been converted into a rhetoric of color-blindness that is complicit with the neoliberal discourse of multiculturalism. Conversely, while the alter-globalization movement suffers from color-blindness, contemporary racial justice struggles on behalf of Afro-descendant populations in the Americas tend to focus on reforming the state apparatus and often do not fully address the mechanisms through which global capitalism perpetuates racial violence and racial inequity. As the Movement for Black Lives in the United States, for example, has begun to move toward a broader critique of racial capitalism and toward a transnational vision of solidarity, it too exhibits a partial revival of a largely forgotten Tricontinental past.

By pointing to these partial returns to Tricontinentalism in our contemporary moment, this book does not propose a celebratory embrace of the Tricontinental as an ideal model for political activism. As I will detail, the Tricontinental was burdened with profound inconsistencies such as its overwhelming silence on racial inequities within countries with leftist governments and its tendency to address itself to a heteronormative, masculinist subject. Rather than attempting to redeem the use value of Tricontinentalism as a political prototype, this book shines a light on the key insights to be gleaned from the study of this movement. That is, through recovering this buried history, I do not propose a return to the Tricontinental but rather intend to call contemporary solidarity politics into a deeper engagement with black internationalist thought that foregrounds the fight against racial inequities as a prerequisite to the future of transnational political resistance.

NETWORKED POLITICAL IMAGINARIES AND COLD WAR TRANSNATIONALISM

The networked character of politics today has challenged the models with which critics approach politically resistant cultural production, leading to the emergence of what I would characterize as horizontalist approaches to cultural criticism. Here I refer to two sets of overlapping critical categories. First, I refer to those that address how capitalist globalization facilitates the creation of networks among grassroots movements, yielding a new transnational political imaginary and global resistant subjectivity. This includes concepts like Arjun Appadurai's "grassroots globalization" and "globalization from below," Boaventura de Sousa Santos's "counter-hegemonic globalization," and Michael Hardt and Antonio Negri's "multitude."[8] Second, I refer to a set of horizontalist reading praxes of both contemporary and past resistant cultural production in which texts are examined in dialogue with a global network of writers and artists. In the second category, concepts like Shu-mei Shih and Françoise Lionnet's "minor transnationalism"; Monica Popescu, Cedric Tolliver, and Julie Tolliver's "alternative solidarities"; and Ngũgĩ wa Thiong'o's "reading globalectically" commonly deviate from a center-periphery model and move toward a decentered, networked model of reading antisystemic textual production. In this model, texts are examined within a transnational web of writers and artists who understand their conditions of oppression and resistance as interconnected.[9] All of these concepts describe power as unmoored from territorial boundaries and emphasize lateral dialogue and mutual identification among oppressed groups in terms transcendent of a shared experience of European colonization or of national, ethnic, and linguistic affinities. They aim to devise a "thick" globalization theory that provides an alternative to the discourse of neoliberalism by viewing the transnational experience of global capitalism from below.

Within this constellation of terms, the "Global South" has likely gained the most currency. While the Global South is often used to refer to economically disadvantaged nation-states and as a post–Cold War alternative to the term "Third World," in recent years and within a variety of fields, including literary and cultural studies, the Global South is being employed in a postnational sense to address spaces and peoples negatively impacted by capitalist globalization.[10] As a concept, the Global South captures a deterritorialized geography of capitalism's externalities and means to account for subjugated peoples within the borders of wealthier countries, such that there are Souths in the geographic North and Norths in the geographic South.[11] Through this transnational conceptualization, the Global South is emerging as a critical category that encapsulates both horizontalist approaches mentioned previously: it is used to refer to the resistant imaginary of a transnational political subject that results from a shared experience of subjugation and also to a model for the comparative study of resistant cultural production.[12]

While the Global South and similar horizontalist concepts are valuable for engaging our contemporary political imagination, their newness risks eliding the historical context from which contemporary solidarity politics have emerged, creating utopic categories that reproduce the atemporal "end of history" narrative of globalization.[13] In response, this book provides a systematic account of the cultural history of this horizontal turn in antisystemic struggles. It argues that the Global South and similar critical categories represent an attempt to recover a legacy that has been overlooked within the all-encompassing frame of postcolonial theory: the understudied yet powerfully influential Cold War ideology of Tricontinentalism.

In this sense, this book is rooted in a broader transnational turn in literary and cultural studies, joining an expansive body of interdisciplinary works in south-south comparison, world literature, global modernisms, transnational American studies, new Southern studies, and—most significantly for this book—studies of the Global South. In current scholarship on the Global South, however, our understanding of the relationship between Global South and postcolonial theory remains underdeveloped since both bodies of theory have arisen from a history of Cold War decolonization. Through tracing its roots to the Tricontinental movement, this book intends to make a unique and vital contribution to the study of the Global South as a critical concept.

Within the broader transnational turn, recent scholarship on the Cold War is exploring a more nuanced understanding of this conflict by viewing it through the experiences of marginalized nations and peoples and through histories of decolonization.[14] Although much has been written on African Americans' involvement in Cold War anticolonial activism, generally studies of decolonization have focused on post–World War II Africa and Asia, overlooking the Americas almost entirely. David Luis-Brown's *Waves of Decolonization: Discourses of Race and Hemispheric Citizenship in Cuba, Mexico, and the United States* (2008) responds to this gap by tracing anti-imperialist discourses in the Americas in the late nineteenth and early twentieth centuries that precede the decolonization of Africa and Asia. *From the Tricontinental to the Global South* builds on Luis-Brown's earlier work by examining the later transformation of these hemispheric American radicalisms from the early twentieth century into the present day.

Similarly, this study engages the extensive body of critical work on black internationalism and is influenced by scholarship on black-brown political solidarities, such as studies of exchanges between African Americans and Cubans.[15] However, I aim to provide a new perspective by analyzing the roots and development of Tricontinentalist discourse as well as its contribution to internationalist and interethnic resistant subjectivities from the 1960s to the present. Within this field, this book shares with Cynthia A. Young's *Soul Power: Culture, Radicalism, and the Making of a U.S. Third World Left* (2006) a focus on both Cold War radical cultural production and a transnational vision of revolution that was built largely through solidarity between African American and Cuban activists. Young argues that the formation of a U.S. Third World Left was inspired by two factors: first, decolonization, and especially the Cuban Revolution, and second, the print culture and media that helped to spread Third World leftist ideas around the globe.[16] However, although the legacy of the Tricontinental permeates Young's book and although she consistently recognizes Cuba as central to the dynamics she analyzes, at no point does she mention the Tricontinental as the primary infrastructure for the production of the print culture and media disseminated among that Third World Left that is the subject of her book. Thus, this study's unique attention to the cultural production of the Tricontinental illuminates an overlooked genealogy, broadens *Soul Power*'s focus on intellectuals from and within the United States, and uniquely brings this Cold War history to the present moment, providing further-reaching implications for how this history informs our contemporary political context.

Within scholarship on Third World internationalisms, black radicalism, and decolonization discourses, attention to the Tricontinental prior to this book has been conspicuously sparse, but with a few important interventions.[17] Vijay Prashad devotes a chapter of *The Darker Nations: A People's History of the Third World* (2007) to the Tricontinental, but he treats it as a single event rather than a movement. In *Postcolonialism: An Historical Introduction* (2003), Robert J. C. Young locates the beginning of an epistemology of postcolonial subjectivity in the Tricontinental and even suggests "Tricontinentalism" as a more appropriate term for postcolonialism. This book complements these studies but argues that the Tricontinental's vision of power and resistance is more akin to the horizontalist worldview encapsulated by the Global South. I suggest that the shift from Bandung's solidarity, which was based around postcolonial nation-states and a former experience of European colonialism, to the Tricontinental's more fluid notion of power and resistance is parallel to a shift currently taking place in academic scholarship from postcolonial theory to the Global South.

Moreover, I contend that Tricontinentalism constitutes a discourse that reverberates in a wide and transnational array of radical Cold War cultural production. In this sense, the understanding of Tricontinentalism put forth in this book aligns with Thea Pitman and Andy Stafford's position, expressed in the introduction to their 2009 special issue on "Transatlanticism and Tricontinentalism" in the *Journal of Transatlantic Studies*, in which they define Tricontinentalism as a "discourse and practice" whose "ethos has been taken up . . . in cultural products from across the continents involved."[18] Similarly, Besenia Rodriguez's "Beyond Nation: The Formation of a Tricontinental Discourse" (2006) describes Tricontinentalism as an "anticolonial and anti-imperial as well as anticapitalist" ideology that represents an alternative to integrationist views and to positions of black nationalism and pan-Africanism.[19] It is, she writes, "staunchly anti-essentialist and critical of cultural or biological notions of race."[20] She identifies the presence of this ideology within the writings of specific U.S. antiracist activists from the 1930s through the 1970s, such as Shirley Graham Du Bois, Grace Lee Boggs, several African American journalists who participated in the Fair Play for Cuba Committee in the early 1960s, and the Black Panther Party founder, Huey P. Newton.[21] Rodriguez's understanding of Tricontinentalism, especially her analysis of its anti-essentialist leanings and its circulation among black internationalist intellectuals, has profoundly influenced my own. However, while she mentions the 1966 Havana Tricontinental Conference as an important moment for Tricontinentalism, her study does not include any discussion of the Tricontinental organization itself or of its prolific cultural production. For this reason, her definition of its discourse remains at times undefined, collapsing, for example, the Bandung moment with that of the Tricontinental.

Whereas Pitman and Stafford, Rodriguez, and Young suggest Tricontinentalism as an ideology and discourse devised through a transnational dialogic exchange, which is the notion that I take up here as well, both Sarah Seidman and John A. Gronbeck-Tedesco take a different approach. Seidman's comprehensive study of the relations between African American activists and the Cuban Revolution in "Venceremos Means We Shall Overcome: The African American Freedom Struggle and the Cuban Revolution, 1959–79" (2013) discusses the 1966 Tricontinental Conference in detail. She argues that African American and Cuban exchanges during this period "occurred within the rubric of tricontinentalism," an ideology that she describes as emphasizing "the unity of Latin America, Asia and Africa specifically against Western imperialism, colonialism, racism, and capitalism," but which she characterizes as an ideology belonging to and devised by the Cuban state.[22] Although Seidman recognizes the role of Tricontinental posters well into the 1970s in African American and Cuban political interchanges, as well as the influence of Tricontinentalist ideology on Cuba's involvement in the Angolan Civil War from 1975 to 1990, she suggests Tricontinentalism as a historical moment contained to the short period between 1966 and 1968, peaking in 1967.[23] Gronbeck-Tedesco's *Cuba, the United States, and Cultures of the Transnational Left, 1930–75* (2015) similarly positions the Tricontinental as a foreign policy strategy created by the Cuban state, but he emphasizes that it inspired a "Left humanism that crossed borders" and that it was "both a cultural language and a geopolitical strategy."[24] He also dedicates a significant portion of his book to an analysis of the disconnect between Cuba's Tricontinentalist antiracist politics and its domestic myth of racial equality. Building on the foundational work of these innovative studies, but also moving in new directions, I conceive of Tricontinentalism as a transnational discourse that begins to take shape prior to the Tricontinental Conference, that circulates outside of materials produced by the Tricontinental itself, that supersedes the Cuban state, and whose influence can be seen in contemporary transnational social movements. While all of these studies are influential, I seek to expand and define more precisely the notion of Tricontinentalism that is introduced within this prior scholarship and to address its aesthetic and ideological influence on related radical intellectuals in the hemisphere.

OUTLINING THE TRICONTINENTALIST TEXT

Because the Tricontinental achieved its greatest impact through its immense propaganda apparatus, it represents, in large part, a body of cultural production. This vast array of cultural production includes *Tricontinental Bulletin* (1966–1988, 1995–), published in English, Spanish, French, and sometimes Arabic; posters that were folded up and included inside of the bulletins; *Tricontinental* magazine (1967–1990, 1995–); books and pamphlets; radio programs; and the ICAIC Latin American Newsreel produced by the Cuban Film Institute (ICAIC). These materials, which continue to be published on a much smaller scale to this day, were all produced in postrevolutionary Cuba with the financial backing and bureaucratic support of the Cuban state. However, much of the content of the articles printed in the bulletin and magazine was sent in by the various delegations, and the films and posters were often produced in dialogue with members of the particular struggles that those materials represented. In this way, the Tricontinental provided both physical and textual spaces in which diverse political groups came into contact and functioned as an ideological nerve center that simultaneously shaped and was shaped by the perspectives of its various delegations.

Through the circulation of its publications and films, and through the iconic posters for which it is now recognized, the Tricontinental created something akin to Benedict Anderson's notion of an "imagined community."[25] However, whereas Anderson traces the role of textual production in the construction of a nation-state model of collective identity, the imagined community forged among political movements around the world through the circulation of the Tricontinental's materials was more similar to a communitas, a term that I take from Christopher Lee's description of the collective spirit inspired by the Bandung moment.[26] Communitas refers to a community of feeling, an affective community of solidarity that transcends national and regional geography and whose affinities are not based on location, language, or blood.

Building on Lee's analysis of Bandung, I refer to Tricontinentalism as an early model for what I call a "trans-affective solidarity" in which the ideology of Tricontinentalism is undergirded by and produces as surplus value a transnational, translinguistic, transethnic, and transracial affective encounter. That is, the Tricontinental's ideal vision of a collective social subject is not forged through the social contract provided by the state or through a narrow definition of class or race but rather through a radical openness facilitated by affective relation. The Tricontinental envisions a political subject whose becoming rests in "making solidarity itself," to use Lauren Berlant's terms, or in forging a collectivity through the "attachment to the process of maintaining attachment" and to "the pleasure of coming together."[27] The Tricontinentalist project of generating a new transnational political subject held together through affective attachment presents itself as a rehearsal for the eventual realization of a new global social relation. The means and the ends of Tricontinentalist politics are the same: the repetitive and persistent proclaiming of affective relation and community across national, linguistic, and ethnic borders is both the political act and the ultimate aspiration of Tricontinentalism.

In this sense, although they are mutually imbricated, this book does not present the discourse and praxis of Tricontinentalism and the Cuban state's policies as necessarily one and the same. There is a tension within Tricontinental materials where, on the one hand, they represent a site of convergence for radical organizations with diverse views and, on the other, they are produced by the Cuban state and reflect the Cuban state's ideological positions. Understanding this tension is key for comprehending the progressive politics on gender and sexuality espoused in some Tricontinental materials in the midst of Cuba's so-called *quinquenio gris* (five gray years) (1971–1976), a period of repression of artistic and sexual freedoms on the island. Understanding this tension is also especially important for considering how the Castro government used Tricontinental materials to externalize its own racial divisions to the United States and South Africa while negating its presence at home.

Although Cuba's revolutionary government had a vested interest in maintaining focus on black struggles abroad and silencing discussion around racial inequity within Cuba itself, and although Tricontinental materials became a primary tool for the exercise of these duplicitous racial politics, Tricontinentalist racial discourse—which was the result of a transnational exchange of activists and intellectuals—is not exactly identical to the racial discourse of the Cuban state. Conflating the two risks flattening the multiplicity of issues and interests to which Tricontinentalism responds and eliding the central contribution of black internationalist intellectuals—including black Cuban intellectuals—to the discourse and ideology of Tricontinentalism. Rather than simplistically reducing Tricontinentalism to a propaganda tool of the Cuban state, I propose Tricontinentalism as a transnational movement that was deeply rooted in a long tradition of black internationalist thought.

Specifically, it revised a black internationalist resistant subjectivity into a global vision of subaltern resistance that is resurfacing in social movements today.

Since the Tricontinental marks the official extension of the so-called spirit of Bandung into the Americas, it points to a moment in which a diverse range of radical writers and filmmakers in the Americas began to closely engage its discourse. Works situated within the Nuyorican and Black Arts political and artistic movements, Third Cinema, and Cuban revolutionary film represent a map of closely linked loci of radical New World cultural production whose connections remain largely unexplored because of the specificities of the identity politics, geographies, and artistic media asserted in their classification and study. Scholars have discussed the exchange between writers from the Black Arts and Nuyorican movements, the political alliances between the Cuban Revolution and Black Power activists, the influence of Cuban revolutionary film on the Third Cinema movement in the United States and elsewhere, as well as the cultural production of a U.S. "Third World Left."[28] This book builds on this scholarship yet offers a new perspective by analyzing the Tricontinental's contribution to the internationalist and multiracial resistant subjectivities often envisioned in these materials. I place these intellectual, artistic, and political exchanges within a broader context, tracing the Tricontinentalist argument for a deterritorialized imperial power and equally transnational and transracial resistant politics that is woven throughout texts from these diverse movements.

The remainder of this book is organized into five chapters. The first chapter, "Beyond the Color Curtain: From the Black Atlantic to the Tricontinental," provides a long view of the Global South, a concept it discusses in further detail, by considering its roots in black internationalist political thought and specifically in the legacy of Tricontinentalism. The Tricontinental responded to prior framings of transnational anti-imperialism within the hemispheric American context: that is, the black internationalism of the 1920s to 1940s that is found in cultural movements like the Harlem Renaissance, *negrismo*, and *négritude*. With the U.S. expansion of the Spanish-American War and the military occupation of multiple Caribbean islands in the years during and immediately preceding the rise of these movements in the early twentieth century, Jim Crow racial politics would define foreign policy toward the millions of people of color newly brought under U.S. jurisdiction. This led to the emergence of a specific formulation of blackness in the négritude/negrismo/ New Negro movements as both the emblem of a transnational experience of imperialist exploitation as well as the symbol of anti-imperialist resistance to that exploitation.

This political signifier of blackness traveled, so to speak, to the 1955 Bandung Conference with Richard Wright, who went to Bandung from Paris where he was living and collaborating with négritude writers. In Wright's *The Colour Curtain: A Report on the Bandung Conference* (1956), he uses the term "color" to expand this use of blackness as a political signifier in order to include people of non-African ancestry but continues to maintain the racial determinism and essentialism for which these movements were criticized. The Tricontinental, in its expansion of the Bandung alliance to the Americas, attempted to push *beyond the color curtain*, meaning that the Tricontinental meant to transform the category of color into a political signifier of color that did not denote a racially deterministic signified.

While the first chapter traces the evolution of a black Atlantic resistant subjectivity into Wright's articulation of a color curtain, chapter 2, "In the Belly of the Beast: African American Civil Rights through a Tricontinental Lens," delineates how Tricontinental materials discursively separate the politicized use of color found in Wright's text from its racially deterministic content. Wright claimed that "the negro problem" was not discussed at Bandung, but as the Afro-Asian solidarity of Bandung moved into the Americas, this alliance explicitly began to reach out to African Americans.[29] This chapter analyzes the plethora of official Tricontinental cultural production on African American civil rights, including articles from *Tricontinental Bulletin* and *Tricontinental*, posters focused on the Black Panthers and African American activism, the film shorts *Now* (1965) and *El movimiento Panteras Negras* (The Black Panther movement) (1968) by the Cuban filmmaker Santiago Álvarez, and writings and speeches quoted in Tricontinental materials by the African American activists Stokely Carmichael and Robert F. Williams. Through the analysis of these texts, this chapter illuminates the central tenets of a Tricontinentalist ideology in which the Jim Crow South and African American liberation became the primary focus.

Within what I term the Tricontinental's "metonymic color politics," the Jim Crow racial divide functions as a metonym not for a global color line but for a Tricontinental power struggle in which all radical, exploited peoples, regardless of their skin color, are implicated. The Tricontinental forges its transnational, transethnic, and translinguistic solidarity through a discursive coloring of resistant peoples. With this transformation of color from a racial to a political signifier, the Tricontinental articulates its critique of a global system of imperialism through a denunciation of racial inequality but simultaneously takes a radically inclusive stance that attempts to destabilize racial essentialisms.

This global concept of power, lateral solidarity among liberation struggles, and destabilization of trait-based claims to belonging make the Tricontinental a model that anticipates and is intrinsically relevant to contemporary theories and praxes of resistance.

The Tricontinental's deterritorialized notion of empire, its privileging of African Americans as representative of the global struggle, as well as its metonymic color politics, all represent a discourse that circulates in a range of cultural production beyond official Tricontinental materials. This ideology does not originate with the 1966 Tricontinental Conference, but rather, the Tricontinental becomes an official mouthpiece for ideas that were already being exchanged among American radicals. Through an analysis of works from the Nuyorican movement by Miguel Algarín, Piri Thomas, Pedro Pietri, and Felipe Luciano; writings by a group of radical Puerto Rican and African American youth in Harlem called the Young Lords Party; and an issue of *Tricontinental Bulletin* devoted to the Young Lords, chapter 3, "The 'Colored and Oppressed' in Amerikkka: Trans-Affective Solidarity in Writings by Young Lords and Nuyoricans," demonstrates how a global vision of revolution circulated in radical writings outside the Tricontinental's own cultural production.

Through a study of the treatment of Puerto Rican and African American solidarity found in Young Lords' and closely related Nuyorican texts, this chapter examines how the Jim Crow South became the lens through which Nuyorican writers took up structural inequalities in their particular contexts as part of a larger pattern of imperial power. This position is frequently summarized in materials written by the Young Lords through their consistent spelling of America as "Amerikkka." Like in Tricontinental materials, the racial oppression of the Jim Crow South emerges as a microcosm of an unequal power structure not only in America but also metonymically around the globe. The KKK stands in for global oppressive power and African Americans epitomize for the Young Lords what they call the "colored and oppressed people" of the world, which they explicitly state does not necessarily exclude white people. Ultimately, I argue, these materials contain within them a characteristically Tricontinentalist model of trans-affective solidarity, which produces a political imaginary that is always situated in the envisaged affective traversing of borders.

At the same time that a study of Tricontinentalism in New York Puerto Rican texts provides a case study for how this discourse circulated outside of Cuba, the Tricontinental also disseminated Young Lords' writings among its international constituency. Considering the inclusion of texts by the Young

Lords within the pages of *Tricontinental Bulletin* provides a helpful lens for understanding the Tricontinental's precarious political positioning between Cuba's communist government and the diverse constituents of the alliance. Through a discussion of the Young Lords' progressive politics on gender and sexuality, this chapter outlines the tension between the increasing Sovietization of the Cuban state in the early 1970s and the Tricontinental's role as a site of convergence for radical organizations with diverse views.

Finally, within a broader discussion of Nuyorican writings, this chapter offers a sustained close reading of *Down These Mean Streets* (1967), the well-known text by Piri Thomas (the most widely read Puerto Rican writer in the United States and the first to be embraced by mainstream U.S. publishers). The inclusion of *Down These Mean Streets* in this analysis may, at first glance, seem out of place because Thomas was not affiliated with the Young Lords, and, although he influenced Nuyorican writers greatly, he was considerably older than the other writers considered in the chapter. However, the discussion of Thomas's book—especially regarding its representation of the Jim Crow South as a microcosm of global inequities, its discussion of Puerto Rican solidarity with African Americans, and the protagonist's identification with a Southern, black subjectivity—not only reveals the presence of Tricontinentalist ideology in Nuyorican writings prior to the official formation of the Tricontinental alliance but also demonstrates how the lens of Tricontinentalism changes how we read such an exhaustively studied text. While not as hard-hitting as Santiago Álvarez's newsreels or the propagandistic writings in *Tricontinental Bulletin*, Thomas's Tricontinentalist worldview as expressed in *Down These Mean Streets* is quite explicit but has consistently been overlooked in the abundant scholarship on his text. In this sense, this chapter models a Tricontinentalist reading praxis, providing an opening for future scholarship that would engage in a reorientation of movement-era texts through the transnational lens of Tricontinentalism.

The fourth chapter, "'Todos los negros y todos los blancos y todos tomamos café': Racial Politics in the 'Latin, African' Nation," examines the inherent contradiction in Cuba's primary role in producing the Tricontinental's materials through which the Cuban Revolution presented itself to the world as deeply committed to the struggle for racial equality. Cuba's Tricontinentalist support for black liberation in the sphere of international politics contradicted the Castro government's domestic racial discourse. As Mark Q. Sawyer has argued, in the domestic sphere, Cuba embraced a generic Latin American racial exceptionalism in which the seemingly inclusive concept of *mestizaje* is used to support a myth of racial democracy that veils inequalities. To this

Latin American exceptionalism, the Cuban government added a Marxist exceptionalism, in which socialist reforms are purported to have eradicated racial inequities.[30] Within a discussion of this dual racial discourse, I consider both the Cuban government's fraught relationship with African American and Afro-Cuban activists in the late 1960s and 1970s as well as how the dissonance between Cuba's domestic and internationalist racial discourses is clearly demonstrated in state rhetoric surrounding Cuba's involvement in the Angolan Civil War.

In the 1960s and 1970s, harsh condemnations of Cuba's racial politics came from African American militants who spent time in Cuba and wrote about their experiences upon leaving. At the same time, and while U.S. black radical groups like the Black Panthers faced ongoing political persecution and factionalism, Cuba was becoming further entrenched in the conflict in Angola. This contributed to a shift in Tricontinental materials in the late 1970s from a focus on the U.S. South, which was used as a microcosm for an expansive global empire characterized by racial capitalism, toward a focus on apartheid South Africa. In this process, the Tricontinentalist concept of the "South" becomes further deterritorialized and global in scope. The U.S. South, for example, is compared to South Africa, which is then compared to political relations in the Southern Cone of Latin America. In other words, a Tricontinentalist vision of the South as indexing spaces of inequity around the globe—which anticipates the contemporary usage of the term "Global South"—is even more fully articulated in Tricontinental materials in the late 1970s.

Despite the Tricontinental's focus on black struggles abroad, the immediate years following the 1966 Tricontinental Conference generally produced a textual silence on post-1959 racial inequalities on the island and was a period marked by repression toward intellectuals, including Afro-Cuban intellectuals. Despite this general climate of censorship, some Cuban writers and artists continued to produce texts that challenged the Castro government's triumphalist domestic racial discourse.

One significant example is the emergence in the mid-1960s of a loosely affiliated group of young black Cuban intellectuals and artists. Through a close reading of the work of one of these intellectuals, Nicolás Guillén Landrián— the long-censored Afro-Cuban filmmaker and the nephew of the famed poet Nicolás Guillén—this chapter considers how he used Tricontinentalism as a platform from which to launch a critique of the Cuban government's handling of domestic racial inequalities. Guillén Landrián appropriates a Tricontinentalist rhetoric as well as its newsreel aesthetic in order to expose racial discrimination and inequality within communist Cuba. In this sense, Guillén Landrián's work is a testament to an inherent contradiction and lack of self-criticism within the Tricontinental's focus on racism in the imperialist North. However, it also reveals the way in which Tricontinentalism as a discourse transcends the Cuban Revolution and could even be employed as a critique of it.

Although its materials continue to be produced today, the Tricontinental has been largely forgotten. This erasure is due to a combination of several factors, such as disillusionment with Cuba's repression of intellectual freedoms and the severe weakening of the Left in the Americas in the 1970s and 1980s. Equally significant is the way in which Cold War decolonization discourses would become preserved within the academic field of postcolonial studies, a field that has had a contentious relationship with Latin Americanism and that has tended to emphasize an experience of colonization rather than a horizontalist ideological project. In contrast, the Tricontinental was focused on global solidarity organized around ideological affinities. While it recognized similarities between experiences of oppression, the basis of its solidarity was not dependent either on those similarities or on trait-based characteristics, such as skin color or geographic location. In other words, even though Tricontinentalism has been recognized as a foundational moment for postcolonial subjectivity, the two are quite different in perspective.

Beginning in the 1990s, we witnessed a return of the Left in the Americas and, alongside it, I suggest, a return to the Tricontinental moment. With the slow recovery from the 2008 economic slump, leftist electoral politics are in crisis in the hemisphere, yet grassroots progressive social movements continue to gain ground. By suggesting that we have seen a return to the Tricontinental in these social movements, I do not mean that the Tricontinental has once again become the central voice of leftist radicalism. Rather, recent inter-American solidarity politics within the contemporary alter-globalization movement—of which the most obvious referent are the annual World Social Forums that have taken place since 2001—exhibit a revival of Tricontinentalism both in their aesthetics and ideology. Thus, the final chapter, "The (New) Global South in the Age of Global Capitalism: A Return to the Tricontinental," examines digital media from the World Social Forum, such as its "Bamako Appeal," which explicitly calls for a revival of the Tricontinental; the Occupy Wall Street movement; and the Black Lives Matter movement. It argues that, aesthetically, recent social movements draw from Tricontinentalist cultural production through the proliferation of "political remix videos," the creation of political posters that are at times direct copies of Tricontinental screenprints, and the use of "culture jamming" to subvert media culture. Similarly, contemporary concepts like the Global South that have emerged to describe the transnational imaginary of alter-globalization movements are reviving Tricontinentalism's ideological project and global concept of power and resistance.

While within the realm of Global South theory racial inequality has remained a central focus, there is currently a disconnect between theory surrounding transnational political solidarity and the reality of solidarity politics on the ground. For example, although the struggle against antiblack violence and racism is gaining visibility on the world stage, these struggles tend to be framed as critiques of the state that do not necessarily address racial violence through the lens of global capitalism. Conversely, alter-globalization movements directed against multinational financial institutions and corporations tend toward color-blind discourses of solidarity that overlook questions of race. In other words, in the contemporary revival of Tricontinentalism, the Tricontinental legacy is stripped of its most valuable contribution: its metonymic color politics, which conceived of a global, inclusionary, and nonracially deterministic resistant subjectivity but which still kept racism and the image of global capitalism as a racializing apparatus in the spotlight. In contrast to the Tricontinental, the transnational solidarity of much of alter-globalization organizing today tends to reproduce the color-blind multiculturalism of neoliberal discourse, producing silences around racial inequalities.

This sustained study of the Tricontinental provides a long view of contemporary theories and practices of horizontal resistance, offering a point of comparison from which to develop in a more critical manner. With this in mind, *From the Tricontinental to the Global South* aims to call contemporary transnational solidarity politics into a deeper engagement with black internationalist thought and suggests that the fight against racial inequities is fundamentally necessary for the formation of Global South political resistance. Many of the writers and filmmakers discussed in the pages that follow had to physically travel somewhere else—to Alabama, Havana, Harlem, and Beijing—in order to fully place the social inequities that they witnessed and experienced at home into a larger context of global systems of oppression. In this sense, Tricontinentalist writers beg Tricontinentalist readers who are as internationalist in their thinking and understanding of oppression and resistance as they are. This book represents a step toward developing a Tricontinentalist reading, one that outlines a worldview that continues to be imagined, theorized, written, and believed.

ONE

Beyond the Color Curtain

From the Black Atlantic to the Tricontinental

The cover image of the tenth issue of *Tricontinental*—with its flat, bold colors and geometric designs (fig. 1.1)—is typical of the posters, magazines, and films that the Tricontinental alliance began distributing in 1966. Through graphic art and film, Tricontinental materials often communicated complex concepts, such as inequality, racism, and economic exploitation, in simple visual terms, creating nuanced political arguments through immediate visual impact. On the cover of this January–February 1969 issue, a drawing of what could be a preschool puzzle—where the child lines up the heads, bodies, and feet for three separate figures—is used to depict three militants who stand in for the three continents of the alliance (Africa, Asia, and Latin America). An African militant in camouflage wears the body of his Latin American ally (a Che Guevara lookalike with a beard and beret) and stands with the feet of an Asian fighter wearing the signature *dép lốp* sandals of the Viet Minh. Three profoundly diverse continents, which are represented in the Tricontinental alliance through a multiplicity of militant liberation movements with varying interests and goals, are metonymically synthesized into typecast caricatures.

Despite the simplistic nature of this image, the interchangeability of the three militants' bodies communicates a shared purpose, unity, and collective political subjectivity that is much more nuanced than it would initially ap-

FIG. 1.1 *Tricontinental*, tenth issue (January–February 1969). COURTESY OSPAAAL.

pear. The vision portrayed here of an intercontinental exchange resulting in a globally unified and mutually supportive militant front against a common enemy—where any guerrilla fighter from any of the three continents could theoretically stand in for the eyes, hands, and feet of another, no matter how geographically, linguistically, or nationally distant—is a vision laden with idealism. Yet it was this far-fetched notion that drew delegates from leftist and militant movements of eighty-two nations, some with the support of their national governments and some in opposition to those governments, to the Tricontinental Conference in Havana, Cuba, from January 3 to 15, 1966.[1] Five hundred and twelve delegates from Africa, Asia, and Latin America as well as 270 more observers, including journalists, invited guests, and representatives from socialist countries, met in the Hotel Habana Libre (formerly the Havana Hilton) in the busy cultural district of Vedado.[2] The conference was historically unprecedented and drew political leaders like Chile's Salvador Allende, Uruguay's Luis Augusto Turcios Lima, and Guinea-Bissau's Amílcar Cabral, as well as celebrities like the performer Josephine Baker and the writers Elizabeth Burgos and Mario Vargas Llosa. The Tricontinental alliance against imperialism that was forged by the delegates, formally named the Organization of Solidarity with the Peoples of Africa, Asia, and Latin America (OSPAAAL), would quickly become the driving force of international political radicalism and the primary engine of its cultural production around the globe.

In the pages of the issue of *Tricontinental* mentioned earlier, we catch a glimpse of the broad range of struggles brought together through this movement. The articles contained in this issue cover politics in India, the Vietnam War, activities of the Tupamaro urban guerrilla groups in Uruguay, liberation movements in South Yemen, an interview with U.S. Black Panthers George Murray and Joudon Major Ford, a reflection by Fidel Castro on ten years of the Cuban Revolution, and an article by the U.S. socialist writer Irwin Silber on revolutionary art in the United States. On the back cover appears an iconic mother-child drawing by the Black Panther Party's Minister of Culture, Emory Douglas, in which a black woman sits on the edge of the bed in a room with peeling walls and smiles happily at her toddler, who is standing below her and holding a rifle over his shoulder.[3]

The overt presence and influence of African American intellectuals and artists are not unique to this issue of *Tricontinental*. In fact, an engagement with African American struggles formed an integral part of the Tricontinental's worldview and international appeal. The U.S. South and a Jim Crow racial binary of white and colored are consistently mobilized in Tricontinental materials as the primary lens through which to theorize a transnational empire and transracial resistant subjectivity. In a way similar to the visual language analyzed in the cover image mentioned earlier, Tricontinentalism often employs apparently simplistic racial divisions to refer to a complex and nonracially deterministic understanding of global power and resistance. In this way, Tricontinentalism intentionally deviates from presenting its political collectivity through the lens of global class struggle. Rather, it foregrounds racial struggles, and specifically the struggles of black peoples, in order to open onto a broader, transracial political subjectivity.

This issue of *Tricontinental* is just one of many visually and historically rich materials that speak to a transnational political, artistic, and intellectual exchange between and beyond the three continents that the Tricontinental alliance claimed to represent. Activists and intellectuals from across the globe contributed to the Tricontinental's large body of cultural production, but, more important, they participated in the creation of a Tricontinentalist political ideology and cultural aesthetics that they would incorporate into their local artistic and intellectual networks. For this reason, Tricontinentalism can be found in a wide range of cultural production beyond what was produced by the Tricontinental organization (OSPAAAL) itself. Its influence is clearly evident in closely related radical texts in the Americas, such as those within Third Cinema, the Nuyorican movement, and writings by Black Power activists. While the chapters that follow will be devoted to tracing this influence more fully, in general, we might consider a Tricontinentalist text to be any text that engages explicitly with the aesthetics and especially the discourse of Tricontinentalism. That is, a Tricontinentalist text is one that incorporates Tricontinentalism by reflecting a deterritorialized vision of imperial power and a recognition of imperialism and racial oppression as interlinked, and often by using a racial signifier of color to abstractly refer to a broadly conceived transracial political collectivity. In this sense, through identifying and analyzing Tricontinentalist texts, this book resituates sites of cultural production whose analysis is often constrained by the national and linguistic boundaries that have traditionally determined how texts are studied and anthologized.

According to the Tricontinental's International Preparatory Committee, the Tricontinental originated in the 1955 Afro-Asian Bandung Conference. In reality, the Tricontinental (OSPAAAL) represented an extension of the Afro-Asian Peoples' Solidarity Organization (AAPSO) into the Americas, and although the preparatory committee described the AAPSO, an alliance of seventy-five organizations founded in Cairo in 1957, as originating "in 1955 at the meeting of the heads of State in Bandung," the AAPSO is generally considered significantly more communist-aligned than the 1955 Bandung Conference.[4] Yet the Bandung and Tricontinental moments might be taken as two major cornerstones of Cold War anticolonialisms, separated by an ocean and a decade.[5] Whereas Bandung has been the subject of a plethora of studies and is frequently referenced as a foundational moment for historically influential and impactful developments like the Non-aligned Movement (NAM) and academic postcolonial theory, the Tricontinental has not fared as well.[6] The few studies on Tricontinentalism often simplistically limit it to the January 1966 conference, characterize it as a Soviet front organization, or dismiss it as a mere propaganda instrument of the Cuban state. Tricontinentalism, however, was conceived through a transnational dialogue whose discourse circulated widely outside of Cuba before and after the 1966 conference and whose origins and influences cannot solely be attributed to any one nation-state, not even Cuba or the Soviet Union. It is a key contention of this book that as Tricontinentalism represented a shift from a Bandung-era solidarity, based around postcolonial nation-states and a former experience of European colonialism, to a more fluid notion of power and resistance, Tricontinentalism largely anticipated a shift currently taking place in related theoretical approaches to transnational politics, such as the shift from postcolonial theory to the Global South.

Tricontinentalism has not only influenced theorizations of resistant political subjectivities under contemporary capitalist globalization, such as the Global South, but key aesthetic, discursive, and ideological elements of Tricontinentalism are also being manifested in present-day anticapitalist and antiracist social movements. In this regard, what has heretofore been completely overlooked in studies of Tricontinentalism is the way it represents, in large part, a response to previous efforts to combine anticapitalist and racial justice organizing in the American hemisphere. That is, Tricontinentalism sought to respond to long-standing debates within black internationalist political networks around the possibilities and limits of a transnational and transracial resistant collectivity. In contrast to a race-centered, pan-Africanist model or to the color-blind approach of communist internationalism, it aimed to articulate a critique of global capital and a vision of transracial resistance precisely through a focus on racial violence and racial inequality. Using the U.S. South and later apartheid South Africa as microcosms of global systems of inequity, Tricontinental materials posed the struggles of African Americans and of black South Africans as representative of the entirety of the Tricontinental's transracial resistance.

Ironically, the Tricontinental's international and antiracist stance would frequently be mobilized by Cuba's postrevolutionary government in order to externalize its own racial divisions to the United States and South Africa. Tricontinental materials, all produced in Havana and radically committed to black movements abroad, were consistently silent on any racial discrimination or black political organizing within communist Cuba. This inherent contradiction will be discussed more fully in later chapters, but it should be noted that although the focus on black struggles abroad and silence on racial inequity within Cuba have significant overlap with the Cuban state's racial politics, Tricontinentalist racial discourse is not identical to the racial discourse of the Cuban state. Tricontinentalism should be understood, rather, as a transnationally dialogic discourse rooted in a long tradition of black internationalist thought that at times converges with and at times deviates from the Cuban state's racial rhetoric. Specifically, it revises a black international resistant subjectivity into a global vision of subaltern resistance that is resurfacing both in contemporary social movements and in contemporary horizontalist theories of power and resistance. In this sense, looking back at a Tricontinental model of political resistance provides significant insight for understanding social movements today, and specifically, it will help us to better understand a contemporary disconnect in the American hemisphere between alterglobalization and racial justice discourses.

What remains of this chapter outlines the Tricontinental's theoretical afterlives and roots. First, I begin with its afterlives by discussing modes of analysis, specifically world-systems and postcolonial theory, which emerged out of the transnational approaches of Cold War "Third Worldist" movements. I consider the recent trend away from these prior models toward more networked, horizontalist understandings of the operation of power and political resistance within neoliberal globalization. These networked theories of power and resistance, especially the critical concept of the Global South, are recovering, I argue, key components of a long-elided Tricontinentalism.

Second, I turn to the Tricontinental's roots, providing a long view of the Global South by considering how it is based in transnational anti-imperialist solidarities that arose in response to the early twentieth-century expansion of U.S. empire and to the accompanying exportation of regimes of control from the U.S. South to a larger Caribbean plantation zone. Tricontinentalism responded to prior framings of anti-imperialism in the American hemisphere, and specifically to a formulation of blackness in the *négritude/negrismo*/New Negro movements of the 1920s to 1940s, as the emblem of both a transnational experience of imperialist exploitation and an anti-imperialist resistance to that exploitation. The political signifier of blackness conceived in these movements would travel with Richard Wright from Paris, where he was living and collaborating with négritude writers, to the 1955 Bandung Conference. Wright would use his notion of the "color curtain," from his memoir *The Colour Curtain: A Report on the Bandung Conference* (1956), to expand this use of blackness as a political signifier to include people of non-African ancestry. However, his presentation of the "color curtain" would continue to maintain the racial determinism and essentialism for which the négritude/negrismo/New Negro movements were often criticized.

Tricontinentalism, I suggest, would respond less to the realities of the Bandung moment and more to the meanings ascribed to Bandung within black internationalist networks in the American hemisphere. In this sense, the Tricontinental, in its self-described expansion of the Bandung moment into the Americas, would attempt to push *beyond the color curtain*, meaning that the Tricontinental would transform the category of color into a political signifier that does not denote a racially deterministic signified and that refers to a global and broadly inclusive resistant subjectivity that is increasingly relevant today. But in order to trace the shift from the négritude/negrismo/New Negro nexus to Wright's "color curtain" to the Tricontinental, it is first necessary to discuss how political collectivities are currently being conceived under capitalist globalization, such as in the notion of the Global South, and how these new concepts are reviving key elements of Tricontinentalism.

TRICONTINENTAL AFTERLIVES

The Post–Cold War: Power and Resistance in the Networked Society

The internationalist rhetoric of Cold War decolonization movements and "Third Worldism" is generally considered to have given rise to two pioneering modes of analysis in the Western academy—world-systems analysis and postcolonial theory—that were intended to look beyond state-centric ontologies of power and political resistance. However, in recent years, and especially since the dissolution of the Soviet Union, power and resistance are being theorized anew within light of contemporary capitalist globalization. Recent, post–Cold War network power theories are diverging from the territorialist tendencies of these prior models and are questioning world-systems and postcolonial theories' framing of contemporary forms of sovereignty as a continuation of colonial forms of domination. Although recent network power theories intentionally distance themselves from Cold War forms of analysis, they are simultaneously recovering core elements of Tricontinentalism's long-elided Cold War ideology. Specifically, Tricontinentalism anticipates three key concepts within recent theories of network power and resistance: (1) power is conceptualized as transcendent of individual nation-states, such that those located in wealthier countries also suffer the negative aspects of neoliberal globalization; (2) potential resistance to power is theorized as occurring through global, lateral networks that similarly transcend geographic, national, linguistic, or racial boundaries; and (3), since power is global, there is no outside to it and thus resistance must occur from within. Among these recent theories, the Global South especially has striking resonances with Tricontinentalism in that the "South" functions metaphorically to refer both to a global and decentralized system of inequity that affects diverse peoples across a fluid geographical space and to a transnational resistance that is unified around ideological rather than trait-based affinities.

It is well known that world-systems and postcolonial theories emerged alongside one another in the 1970s with the aim of better understanding global patterns of inequity and with the intention of drawing parallels between the economic, political, and social circumstances of vastly diverse nations within the so-called Third World. Immanuel Wallerstein's world-systems model sought to explain why capital continued to transfer to Western European countries even after their former colonies had gained independence.[7] Wallerstein conceived of a modern world-system that began in the long sixteenth century (circa 1450–1640) with the introduction of a division of labor between a skilled Western European core and an unskilled Eastern European periphery, resulting in the gradual accumulation of capital in the core. As this system expanded outward toward lower-cost pools of labor, Wallerstein claimed, core capitalist accumulation was continually reproduced, extending Europe's uneven relations out globally and generating intermediate semiperipheral nations.[8]

Although Wallerstein's paradigm depended heavily on the contributions of Latin American dependency theory, it has been criticized for being too Eurocentric and especially for failing to fully address the complexities of capital and labor relations in the colonial Americas. The Latin Americanist historian Steve J. Stern, for example, points to sixteenth-century labor in silver mines in

Bolivia and in sugar mills in Brazil and Hispaniola as case studies for how "the fundamentals of Wallerstein's interpretation are severely flawed when viewed from the American periphery."[9] Specifically, he employs these case studies to point to problems in Wallerstein's division of labor into free-wage labor in the core states of Western Europe, forced labor in the periphery, and intermediate forms such as sharecropping in the semiperiphery. Ultimately, Stern calls for a closer engagement with Latin Americanist scholars who have led the way in theorizing colonial modes of production in the Americas.

Whereas Wallerstein's work was concerned primarily with the economic continuities from the colony to the postcolony, postcolonial studies—initiated in the academy with Edward Said's *Orientalism* (1978) and solidified with the 1989 publication of Bill Ashcroft, Gareth Griffith, and Helen Tiffins's *The Empire Writes Back: Theory and Practice in Post-colonial Literatures*—sought to address the enduring cultural and social legacies of colonialism after decolonization.[10] Similar to world-systems analysis, postcolonial theory would mostly focus on the experience of European colonization in Africa and Asia, developing models that largely overlook the Latin American context.[11] The marginal position of Latin America within the majority of postcolonial studies scholarship has generated much debate around the relevance of postcolonial theory for addressing sociocultural relations following the nineteenth-century decolonization of Latin America as well as for addressing the role of U.S. expansionism in Latin America throughout the twentieth century.[12]

While a common critique of both world-systems and postcolonial theories is that they tend to elide the history and intellectual contributions of Latin America, they share another significant commonality, which has also been the subject of some criticism. That is, despite the transnational and comparatist perspective they provide, both tend to engage in what could be considered territorialist methodologies: dividing the globe geographically into centers, peripheries, and semiperipheries or—in the case of postcolonial studies—into East and West, postcolonial nations and imperial centers. In this sense, the urban theorist Neil Brenner's critique of Wallerstein's world-systems analysis could easily be addressed to postcolonial studies as well, meaning that both methodologies expand the "unit of analysis to the world scale, but . . . paradoxically continue(s) to conceive the space of the world in methodologically territorialist terms."[13] The comparative lens is global but the underlying axis of that comparison still centers around "nationally-scaled territorial economies."[14]

However, with the collapse of Soviet obstacles to capitalist expansion and the ascendancy of the neoliberal model of economic power, there has been an ongoing shift away from territorial and state-centric modes of analysis toward further deterritorializing our understanding of the operation of power and the place of sovereignty within capitalist globalization. In recent years, there is an increasingly robust body of theory that conceives of power as profoundly decentralized, operating through the overlapping realms of multiple transnational, networked actors that include not only national governments, but also the global media, the financial sector, multinational corporations, consumers, and other power brokers. Theorists like Arjun Appadurai, Jon Beasley-Murray, Manuel Castells, Alexander R. Galloway, Eugene Thacker, and David Grewal maintain that sovereignty within contemporary capitalist globalization cannot be understood through solely national, sociospatial geographies, framing contemporary sovereignty rather as distributed, immanent, networked, and supraterritorial.[15]

In an attempt to reconcile the deterritorializing impulse of capitalist globalization with the contributions of world-systems and postcolonial analyses, Latin Americanist scholars like Enrique Dussel, Aníbal Quijano, and Walter Mignolo began developing the notion of "modernity/coloniality/decoloniality" in the 1990s.[16] This body of scholarship arose largely in response to Wallerstein's blind spot toward the history of Latin America and the perceived privileging within postcolonial studies of Anglophone and Francophone contexts as well in an attempt to consider the relationship between older forms of colonial power and the post-Soviet context. In this vein, Mignolo has taken the deterritorial stance that the "classical distinction between centers and peripheries" can no longer obtain in a post–Cold War moment and that, "yesterday, the colonial difference was out there, away from the center. Today it is all over, in the peripheries of the center and in the centers of the periphery."[17]

Mignolo employs Quijano's "coloniality of power"—a mode of capitalist domination beginning with European colonization that is anchored in the articulation of the social category of race—as his model for understanding the operation of power within contemporary capitalist globalization.[18] While the Cold War ushered in a "new form of colonialism, nonterritorial . . . in which power was no longer visible and measured in territorial possessions," beneath this façade of modernity, Mignolo argues, is an underside of coloniality.[19] In other words, capitalist globalization still legitimates its dominance over peoples and spaces through colonial racial classifications, the use of institutional structures to manage those classifications, and the construction of an epistemology to naturalize those forms of domination.[20] This is why Mignolo argues that the modern world-system should be understood as a "modern/colonial world system."[21] Although this post–Cold War form of coloniality is "nonterritorial" and cannot necessarily be tied to specific nations, these theorists maintain that the mode of domination is still that of a colonial difference that was birthed through European colonial rule.

Although their vision of contemporary power is similarly not limited to territorial boundaries, network power theorists do not generally ascribe to the framework provided by the modernity/coloniality research program.[22] In contrast to the position of this body of scholarship, network power theorists acknowledge continuities but argue that sovereignty in contemporary global capitalism is fundamentally dissimilar to prior forms of domination. In Michael Hardt and Antonio Negri's well-known configuration, they argue that the immanent form of sovereignty found within network power—what they call "Empire"—is distinct from colonial forms of expansion in that "this new sovereignty does not annex or destroy the other power it faces but on the contrary opens itself to them, including them in the network."[23] Whereas the old colonial powers sought to dominate through differential classification, Empire as "a *decentered* and *deterritorializing* apparatus of rule progressively incorporates the entire global realm within its open, expanding frontiers."[24] Within network power theory, subjects are not necessarily forged through interpellation by an institution or state that would exercise coloniality of power but are individuated through their function as nodes in the network and adherence to the protocols that allow power to operate.[25]

Network power theorists have done much to help us reframe our understanding of neoliberal sovereignty. However, in moving away from theorizing contemporary power as a continuation of colonial forms of domination, network power theorists—in contrast to their decoloniality counterparts—are often silent on how processes of racialization and ongoing racial inequities operate within neoliberal globalization. This raises a central question: if contemporary power is immanent and inclusive rather than centralized and differential, why does capital continue to be unequally distributed along historically colonial, racial lines?

Building on Charles Hale's concept of "neoliberal multiculturalism," Jodi Melamed's work offers a helpful lens for understanding racialization within contemporary global capitalism.[26] Melamed defines neoliberal multiculturalism as "a market ideology turned social philosophy" that posits an equivalence between neoliberal market structuring and postracial opportunity around the globe.[27] Neoliberal globalization relies on an apparently innocuous color-blind multiculturalism to frame market ideologies of free trade, financial liberalization, and deregulation as multicultural rights. It expands through the language of an official antiracism, a language of inclusion that veils systemic inequalities and that, according to Melamed, has "disguised the reality that neoliberalism remains a form of racial capitalism."[28]

The color-blind rhetoric of neoliberal multiculturalism implies an apparent shifting of signs regarding conventional racial categories where power in the networked society is seemingly based not necessarily on physical or other historically racialized traits but on one's value to global capital and one's access to the multicultural "rights" of the free market.[29] In other words, the new racial capitalism does not necessarily embrace biological determinism and colonial theories of racial superiority but rather is founded on a "strategy of differential inclusion" into a system of control.[30] Racialized privilege is ascribed to those who adhere to the protocols of network power, or the "health regimes, acquisition of skills, development of entrepreneurial ventures, and other techniques of self-engineering and capital accumulation" that Aihwa Ong has referred to as "technologies of subjection."[31] Those whose adherence to these technologies of subjection is only partial or is somehow frustrated are ascribed with racialized stigma, such as backwardness, irrationality, monoculturalism, illegality, and violence.[32]

In sum, racialization within neoliberal multiculturalism significantly overlaps with the racial logics of earlier forms of racial capitalism and, as decoloniality theorists have argued, it is imperative that we continue to study how histories of colonization and slavery shape the present moment. However, to contend that contemporary power simply reproduces colonial models of domination risks mischaracterizing the complexity of the relationship between prior racial regimes and neoliberal network power. Although network power may operate quite differently from the biological determinism of colonial racial regimes, the brutal racial hierarchies it produces are more similar to the past than they are different. Although "traditionally recognized racial identities—black, Asian, white, Arab—occupy both sides of the privilege/stigma divide," capitalist networked society continues to be upheld through the exploitation of labor from traditionally racialized bodies, control and violence exercised over historically racialized populations, and policies that ensure capital accumulation in predominantly white and wealthy zones.[33]

This reflection on the operation of race and power in the contemporary moment brings us to the question of anticapitalist and racial justice organizing. Perhaps one of the most profound impacts of the deterritorialized nature of contemporary capitalist globalization, many have argued, is the way it creates the conditions for a newly expansive emancipatory politics. Indeed, in recent years, a wave of demonstrations against economic, political, and racial inequality has taken place in the American continent and around the world. From the *piquetero* protests in Argentina, to Occupy Wall Street, to the World Cup riots in Brazil—to name a few examples from the Americas—it would be difficult to deny that we have witnessed a new era in solidarity politics in which resistance movements increasingly view their local struggles as interconnected within a global one. This is, in fact, a central paradox of our time: the deregulation and international integration that are the hallmarks of the global financial system are also the very tools through which transnational movements of opposition to that system are formed. However, as I will discuss more fully in the final chapter of this book, alter-globalization movements—such as Occupy or the World Social Forum—have thus far tended to reproduce a rhetoric of neoliberal multiculturalism, failing to address forms of racialization both within the system they protest and within their own ranks. In turn, recent racial justice movements against antiblack racism in the American hemisphere have largely focused their efforts toward reforming the state apparatus, and a transnational critique of the role of global capital flows in systemic racial inequities within these movements is often secondary.

Despite this disjuncture between alter-globalization and racial justice organizing, the way in which contemporary capitalist globalization appears to facilitate the creation of horizontal networks among grassroots movements, yielding a new transnational political imaginary and global resistant subjectivity, has been described with varying terms in recent scholarship. New categories like subaltern cosmopolitanism, grassroots globalization, counterhegemonic globalization, alternative Southern cosmopolitanism, and the Global South have arisen as attempts to describe subaltern political collectivities not through a focus on the transnational experience and legacy of European colonization (as in postcolonial theory) but through a shared experience of the negative effects of capitalist globalization. These concepts attempt to name the networked, horizontal nature of political organizing today in which resistance emerges from within the networked capitalist society itself through the use of, for example, technologies of mass self-communication to forge relationships with allies around the globe. Among these concepts, the Global South, which I will describe more fully in the coming pages, has gained the most currency.

The "Global South" came into use in the late 1970s to refer to economically disadvantaged nation-states and as a replacement for the term "Third World."[34] It was initially conceived in territorial terms that shifted the East-West framework of a worldview based around European colonialism and Cold War decolonization to a Gramscian North-South vision of power relations in which multidirectional capital flows mostly benefit the geographic North.[35] However, as part of a larger deterritorializing turn within globalization theory, a second definition has emerged in which the Global South is no longer being used as a mere territorial designation that describes an economic divide between a geographical North and South. Rather, it is now used to address spaces and peoples negatively impacted by globalization, including within the borders of wealthier countries, such that there are Souths in the geographic North and Norths in the geographic South.[36] Much of the work on so-called Southern epistemologies, such as Jean and John L. Comaroff's *Theory from the South: Or, How Euro-America Is Evolving toward Africa* (2012) or Raewyn Connell's *Southern Theory: The Global Dynamics of Knowledge in Social Science* (2007), has conceived of the South in precisely such geographically fluid terms.[37]

Implied in the concept Global South is a Western tradition in which the "South" has long represented an internal periphery for both Europe and the United States wherein "Southern" does not only refer to a region but also to a subaltern relational position vis-à-vis a more economically vital and modern North. A major contribution to this notion of the South as a "situational location" that indexes spaces of inequity and marginalization around the globe has been forged in the work of both new Southern studies of the U.S. South and by studies of southern Europe, such as the neo-meridionalist approach to southern Italy.[38] Drawing from Antonio Gramsci's reflections on the "Southern Question," scholars have long analyzed how southern Italy and southern Europe are framed as an internal other that is a repository of a premodern European past.[39] Similarly new Southern studies scholars have considered the "imagined location" of the U.S. South within a larger global political and economic imaginary. This scholarship frequently addresses how a model of governance in the post-Reconstruction U.S. South—including racial segregation and the proletarianization of plantation agriculture—was globalized through U.S. expansionism.[40] While the Global South contains this tradition of thinking the South within the North, in which the spatial and directional notion of the South is often more relational than literal, the epithet "global" further unhinges the South from any one-to-one relation to geography.

Conceived in such terms, we might see the Global South as a kind of inter-mediary between deterritorializing and territorializing models. It is an attempt to reconcile—as theorists of uneven development like David Harvey have called for some time—the need to transcend state-centric forms of analysis with an acknowledgment of the way that contemporary global capitalism pro-duces "new, rescaled sociospatial configurations."[41] These new configurations "cannot be effectively described on the basis of purely territorialist, nation-ally scaled models" but they are still fundamentally sociospatial in nature.[42] In other words, the Global South here does not refer simplistically to the ge-ography of the Southern Hemisphere but rather to a geographically flexible, sociospatial mapping of the so-called externalities of capitalist accumulation.

Yet beyond this sociospatial definition, the Global South has also taken on a third meaning, referring to an emergent political imagination under-girding contemporary social movements that results from the recognition by the world's Souths of a shared experience of the negative effects of neoliberal globalization. For example, Alfred J. López, founding editor of the academic journal *The Global South*, describes it as the "mutual recognition among the world's subalterns of their shared conditions at the margins of the brave new neoliberal world of globalization."[43] Vijay Prashad defines it similarly but adds an implication of political action provoked by this shared consciousness: "this concatenation of protests against the theft of the commons, against the theft of human dignity and rights, against the undermining of democratic institutions and the promises of modernity. The global South is this: a world of protest, a whirlwind of creative activity."[44] This definition of the Global South as a transnational political imaginary that results from the identification of one's shared conditions with others across the globe, a recognition that produces a "world of protest," offers cultural critics a helpful lens through which to ap-proach resistant cultural production in both contemporary texts and in those past contexts that prefigure the contemporary political landscape.[45]

In this sense, the Global South—as both a theory of power and a vision of transnational political resistance—might productively be considered a direct departure from the limitations of postcolonial theory and its conceptualiza-tion of a postcolonial subjectivity.[46] As a category of political subjectivity, postcoloniality has emphasized a circumstance of former colonization, a circumstance that is generally homologized with nonwhiteness and other trait-based definitions of collectivity. Postcoloniality, with its focus on the experience of European colonization, has long been the subject of debate around its relevance to people living within Western Europe and North America and whether its attempted use in reference to Latin America is merely part and parcel of an orientalizing Western academy that forces equivalences between the nineteenth-century decolonization of Latin America and that of Africa and Asia much later. In essence, postcoloniality has not had a reach commensurate with the transcendent geocultural boundaries of globalization, and the Global South represents an attempt to provide a more useful rubric for theorizing contemporary power and resistance.

In this sense, a Global South resistant imaginary and political subjectivity do not center around a shared postcolonial condition or an experience with power that necessarily mimics earlier forms of colonialism, and they are not centered around a trait-based definition of political collectivity. The Global South and other similar concepts conceive of subaltern political collectivities not through a focus on the transnational experience and legacy of European colonization but through a shared experience of the negative effects of capitalist globalization. As the Global South takes postcolonial theory as a point of departure yet moves toward more networked understandings of power, it offers a potential framework for thinking horizontalist political resistance in ways that would address forms of racialization within neoliberal globalization. Similar to how this concept attempts to mediate between territorialist and deterritorialist models through a nonterritorial sociospatial mapping of inequity, the Global South could provide a framework for beginning to address the relationship between global capital and processes of racialization in ways that acknowledge the flexibility with which neoliberal multiculturalism navigates historical racial categories.

Whereas the Global South may be seen as the post–Cold War counterpart to postcolonial theory, it is my contention that this emergent critical category also has its origins in Cold War political thought and actually represents an attempt to recover an ideology that has been all but completely elided in postcolonial studies.[47] That ideological legacy is located in the Tricontinental and in the artistically innovative and politically radical films, posters, and magazines that it distributed globally. Whereas Robert J. C. Young locates the beginning of an epistemology of postcolonial subjectivity in the 1966 conference and even suggests "Tricontinentalism" as a more appropriate term for postcolonialism, I suggest that its vision of power and resistance is more akin to the worldview encapsulated by a concept like the Global South. Specifically, what I find significant about Tricontinentalism is the way in which, in contrast to postcoloniality's focus on formerly colonized nations, it explicitly includes those located within imperial nations into its subjectivity. In its copious materials, the Tricontinental theorizes imperialism as a global system of power affecting not only peoples in occupied territories or in regions suffering from foreign economic exploitation but also those oppressed peoples located inside the geopolitical boundaries of imperial centers. This particularly applies to African Americans in the U.S. South. According to Tricontinentalist thought, racial inequalities in the United States represent a microcosm of a transnational experience of imperialism such that the African American freedom movement is chiefly representative of the Tricontinental's global struggle.[48]

By consistently presenting the Jim Crow South as a synecdoche of global empire, the Tricontinental maintained, much like the concept of the Global South, a deterritorialized vision of imperial power. Moreover, Tricontinentalist discourse often used a racial vocabulary to mark ideological position rather than physical appearance, attributing color as a signifier of subaltern resistance to phenotypically white people who shared its views, and in this way, it sought to destabilize racially essentialist claims to belonging. It is this deterritorialization of power and destabilization of trait-based requirements for inclusion that, I argue, make the Tricontinental a model for an international political subjectivity that anticipates and is intrinsically relevant to emerging theories of transnational subaltern resistance.

In devising its political signifier of color, Tricontinentalism revises a preexisting discourse, which poses blackness as a signifier of both an experience of imperialist exploitation and anti-imperialist resistance to that exploitation, into a nonracially deterministic revolutionary subjectivity in which color is used to refer not to the color of one's skin but to an ideological position of Tricontinentalism. Tricontinentalism attempted to revise a specifically black internationalist anti-imperialist tradition that circulated on the American continent during the 1920s to 1940s through the exchange between négritude, negrismo, and the Harlem Renaissance. Although it is well known that black intellectuals like W. E. B. Du Bois, Aimé Césaire, and Richard Wright among others were integrally involved in anticolonial coalition building, Tricontinentalism does not simply reflect an engagement with a black internationalist tradition or the participation of a transatlantic black intelligentsia. Rather, in its focus on the African American freedom movement, it aims to respond to a specific dilemma within black Atlantic anti-imperialist thought in the American hemisphere leading up to this moment.[49]

In what follows, I track the Tricontinental's attempted revision of a black internationalist anti-imperialism into its vision of a global and broadly inclusive resistant subjectivity. This shift, this book argues, is foundational to contemporary horizontalist approaches, such as the Global South. Yet in order to understand how a black Atlantic anti-imperialism becomes a Tricontinental one, we must first address how the négritude/negrismo/New Negro exchange of the interwar period grew out of a context of U.S. expansionism and a growing solidarity between people of color from within the United States and those subjected to its hegemony abroad. For this reason, in the sections that follow, I trace the Tricontinental's roots in black anti-imperialism from the Cuban wars of independence and the 1898 Spanish-American War, to the pan-Africanist and communist movements that arose following the U.S. occupation of Caribbean islands in the early twentieth century, and on to black Americans' investment in Bandung-era decolonization movements. Through this tracing, this chapter will ultimately discuss how the Tricontinental proposes itself as both a resolution to key problems and debates within these prior iterations of black anti-imperialism as well as a vision for a new, nonracially deterministic subaltern resistance.

TRICONTINENTAL ROOTS

Globalizing the South in 1898

It is not coincidental that a movement such as Tricontinentalism—with its vision of a global empire and equally global political resistance—would be headquartered in the Caribbean region, or in Cuba. The U.S. intervention in the Cuban War of Independence through the 1898 Spanish-American War and the subsequent U.S. treaty with Cuba on May 22, 1903, marked, as Rachel Price has eloquently argued, "a transition from older, territorial empire to less territorial forms of economic hegemony and a more fully global capitalism."[50] In this characterization of 1898, Price builds on Carl Schmitt's understanding of 1898 as introducing "the modern form of control, whose first characteristic is renunciation of open territorial annexation of the controlled state."[51] This model of control, in contrast to earlier forms of colonial expansion, is one in which the "controlled state" maintains its territorial sovereignty but is "transformed into an empty space for socio-economic processes."[52] The post-1898 model, more focused on economic than territorial control, would inspire Vladimir Lenin's theorization of a new form of imperialism, what he called the "highest stage of capitalism," in which multinational monopolies, through the complicity of big banks and with backing by military power, eventually come to dominate the entire global market.[53]

Just as 1898 marks a hinge between previous and more "modern" forms of expansionism, it is also the fulcrum of distinct yet overlapping racial regimes of control. As was famously argued by C. Vann Woodward in *The Strange Career of Jim Crow* (1955), in the years following the 1898 Spanish-American War and the resulting Philippine-American War (1899–1902), the United States would export to prior Spanish colonies a racial regime that was initially formulated in the post-Reconstruction U.S. South. The Jim Crow laws characterizing the U.S. South since the end of Reconstruction (1877) would come to define U.S. foreign policy toward the millions of people of color now brought under U.S. jurisdiction. The United States justified the occupation of Cuba between 1898 and 1902, for example, based on a rhetoric of white superiority and the "perceived incapacity of nonwhites for self-government."[54] During this occupation, the Cuban military was racially segregated for the first time and strict restrictions were placed on Haitian and Jamaican immigration to the island.[55] This process of "globalizing the South" included not only racial segregation and strategies for black disenfranchisement but also other post-Reconstruction methods like governance from afar and commercial plantation agriculture based around vertical integration and wage labor rather than colonial-slave modes of production.[56]

As 1898 saw the overlap of U.S. and Spanish colonial racial regimes, it also represents an axis of diverse anticolonial and antiracist discourses in the American hemisphere. The difference between two of these discourses, which converge on the 1898 moment, will underlie the eventual distinction between the racial discourse of postrevolutionary Cuban nationalism and the internationalist rhetoric of Tricontinentalism. One builds on a vision of a Cuba Libre founded in raceless fraternity (such as in the writings of José Martí and Juan Gualberto Gómez) and the other is based in a black internationalism that foregrounds justice for Afro-descendant peoples but links those struggles to antiracist and anticolonial struggles around the world (such as in the work of Du Bois). The vision of raceless fraternity associated with the Cuban independence movement against Spain was the product of the movement's dependence on the participation of black Cuban soldiers and the integral connection of the independence movement with a struggle for black liberation. However, the relationship between Cuban independence and a struggle for racial justice is complex, and its pre-1898 history bears repeating.

Cuba's prolonged colonial status and late independence in comparison to the rest of Latin America was a direct result of a different Caribbean movement for black freedom, the Haitian Revolution. The collapse of slavery and colonialism in Haiti, only ninety miles from Cuban shores, quite literally produced the success of Cuba's nineteenth-century sugar industry, because sugar formerly produced in Haiti was then replaced by Cuban sugar. As Ada Ferrer writes, "Two decades after Haitian independence, Cuba had emerged as the world's largest producer of sugar and one of the greatest consumers of enslaved Africans in the nineteenth-century world."[57] Cuba's sugar boom allowed Spain to maintain its control over the island through instilling fear in white Cubans that independence would necessarily result in a race war and that the large Afro-descendant population in Cuba would reproduce another Haiti in the region.[58] This rhetoric proved highly effective, especially while slavery was still legal in Cuba, since white elite Cubans thought it better to forego independence and maintain the prosperity of the sugar industry.

The Spanish colonial regime in Cuba was deeply undermined, however, when a sugar plantation owner, Carlos Manuel de Céspedes, on October 10, 1868, recruited his slaves to join the uprising in eastern Cuba that would become known as the Ten Years' War (1868–1878). With this symbolic beginning, black participation in the first of Cuba's independence wars steadily increased as slaves fled their plantations to join the rebellion and as figures like the mixed-race Antonio Maceo rose through the rebel ranks and were recognized for military achievements. For many in favor and against Cuban independence, the anticolonial war against Spain increasingly became commingled with a war against slavery. Colonial authorities and other critics of Cuban independence would emphasize this fact, as well as the multiracial makeup of the rebel army, to argue that Cuba, if not a Spanish colony, was bound to become an African island like Haiti. Fears among white insurgents about increasing black involvement and leadership in the rebellion and the potential of Cuba becoming a black republic largely contributed to the insurgents' eventual surrender. With the 1878 Pact of Zanjón, which, significantly, Antonio Maceo refused to sign because it did not ensure the abolition of slavery, the Spanish offered amnesty to insurgents and manumission to slaves who had fought in the war in exchange for the insurgents' surrender.[59]

By freeing the sixteen thousand rebel slaves who had participated in the rebellion, the Spanish crown essentially punished all enslaved laborers who did not participate. Thus, the subsequent rebellion that broke out shortly afterward in the Guerra Chiquita (Little War) (1879–1880) would count on even more black participation and consequently less white support.[60] Despite this, the Little War achieved the abolition that the first war did not, and it was during this war that Spain finally declared the end of slavery and the beginning of a system of apprenticeship that would eventually end in 1886.

The end of slavery and the increase in Spanish migration during the fifteen years of peace that followed the Little War would help independence activists, who had seen their cause dismantled through the fear of a race war, construct a new rhetoric of independence that undermined this fear at its core.[61] During this period of peace, a racially diverse group of nationalist intellectuals— many of whom were in exile in the United States—attempted to reconceive the relationship between race and nation in Cuba, promoting racial equality as the foundation of the future Cuban nation. Building on the antiracist rhetoric of insurgents from the previous two struggles, Cuban intellectuals like Juan Gualberto Gómez, Martín Morúa Delgado, José Martí, Manuel Sanguily, and Rafael Serra y Montalvo reflected on the first two independence wars and argued that the experience of fighting alongside one another against colonialism and slavery had allowed Cubans to overcome racial divisions. Racial inequities were conflated with the island's history of Spanish colonialism, and a future independent Cuba, they claimed, would be founded on an inclusivity that transcended race.

At the height of Social Darwinist philosophy and during the so-called nadir of American race relations, in which de jure racial segregation was being enforced throughout the U.S. South, the movement's leading intellectual, José Martí, who founded the Cuban Revolutionary Party in New York in 1892, argued not only that all races were equal but also that biological races did not exist.[62] Significantly, although Martí did celebrate racial mixing within those former Spanish colonies he referred to as "nuestra América" (our America), Martí's vision of a raceless Cuban nation was not founded on the discourse of mestizaje (racial mixing) that is most frequently associated with Latin American notions of racial democracy. For Martí, Cuba's racial unity had not occurred through an idealized miscegenation but rather through the shared fraternal experiences of a multiracial army in which men fought alongside one another for a common cause.[63]

While this masculinist vision tended to ignore the role of women in the future nation, the ideal of a future multiracial Cuban citizen forged through cross-racial political alliances—rather than through a romanticized vision of racial mixing—was a truly radical concept at the turn of the twentieth century. At the same time, however, this vision of racial fraternity and equality conceived by black and white writers alike, which reconfigured the first two wars as a cleansing by fire of the racial legacies of slavery and the colonial system, was more of a goal than a reality. Indeed, this antiracist discourse often contained troubling rhetorical moves that would ironically serve to disenfranchise black Cubans in the new republic. For example, not only had the independence struggles supposedly resolved racism and racial inequity, but dwelling on racial divisions was often couched as unpatriotic because it was viewed as taking away from the cause for a raceless Cuba Libre and serving the divisive rhetoric of the Spanish Empire. Moreover, the dismissal of any possibility of race war was often constructed, as Ferrer writes, through "a powerful image of the black insurgent as militarily able but as politically subservient to white people."[64] Black *mambises* (independence fighters) were presented not as those who had attained freedom through their own violent struggle but as eternally grateful to the white insurgents who had freed them from the yokes of slavery.

The color-blind racial silencing and white savior complex inherent in much of the nationalist discourse at the heart of the new Cuban republic would later be reproduced in the rhetoric of the 1959 Cuban Revolution, which would claim that socialist reforms had resolved racial inequities once and for all and that black Cubans should be grateful to the Revolution for freeing them from the oppression of American imperialism. However, even in the more immediate context, this rhetoric had profoundly negative implications for black Cuban citizens. Although republican political leaders would insist on universal male suffrage despite American objections, the vision of racial unity and black leadership of the independence wars would pose a problem for securing American withdrawal. The United States' racial ideology posed Cubans, and especially black and mixed-race Cubans, as unfit for self-government, resulting in the solidification and expansion of a process that began toward the end of the war in which white soldiers from elite families were placed in key positions in order to step into governance under the new republic.[65]

In essence, black Cubans faced a double bind in which protests over their disempowerment—even if framed as a nationalist critique of American intervention—were silenced through the very race-blind nationalist discourse that had promised racial equity. The overlapping influence of Jim Crow racial oppression and Cuban race-blind nationalism would come to a head with the violent response to the formation in Cuba of the first black political party in the hemisphere, the Partido Independiente de Color (PIC), which was mostly made up of former black insurgents and which called for more equitable black representation in all branches of government.[66] Black mobilization in the formation of a political party revived, for the Americans and for many Cubans in both parties, the old fear of Haiti, and Cuba's race-blind nationalism was wielded to outlaw the party based on the argument that a political party organized around race was anathema to the vision of democracy under the new republic.[67] When PIC members staged an armed protest in eastern Cuba over the so-called Morúa Law, in which a black senator named Martín Morúa Delgado had introduced a bill prohibiting political parties based on race, the U.S. government became alarmed and threatened a second occupation to protect U.S. lives and properties under the Platt Amendment (1903).[68] Cuba's Liberal president, José Miguel Gómez, responded in May 1912 with ordering the massacre and mass arrest of thousands of Afro-Cubans in the Oriente Province. With the racist killing of what is estimated between two thousand and six thousand black Cubans, a Jim Crow racial regime of political and economic control had seemingly taken hold in the new Cuban republic.[69]

As these Jim Crow racial logics gained footing abroad through U.S. expansionism, the possibility for challenging its inequalities within the domestic realm would become even further out of reach for African Americans. With 1898, the U.S. North and South were united against a common enemy, and the logic of Southern Jim Crow laws were legitimized on a national scale.[70] This recognition of a tie between Jim Crow white supremacist ideology and U.S. imperial projects would inspire solidarity between African Americans and peoples directly impacted by U.S. imperial designs in the wake of the Spanish-American War. W. E. B. Du Bois famously viewed the U.S. expansionism of 1898 as a conduit to the spread of white supremacism around the world and declared at the First Pan-African Conference on July 15, 1900, in London that the defining problem of the twentieth century is that of a global color line, a racial division that he predicted would characterize global inequality for the next century.[71] As Du Bois tied the oppression of African Americans to racially oppressed peoples everywhere, he argued that overcoming the global color line would require a transnational struggle by those he called the "darker races of mankind," thus linking the rights of Afro-descendant peoples to anticolonial and racial justice struggles throughout the globe.[72]

For Du Bois, to be African American was, as he suggests twenty years later in *Darkwater* (1920), to participate in a "broader sense of humanity and world fellowship," a statement that David Luis-Brown views as Du Bois's suggestion of a black identity that "was not a racial essence but rather a political aspiration."[73] As Du Bois explained in "The Negro Problems" (1915), he viewed pan-Africanism not as a "narrow racial propaganda" but as a movement that would usher in "a unity of the working classes everywhere, a unity of the colored races, a new unity of men."[74] In essence, Du Bois's vision of pan-Africanism was not an ethnically or racially deterministic movement but rather a global unity of subjugated peoples.

Although Du Bois's notion of a transnational black identity as a political subjectivity founded on "fellowship" and solidarity with subjugated peoples everywhere emerged largely in response to U.S. intervention in Cuba and contains a similar appeal to transracial unity, Du Bois's vision is significantly distinct from the vision of racelessness conceived through the Cuban independence movement. Not only is Du Bois's vision a global rather than nationalist one, it is also based in a transracial unity that foregrounds and emphasizes the struggle of Afro-descendant peoples rather than one that forecloses race-based organizing and dismisses a focus on black political rights as divisive. This distinction is important, because it has major implications for understanding the later divergence between the Cuban Revolution's domestic racial discourse and its participation in the internationalist discourse of Tricontinentalism. Whereas a vision of a raceless Cuba Libre (and the wielding of this rhetoric to politically disempower black Cubans) would continue to shape the island's domestic racial discourse even after the 1959 Cuban Revolution, Du Bois's vision of a global color line that would engender a new global political subjectivity would undergird, I suggest, key components of the transnational négritude/negrismo/New Negro exchange and eventually that of Tricontinentalism. It is the interethnic and transnational vision that can be found in Du Bois's writings that, through the political thought of black internationalist circles in the interwar years, became a major pillar for the later emergence of Tricontinentalism.

Black Atlantic Anti-imperialism and Dixie's Travels in the Caribbean

As Du Bois's writings make clear, the U.S. expansionism of 1898 inspired solidarity between black Americans and peoples affected by U.S. imperialism abroad. However, the U.S. military occupation of multiple Caribbean islands in subsequent years—Haiti from 1915 to 1934, the Dominican Republic from 1916 to 1924, and Cuba from 1917 to 1922—would greatly enhance these connections. In many ways, these occupations furthered the U.S. takeover of the Caribbean sugar industry, continuing to export and solidify a post-

Reconstruction model of sociopolitical organization in sugar-producing countries.[75] According to Glenda Gilmore, although Jim Crow became more entrenched in the U.S. South with the Spanish-American War, it "took flight" with the U.S. occupation of Haiti in 1915.[76] In *Defying Dixie: The Radical Roots of Civil Rights, 1919–1950* (2008), Gilmore discusses how the U.S. occupation of Haiti was headed by the Secretary of the Navy Josephus Daniels, who had managed an 1898 disenfranchisement campaign against African Americans in North Carolina. Daniels put white Southerners in charge of governing Haiti, and they quickly instituted segregated facilities and impressed Haitians into forced labor. As a result, Haitian dissidents, such as the writer Jacques Roumain, reached out to black political groups in the United States. In turn, African American activists, like National Association for the Advancement of Colored People Secretary James Weldon Johnson, protested against the occupation.[77] The occupation of the only black republic in the Western Hemisphere would serve as proof for many that U.S. imperialism and Jim Crow were mutually imbricated and inextricable.

The transnational system of racial oppression fueled by U.S. expansion, which Gilmore simply calls "Dixie," would foment the development of a pan-Africanist anti-imperialism that circulated among Antillean and U.S. writers alike. During the interwar period, the Caribbean was uniquely poised, as Michelle Stephens writes, "at the intersection of the decline of the European empires after World War I and the rise of the United States as an empire in the same moment."[78] The overlap between these various imperial forms and the overlapping mechanics of racial segregation and oppression were not lost on Caribbean intellectuals. Although the legacy of European colonialism and slavery loomed large within Caribbean islands and cannot be attributed solely to U.S. involvement, the series of U.S. occupations would contribute to the common recognition of a racial hegemony that superseded national and linguistic boundaries.

It is in this context that the black artistic movements of the 1920s to 1940s—such as that found in the Harlem Renaissance, negrismo, négritude, *afrocubanismo, afroantillanismo,* and Haitian *indigénisme*—emerge. Richard L. Jackson has described the Francophone and Hispanophone Caribbean manifestations of this larger transatlantic phenomenon as the *afrocriollo* movement. Within the dialogue between the afrocriollo movement and the Harlem Renaissance, I argue, there emerges a specific formulation of blackness as a symbol of anti-imperialist resistance. This black anti-imperialism, and a transnational black resistant subjectivity that develops from it, will influence anti-imperialist discourse in the Americas and largely inform the ideology of Tricontinentalism decades later.

The afrocriollo movement, which includes negrismo in the Hispanophone Caribbean and négritude in Francophone African and Caribbean countries, was a transnational cultural and artistic movement that, while highly heterogeneous, can generally be characterized by a pan-Africanist cultural vision; an engagement with cubism, surrealism, and Harlem Renaissance writings; and a political stance of anti-imperialism. In the Hispanophone Caribbean, the backdrop for the emergence of these movements was the massive unemployment and political instability caused by the collapse of the sugar industry following the 1920 sugar crash and subsequent Wall Street Crash of 1929. The instability in the sugar industry contributed to the eruption of workers' strikes in Puerto Rico and Cuba and led to the overthrow of the dictatorship of Gerardo Machado in Cuba.[79] In this context, thus, afrocriollo writings in the Hispanophone Caribbean generally reflect strong resentment toward the United States, which, in its efforts to expand the sugar industry, forced the rapid proletarianization of farmers in the countryside as well as the mass importation of immigrant workers into sugar-producing regions, exacerbating the economic crisis for many domestic workers.[80] In Cuba, where the United States owned 82 percent of sugar plantations and up to 22 percent of national territory and could intervene militarily at any time according to the Platt Amendment, there was significant overlap between communist and anti-imperialist political groups, organized resistance to the U.S.-backed dictatorship of Gerardo Machado, and the black anti-imperialist writings of afrocriollo authors.[81]

While it is the commonalities within the afrocriollo movement that undergirded the later emergence of Tricontinentalism, there are important differences between negrismo and négritude, which were internally diverse movements and which served diverse functions in their varying contexts. For example, many negrista writers, artists, and composers, in contrast to their négritude counterparts, were not of African descent. Whereas négritude implies the radical indictment of French colonialism and the antiracist assertiveness of black writers like Aimé Césaire, Léopold Sédar Senghor, or Léon-Gontran Damas, negrismo is often associated with the gesture of European primitivism through which white writers, such as Emilio Ballagas, Alejo Carpentier, Luis Palés Matos, and composers, like Ernesto Lecuona and Gonzalo Roig, ventriloquized blackness for nationalistic purposes.[82]

Richard Jackson's grouping of both these movements under the umbrella of the larger afrocriollo movement suggests the way that many of these works propose Afro-Caribbean peoples and cultures as defenders of *lo criollo*, meaning national culture, against foreign imperialist influence and intervention.[83] The term also captures a tension within the Hispanophone Caribbean iteration of this movement in which criollo writers and artists, meaning descendants of the criollo colonial social class of locally born people of European descent, often appropriated Afro-diasporic cultural forms. Whereas afrocriollo as a term captures the various aspects of these movements, in its reference to criollo nationalism, it fails to address both its transnational elements—how these movements were concerned with cultural forms and politics beyond criollo nationalism—as well as the more militantly antiracist and black internationalist works of some artists, such as Césaire or Cuba's Nicolás Guillén, Regino Pedroso, or Marcelino Arozarena, who are included under this umbrella.

The Cuban iteration of negrismo—more frequently called afrocubanismo—sought to undermine the ideology of Anglo-American exceptionalism, through which the United States justified its continued intervention in the Cuban government and economy, by valorizing black cultural contributions to national identity and by celebrating the cultural and racial mixing that had forged the essence of *cubanidad* (Cubanness).[84] Whereas the earlier vision of a raceless Cuba Libre in the independence movements did not necessarily rest on a celebration of racial mixing, the nationalism of the early Cuban republic would frame the unity of cubanidad through a vision of a mixed-race nation. According to Darién J. Davis and Judith Michelle Williams, afrocubanistas, in contrast to négritude writers, "did not claim . . . that the African element was the center and the redemption of Caribbean culture. . . . Their agenda was to emphasize the unity of blacks and whites in the forging of the Cuban community—a community that was culturally mulatto."[85] In other words, the goals of afrocubanista and other negrista writers in their representations of black culture are generally characterized as being distinct from those of négritude writers.[86] In contrast to négritude's overt antiracism, negrista artists tended to embrace a form of multiculturalism that, in its promotion of national consolidation, romanticized racial miscegenation and celebrated nonwhite subjects while paradoxically veiling the harsh reality of racial inequalities.[87]

Some negrista artists challenged the celebratory vision of racial and cultural synthesis at the heart of this nationalist movement and pushed for a more committed effort against racism. Regino Pedroso, a Cuban poet of African and Chinese descent, writes for example in his "auto-bio-prologue" to his collection of poems *Nosotros* (Us) (1933) that his "race" is simply "human," thus resisting the notion of a national race, a Cuban race, at the heart of the conceptualization of cubanidad in this period.[88] Moreover, he writes that his "pigmentation" is "negro-amarillo. (Sin otra mezcla)" (black-yellow. [Without any other mixture]), thus destabilizing a homogeneous representation of Cubans as a mixed-race populace of partial Spanish descent.[89] On a similar note, some have considered writers such as Pedroso, Guillén, and Arozarena as négritude writers rather than grouping them with the white negrista writers of the Spanish-speaking Caribbean because their writing is viewed as more explicitly opposed to racist stereotyping.[90]

While it is important to keep the differences between negrismo and négritude in mind, afrocriollo writings in general share some important similarities that will form the roots of Tricontinentalism. First, much like Du Bois's conceptualization of black identity, afrocriollo writings generally tend to uphold blackness as both the emblem of a transnational experience of imperialist exploitation, beginning with slavery and European colonialism and continuing into twentieth-century U.S. expansionism, as well as the symbol of anti-imperialist resistance to that exploitation. For many afrocriollo writers, whether a black person was living in Cuba, Puerto Rico, Haiti, Harlem, or the U.S. South; in Martinique under French colonial rule; in the French, Portuguese, or British colonies in Africa; or in a country where slavery was abolished as early as 1791 or as late as 1880, the presence of an imperial power and the experience of racial oppression appeared to go hand in hand.

This is the awareness that sparked Aimé Césaire, in his *Notebook of a Return to the Native Land* (1939), to trace a pan-African geography of oppression, referencing the Caribbean countries of Guadeloupe and Haiti and the Southern U.S. states of Florida, Alabama, Tennessee, Georgia, and Virginia. This is also the conceptual basis from which Fernando Ortiz, in *Cuban Counterpoint: Tobacco and Sugar* (1940), presented his pan-Caribbean argument for the similarities of plantation-based economies throughout the Antilles, claiming that the plantation has led to "foreign ownership, corporate control and imperialism."[91] Phenotypic blackness, pan-African symbology, and the experience of slavery and exploitation suffered by black people were, for afrocriollo writers, the platform for resistance against the history and continued presence of white/imperial oppression. For Ortiz, this oppression was embodied in the U.S.-owned sugar plantation; for Césaire it was French colonialism that starved "the hungry Antilles."[92] Conversely, Palés Matos presented the shaking of the *mulata's* hips as a provocation against Uncle Sam, and for Alejo Carpentier the bongo in his *Ecué-Yamba-Ó* (1933) served as the mode of resistance to the pervasive Yankee invasion.[93]

This afrocriollo formation of black anti-imperialism arose directly out of the relationship between many of these writers and forms of black internationalism, such as pan-Africanism and communism. Michelle Stephens points to two pivotal historical events, World War I and the Russian Revolution of 1917, for the emergence of these interwar forms of "black transnationalism, both as a narrative imaginary and as an intellectual formation" in the early twentieth century.[94] Whereas the post–World War I League of Nations drew a sharp distinction between nations and colonies and largely configured the nation-state as white and European, black intellectuals sought out forms of political identity that were alternative to this model.[95] Much of this took the form of black nationalism, which imagined a race-based and pan-Africanist national belonging that transcended the very nation-states that had long denied citizenship and participation to black people. For example, Marcus Garvey's Universal Negro Improvement Association provided a network and transnational collective identity for Afro-descendant peoples from primarily the United States, Africa, and Latin America.[96] Similarly, the Pan-African Congresses of 1919 (Paris), 1921 (London, Brussels, and Paris), 1923 (London and Lisbon), and 1927 (New York), in which Du Bois played a central role, connected black Caribbean, African American, and African intellectuals across the Atlantic, providing a transnational space for the articulation of a global black collectivity.

Another alternative to the post–World War I nation-state model of political identity was provided by the Russian Revolution's class-based internationalism. As Stephens argues, black intellectuals traced Marxist analysis of capitalist relations back to a history of colonialism and slavery in the New World. More specifically, the Third Communist International, or Comintern, which was formed in 1919 to foment and organize an international communist movement, was pivotal both in shaping the largely Caribbean, anti-imperialist resistant subjectivity that appears in afrocriollo writings and especially in forging links between racial justice and anti-imperialist struggles in the Americas. The Comintern devised an agenda to radicalize black workers in the American continent, and in doing so, it created a Caribbean political program focused on the region's racial minorities. These overlapping communist projects to radicalize both the Caribbean region and African Americans throughout the continent would be articulated in the work of afrocriollo writers, many of whom were involved in communist organizing.

While Marx and later Lenin both drew connections between capitalistic expansion and the exploitation of black labor, an official strategy and statement on the position of Afro-descendant peoples would not be articulated until the formation of the Comintern.[97] Speeches before the Fourth World Congress of the Comintern in Moscow on November 25, 1922, by the Jamaican-American and Harlem Renaissance writer Claude McKay and the Suriname-born activist and representative of the U.S. Communist Party (cpusa) Otto Huiswoud helped to bring black American issues to the fore of communist strategy in the Americas.[98] These speeches introduced the "Thesis on the Negro Question" composed by the Negro Commission of the Comintern, which had formed in the same year. The Negro Commission's "Thesis on the Negro Question" pointed to the dependence of post–World War I capitalist accumulation on the expansion of European powers into the African continent and argued that the "Negro race" around the world was essential to the destruction of capitalist power.[99] Thus, it claimed that Moscow should do everything in its ability to help delegates of the Comintern from countries with large black populations to organize black workers and to forge alliances between black workers and the white proletariat.[100]

The speeches that introduce the "Thesis on the Negro Question" couch this endeavor in the various challenges that must be considered. In his opening statement, Huiswoud argues that the Second International (the original Socialist International founded in Paris in 1889) was primarily focused on white workers, largely side-stepping the possibility of communist organizing in the colonial world and ignoring completely "the Negro Question."[101] The Negro Question, he claims, is fundamental to "the Colonial question," or the Comintern's efforts to link freedom struggles in the colonies with the working-class struggles in the metropoles.[102] Because the Third International has posited itself as "an International of the workers of the world," it should make every effort to unite colonized and nonwhite workers to the proletarian revolution.[103] Moreover, because of their large numbers, he suggests, outreach to black Americans has enormous potential for fomenting revolt in the continent.

Huiswoud's speech carefully navigates the class before race rhetoric of the Comintern. He defines the subjugation of U.S. blacks as "fundamentally an economic problem" yet he also argues that the poor conditions of black workers are intensified by prejudice and racism on the part of the white proletariat.[104] This prejudice is not simply based on labor competition between black and white workers but is largely due to the history of slavery and the racist ideologies that have historically upheld that institution. These "psychological factors," he argues, must be taken into account in any consideration of the organization of black and white workers together in the American region.[105]

McKay's portion of the speech echoes Huiswoud's position that the Third International "stands for the emancipation of all the workers of the world regardless of race or color," and he defines black people as "the most oppressed, exploited, and suppressed section of the working class of the world," thus arguing for their central importance to the global revolution.[106] However, he delivers a more pointed critique of the Comintern's commitment to racial issues, and especially of the CPUSA, saying that "there is a great element of prejudice among the socialists and communists of America" and that in order to achieve a unity among black and white workers in the United States, the CPUSA must address head-on racism and discrimination within its own ranks.[107]

These speeches and their accompanying "Thesis on the Negro Question" trace a link between Afro-descendant peoples and other racially oppressed populations, argue for Afro-descendant peoples (especially African Americans) as vanguards in the global struggle, and call for a revolutionary strategy that would foreground the issue of racial inequality and discrimination. This rhetoric would resonate in the later 1927 Brussels World Anti-colonial Congress, which was sponsored by the Comintern and which brought together two hundred delegates from the world's colonial regions.[108] The Brussels Congress, which founded the League of Anti-imperialism, was viewed as "the first Bandung" by attendees at the 1955 Bandung Conference decades later.[109] While black representation at the Brussels Congress was sparse, the representatives included such high-profile figures as the Senegalese activist Lamine Senghor, James La Guma of the African National Congress of South Africa, and Richard B. Moore, who represented the CPUSA's American Negro Labor Congress.[110] These representatives composed the "Common Resolution on the Negro Question," and this document, along with Lamine Senghor's speech before the congress, would largely echo McKay and Huiswoud, especially emphasizing the vanguard position of black people in the anticapitalist struggle.

In the year following the Brussels Conference, during the Comintern's Sixth Congress of 1928, the Comintern began to focus on black self-determination in the United States and South Africa. This included the famous "Black Belt" thesis of the United States, which claimed that African Americans in the U.S. South should seek independence and govern themselves as a nation. This was also the moment in which the Comintern, which had largely ignored Latin America's communist parties, began to express an active interest in the region. This interest in Latin America led to the founding in 1926 of a South American Secretariat, which used its biweekly newspaper *La correspondencia sudamericana* (*South American Correspondence*) to organize the First Latin American Communist Conference—with thirty-seven delegates from fifteen countries—in Buenos Aires in June 1929.[111] In response to the debates around the "Negro Question" at the Sixth Congress in Moscow, the strategy of black self-determination became a topic of heated debate at the conference in Buenos Aires, and it was especially employed in discussions around the potential for self-determination for indigenous communities in Latin America.

The well-known Peruvian indigenista philosopher José Carlos Mariátegui was not able to attend the Buenos Aires conference, but he composed a lengthy position paper, "The Problem of Race in Latin America," to be read at the conference by his chosen representative, Dr. Hugo Pesce (the Peruvian physician who later introduced Che Guevara to Marxism while Guevara was working at Pesce's leprosarium in 1951).[112] In this paper, Mariátegui categorically rejected the belief, popular among some indigenista intellectuals at the time, that mestizaje presents a solution to inequities faced by indigenous peoples because, as some indigenistas argued, elements of indigenous racial inferiority would be erased through racial mixture. He argued that the exploitation suffered by indigenous communities was not due to any racial inferiority but was rather an economic problem and the product of a long history of colonial feudalism. For this reason, he viewed indigenous participation in the class struggle as the only path to liberation. At the same time that he expressed a strong belief in the centrality of an indigenous proletariat in a socialist revolution, he dismissed as misguided the Comintern proposal for a republic of Quechua and Aymara in the South American Andes. This deviation from Moscow created a polemic at the conference, fomenting much debate among the delegates.[113]

Although Mariátegui argued in this paper for the central importance of indigenous peoples within a larger struggle for Latin American socialism, in his rejection of the Comintern's project for indigenous nationalism and self-determination, Mariátegui went so far as to dismiss the viability of any race- or ethnicity-based organizing for indigenous communities and ended up defending a more orthodox Marxist position on class struggle than even Moscow was promoting at this moment. In these and other writings, Mariátegui has been celebrated for his innovative ideas on land reform and economic justice for indigenous communities and for theorizing a rural, peasant-based movement that, similar to Antonio Gramsci in Italy, sought to adapt Marxist theory to the concrete realities of Peru rather than to follow the Comintern's centralized attempts to export revolutionary models to contexts for which they were not appropriate.[114] However, it must also be said that Mariátegui as an indigenista intellectual was—similar to many of his negrista counterparts— not indigenous but rather speaking on behalf of indigenous peoples. As Marc Becker writes, "During the debates in Buenos Aires apparently no one considered consulting with Indians as to their views on establishing an independent native republic or even bringing them into the discussion."[115] The same can be said for much of the debate at the conference around people of African descent. This is glaringly evident in Mariátegui's comments on the subject, which repeat the contention of Mario Grazini of the Brazilian delegation that racial prejudice and discrimination in employment were not problems for Afro-Latin Americans and that, in contrast to the United States, "in Latin America, in general, the negro problem does not take on a noticeable racial character."[116] He uses this argument to further sustain that "the problem of the races" is an economic and social problem that must be combatted with class struggle.[117]

Those who spoke out most strongly against this assumption at the conference were the members of the Cuban delegation, and especially the Afro-Cuban communist Sandalio Junco. Junco argued that in Cuba, despite the state's proclamations of legal equality, black Cubans consistently faced discrimination in employment and that only certain jobs were reserved for them. Junco maintained that his authority on this subject came from his own experiences of discrimination in the workplace; the bakers' union that he directed was engaged in a fight to force bakeries to hire black Cubans.[118] He concluded by calling for everyone to struggle not only on behalf of blacks in Latin America but also for those in the United States. The white Cuban delegate Alejandro Barreiro Oliveira concurred with Junco and rejected the Brazilian Grazini's argument that antiblack prejudice only existed among the bourgeoisie and was absent among the proletariat. Communists, he argued, must work to abolish these prejudices among white workers.[119]

While there was much discussion at the conference, the delegations were not able to come to an agreement on national self-determination, leading *La correspondencia sudamericana* to publish one analysis of the problem accompanied by two potential resolution drafts to be debated among readers and further discussed at the next continental conference, an event that never took place. The published analysis argues that, despite the perspective of many communists, race is a complex and relevant problem in Latin America and that indigenous and black Latin Americans form a central base of production and are integrally important to class struggle in the region. While one resolution calls for national self-determination, the other does not advocate for national self-determination and calls on communist parties to revise their indifferent attitudes toward race in Latin America and to seek alliances with indigenous and black workers.

Despite the short-lived nature of this debate among continental Latin American communists, Hakim Adi has claimed that "the Communist International, more than any other political movement in the interwar years, emphasized the capacity of black workers for self-organization and for leadership in the struggle for black liberation globally."[120] Moreover, the Comintern's campaign on behalf of the "Scottsboro boys," the nine African American youth imprisoned in Scottsboro, Alabama, on false charges of raping two white women, would call global attention to racial injustice in the United States, helping to unite racial justice activists around the globe.[121] At the same time, although the Black Belt Thesis was significant in that it circulated among African Americans in the U.S. South, it never had much support among U.S. African American communists.[122] Similarly in Cuba, the Cuban Communist Party (PCC) was successful in mobilizing Afro-Cuban workers (especially in the sugar sector), promoting Afro-Cubans to positions of leadership, and making antiracism a central part of its platform.[123] However, the growth of communism among Afro-Cubans was somewhat undermined by the PCC's *faja negra* (literally, black belt) thesis, which envisioned a separate, self-determined nation of Afro-Cubans in the Oriente region.[124] For black Cubans who had fought to liberate Cuba from Spanish colonialism and for the founding of a new nation based in racial fraternity, black national self-determination in the eastern region hardly seemed like an adequate solution to the island's inequities.

Although the "Negro Question" and the vanguard position of black Americans in catalyzing a broader anticapitalist struggle would continue to be debated, the Comintern's focus on race in the interwar years would wane as it became more sectarian, eventually dissolving in 1943.[125] As black intellectuals from the Americas like Richard Wright, Ralph Ellison, and Harold Cruse became disillusioned with communism and the polarized political climate of the Cold War, they would find new hope in decolonization movements and in neutralism from either of the two heavyweight Cold War powers, ideals that would become embodied in the 1955 Afro-Asian Bandung Conference.[126]

The Comintern played a significant role in forging a black international, and it was also crucial in devising a regional Caribbean resistant imaginary.[127] The combination of these two Comintern projects would profoundly influence afrocriollo writers. Sandra Pujals has argued that the establishment of the Comintern's Caribbean Bureau in 1931, which was responsible for radical organizing and the fomentation of unity among the region's workers, played a pivotal role in defining the Caribbean as a region. The Comintern's definition of the Caribbean, which included the continental Central American and South American nations that border the Caribbean Sea, was based on the stated unique economic history that distinguished the Caribbean region from the rest of Latin America. This political and economic definition that the Comintern used to attempt to unify the workers of a region of such linguistic and racial diversity would help to shape a conceptualization of a shared Caribbean historical experience and the formation of a regional identity among Caribbean leftist intellectuals.

In line with its race agenda on "the Negro Question," the Comintern's Caribbean Bureau specifically focused on the radicalization and unification of the region's racial minorities. Pujals writes,

> The anti-imperialist armies in Sandino's Nicaragua for example now struggled in tandem with forces against the Juan Vicente Gómez dictatorship in Venezuela and the Gerardo Machado regime in Cuba. Even when so far apart, and despite their national particularities, these anti-imperialist legions and the movements to end dictatorships in Venezuela and Cuba also joined those who opposed the lynching of Blacks in the Southern states of the U.S. . . . and simultaneously marched along those who opposed racial discrimination of Black workers in Jamaica and Trinidad or indigenous plantation workers in El Salvador.[128]

All these individual struggles, within the rhetoric of the Comintern's Caribbean Bureau, were joined together in a regional struggle against what was simply defined as "Yankee imperialism."[129]

At the same time that the Caribbean Bureau focused on the radicalization of the region's racial minorities, much of the rhetoric around black workers in its paper *Mundo obrero* (*Workers' World*) contains a condescending tone for which many black communists would criticize the Comintern and local communist parties.[130] Moreover, the rhetoric used to forge a Caribbean political collectivity was most often based around a shared proletariat identity. In the discussion of the Scottsboro boys that appears in *Mundo obrero*, for example, national and linguistic differences are bridged through an insistence on the young men's proletarianization in which—even though they are children and not laborers—it is emphasized they are "sons of workers and farmers, sons of our class."[131] The continued focus of the Comintern on class struggle and the Comintern's inability to articulate processes of racialization in other terms were, many have argued, among its greatest limitations. It is this limited viewpoint to which, I argue, the later movement of Tricontinentalism attempts to respond by framing its global and transracial, anticapitalist project primarily through a struggle for black liberation.

Despite its limitations, the formation of the Caribbean Bureau influenced leftist Caribbean intellectuals to consider their transnational and translinguistic connections to a larger Caribbean or West Indies community. C. L. R. James's concept of a West Indian identity that emerges out of a shared experience of slavery derives directly, Pujals claims, from the Caribbean Bureau's propaganda.[132] We might also consider other afrocriollo writings as indebted to or perhaps in dialogue with the discourse of the Caribbean Bureau, such as Fernando Ortiz's analysis of the sugar plantation in *Cuban Counterpoint*, through which Ortiz develops a theory of a shared Caribbean identity and upon which Antonio Benítez-Rojo later bases *The Repeating Island: The Caribbean and the Postmodern Perspective* (1989). This pan-Caribbean identity, based on a shared economic history of the exploitation of black labor, appears as well in Nicolás Guillén's *West Indies, Ltd.* (1934) and is taken up a few years later in Césaire's *Notebook of a Return to the Native Land*. Indeed, it is well known that many afrocriollo writers were communists and involved in organizations funded by the Comintern, often under the organizing principle of anti-imperialism.[133] Many of the members of the Cuban group of intellectuals named Grupo Minorista (Minority Group)—whose magazine *Revista de avance* (*Advance* magazine) (1927–1930) was key in the popularization and dissemination of negrista texts—were involved in communist organizations, such as the Anti-imperialist League of Cuba (1925–1935) as well as the Cuban Communist Party.[134]

The emergence of the afrocriollo movement and its ties to communism coincided with the rise of the pan-African movement, and communist internationalism and pan-Africanism often overlapped and shaped one another.[135] Despite Du Bois's communist leanings, due to the predominant presence of a black elite at the four Pan-African Congresses that he organized between 1919 and 1927, these congresses tended to have a more conservative position that shied away from any discussion of anticolonial revolution.[136] In comparison to the previous four congresses, however, the Fifth Pan-African Congress, organized by George Padmore in October 1945 in Manchester, England, and which included two hundred delegates mostly from Africa and the West Indies, took a more activist approach and had the stated goal of eliminating colonialism from the African continent. This congress catalyzed the groundswell of African independence movements that would emerge over the next two decades.[137] According to Du Bois's memorandum to the United Nations following the Fifth Pan-African Congress, this Congress "helped to bring persons of Negro descent in the Americas in sympathy and co-operation with their African brethren."[138] In addition to building transatlantic ties among peoples of African descent, through releasing statements of solidarity with anticolonial struggles in India, Indonesia, and Vietnam, this conference also helped to lay the groundwork for the eventual Afro-Asian solidarity movement carried out through the 1955 Bandung Conference.[139]

Through ties to communism and pan-Africanism, afrocriollo writers participated in devising an anti-imperialist signifier of blackness that would be central to black internationalist and anti-imperialist movements moving forward. However, in order to illuminate how Tricontinentalism specifically used and attempted to transform this anti-imperialist signifier of blackness that came to characterize the afrocriollo movement, it is necessary to address a second and equally important commonality shared by afrocriollo writers, which is that they have often been criticized, despite their internationalist and interethnic leanings, for a tendency to slide into essentialist representations.

Some critics have argued that while the Francophone négritude movement sought to challenge racism, negrismo, despite its anti-imperialist vision, did little to dismantle negative stereotypes and often heralded colonialist caricatures of blackness—such as the cannibal figure—as well as other stereotypical associations with myth and lasciviousness.[140] Yet both negrista and négritude writers have been criticized, to varying degrees, for engaging what Stuart Hall has called "inferential racism," or the unquestioning inscription of racist premises into apparently naturalized representations of black subjects.[141]

This is precisely the well-known critique that Frantz Fanon would launch in his *Black Skin, White Masks* (1952) against both Aimé Césaire and Léopold Sédar Senghor's négritude as well as the writings of Langston Hughes. While Fanon recognizes the importance and value of négritude for black self-definition, he argues that it touts an essentializing representation of black culture and that the identity it fashions is antithetically dependent on a relationship to whiteness. Fanon responds to négritude's poetics by remarking:

"On the other side of the white world there lies a magical black culture. Negro sculpture! I began to blush with pride. Was this our salvation? I had rationalized the world, and the world had rejected me in the name of color prejudice. Since there was no way we could agree on the basis of reason, I resorted to irrationality."[142] Fanon claims that by rejecting rationality and embracing a "magical black culture," négritude writers claimed ownership of a world inaccessible to whites.

Fanon quotes the French philosopher Jean-Paul Sartre's *Black Orpheus* (1948), saying,

> Negritude appears as the weak stage of a dialectical progression: the theoretical and practical affirmation of white supremacy is the thesis; the position of Negritude as antithetical value is the moment of negativity. But this negative moment is not sufficient in itself and the Blacks who employ it well know it; they know that it serves to pave the way for the synthesis or the realization of the human society without race. Thus Negritude is dedicated to its own destruction, it is transition and not result, a means and not the ultimate goal.[143]

Fanon sees Sartre's intervention as grounded in a paternalistic view that reduces négritude to merely a stage. However, he does in fact agree with Sartre's critique of the antithetical value of these writings in which négritude is proposed in response to, but never achieves transcendence of, a colonial construction of whiteness. For Fanon then, négritude represents a step toward but not the ultimate end goal of what Sartre calls an eventual "realization of the human society without race."[144] Fanon concludes his *Black Skin, White Masks* with an appeal for a synthesis to this dialectic in which people move away from "the inhuman voices of their respective ancestors so that a genuine communication can be born."[145]

Despite Fanon's critique, one can find instances of négritude and negrista writings that employ internationalist models to envision a transnational and transethnic subjectivity that resists this antithetical and essentialist position. Césaire's *Notebook of a Return to the Native Land* describes his négritude, in contrast to the towers and cathedrals of the "white world," as that of "the eldest sons of the world . . . spark of the sacred fire of the world," and so plays into the notion of a magical black culture that defines itself in contrast to colonial whiteness.[146] However, Césaire also draws an equivalence between the experience of his people and that of "a jew-man . . . a Hindu-man from Calcutta" as well as the more general "famine-man, the insult-man, the torture-man you can grab anytime."[147] As Anke Birkenmaier has pointed out, these lines would reemerge in the Haitian writer Jacques Roumain's 1945 poem "Sales Nègres" (Filthy Negroes) in the lines "We're finished you'll see / our Yes Sir . . . when they order us / to machine gun our Arab brothers / in Syria / in Tunisia / in Morocco / and our white comrades on strike / starving to death / oppressed / plundered / despised like us."[148] The comparisons between diverse experiences of exploitation that are laid out in these poems—drawing links between the experiences of oppression of a white worker, a Jew, a man from Calcutta, Morocco, or Syria—would be further developed by Césaire in his *Discourse on Colonialism* (1955).[149]

Along the same lines, Pedroso's poem "Hermano negro" (Black Brother) admonishes his reader to "silence your maracas just a bit," since these are often used to exploit black culture for entertainment, calling rather to "give the world with your rebellious anguish / your human voice," a line that anticipates Fanon's call to move away from the "inhuman voices" of the past and toward "genuine communication."[150] Much like Césaire's and Roumain's transnational and transethnic visions, Pedroso writes "about the masses, the lumpenproletariat (Blacks, Chinese, Indians), all the workers of the factories, cane fields and sugar plants."[151] He dedicates his book of poems to the broadly defined "my exploited brothers" and appeals, as Miriam DeCosta-Willis describes, to "a Third-World union—a union based not necessarily on race but on the oppression experienced by all the downtrodden."[152]

Similarly, some Francophone radicals in the 1920s used the term *nègre* not only to construct an anti-imperialist solidarity among people of African descent but, as Brent Hayes Edwards writes, they broadened "the term nègre into the service of anti-imperialist alliances among what . . . Du Bois called 'the darker peoples of the world.' "[153] These moments, among others, suggest that although Tricontinentalism would reject some of the more essentialist representations of afrocriollo writings, we can also find the presence of a budding Tricontinentalism in some of these writings. The afrocriollo movement provides the foundations for an ideology that the Tricontinental would later globalize.

Fanon's critique played an important role in the Tricontinental's response to the anti-imperialism of the afrocriollo movement. As a Martinican, Fanon's participation in the Algerian struggle for independence precedes, by over a decade, Latin America's entrance into the Afro-Asian alliance and Che Guevara's guerrilla activity in the Congo. Fanon's writings, especially his theory of colonial societies and discussion of the Algerian liberation movement in *The*

Wretched of the Earth (1961), would profoundly influence the later formation of the Tricontinental. Fanon claimed that Marxist analysis must be significantly stretched when applied to colonial contexts, because the working class of colonial countries often functions as a bourgeoisie that upholds the colonial system. He privileged the militant potential of rural populations and the lumpenproletariat and claimed that unification based around racial hatred of the colonizer would only spark but could not sustain a liberation movement. All of these interventions would resonate with those activists closely familiar with the colonial and postindependence experiences of the American hemisphere, and the Tricontinental would eventually uphold Fanon as a model theorist of transnational militancy.

Since *The Wretched of the Earth* became a manifesto of global decolonization, Fanon's influence on later anti-imperialist movements is widely known. Yet what is not discussed, but what I will argue is fundamentally important for understanding the development of anti-imperialist thought in the Americas, is the way in which Tricontinentalism responds specifically to Fanon's critique of négritude. While Tricontinentalism does not go so far as proposing "the realization of the human society without race" that Sartre described, I argue that Tricontinentalism does posit itself as the synthesis to Fanon's dialectic through its attempt to revise the afrocriollo use of blackness as a signifier of anti-imperialism into a nonracially deterministic revolutionary subjectivity in which color refers to one's political stance of anti-imperialism rather than the color of one's skin.[154] In this way, Tricontinentalism attempts to destabilize the afrocriollo notion of blackness as the essentialized antithesis to the colonial construction of whiteness through outlining a new vision for global subaltern resistance. While I do not claim that Tricontinentalism actually delivers this neat synthesis, I will argue that the crux of Fanon's critique plays an important role in shaping the Tricontinental project.

From the Black Atlantic to the Color Curtain

Three years following the publication of Fanon's *Black Skin, White Masks,* in which he critiques the négritude movement, the black anti-imperialism of the afrocriollo movement traveled—so to speak—to the 1955 Bandung Conference with the African American writer and former communist Richard Wright. In his memoir, *The Colour Curtain: A Report on the Bandung Conference* (1956), Wright would document his experience traveling to Bandung, Indonesia, and witnessing this meeting of newly decolonized African and

Asian nation-states, whose participants included such figures as the conference's host, President Ahmed Sukarno of Indonesia, as well as Prime Minister Jawaharlal Nehru of India and President Gamal Abdel Nasser of Egypt.

During the early years of decolonization efforts in Africa in the late 1940s and 1950s, Wright was living in Paris, a city that since World War I had been central to the interactions among African American, Afro-Antillean and African writers who had produced the afrocriollo movement and where, following in this tradition, Wright collaborated with Aimé Césaire on the literary review *Présence Africaine* (1947–).[155] Although Wright left communism in the 1940s, he continued to remain involved in internationalist leftist and anti-imperialist politics.[156] Due to his growing interest in anticolonial movements, in 1953, Wright traveled to the Gold Coast to observe Kwame Nkrumah's leadership as he transitioned Ghana from British colonial rule to independence. Wright wrote about his experience as Nkrumah's guest in *Black Power* (1954). Shortly afterward, Wright would be one of the only people from the United States to make the trek to Indonesia to attend the 1955 Afro-Asian Bandung Conference.

Following the end of World War II, Europe had lost much of its grip over its former colonies. By the time of the Bandung Conference, U.S. communist containment policy was in full swing and there was growing discontent against Stalinism within the Eastern bloc. After gaining independence from the colonial powers, the nascent nations who participated at Bandung—which took place on April 18–24, 1955, and included representatives from twenty-nine nations that had a collective population of more than one billion—sought to ensure the maintenance of state sovereignty and noninterference amid increasing tensions among the United States, the Soviet Union, and China.[157] One of the primary underlying objectives for the conference's five sponsors (Burma, Ceylon, India, Indonesia, and Pakistan) was a strategy to reduce China's diplomatic isolation and dependence on the Soviet Union, and China's Premier Zhou Enlai used the conference as an opportunity to forge better relations with China's neighbors.[158] Some of the central concerns and debates at Bandung surrounded political and economic independence, nonviolent international relations and nuclear disarmament, principles of interstate engagement, neutralism and coexistence between countries, economic development, the elimination of all forms of racism and colonialism, and the democratization of the United Nations.[159] While the majority of the represented states were outspokenly aligned with either the Soviet Union or the United States, the conference made a point to condemn colonialism "in all its manifestations," which functioned as a condemnation of both the West and the Soviet bloc.[160]

There has been much debate around the historical significance of the Bandung meeting and whether its apparent success was more myth than reality.[161] Generally, however, the so-called Bandung spirit—which some used to refer to a method of international diplomacy and others to a "feeling" of Third World solidarity—is understood as a forerunner to both the Afro-Asian Peoples' Solidarity Organization (AAPSO), established two years later in December 1957 in Cairo, and to the NAM, which first convened in Belgrade in 1961.[162] NAM, which still exists today, would give rise to the establishment in 1964 of the Group of 77, which has since grown to 130 nations and which is the largest intergovernmental organization of developing countries within the United Nations.[163] The AAPSO, on the other hand, would eventually join with Latin America to form the OSPAAAL (Tricontinental).

According to Sohail Daulatzai's analysis of the role of Bandung in what he keenly calls "the Muslim International," this Afro-Asian conference "was arguably the most important international gathering of the century, one with incredible implications not only for the Third World, Europe, and the Cold War but also for Black peoples in the United States."[164] He cites as evidence of Bandung's impact on black Americans both Malcolm X's framing of a call to unity among black peoples within the example and legacy set by Bandung from his 1963 speech "Message to the Grassroots" as well as the Revolutionary Action Movement's use of "Bandung Humanism" as its organizing rubric in the mid-1960s.[165] Bandung's production of official statements decrying racism and colonialism influenced, many have argued, racial justice and anticolonial activists around the world.

Indeed, the year following the Bandung Conference, in September 1956, Wright participated in the First Congress of Black Writers and Artists in Paris, which was frequently described by the participants as a follow-up to Bandung and in which Césaire, Fanon, Senghor, and James Baldwin were participants.[166] According to Baldwin, who published the essay "Princes and Powers" (1957) about his participation at the conference, one of the central questions for the writers present was "Is it possible to describe as a culture what may simply be, after all, a history of oppression?"[167] The myriad responses to this question dealt with how transnational black intellectuals might articulate a common subjectivity and position that does not present itself either as a mythic return to a precolonial origin or as an antithesis to a colonialist notion of whiteness. In Césaire's speech, "Culture and Colonization" (1957), at the conference he responds to this central question with a statement that clearly evokes Fanon's call for a synthesis to the white imperialist/black anti-imperialist dialectic. Césaire states, "Today we are in cultural chaos. Our role is to say: free the demiurge. That alone can organize this chaos into a new synthesis, a synthesis that will deserve the name of culture, a synthesis that will be the reconciliation and surpassing of old and new. We are here to say and to demand: Let the peoples speak. Let the black peoples come onto the great stage of history."[168] This synthesis that will "deserve the name of culture," Césaire maintains, will eventually emerge, and the responsibility of black intellectuals in bringing this to fruition is to continue to demand black freedom.[169]

Considering Wright's participation at this conference, his interest in African decolonization movements and the Afro-Antillean circles in which he found himself in Paris, it seems logical that Wright might propose Bandung—the new movement of solidarity among decolonized peoples of diverse ethnicities and nationalities—in his Colour Curtain as a possible path for articulating the synthesis outlined by Fanon. In other words, by expanding the image of anti-imperialist resistance formulated by afrocriollo writers to people of non-African descent, Bandung could provide an outlet for destabilizing prior framings of both blackness and anti-imperialist resistance as being antithetical to colonial whiteness. Additionally, this movement might provide a middle ground between communist anticolonialism, which framed its engagement with black internationalism through the race-blind notion of the workers of the world, and the race-before-class vision of pan-Africanist movements. However, I would argue that this is not the approach that Wright takes.

With his notion of the "color curtain"—much like Du Bois's use of the "color line" to reference "the relation of the darker to the lighter races of men in Asia and Africa, in America and the islands of the sea"—Wright uses the term "color" to refer to all racialized peoples, not just those of African descent.[170] In other words, Wright's "color curtain" broadens a pan-Africanist political subjectivity to include Asian peoples represented at Bandung. However, despite this expansion from a black resistant subjectivity to a color curtain, which he uses to describe "the despised, the insulted, the hurt, the dispossessed—in short, the underdogs of the human race," he continues to maintain the antithetical discourse that was the subject of Fanon's critique.[171]

Throughout The Colour Curtain, which is composed of Wright's own reflections as well as interviews with conference delegates, Wright remarks that all "these people were ex-colonial subjects, people whom the white West called 'coloured' peoples."[172] According to Wright, this shared "coloured" identity allows him and his interviewees to mutually identify and speak frankly with one another.[173] While one of his interviewees claims that "the West calls some nations 'coloured' in order to impose a separation between the dominator and the dominated," "coloured" for Wright clearly implies not just the experience of domination or an anti-West sentiment but, throughout the text, is directly tied to racialized physical characteristics, such as skin color.[174] Wright views the colonial experience of exploitation, as well as the anti-imperialist resistance that Bandung embodies, as joining people of African descent with those of other ethnicities.

These "coloured peoples," Wright claims, became united at Bandung not necessarily around a common ideology but against a common white enemy. He writes, "They could now feel that their white enemy was far, far away. . . . Day after day dun-coloured Trotskyites consorted with dark Moslems, yellow Indo-Chinese hobnobbed with brown Indonesians, black Africans mingled with swarthy Arabs, tan Burmese associated with dark brown Hindus, dusky Nationalists palled around with yellow Communists, and Socialists talked to Buddhists."[175] Wright's "color curtain" is profoundly ethnically and ideologically diverse, but racialized physical attributes, like skin color, are central for Wright in defining who is included within the "color curtain."

At the same time that he celebrates the union of the "coloured peoples" at Bandung, Wright associates the African and Asian people with whom he comes into contact with religious fanaticism and irrationalism. He ends the book with a call for the African and Asian elite, who, he claims, have all been educated in the West, to take the lead or else the "Asian-African secular, rational attitudes will become flooded, drowned in irrational tides of racial and religious passions."[176] This position is echoed in the lecture that Wright delivered at the 1956 First Conference of Black Writers and Artists in Paris, in which he argued that "the partial overcoming of the forces of tradition and oppressive religions in Europe," through the Enlightenment, "resulted, in a round-about manner, in a partial overcoming of tradition and religion in decisive parts of Asia and Africa," or within elite circles in those continents. Because this process has only been partial, he argues, Sukarno, Nehru, and Nasser will need to use "quasi-dictatorial methods" in order to defeat "the irrational forces of racism, superstition" in their countries.[177] At the time, James Baldwin admitted to finding these comments strange and unsettling.[178] More recently, Henry Louis Gates Jr. wrote a biting critique of Wright's embrace of Western notions of rationalism and portrayal of the nonelite in Africa and Asia.[179]

In sum, even though Wright takes the opposite approach of many af-rocriollo writers in upholding rather than rejecting Western rationalism, he uncritically represents racialized peoples through the very tropes that have been used in their oppression and thus falls into the same trap that Fanon describes. With his representation of Bandung, Wright expands the afrocriollo black anti-imperialist resistance, including some of its essentializing representations, into a "color curtain." Although Wright uses "color curtain" to refer to the Afro-Asian solidarity of the Bandung Conference, we can submit the term to a deeper analysis by considering it a metaphor for a general tendency toward a flattening racial essentialism within some black Atlantic anti-imperialist thought. The color curtain, as a concept, encapsulates a political resistance of "color" that, like the iron curtain from which Wright takes its name, is overdetermined and constitutive of binary oppositions.

Tricontinentalism, I argue, represents an attempt to push *beyond the color curtain* or an attempt to move toward the synthesis for which Fanon calls. By this I do not mean that the Tricontinental responds specifically to Wright's memoir about his experience at Bandung. Also, I do not intend to collapse Wright's notion of the color curtain with the ideas expressed in the speeches and debates of the conference itself. Although Sukarno's opening address at Bandung referred to the meeting as "the first intercontinental conference of coloured peoples in the history of mankind" and many of the speeches and the Final Communiqué condemn racism, not everyone at the conference felt that what united the delegates was a race-based community.[180] As the political scientist Robert Vitalis writes, "Color was a fact for some, not for others, but for no one was it what united them. To the contrary, many rejected the idea that color mattered. They called it racialism and warned against appealing to it as a dangerous and retrograde step. Nehru, for one, detested such talk."[181] Similarly, the Turkish delegates objected to Sukarno's framing of the conference because they did not necessarily view themselves as colored, and many Indonesians, who had only recently been occupied by the Japanese military, viewed Sukarno's vision of a communion of colored peoples with much skepticism.[182]

After reading Wright's essay, "Indonesian Notebook," which later became part of *The Colour Curtain*, Wright's host in Indonesia—the novelist and newspaper editor Mochtar Lubis—wrote that Wright had seen Indonesia "through 'coloured glasses,' and he had sought behind every attitude he met colour and racial feelings."[183] The Indonesian writer, Beb Vuyk, later repeated this impression in "A Weekend with Richard Wright," in which she reflects on her experience with Wright the weekend following the Bandung Conference when Wright was the invited lecturer to the Konfrontasi Study Club, which often held lecture-discussion events at a villa in the mountains between Jakarta and Bandung. In this essay, Vuyk relates several conversations with Wright that she regards as evidence for her description of him as "color crazy."[184] Beyond these differences in perspective, Lubis explained that many of the intellectuals whom Wright met during his time in Indonesia were "amazed" to find that "Mr. Wright quotes them saying things which they never had said."[185] The inaccuracy of at least some of Wright's account is made clear in his description of the sanitary practices of Indonesians in which he claims that toilet paper is not used because of the difficulty of importing it from Europe rather than for cultural and religious reasons.[186] As the Indonesian writer Fritz Kandou pointed out, this detail, and other descriptions of Indonesian customs, is "proof that this writer's attitude is not always objective."[187] In other words, Wright's representation of the Bandung Conference in *The Colour Curtain* provides a window into the perspective of a prominent black American writer—and perhaps even of other writers within Wright's black internationalist circles—on the Bandung moment, but it certainly should not be collapsed with the conference itself.

By claiming that the Tricontinental aims to push beyond the color curtain, thus, I am not intending to confuse Wright's vision of Bandung with the actual conference nor am I arguing that the Tricontinental directly addresses Wright's text per se, but rather I suggest that the Tricontinental responds to the essentializing tendencies within some black Atlantic thought that Wright's text embodies. The Tricontinental's expansive cultural production will attempt to destabilize the black Atlantic-cum-color-curtain anti-imperialism by intentionally avoiding colonialist stereotypes of people of color and by expressing a broader revolutionary subjectivity that is explicitly inclusive of all resistant, oppressed peoples, regardless of skin color, ethnicity, or locality. It revives the Comintern's rhetoric on black liberation, which attributes a vanguard position to African Americans, but rather than the class-over-race rhetoric of the Comintern, it describes its revolutionary subjectivity through employing the category of color in a way that aims to foreground racial inequality without collapsing into racial essentialisms.

In this sense, we could see the Tricontinental as continuing the so-called spirit of Bandung, which has been described by Christopher Lee as a communitas based on political feeling and precisely not on essentialist notions of "locality or blood."[188] Although the Tricontinental movement would diverge from Bandung's nonviolence, its neutralist position, and its primary association with heads of postcolonial nation-states, it is that communitas—that political solidarity that is transcendent of ethnic or territorial affiliations—that the Tricontinental will uphold and extend into the Americas.

Significantly, the Tricontinental's expanded resistant subjectivity does not empty prior black Atlantic anti-imperialisms of their critique of racism. Rather, it articulates its global vision of power and resistance through a language that explicitly condemns racial inequality and racial violence. However, this language takes on a unique form since racial categories are sometimes used in Tricontinental materials not to refer to perceived embodied difference but rather as metonyms for the global political positions that inform the Tricontinental project. This is what, in the following chapter, I will call the Tricontinental's "metonymic color politics" in which the category of whiteness is used metonymically to refer to global empire, and color explicitly functions as a metonym for a transethnic resistant subjectivity that does not necessarily exclude phenotypically white people. In other words—in contrast to the overdetermined category of the color curtain—within the Tricontinentalist political signifier of color, color remains an umbrella for a politics of anti-imperialism but does not necessarily denote the skin color of the peoples included under that umbrella.

Considering the trajectory I have laid out above, it is not surprising that the original idea for convening a Tricontinental Conference came from yet another participant at the 1956 First International Conference of Negro Writers and Artists in Paris, the Afro-Cuban scholar Walterio Carbonell. Carbonell lived in Paris from 1953 to 1959 and was an acquaintance of Richard Wright. In a February 1960 article entitled "Lo que Bandung significó para mí" (What Bandung Meant for Me), Carbonell attributes the Bandung Conference with the beginning of his broader awareness of revolutionary movements of "pueblos árabes y negros" (Arab and black peoples).[189] He explains in this article that he read Wright's book on Bandung, which shaped his understanding of the conference, and that this motivated him to begin to think about how Latin America could begin to overcome U.S. dominance by organizing a similar conference.[190]

He started pushing for a Tricontinental Conference in 1959 during his brief period as the Cuban Revolution's ambassador to Tunisia.[191] In the December 5, 1959, issue of the Cuban newspaper *Revolución*, Carbonell explained that although the African and Asian countries that met at Bandung were now independent of the European colonial powers, they remained threatened by the "colonialismo disfrazado" (disguised colonialism) of the United States.[192] Latin America, although long independent from Spain, "is today less free than the group of Afro-Asian states."[193] Therefore, Carbonell proposes that Latin America participate in the formation of a third power bloc because "no power will be able to try to attack directly or indirectly the block of American-Afro-Asian countries, not any of the States in Solidarity from the Community of Underdeveloped Countries."[194] He claims that Cuba should take a leadership role in this global anticolonial movement, and he even proposes Havana as the location for "the next Conference of Underdeveloped Countries."[195]

While Carbonell's intervention has more to do with political strategy than an explicit aim at moving beyond a racially essentialist notion of transnational subaltern subjectivity and although Carbonell would eventually temper his support of the Castro government, his vision of Tricontinentalism would endure and would respond to the debates in which Carbonell was engaged in Paris. For example, a few months after the Tricontinental Conference, an article on Fanon appears in the December 1967 issue of *Tricontinental Bulletin*. It contains the following statement: "Certain dogmatists have dubbed Fanon a 'reformist.' Although this word carries an evil meaning, this same meaning may be turned in his favor. If Fanon did 'reform' something, it was the narrow viewpoint of post-war Afro-Asian nationalism. . . . His violence is basically the same violence that is today impelling the peoples of Africa, Asia and Latin America forward in the Tricontinental armed struggle against imperialism."[196]

Fanon's position here is characterized as reforming the "narrow viewpoint" of Afro-Asian nationalism, by which it refers to nonviolence, and pushing the anti-imperialist struggle toward the Tricontinental.[197] While this quote references Fanon's thoughts on violence and not his critique of négritude's representation of black anti-imperialism per se, I mention this article as an example of how the Tricontinental viewed itself largely in response to Fanonian thought. The Tricontinental responds not only to Fanon's call for violence but also to his critique by taking up the political signifier of blackness envisioned within the afrocriollo movement but attempting to move beyond its association with essentialist representations and racial determinism. It reframes an afrocriollo black anti-imperialism into a nonracially deterministic vision of subaltern resistance that is deeply relevant to political organzing today.

Tricontinentalism was birthed in a black internationalist intellectual exchange that began decades prior. The chapter that follows outlines the emergence of the OSPAAAL and delineates the Tricontinental's ideology, focusing especially on the exchange between African American activists and artists in the United States and the Tricontinental's cultural production. Subsequent chapters examine authors and texts together that, while often created through a shared political dialogue, have been kept apart through the classifications that have traditionally determined how scholars approach the study of cultural production. The afrocriollo movement underlies a range of hemispheric New World texts, and the texts produced out of 1960s leftist radicalism in the Americas are equally vast. I do not suggest that all such texts reflect the influence of Tricontinentalism. Rather, Tricontinentalist texts are those that engage explicitly with the rhetoric and aesthetics of the Tricontinental movement. They view imperial power as global, see imperialism and racial oppression as fundamentally interdependent, and attempt to move beyond the caricaturesque tropes of afrocriollo writings, beyond the color curtain of a racially deterministic signifier of anti-imperialism, and toward an abstract use of color to signify an ideological position of resistance to imperialist subjugation.

TWO

In the Belly of the Beast

African American Civil Rights
through a Tricontinental Lens

In the photograph that appears on the cover of the second issue of *Triconti-nental Bulletin* (fig. 2.1), a white soldier stands with his back to the camera, threatening to strike an unarmed black protestor with the butt of his rifle. The protestor, positioned below the soldier, faces the camera slightly and stands with clenched fists, looking ready to fight. This image is one of hundreds like it that the Tricontinental would disseminate around the world. It provokes identification and solidarity with the man whose face the viewer can clearly see, as well as dissociation from the soldier whose back is turned away from the viewer.

The photograph, taken by the journalist Juan Pérez Terrero, captures a confrontation between an unarmed Dominican citizen named Jacobo Rincón and a U.S. Marine. It became an iconic image of the 1965 U.S. invasion of the Dominican Republic.[1] However, in this issue of *Tricontinental Bulletin*, published less than one year after the photo was taken, the location and the names of the people depicted are not listed. The implicit argument here is that this photograph could have been taken almost anywhere and could refer to almost any of the articles, listed below the photograph, that are included in the issue. In other words, it could indeed have been taken in the Dominican Republic where U.S. soldiers invaded the year before, occupying the island until four months after the issue's publication, or it could have been taken in

BULLETIN
TRICONTINENTAL

PUBLISHED BY THE EXECUTIVE SECRETARIAT OF THE TRICONTINENTAL.

English

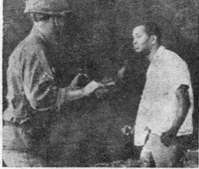

World Solidarity with the Dominican People / The Revolutionary Struggle in Guinea (Bissau)/The Struggle for the Reunification of Korea / May First: Day of Solidarity and Struggle/Viet Nam Escalated Aggression/ Political Prisoners in South Africa/Message to the U.S. People/Imperialist Military Bases / The Yankee "Interamerican Peace Force" / Rhodesia: Concentration Camp/ Yankee Aggressions in Southeast Asia/Tricontinental News.

May '66

FIG. 2.1 *Tricontinental Bulletin,* second issue (May 1966).

Guinea-Bissau where rebels were fighting the Portuguese, in apartheid South Africa, or during the civil rights or Vietnam War protests in the United States.

The image communicates the Tricontinental's basic message that the people of the three continents—and their sympathizers in places like the United States—are all "facing the same cruel enemy."[2] The racial division between the soldier and the protestor is meant to signify, in an abstract way, the division between the Tricontinental's imperialist enemy and its political solidarity of resistance. This process of abstraction, in which the Tricontinental's cultural production condenses the complexity of its vision of global empire and global resistance into the seemingly simplistic vocabulary of a white/black racial division—which I will refer to in this chapter as the Tricontinental's "metonymic color politics"—is key for understanding the Tricontinental's discourse.

As the Afro-Asian movement expanded into the Americas to become the Tricontinental, this discourse would respond to predominant formulations of anti-imperialism in the American region from the preceding decades. Specifically, Tricontinentalism would take up a preexisting signifier of black anti-imperialism, which Richard Wright expanded into a "color curtain" to include people of non-African descent, and would attempt to move beyond its relationship to perceived physical difference and essentialist representations and toward an abstract use of color that refers to a shared political ideology that traverses linguistic, geographic, and racial borders. Although the Bandung Conference was celebrated by many prominent African American activists, Wright claimed that "the Negro problem" was not a major issue discussed at Bandung.[3] In contrast, the Tricontinental would explicitly reach out to African Americans, using African Americans' unique internal position within the United States to theorize a deterritorialized empire and an equally global resistance.

This chapter analyzes the plethora of official Tricontinental cultural production on African American civil rights, including articles from *Tricontinental Bulletin* and *Tricontinental* magazine, posters focused on the Black Panthers and African American activism, the film shorts *Now* (1965) and *El movimiento Panteras Negras* (*Black Panther Movement*) (1968) by the Cuban filmmaker Santiago Álvarez, and writings and speeches by the African American activists Stokely Carmichael and Robert F. Williams. Through the discussion of these texts, and specifically through an extended analysis of Álvarez's newsreel *Now*, this chapter illuminates the central tenets of a Tricontinentalist ideology in which the Jim Crow South and African American liberation are placed in the spotlight. Following an overview of the historical context and background of the Tricontinental organization, I use *Now* to trace how a focus on the African American freedom movement is employed in Tricontinental materials to discursively separate the politicized use of color found in Wright's color curtain concept from its racially deterministic and culturally essentialist content. This discursive shift allows the Tricontinental to theorize a global, transracial resistant subjectivity that undergirds contemporary notions of subaltern resistance.

THE TRICONTINENTAL: A SUMMARY

The January 1966 Tricontinental Conference was planned to coincide with the seventh anniversary of the Cuban Revolution. Although Cuban representatives had been attending Afro-Asian meetings for some time, the Tricontinental was announced as "the first time in history that revolutionaries from three continents . . . representatives of anti-imperialist organizations from the most distant parts of Africa, Asia, and Latin America" had met at such a conference.[4] The Cuban government spared no expense in the preparations for this unprecedented event, printing programs in each of the languages represented and planning cultural events, performances, art exhibits, athletic tournaments, excursions to provinces outside of Havana, and reportedly a dinner for fifty thousand people in the Plaza de la Revolución (Revolution Square) to accompany the conference proceedings.[5] In the months leading up to the event, study circles and lectures were organized in Havana to discuss the various issues and struggles that would be represented, and a campaign to beautify Havana was undertaken in which "solidarity trees" were planted in empty city lots and streets were decorated with flags of visiting delegations.[6]

Plenary sessions began the morning of January 4th; for the next two days, each delegation chairman—which included recognizable figures like Salvador Allende, Luis Augusto Turcios Lima, and Amílcar Cabral—spoke to the full assembly. Working sessions of individual committees that were assigned to draft resolutions took place from January 7 to 12, and final resolutions were presented and adopted at plenary sessions held over the final three days.[7] The conference ended with a large assembly for the closing ceremonies in which Fidel Castro gave the final speech in front of towering portraits of revolutionaries of the three continents—Ho Chi Minh, Patrice Lumumba, and Augusto César Sandino—as well as Cuban national heroes José Martí, Antonio Maceo, and Camilo Cienfuegos.

The portraits themselves capture the dual intention of the Cuban government in hosting the conference. On the one hand, the conference gave Cuba an opportunity to display its growing political network on an international stage, and the portraits drew a clear parallel between Cuba's revolution and other nationalist struggles in the three continents. On the other hand, as Sarah Seidman has written, Cuba used the conference "as a nationalist, hegemonic project intended to unify the Cuban people" under new work-production quotas and educational curricula.[8] In that spirit, the portraits visually articulate an idea often repeated by the Castro government's official discourse in which the Cuban Revolution is presented as completing the founding fathers' heretofore unfinished struggle for both independence from colonial rule and the creation of a raceless Cuba Libre. This argument, as I will discuss more fully in later chapters, forces a precarious equivalence between the liberal causes of Cuban independence heroes, like José Martí and Antonio Maceo, and those of the Cuban Revolution decades later and fails to address how the Cuban Revolution, despite its participation in the Tricontinental's antiracist rhetoric, would perpetuate racial inequities from the prerevolutionary period.

The purpose of the Tricontinental alliance, called the Organization of Solidarity with the Peoples of Africa, Asia, and Latin America (OSPAAAL), was to "outline a programme of joint struggle against imperialism, as well as to fortify, increase and co-ordinate the militant solidarity which should exist between the peoples of the three Continents."[9] This alliance stemmed largely from the common recognition among decolonized nations that political independence did not necessarily imply economic independence.[10] So while it would facilitate international support for militant liberation struggles in places as diverse as Vietnam, South Africa, and Palestine, it also sought to create an economic alliance in order that members could trade with "the advanced countries on such bases that will allow our own development."[11] Following the 1966 Tricontinental Conference, the OSPAAAL published in the first issue of its *Tricontinental Bulletin* a statement of the organization's goals and political positions in which it proclaimed the right to complete political independence for all represented parties and promised mutual military and moral support for the representatives' armed struggles in achieving this goal.[12] It stated its intent to eliminate all "vestiges of imperialist economic domination" and the right to national control of resources, trade, and the national economy.[13] It condemned the war in Vietnam and the embargo against Cuba, claiming racial discrimination as a central component of the maintenance of imperial power and calling for a trade blockade against apartheid South Africa by all represented countries.[14]

For many years prior to the formation of the OSPAAAL, pan-Africanism and communism facilitated the formation of political networks across the Atlantic, and in the years leading up to the Tricontinental, Cuba was already supporting, both militarily and financially, anticolonial struggles in the Congo and Angola. However, despite these transatlantic political solidarities, at the time of the 1955 Bandung Conference, there were "effectively two analogous but separate spheres of subaltern struggle": one in Asia and Africa and the other in Latin America.[15] With the mounting U.S. military campaign in Vietnam and a common recognition of Cuba and Vietnam as participating in a joint struggle, these formally separate spheres would fuse together at the Tricontinental.

As early as 1959, Castro was already exploring the possibility of overcoming Cuba's growing isolation through forging relations with the Afro-Asian bloc, sending Che Guevara, for example, to Cairo in June 1959 to seek out the diplomatic support of Egyptian President Gamal Abdel Nasser. Guevara's meeting with Anwar al-Sadat, the secretary general of the Afro-Asian Peoples' Solidarity Organization (AAPSO), during this visit would lead to the eventual invitation for Cuba to attend future Afro-Asian conferences.[16] Within two years, a Cuban observer would attend the Fourth Session of the Council of Solidarity of the Afro-Asian Peoples, held in Bandung in April 1961, the same month and year of the Bay of Pigs invasion.[17] There, the Afro-Asian group would compose a resolution condemning the U.S.-backed invasion of Cuba.[18] The 1962 ousting of Cuba from the Organization of American States (OAS) would exacerbate Cuba's need to seek friends beyond the American region and to advocate to officially join the AAPSO, eventually leading to the 1966 Havana Tricontinental and to the formation of the OSPAAAL.[19]

The AAPSO had its origins in the first Afro-Asian Peoples' Solidarity Conference in Cairo in 1957, two years after the famous 1955 Bandung Conference. However, Tricontinental leadership would consistently present the OSPAAAL and the AAPSO as having been birthed in the historic Bandung moment.[20] Despite this, there are key differences between the 1955 Bandung Conference and later AAPSO meetings. Whereas the Bandung meeting had intentionally excluded the Soviet Union, the AAPSO included representation from the Soviets and the Chinese and could not be characterized with the same commitment to neutralism that is often attributed to the Bandung meeting. Similarly, although Bandung was a governmental conference made up of heads of state, the AAPSO would include government officials but also nongovernmental representatives from leftist political parties and movements.[21] The Tricontinental alliance would generally follow the structure of the AAPSO, including heads of state as well as representatives of liberation movements.

Although the Tricontinental would present itself as the continuation of the 1955 Bandung meeting and would similarly be interested in preventing foreign military occupation and encouraging economic alliances to allow for more advantageous trade agreements with the North, the heads of state at Bandung had a rhetoric that Dipesh Chakrabarty has characterized as "an uncritical emphasis on modernization" and a development model posed as "catching-up-with-the West."[22] The Tricontinental would mark a clear shift away from the development rhetoric and principles of nonviolence associated with Bandung and toward a commitment to global militant resistance. More importantly, the OSPAAAL would explicitly state its unity with struggles within imperial centers, such as African Americans in the United States, thus necessitating a more flexible concept of imperial power and subjugation.

The Tricontinental Conference and the formation of the OSPAAAL, as reported by the Cuban newspaper *Granma*, intended to forge a "strategy of the revolutionary movements in their struggle against imperialism, colonialism, and neocolonialism and, especially against Yankee imperialism," and to create "closer military ties and solidarity between the peoples of Asia, Africa, and Latin America, the working class, the progressive forces of the capitalistic countries of Europe and the United States, and the Socialist Camp."[23] Through this goal, the Tricontinental joined together movements from vastly diverse contexts and developed a broad definition of its common enemy of global imperialism. Some of the delegations represented countries like Cuba that had long since obtained national liberation from its original colonizer but found itself continually threatened by the economic and military bullying of the United States. Others, like those from the Congo and Guinea-Bissau, were actively engaged in armed struggle with long-established European colonial powers. The Vietnamese were fighting U.S. military invasion and occupation, and others, like the Dominican Republic, were struggling to end a U.S.-backed political regime. As Che Guevara would declare in his 1967 "Message to the Tricontinental," the OSPAAAL was called to create "two, three . . . many Vietnams," a vision akin to Guevara's *foco* theory of guerrilla warfare—where the efforts of small cadres of guerrilla fighters eventually lead to massive insurrection—but on a global scale.[24] Significantly, the OSPAAAL framed this global struggle encompassing not just movements in Africa, Asia, and Latin America but also those "progressive forces" within countries like the United States.[25]

Considering Cuba's close alliance with the Soviet Union and announcement in 1961 of the socialist nature of its revolution, and considering the profound influence of Marxism on many of the anticolonial and independence struggles represented at the Tricontinental, we might expect that the unity between these diverse movements would be described as a common commitment to international class struggle. However, partly because of key disagreements and compromises made in the initial founding of the organization, the Tricontinental was not framed in these terms.

Before merging with Latin America to become the OSPAAAL, the AAPSO had strong representation from both the Soviet Union and China, and many of the African and Asian delegates of this organization were closely affiliated with the Soviet World Peace Council (WPC).[26] As Sino-Soviet relations worsened, the split caused deep fissures in the organization and "began to absorb the energies of the meetings and became the principal focus of attention."[27] Planning for the Tricontinental was similarly shaped by Sino-Soviet discord, but in its inclusion of Latin American movements, the Tricontinental presented an opportunity to shift the binary power struggle that had characterized the organization thus far.

A proposal for the AAPSO to combine with Latin American leftist movements was initially presented by the Cuban observer at Afro-Asian meetings in 1961 and 1963, but disagreements over the sponsorship of its first conference stalled the conversations. The Soviet Union wanted the conference to be sponsored by the WPC and by Latin American groups affiliated with the WPC under the leadership of one of its vice presidents, Lázaro Cárdenas of Mexico. The Chinese sided, however, with Castro's bid to host the conference. According to the OAS report, because of these disagreements, discussion was eventually transferred from AAPSO council meetings to a secret meeting to which China and the Soviet Union were excluded, held in Cairo in 1964 with Mohamed Yazid of Algeria who was representing President Ben Bella; Mehdi Ben Barka of Morocco; the Cuban ambassador to Algeria, Jorge Seguerra; and the secretary general of AAPSO, Youssef El Sebai of the United Arab Emirates.[28] There, it was decided to move forward with the Tricontinental Conference, and at the fourth AAPSO Solidarity Conference, held in Winneba, Ghana, in May 1965, President Kwame Nkrumah of Ghana presented the formal resolution, as Castro had requested, to hold the conference in

Havana in January 1966 to coincide with the seventh anniversary of the Cuban Revolution. The International Preparatory Committee was then composed at Winneba with six representatives from each continent, with Medhi Ben Barka operating as chairman of the committee until his October 1965 abduction and murder and the transfer of his chairmanship to the Cuban politician Osmany Cienfuegos.[29]

In the first meeting of the Tricontinental's International Preparatory Committee in Cairo in September 1965, another disagreement arose between the Soviet Union and China over the composition of the Latin American delegations. This time, Cuba sided with the Soviets. Cuba presented a list of pro-Moscow parties and China created a list of pro-Chinese groups. It was eventually agreed that, "insofar as possible, there would be solidarity committees representing all leftist, anti-imperialist and liberation groups in each of the Latin American countries, but under the direction of the respective communist parties."[30] In practicality, this meant that Latin American communist parties were responsible for inviting groups to the Tricontinental Conference but that those groups did not necessarily have to be communist in affiliation or in ideology. This established a precedent of ideological fluidity within the Tricontinental that would be developed much more fully in Tricontinental cultural production over the next three decades.

A U.S. Senate subcommittee assigned to create a report on the Tricontinental Conference described the event as "humiliating" since a "country 60 miles from American shores" had been "transformed into a headquarters for international revolutionary subversion."[31] Within the binary logic of the Cold War, it would seem that such a humiliation of the United States would represent an obvious boon to the Soviet Union, and indeed the United States and the OAS used the Tricontinental Conference to drum up anti-Soviet sentiment in the U.S. and Latin American media.[32] The Soviet Union did send a large delegation to Havana for the conference, whose head, Sharaf Rashidovich Rashidov, gave a speech before the initial plenary meeting.[33] However, more privately, the U.S. government clearly demonstrated an understanding that the Tricontinental alliance was actually a source of discomfort for the Soviets.[34]

For example, in the context of the Soviet strategy of so-called peaceful coexistence with the United States, the Chinese delegation used the conference to point out Soviet hypocrisy and to question the USSR's commitment to anti-imperialism. Attempts by the leader of the Soviet delegation to include a section promoting peaceful coexistence in the General Declaration were resolutely rejected by the Chinese and by a number of Latin American delegations.[35] Because of the conference's divergence from peaceful coexistence, the Soviet ambassador in Uruguay was forced to defend the Soviet Union against the accusation that its participation in the conference was not in compliance with the United Nations charter. The ambassador claimed that the Soviet Union had not sent government representatives to the conference and assured the Uruguayan government that the Soviet Union is guided by "the principles of non-intervention and rejects the so-called 'export of revolution.'"[36]

Another major conflict erupted over the location of the headquarters of the OSPAAAL. The Chinese delegation, which was concerned about maintaining China's influence in the AAPSO, pushed for the headquarters to be located in Havana and for the OSPAAAL and the AAPSO to remain two separate organizations. The Cuban delegation argued that it should be one unified organization headquartered in Havana. The Soviets similarly wanted one organization but with its headquarters in Cairo. Latin American nationalist movements supported the Cuban position, and Castro was able to convince the Latin American communist parties to counter the Soviet perspective. The Chinese delegation threatened to exit the conference completely if Cairo was chosen as the headquarters. Apparently, tensions were so great that Castro closed the Havana airport to prevent any delegations from leaving the country before they had reached a compromise. Ultimately, the Chinese won out, and the delegates agreed to leave the AAPSO as a separate organization, establishing a new Tricontinental organization, which would be headquartered provisionally in Havana. The final structure of the OSPAAAL, it was agreed, would be decided at a second Tricontinental Conference (which never took place) to be held in Cairo in 1968 at President Nasser's invitation.[37]

In sum, in the realm of Sino-Soviet discord, the Tricontinental Conference seemed to give China the lead in some major ways. Even as the Soviet Union paid for the transportation of many of the delegates from Africa and the Middle East to Havana, and even as the Soviets were largely subsidizing Cuba in this moment, the conference actually revealed how China's Maoist model, which shifted leftist ideology away from a Eurocentric orthodox Marxist focus on the industrial proletariat and toward an emphasis on peasant struggle, was the very ideological glue helping to unify the delegations, drawing together guerrilla struggles from Cuba to Vietnam.[38] As the ideology and discourse of Tricontinentalism would be developed in its propaganda materials in the coming years, the Soviet Union would continue to occupy a marginal position in Tricontinental propaganda. For example, although references to the Soviet Union increase in frequency in Tricontinental materials in the mid-1970s, in the more than three hundred posters produced by the Tricontinental, Vladimir Lenin appears only twice and no other Soviet leaders are represented.[39]

Although *Tricontinental* often includes Marxist analyses of the contexts in which individual liberation struggles are being waged, the socialist camp overall is presented as one force among several "great revolutionary currents, which are repeatedly dashing against the bastion of imperialism."[40] Reports on the Tricontinental from the U.S. government and the OAS would focus primarily on the Sino-Soviet controversy. However, I would argue that beyond the influence and presence of Sino-Soviet communisms, traditions of anti-imperialism from the hemispheric Americas, and especially black internationalist formulations that emphasized race over class, would have an equally significant, and at times even greater influence on the discourse of Tricontinentalism.

In order to address the myriad concerns of the diverse movements represented within the OSPAAAL, the Tricontinental defined its global enemy of "imperialism" quite broadly, encompassing the forces of exploitation and oppression suffered by all member organizations. This Tricontinentalist version of imperialism combined the territorial notions of settler colonialism (faced, for example, by the Palestinian struggle) and exploitation colonialism (such as in the Portuguese colonies in Africa) with a Leninist theory of imperialism. The imperialism that Lenin called the "highest stage of capitalism"—a concept profoundly relevant to Latin America's relationship to the United States—refers to the ever-increasing concentration of production and capital by multinational monopolies that, through the complicity of big banks and with backing by military power, come to dominate the entirety of the global market.[41] The Tricontinental would combine Lenin's theory with other traditional understandings of colonialism to employ a broad definition of imperialism that would serve to unify its diverse delegations while also recognizing their heterogeneity.

While the Tricontinental was against any of these forms of military and economic imperialism, it pointed to the United States as the quintessential representative of imperialist aggression. As a central component of its condemnation of the U.S. government, it consistently identified the cause of African Americans as an integral part of its platform. This solidarity with the African American struggle formed part of the original agenda of the conference, which called for "support to the peoples ... of the United States in defending their rights to equality and freedom; struggle against discrimination and racism in all forms," but it would be developed much more fully in the many propaganda materials that the Tricontinental would publish in the coming years.[42] In these materials, the Tricontinental maintained that African Americans were subject to the very same oppression that the delegations of the three continents were, and thus, not only considered African Americans to belong to the Tricontinental but also—because they were said to be fighting within the belly of the beast of the imperialist United States—deemed them particularly representative of its global subaltern subjectivity.[43]

By consistently presenting the Jim Crow South as a microcosm of global empire, the Tricontinental maintained a deterritorialized concept of imperial power in which one could be located inside the United States and still be understood as a victim to the imperialist oppression suffered by those located on the outside. Moreover, rather than a socialist rhetoric of commonality based around class, Tricontinentalist discourse sometimes used the term "color" (such as in "colored peoples" or "colored leader") to refer not necessarily to one's race or to one's skin color but to one's alignment with the Tricontinental's anti-imperialist politics. In this sense, in addition to a vision of a transnational power structure, Tricontinentalism is marked by a racial vocabulary that is used to describe its global subaltern subjectivity and that serves to destabilize racially deterministic notions of inclusion into the alliance. This is what I refer to as the Tricontinental's metonymic color politics in which the Jim Crow categories of "white" and "colored" are employed not as indicators of phenotypic difference per se but as metonyms for ideological positions in a global struggle. With this transformation of color into a political signifier, the Tricontinental articulates its critique of a global system of imperialism through a critique of racial inequality but simultaneously takes a radically inclusive stance that attempts to destabilize racial essentialisms.

The ideology that the Tricontinental would take up and disseminate around the globe was already circulating among an international Third World Left prior to the 1966 conference. For example, Besenia Rodriguez uses the term "Tricontinentalism" to refer to a critique of global racial capitalism that "created a language of solidarity beyond race" and that represented an alternative to integrationist, black nationalist, and pan-Africanist perspectives.[44] This discourse, she maintains, was articulated in the writings of Shirley Graham Du Bois, as well as in her edited publication *Freedomways* (1961–1985), and in the work of the Chinese American activist Grace Lee Boggs. Significantly, Rodriguez also points to an ideology of Tricontinentalism present in several articles composed by African American writers who traveled to Cuba in July 1960 through their participation in the Fair Play for Cuba Committee (FPCC), an organization created in the United States to balance the negative media portrayal of the Cuban Revolution.[45] Upon their return, members of the FPCC delegation, such as John Henrik Clarke, Richard Gibson, LeRoi Jones, Julian Mayfield, Robert F. Williams, and William Worthy, wrote a series of articles about their experiences in Cuba in U.S. left-wing newspapers—most of which were reprinted in the FPCC journal, *Fair Play* (1960–1961)—in which they applauded Cuba's aggressive policies against racial discrimination and drew parallels between the plight of black people in the Southern United States and that of Cubans.[46]

Robert F. Williams, a National Association for the Advancement of Colored People (NAACP) activist from North Carolina who visited the island in June 1960 with the FPCC, would become especially friendly with the revolutionary government and its cultural organizations, providing an interview with the famed poet Nicolás Guillén, taping a two-hour interview with state television, and putting together a special issue of the Cuban arts and culture magazine *Lunes de Revolución* on African American writers.[47] This issue, published on July 4, 1960, and called "Los Negros en U.S.A." (Blacks in the U.S.A.), featured writings translated into Spanish by such recognizable figures as Marguerite Angelos (a.k.a. Maya Angelou), James Baldwin, Langston Hughes, and Williams himself.[48] The article by Richard Gibson that opens the issue, "El negro americano mira hacia Cuba" (The Black American Looks toward Cuba), argues that "the luck of twenty million black Americans—even when some still do not understand it—is very linked to the success of the Cuban Revolution, as well as to the tremendous movement for the liberation of Africa and Asia."[49] Gibson's positioning of the African American struggle within a global movement that includes Cuba as well as Africa and Asia clearly anticipates the discourse of the Tricontinental movement that would form six years later.

These writers' publications and visits to Cuba occurred within the context of an exchange between U.S. black leftists and the Cuban Revolution in which, from its earliest years, Castro's government actively reached out to African Americans. This was most famously demonstrated during Fidel Castro's visit to New York City for the United Nations General Assembly in September 1960 when—in a highly publicized display of Cuba's solidarity with African Americans that was suggested by the FPCC—Castro moved his entire delegation from Manhattan's Shelburne Hotel, where the other countries' delegates were staying, to the Hotel Theresa in Harlem. There, Castro was met with cheering crowds, and over the next few days, he held meetings at the Hotel Theresa with world leaders, including several prominent African Americans like Malcolm X and LeRoi Jones (a.k.a. Amiri Baraka).[50] In the coming years, several U.S. black activists would visit and in some cases defect to Cuba. [51]

Many of these activists, like Robert F. Williams, would eventually become disillusioned with the Cuban Revolution and become openly critical of the Castro government. Williams, for example, criticized how Cuba's postrevolutionary government silenced Afro-Cuban dissent by claiming that socialist reforms had resolved all racial inequities on the island, and he resented how the Castro government employed its Tricontinentalist support for African Americans in order to externalize racial inequity to the imperialist North and deny its continued presence in Cuba. However, despite this, I will maintain that the ideology of Tricontinentalism, which U.S. black leftists had a pivotal role in shaping and which cannot be reduced to either a Soviet or Cuban state project, continued to be influential among African American activists.

Although, as these exchanges demonstrate, the ideology claimed by the Tricontinental was already circulating among an international Left well before the 1966 meeting, the Tricontinental would globalize this discourse through its large propaganda apparatus. Among the key reasons that the OAS described the Tricontinental as "the most dangerous and serious threat" to the inter-American system was "its unconcealed desire to create an effective propaganda impact by rapidly publishing a great quantity of documents, speeches, and informational material on the event, and widely disseminating these through all available media."[52] In fact, although many smaller meetings and panels of Tricontinental delegations were held over the next three decades, the entire Tricontinental alliance only met once at the 1966 conference. The Tricontinental's massive cultural production would become the primary site for communication among its delegations. Through its publications and films, and through the iconic posters for which it is now recognized, the OSPAAAL provided both physical and textual spaces in which diverse political groups came into contact, and its materials shaped and were shaped by the perspectives of the various delegations it represented.

The OSPAAAL had four official arms of propaganda: *Tricontinental Bulletin* (1966–1988, 1995–), published monthly in English, Spanish, French, and sometimes Arabic, which provided updates on liberation struggles and Tricontinental actions, interviews, and statements from delegations; radio programs; the posters that were folded up inside of the bulletin; and the Instituto Cubano del Arte e Industria Cinematográficos's (ICAIC) Latin American

Newsreel.[53] Although only these four are mentioned in *Tricontinental Bulletin*, the OSPAAAL also produced books and pamphlets, and in August 1967, it began publishing a bimonthly magazine in English, Spanish, French, and Italian called *Tricontinental* (1967–1990, 1995–) that included speeches and essays by revolutionaries, like Che Guevara and Amílcar Cabral, as well as interviews and in-depth analyses of the political and economic contexts of each struggle.[54] The ICAIC Latin American Newsreel played weekly in Cuban theaters from 1960 to 1990, was often distributed internationally, and engaged themes such as the achievements of the Cuban Revolution and independence struggles in Vietnam and elsewhere.[55]

These materials were distributed around the world, even in countries in which they were banned, arriving in right-wing Latin American countries and the United States through Mexico and through personal travel such as the annual trips of U.S. activists to Cuba through the Students for a Democratic Society's Venceremos Brigade.[56] Fifty thousand copies were printed of the first issue of *Tricontinental*, and fifty thousand accompanying posters were also produced to include within the magazine's pages.[57] While initially the OSPAAAL produced three different versions of its signature posters, in 1968, it began producing one, singular poster with text in English, Spanish, French, and Arabic, printing fifty thousand offset copies and five hundred screenprints.[58]

The contemporary OSPAAAL has no record of the number of subscriptions or issues produced from 1967 to 1995, and since both *Tricontinental* and *Tricontinental Bulletin* include a statement on the first page authorizing total reproduction of all articles, it is difficult to estimate the reach of these materials.[59] However, from its earliest years, *Tricontinental Bulletin* includes letters from readers and activists around the globe, and both publications list the international activities of Tricontinental delegations as well as frequent visits by foreign leaders to the OSPAAAL headquarters in Havana.[60] Moreover, material evidence speaks to a wide-ranging dissemination. For example, the New York collective of radical filmmakers called Newsreel, whose logo was inspired by the final frame of Álvarez's *Now*, distributed many of Álvarez's Tricontinental films to its sixteen chapters throughout the United States as well as to chapters of Students for a Democratic Society and to the East and West Coast Black Panthers.[61] During the 1960s and 1970s, images from Tricontinental posters appeared in publications by groups as geographically distant as the Palestinian group Al Fatah and the Black Panther Party.[62] Glad Day Press, a leftist printing press (1967–1973) in Ithaca, New York, reissued some of the OSPAAAL's materials with their logo below.[63] People's Press of San Francisco published a slightly revised, North American edition of *Tricontinental*, and People's Press artist Jane Norling even worked at the OSPAAAL headquarters in Havana for several months in 1973 where she designed a poster in solidarity with Puerto Rico.[64] According to Norling, the OSPAAAL posters "appeared on every wall in the San Francisco houses in 1970 where activists met in the struggle for civil rights/women's rights & against the war in Vietnam."[65]

In more recent years, reproductions of Tricontinental posters have been used by the Ontario Coalition against Poverty, the Irish Anti-War Movement, and most notably in many of the posters designed by Shepard Fairey, who created the famous Barack Obama "Hope" poster.[66] Libraries around the world currently hold complete or near complete collections of both *Tricontinental* and *Tricontinental Bulletin*, and it has been estimated that nine million copies of Tricontinental posters have been produced in total and distributed in sixty countries around the world.[67]

While many of the films that were made by Santiago Álvarez through the ICAIC Latin American Newsreel are widely known, their ties to the Tricontinental are infrequently recognized. The Cuban Film Institute, or ICAIC, created less than three months after the triumph of the Cuban Revolution, was the first cultural organization decreed by the Castro government.[68] Its cinema occupied a central space of social dialogue within revolutionary Cuba and would have a profound impact on the development of a new radical aesthetics of filmmaking throughout the world. Cinema of the Cuban Revolution would be made with the style defined by Julio García Espinosa in his famous 1967 manifesto as *cine imperfecto* (imperfect cinema), which celebrated the imperfections of low-budget film that, in contrast to the conventional smooth-surfaced Hollywood studio cinema, which encouraged a passive viewer, emphasized filmmaking as a process and sought to actively draw its audience into the film's revolutionary struggle.[69] Because of limited materials due to the U.S. blockade, the time constraints of a weekly chronicle, and the improvisational creativity of Álvarez as a filmmaker, the inventive short films that made up the Newsreel, which was headed by Álvarez, are arguably the clearest embodiment of the aesthetics of imperfect cinema.

The Tricontinental played a central role in the circulation of this revolutionary film aesthetic among the international Left. The filmmakers Octavio Getino and Fernando Solanas's renowned essay "Hacia un tercer cine" (Toward a Third Cinema) (1969), which named revolutionary filmmaking, and especially the documentary genre, as the defining artistic arena of the anti-imperialist struggle, was first published in *Tricontinental* and the distribution of the Newsreel was a key component of the Tricontinental's propaganda campaign. Considering the central position afforded to the African American cause within the Tricontinental, it is not surprising that the most famous of these newsreels is *Now,* a six-minute, fast-paced film that pairs Lena Horne's eponymous 1963 song to documentary footage of white-on-black police brutality and images of protests from the U.S. civil rights movement. The film was released the same year as the Tricontinental's first publication, *Towards the First Tricontinental* (1965).

Scholarship and reviews of *Now* generally describe the film as a denunciation of violence against African Americans and as a rallying cry in support of civil rights activism.[70] However, I maintain that *Now*'s message is far more complex in that, through presenting a pointed critique of the reformist goals of the civil rights movement and pushing for radicalization and militancy, the film attempts to frame the African American struggle within the Tricontinental's global movement.[71] In what remains of this chapter, I use *Now* alongside other Tricontinental materials, such as articles in *Tricontinental Bulletin,* several Tricontinental posters, and another Álvarez film, *El movimiento Panteras Negras,* to outline how Tricontinentalist ideology, by pointing to imperialism within the geographic borders of the United States and privileging African American protestors as representative of its political subjectivity, attempts to deterritorialize empire and destabilize colonial racial divisions. An analysis of the argument put forth in *Now* sheds light not only on the Tricontinental's use of a local and racialized discourse to formulate a global, nonracial revolutionary subjectivity but also on the way in which a text such as *Now* acquires new meaning when viewed through a Tricontinental lens.

Now's Critique of Martin Luther King Jr.'s "Dream"

The 1965 release of *Now* was met with immediate international acclaim, the film was shown in festivals around the world, and its final frame, in which the word "NOW!" is spelled out with machine-gun shots onto the screen, inspired the logo that appears in the opening credits sequence of each film made by the New York collective of activist filmmakers, Newsreel, which created the Black Panther Party's recruitment film.[72] With time, *Now* has been a testament to the enduring relevance of Álvarez's work. It is widely viewed on YouTube and, in 2005, was included in Travis Wilkerson's DVD compilation *He Who Hits First Hits Twice: The Urgent Cinema of Santiago Álvarez.*

In keeping with Solanas and Getino's theory of Third Cinema, in which the role of the revolutionary filmmaker is not merely to document but to intervene, Álvarez claimed that he intended to "join things up in such a way that they pass before the spectator as a complete entity, with a single line of argument."[73] In this sense, his newsreels, which are not intended to report the news with objectivity but to make a clear political argument, reflect the critical stance and subjectivity that is characteristic of the essay film.[74] The images in *Now*, taken from pirated news footage and photographs cut out of *Life Magazine*, are brought to life through the rapid sequencing, quick cuts, and aggressive zooms that characterize Álvarez's "nervous montage" style.[75] This style has been described as "diametrically opposed to the 'long take' form of the direct cinema approach that dominated US production" at the time.[76]

Yet the true driving force of the film is the audio track: Lena Horne's song entitled "Now!" (1963), which was composed for a performance Horne delivered at a Carnegie Hall benefit for the Students for Nonviolence Coordinating Committee (SNCC).[77] SNCC worked closely with Martin Luther King Jr. and the Southern Christian Leadership Conference (SCLC) to carry out the famous sit-ins and Freedom Rides that occurred across the U.S. South, and it played a leading role in organizing the 1963 March on Washington where King delivered his legendary "I Have a Dream" speech from the steps of the Lincoln Memorial.[78] Horne's song largely reflects King's ideological perspective as expressed in this famous speech in which King defined the civil rights movement as fundamentally concerned with the acquisition by African Americans of all the rights promised to American citizens in the U.S. Constitution.[79] King's political position is fully embraced in Horne's song. Consider, for example, the following citation from the song's chorus:

Now, now
Come on, let's get some of that stuff
It's there for you and me
For every he and she
Just wanna do what's right
Constitutionally
I went and took a look
In my old history book.
It's there in black and white
For all to see.[80]

The lyrics express a clear sense of urgency regarding the granting of civil rights across the racial divide yet emphasize doing "what's right constitutionally" and the United States' history of a discursive commitment to equality. The song suggests that one can look in a history book and find "in black and white" the rights promised to African Americans. The belief in equality has always been a part of American history, the song argues; it just needs to be extended to the black community.

Álvarez noted that in *Now* "the script is in the song itself. As you follow the song, you write the script."[81] In other words, the images in the documentary are arranged in rhythmic timing with the soundtrack and often directly correlate with the lyrics. However, this does not mean that there is a perfect coincidence of argument between song and film. In fact, I suggest that whereas Horne's song echoes the philosophy of Martin Luther King Jr. in drawing its inspiration from the social promise of the Constitution, Álvarez appropriates the song to formulate his own counterargument, claiming that this constitutional promise of equality does not apply to the African American community.

According to Michael Chanan, "Álvarez is a staunch believer in the naked power of the image, illustrated by music. He hates using verbal commentary . . . 'that simply means you have not explained yourself.'"[82] Likewise in *Now*, Álvarez conveys his argument through his use of images, arranging the photographs and film footage in a montage style in which the message is contained in the relationship of one image to the next.[83] Considering that Álvarez's most immediate audience was a Spanish-speaking Cuban public that, despite the cursory subtitles, may not have necessarily understood all the English lyrics of Horne's song on a first viewing, the message conveyed through image becomes that much more important for perceiving Álvarez's intended meaning. In other words, one could watch the film with the sound off and still come away with the film's core message.

However, there are several key moments in which Álvarez places his images in ironic juxtaposition with Horne's lyrics, thus situating the visual track in an intermittent relationship of counterpoint with the audio track. These instances of ironic interaction between the images of the film and the song's lyrics, which I will detail in the analysis below, appropriate the discourse of Horne's song in order to undermine it, giving a sharp edge to the film's critique. Some of these key lyrical moments are not translated in the subtitles, meaning that while a non-English-speaking person would comprehend the overall argument on a first viewing, she would miss many of the subtleties that would be more clearly conveyed to an English-speaking viewer. This suggests that the film's intended audience is also, and perhaps primarily, a U.S. or international Left that sympathizes with the song's rhetoric and that the film seeks to challenge and radicalize.

In keeping with its focus on claiming the rights set forth in the Constitution, the song begins by evoking the origins of U.S. democracy in the figure of its Founding Fathers:

If those historic gentleman came back today
Jefferson, Washington, and Lincoln
And Walter Cronkite put them on Channel 2
To find out what they were thinkin'

Álvarez pairs these lyrics with a photograph of protestors sitting on steps. The camera focuses in on an African American boy, who is holding an American flag. The next image shows a policeman who appears to be violently pulling the flag from the child's arms. The lyrics that follow are accompanied by a close-up of a black person's eyes:

I'm sure they'd say
Thanks for quoting us so much
But we don't want to take a bow
Enough with the quoting
Put those words into action
And we mean action now!

The whites of the eyes transform in a dissolve into the face of Abraham Lincoln, which fades into an image of the Lincoln Memorial, immediately recalling the location from which King delivered his "I Have a Dream" speech two years before the production of the film. The camera descends from Lincoln's head down to the base of the memorial where the face of a protestor, who is being beaten, winces in pain. As Horne sings the word "now!" the word appears as though written across the protestor's pained face.

While the images in the documentary are topically consonant with the song's lyrics—for instance, Álvarez presents images of the Founding Fathers in the same moments that Horne sings about them—the reference to the U.S. forefathers takes on a different meaning in the film than it does in the song. The song evokes the forefathers in order to point to their unfulfilled, but viable, dream of equality such that Washington, Jefferson, and Lincoln are narratively positioned as the ones calling for action. According to John Hess, "the song, and through it Álvarez, argues that the U.S. was once a revolutionary country which then lost its way. To solve our contemporary problems—for example racism—we must reclaim our revolutionary past."[84] Although I agree with Hess's assessment of the song's argument, I argue that the images themselves communicate a very different message. The man wincing in pain is positioned beneath the feet of the Lincoln monument as if he were being crushed by the massive statue. The American flag is ripped from the protesting child's hands. Whereas the song evokes the U.S. identity as a call to action, the film posits an a priori separation of African Americans from citizenship, evoking a call to action based precisely on *disidentification* with the United States and suggesting that if one really "went and took a look in my old history book," one would find a history of violence and anything but equality.

Álvarez reinforces this history of oppression throughout the film, which consists of a montage of images of police brutality against African Americans edited in time with the song's rhythm. He emphasizes racial hierarchies by featuring images in which white police are standing above—often pointing a gun down at—a black victim, who is lying on the ground. While the film footage and several photographic stills are taken from the 1965 Los Angeles Watts riots, in which black residents protested police brutality, Álvarez does not show images of the rioters taking violent action. Instead, he emphasizes their victimization, using photographs like one in which two young boys, who have been arrested, stand beneath a Los Angeles Police sign.

Following the lines "people all should love each other. Just don't take it literal, mister. No one wants to grab your sister," several images of police violence directed at black women appear. In one image of excessive force, a woman is picked up by her arms and legs by a group of five policemen that surround her. As she is forcibly carried to the back of a truck in front of a crowd of people, her shoes fall off into the street and her dress comes up, revealing her thighs and slip. The phrase "no one wants to grab your sister" addresses the racist fear of miscegenation, specifically the fear of sexual relations between white women and black men, that underlay many Jim Crow laws as well as the practice of lynching. Martha Hodes argues that during slavery in the United States, white men maintained not only the sole right to vote but also the perceived right to sexual violence against women, both white and black. The extent to which suffrage was associated with domination over women's bodies became evident in the postemancipation period when "whites conflated the new political power of black men with sexual transgressions against white women."[85] Hodes points out that while this fear had been present since the colonial era, political power and sexual power were so fundamentally intertwined in the minds of Southern whites that it was not until suffrage was extended to African American men that this fear reached the level of social panic.

Tellingly, this single line of Horne's song is purported to have caused it to be effectively banned in the United States by the refusal of some major radio stations to play it.[86] Álvarez juxtaposes this phrase with the conceptually inverted image of ganglike violence by white policemen toward black women, implying that it is not white women who are threatened by black men, but rather, it is white men who "grab" black women. As Álvarez pairs these disturbing images of police violence with the song's reference to the fear of miscegenation, he alludes to a history in which the constitutional right to vote is associated with violence toward African Americans rather than black empowerment. This line of the song, as well as references to the Constitution, are not translated in the film's subtitles, suggesting that many of the subtleties of Álvarez's critique of U.S. democracy are directed to an English-speaking public.

Considering the film's critique of the hypocrisy of U.S. democracy, it is significant that Álvarez originally received a copy of Horne's song from Robert F. Williams, whom Álvarez described as a friend.[87] According to Sarah Seidman, "Williams's assistance indelibly molded both the film's form and content" since Williams provided not only the recording but also many of the photographs that Álvarez used in the film.[88] Williams, the former president of the Monroe, North Carolina, division of the NAACP and a staunch opponent of King's strict pacifism, was living in exile in Cuba when Álvarez made Now. Williams became known for forming a self-defense militia within his NAACP chapter and for his journalistic coverage of the famous Monroe "kissing case" in which two African American boys, aged nine and eleven, were jailed and sentenced to fourteen years in reform school after a white girl kissed one of them on the cheek. As a result of Williams's writings, the case quickly gained international attention and became an embarrassment to the U.S. government. After facing death threats and an FBI arrest warrant, Williams escaped to Cuba in 1961 where he continued to publish his newsletter, The Crusader (1959–1969), and host a radio broadcast called Radio Free Dixie (1962–1966). This broadcast, which aired on Friday nights at 11 PM and which combined jazz and blues music with black radical political content, could be heard in California, New York, Washington, DC, and throughout the U.S. South.[89] Williams also published his influential Negroes with Guns from exile in Cuba in 1962.

Apparently, despite his participation in the making of the film, Williams was disappointed that the film did not focus on militant activism among

African Americans, showing only the nonviolent side of the freedom struggle.[90] He viewed this silence as part of the general discomfort of the Cuban government with black organizing and militancy on the island, a subject that I will explore in further depth in subsequent chapters. However, although this film is still widely known among Cubans, there are, as I have suggested, many subtleties of this film that appear to be directed specifically at an English-speaking public. I read this film thus within the context in which Álvarez described his filmmaking: where his newsreels were not intended to report the news but rather to present a line of argument. In my reading, this film is intended less as an accurate portrait of what was happening in the United States, as Williams may have wanted, and more of a critique directed precisely at the pacifist side of the movement.

I suggest that the critique that Álvarez puts forth in *Now*, while ironically dissonant with the lyrics of the song that Williams gave him, parallels Williams's own ideology. Alvarez's representation of the separation of the black community from U.S. citizenship echoes a statement by Williams in which, when asked by a reporter if he would give up his citizenship in his support for Cuba, he replied, "As an Afro-American, I never had American citizenship."[91] In addition to aligning with Williams's views on citizenship, *Now* also channels Williams in its critique of the nonviolence for which the civil rights movement is recognized. For example, in the 1960 issue of the Cuban magazine *Lunes de Revolución* that Williams edited, Williams critiques Martin Luther King Jr., the NAACP, and the Committee on Racial Equality (CORE) for "preaching an ideology of absolute passive resistance," encouraging activists to turn the other cheek "instead of defending themselves with the same force of aggression from racist whites."[92] He argues that this pacifist approach will not produce the desired results.

Similarly, Álvarez's juxtaposition of photographs in which African Americans are victimized with the song's chorus, "Now is the moment. Come on, we've put it off long enough," proposes action as the path to ending oppression. Whereas the song does not imply that this action need be violent, I suggest that the film calls specifically for militancy. The film's critique of nonviolence is suggested in the extended photographic still that serves as the backdrop for the opening credits. In the photograph, some of the civil rights movement's most prominent leaders—president of the SCLC, Martin Luther King Jr.; president of the NAACP, Roy Wilkins; president of CORE, James Farmer; and executive director of the Urban League, Whitney Young—sit in a meeting with President Lyndon B. Johnson. Hess argues that the photograph sets up the oppositional relationship between protestors and police that characterizes the rest of the film.[93] Indeed, during the time the still photograph remains on screen, the following credits appear in overlay: "Personajes—Negros y Policías Norteamericanos" (Characters—North American Blacks and Policemen).[94] This description of the characters sets up a binary of victims and victimizers, associating Johnson with the policemen and emphasizing the very opposition to which Hess refers.

However, although this photograph can be read as one more depiction of the division between the "negros y policías norteamericanos," Chanan notes that the photo "establishes the film's tone of skeptical irony," an assertion that is not followed with further analysis.[95] The photograph, juxtaposed with video footage of riot police running and marching, stands out as particularly static in an otherwise fast-paced, "nervous" film. In a newsreel lasting merely six minutes, this photograph remains on screen for forty-five seconds. Álvarez does little to dynamize the image (such as fast cuts or zooms) but rather presents the photograph in the Hollywood "long take" style to which he is known as being opposed. Additionally, while I agree that Johnson is associated with the brutality of the policemen, the photo is the only image in which black and white men lean in toward one another in a communicative gesture and appear on the same level, Whitney Young sitting slightly higher than Johnson.

Johnson is the subject of biting criticism in a number of Álvarez's films, such as *LBJ* (1968) and *Hanoi Martes 13* (1967). In *Now,* other than in this photograph with Johnson, the civil rights leaders do not appear again in the film. Thus, instead of focusing on these leaders' activism by showing images of them protesting, Álvarez's only presentation of them is in a static image in which they appear with this reviled politician. In this way, Álvarez offers a subtle critique of the movement's reformism, suggesting that cooperating with politicians like Johnson within a flawed political system does not bring change, only stasis.

The skepticism that Álvarez demonstrates toward the civil rights movement's leaders is then explicitly extended to its nonviolent methods. For example, the lyrics "We want more than just a promise. Say goodbye to Uncle Thomas" are sung simultaneously with the appearance of a famous photograph of a civil rights protestor taken in front of the Traffic Engineering Building in Birmingham, Alabama. The woman is kneeling and her eyes contain an expression of agony. In direct timing with the words "Uncle Thomas," a derogatory term referring to a black person who is subservient to white people, Álvarez focuses in on the protestor's hands, which are folded together as if in prayer, a subtle allusion to the religious character of civil rights protests like the sclc's Birmingham campaign.[96] After zooming in on these praying hands, Álvarez then immediately cuts to the tied hands of a black man in a photograph in which a mob of white men hold him captive by a rope, arguing thus that the nonviolent philosophy of the Birmingham protestors is yet another manifestation of black subjugation, or modern-day Uncle Tom-ism. The praying hands are tied and held by the rope of white domination.

This point is further emphasized in the final frames of the film, which show nonviolent protestors who have chained their hands together in a symbolic act that communicates their continued enslavement even in the era of putative freedom. Once the song reaches its crescendo, Álvarez focuses in on the bound hands of these protestors. As Horne sings the final line, "the time is now," Álvarez cuts to an image of a man running and zooms in on his hands, free of chains and tightened into fists. Next, the film comes full circle, back to an image of a boy who, instead of holding an American flag, furrows his brow and holds up his fists in anger. The final image depicts a woman standing above a crowd with her fist in the air, and the film ends with the sound of a machine gun firing as the word "NOW" is symbolically shot onto the screen. The message is clear: break free of your chains and fight! The pacifist approach of the civil rights movement is implicitly decried as yet another enslavement and a militant approach is affirmed as a more viable path toward liberation.

"Negros y policías norteamericanos" in the Tricontinental Spotlight

In his critique of civil rights discourse, Álvarez seeks to disconnect the African American struggle from a particularly U.S. identity, merging it rather with a global struggle against imperialism. The year following the release of Now is known in Cuba as the "Year of Solidarity" because of the 1966 Tricontinental and the formation of the OSPAAAL.[97] Despite consistently pointing to the United States as the "implacable enemy of all the peoples of the world" and the quintessential representative of imperialist aggression, from the very beginning, the OSPAAAL would identify the cause of African Americans as an integral part of its platform.[98] In the materials published leading up to the 1966 conference, the Tricontinental's International Preparatory Committee defines "support to the negro people of the United States in their struggle for the right to equality and freedom and against all forms of discrimination and racism" as part of the agenda for the upcoming meeting.[99]

This initial solidarity with the African American freedom struggle only becomes more pronounced in the years following the first Tricontinental Conference, as is clearly evinced by the many articles devoted to it in *Tricontinental Bulletin* as well as the many posters in solidarity with African American people that were folded up inside *Tricontinental*. These materials were produced through an exchange with U.S. black activists. For example, one of the many posters designed in celebration of August 18th as the day of solidarity with the African American people, named in honor of the August 1965 Watts riots, was taken from a drawing by Black Panther Party (BPP) Minister of Culture Emory Douglas, whose illustrations for the newspaper *The Black Panther* helped to brand the BPP.[100] The 1968 OSPAAAL poster, created by the Cuban artist Lázaro Abreu, used Douglas's 1968 black-and-white printed graphic of African American men and women in black berets holding machine guns, reversed it from left to right, narrowed the graphic to fit the width of the poster, and added bright colors.[101] Another 1968 OSPAAAL poster by Abreu reprints another Douglas drawing in which two women wearing leopard-print shirts and brightly colored headscarves carry a baby on one shoulder and a machine gun on the other.[102]

This exchange of images went both ways. For example, as Seidman has traced, a 1968 OSPAAAL poster by the Cuban artist Alfredo Rostgaard, in which the words "Black Power" appear inside the roaring mouth of a panther, was reproduced by the BPP in the September 1968 issue of *The Black Panther*. In the BPP's version, however, it is the iconic photograph of Huey Newton seated in his thronelike rattan chair that appears inside the panther's mouth.[103] Alongside this exchange of visual culture, Tricontinental materials also contain interviews with Angela Davis and speeches by Malcolm X, letters from and articles by SNCC leaders like Rap Brown, Stokely Carmichael, Phil Hutchings, Ralph Featherstone, and James Forman, and interviews and speeches by BPP members Joudon Major Ford, George Murray, and Huey P. Newton.[104] Many of these speeches and interviews in *Tricontinental* and *Tricontinental Bulletin* are accompanied by photographs and illustrations of the authors and interviewees.

According to Seidman, Stokely Carmichael called the OSPAAAL "'one of the most important organizations for the development of the struggle of the Negroes in the United States,' and years later dubbed the *Tricontinental* magazine 'a bible in revolutionary circles.'"[105] In fact, four members of SNCC, including Carmichael, traveled to Cuba in the summer of 1967 where Carmichael was given a personal tour of the Sierra Maestra by Castro himself.[106] There, Carmichael was named an honorary delegate and allowed to speak at the convention, held at the Hotel Habana Libre and attended by six thousand people, organized by the Latin American Solidarity Organization (OLAS), which was made up of the twenty-seven Latin American delegations of the Tricontinental.[107] In his speech, "Black Power and the Third World," Carmichael argued that black communities in the United States are "victims of white imperialism" who, much like exploited peoples in other parts of the world, live in urban areas where resources and labor are controlled by whites living outside the city.[108] The similarities between African Americans' exploitation and that represented by peoples of the Third World require thus an internationalist approach to the African American struggle in which, Carmichael stated, "what happens in Viet Nam affects our struggle here and what we do affects the struggle of the Vietnamese people" and where African Americans' internal battle against white rule in the United States will contribute to its defeat in Latin America and South Africa.[109]

Beyond the OSPAAAL's cultural production, the Tricontinental Conference itself made the African American freedom struggle a central priority. The resolution on the "Rights of Afro-Americans in the United States" was drafted at the first Tricontinental Conference by Robert F. Williams, who attended the conference, along with delegates from Jamaica, Indonesia, and Venezuela.[110] The full text of the resolution was printed in the August–September 1966 issue of *Tricontinental Bulletin*. A portion of it states, "Although, geographically Afro-Americans do not form part of Latin America, Africa, or Asia, the special circumstances of the oppression which they suffer, to which they are subjected, and the struggle they are waging, merits special consideration and demands that the Tri-Continental Organization create the necessary mechanisms so that these brothers in the struggle will, in the future, be able to participate in the great battle being fought by the peoples of the three continents."[111] In this statement, the OSPAAAL does not just express its support for African Americans but explicitly brings them within the fold of the Tricontinental alliance itself.

Richard Wright points out in *The Color Curtain* that the only mention of "the Negro problem" at the Bandung Conference came from the African American U.S. congressman Adam Clayton Powell, who, Wright claims, was sent by the U.S. government to hold press conferences in order to defend its "bill of racial health."[112] The U.S. State Department also sent the African American journalist Carl Rowan for a similar purpose, and the journalists William Worthy and Margaret Cartwright, the first black reporter assigned to the United Nations, were also present.[113] W. E. B. Du Bois and Paul Robeson had hoped to attend the Bandung Conference, but their passports were denied.[114] However, statements by Robeson and Du Bois were read aloud at the conference and, contrary to Wright's claim, these statements did in fact mention a relationship to African American struggles.[115] Because Bandung condemned racism in general and, as Sohail Daulatzai writes, "challenged the white world, foregrounding the role of race in both international and domestic affairs," it had profound implications for African Americans and black peoples around the globe.[116] However, overall, the African American struggle, although gaining momentum on the world stage in the mid-1950s, was not on the forefront of issues discussed at Bandung.

It is important to note that with the exception of Robert F. Williams and Josephine Baker, no other African Americans were listed as official attendees at the Tricontinental Conference.[117] Yet discursively, in comparison to Bandung, the Tricontinental marks a clear shift in focus toward the African American freedom movement. This shift seems to be related not only to the increasing radicalization of the African American struggle but also to the extension of Bandung solidarity into the Americas where the legacy of the afrocriollo movement, and its relationship to black intellectuals in the United States, formed the backbone of anti-imperialist thought. The centrality of the African American freedom struggle to the discourse and ideology of the Tricontinental would be integral to the Tricontinental's attempt to revise the color curtain concept discussed previously into the synthesis that Frantz Fanon imagined.

Tricontinental Bulletin is flooded with images of police brutality against African Americans, images strikingly similar to those that appear in *Now*, as well as images of black empowerment and articles on African American militancy. Like *Now*, articles in *Tricontinental Bulletin* consistently point to the oppression of African Americans as revelatory of the hypocrisy of U.S. democratic ideals. For example, an article on the 1967 Newark riots states, "It would take too long to enumerate each and every case of lynching, rape, physical torture and other atrocities perpetrated against the Blacks in a country where the rulers brazenly proclaim themselves the defenders of democracy and freedom."[118] Just as Álvarez pairs images of violence against African Americans with the song's references to the U.S. Constitution, the writers of *Tricontinental Bulletin* point to lynching and rape as evidence of the hypocrisy of the "democracy and freedom" that U.S. political leaders claim to uphold.[119]

Tricontinental Bulletin uses this evidence of hypocrisy to argue for the colonial nature of the U.S. government's relationship to African Americans. A January 1967 article entitled "Black Power: U.S. Version of Struggle against

Colonialism" argues, "Those masses who are discriminated against already understand that their problems do not revolve around the right to eat in certain cafeterias, the right to vote or the right to send their children to certain schools. The question goes much deeper. The radical Negro vanguard is becoming aware that their fight is a part of the independence movement of the colonized peoples and that their enemy is Yankee imperialism."[120] In this statement, the writers for *Tricontinental Bulletin*, like Álvarez in *Now*, present the reformist goals of the civil rights movement as shortsighted. In this critique, the article echoes Carmichael's criticism of the movement's focus on public accommodations in his speech before the OLAS in Cuba. According to Carmichael, this focus does not speak to the needs of the African American masses who "do not have any jobs, any housing worthy of the name decent, nor the money to enjoy restaurants, hotels, motels, etc."[121]

In response, *Tricontinental Bulletin* celebrates what it claims is the increasingly popular belief that, as explained in a January 1970 article, African Americans' "objective of national liberation, the liquidation of racism, cannot be achieved within the present, imperialist, capitalist structure."[122] The path to liberation, *Tricontinental Bulletin* argues, lies primarily in the recognition of U.S. democracy as a farce and of U.S. imperialism as the enemy.

In presenting the United States as an imperial power so pervasive that it has become "the common enemy of the peoples of the world," even including those who live within its borders, the OSPAAAL anticipates by more than three decades theories put forth by Michael Hardt and Antonio Negri on the nature of modern empire.[123] In *Empire* (2000), Hardt and Negri claim that in contrast to the transcendent nature of European colonialism, modern-day empire "establishes no territorial center of power and does not rely on fixed boundaries or barriers. It is a *decentered* and *deterritorializing* apparatus of rule that progressively incorporates the entire global realm within its open, expanding frontiers."[124] They identify the logic of the U.S. Constitution as exemplary of this immanent nature of empire in that, in producing its own internal limit by simultaneously granting and restricting constituent power, it turns outward toward the frontier in order to avoid reflection on its internal contradictions.

This vision of empire as unfettered by territorial boundaries and incorporating the entire world is parallel to the representation of imperialism in the *Tricontinental Bulletin*, which quotes Stokely Carmichael as saying "imperialism is an exploiting octopus whose tentacles extend from Mississippi and Harlem to Latin America, the Middle East, South Africa and Vietnam."[125] The logic behind the Tricontinental is that the resistance to this monster must be equally global, a concept perhaps best articulated by Che Guevara in his 1967 "Message to the Tricontinental," which he wrote prior to leaving for Bolivia in 1966 and which was published in a special supplement by the OSPAAAL on April 16, 1967.[126]

According to Robert J. C. Young, Guevara's message is especially significant because of the way in which it defines a new revolutionary subject—not the proletarian of Marxism—but "'we, the exploited people of the world.' 'We, the dispossessed.'"[127] Guevara's vision of a global subaltern subjectivity is akin to Hardt and Negri's claim that with an immanent empire, there exists more revolutionary potential since it creates "the set of all the exploited and the subjugated, a multitude that is directly opposed to Empire."[128] The two make essentially the same argument: that the expansiveness of empire, lacking geopolitical boundaries, allows for the creation of a new, global revolutionary subject, one who also lacks boundaries and who identifies with exploited people anywhere from Vietnam to Cuba to Alabama.

Among these exploited people of the world, the OSPAAAL consistently privileges African Americans. If imperialism is an octopus covering the earth with its deadly tentacles, then African Americans, *Tricontinental Bulletin* maintains, are fighting "within the guts of the monster itself."[129] This argument, which *Tricontinental Bulletin* makes repeatedly in reference to African Americans, is summed up quite aptly in a 1967 OSPAAAL poster, which was published in Spanish, French, English, and Arabic, in which an abstract drawing of a black man holding a gun appears inside an outline of the map of the United States (fig. 2.2). The caption beneath it states, "We will destroy imperialism from the outside. They will destroy it from the inside." Although arguably the use of "we" and "they" undercuts the Tricontinental's explicit inclusion of African Americans into the alliance, the statement of solidarity at the bottom of the poster reinforces the shared cause of African American activists with liberation struggles in the three continents. More important, the poster captures precisely the tension that Tricontinentalist subjectivity inhabits in which "they" become a part of "we," and exploited peoples inside the geographic boundaries of imperial centers are viewed as united with those from outside.

This especially representative position attributed to African Americans stems from the view expressed in Tricontinental materials that policies of racial inequality within the United States prop up the maintenance of U.S. power abroad. This is parallel to Glenda Gilmore's notion of "Dixie," a racial hierarchy that

FIG. 2.2 Unknown artist, "We Will Destroy Imperialism from the Outside" (1967). COURTESY LINCOLN CUSHING / DOCS POPULI.

accompanies and facilitates U.S. expansionism in the early twentieth century, installing Jim Crow policies abroad while further entrenching them within the U.S. South. For the Tricontinental, African Americans do not simply inhabit a geographic inside but a systemic inside. They are on the front lines of a system of racial subjugation that is integral to U.S. power at home and abroad such that their fight is essential to the struggle facing the three continents.

The importance attributed to the African American cause for—as *Tricontinental Bulletin* claims—"they are striking at U.S. imperialism from inside, while we are dismembering it from outside" is meant to extend as well to other groups struggling from within the United States.[130] An article states "the white population, the Afro-Americans and other national minorities—Puerto Ricans, Mexican Americans, and others in the heat of the present process of radicalization—have the historic responsibility for confronting in the United

States those very monopolies, racist groups, and the imperialist government which takes its cruelty, crimes, and exploitation to a part of the world still governed by capitalism."[131] The fight being fought by African Americans is one for which other U.S. radicals, regardless of skin color, are also responsible. This statement is followed with explicit approval for the alliances being forged in the United States between such radical groups as the "Afro-American Black Panther Party, the Puerto Rican Young Lords, the Mexican-American Brown Berets and white Young Patriots," alliances that, as I will suggest in the following chapter, clearly reflect the influence of Tricontinentalism.[132]

While *Tricontinental Bulletin* explicitly recognizes that other groups are also fighting imperialism from within, African Americans specifically become emblematic of the Tricontinental's slippage between we and they, outside and inside, a liminality that also applies to race and skin color. The especially representative position attributed to African Americans stems not just from their location within the United States but also from a view of the transatlantic slave trade as a foundational moment of colonial hegemony. Consider the statement by Mao Zedong that Robert F. Williams published in the October 1964 issue of his newsletter, *The Crusader*: "The evil system of colonialism and imperialism grew up along with the enslavement of Negroes and the trade in Negroes, it will surely come to its end with the thorough emancipation of the black people."[133] Mao, a central figure to Tricontinentalist ideology, identifies the enslavement of black people as foundational for imperialism and equates their liberation with the end of imperialism itself.

Aníbal Quijano argues that because slavery was the economic driving force behind European colonialism, racial categories were devised to legitimize colonial hierarchies.[134] As a result, "colonizers codified the phenotypic trait of the colonized as color."[135] In this sense, Guevara's revolutionary subject arises out of a preexisting discourse, which Richard Wright called "the color curtain," that broadened the anti-imperialist revolutionary subjectivity of the afrocriollo movement to include colonized peoples of non-African descent and that appropriated the colonial language of race, which separates the colonizer and the colonized into categories of white and colored, in order to create a phenotypic articulation of an international anticolonial resistance. However, while Guevara's "exploited people of the world" may arise from this preexisting discourse of color, the Tricontinentalist use of color is an ideological referent that does not necessarily refer to the skin color of the Tricontinentalist revolutionary but rather the anti-imperialist contours of her politics. By this, I mean that Tricontinentalist materials sometimes define the Tricontinental's global revolutionary subjectivity not through the socialist rhetoric of class struggle but through employing the term "color" (such as in "colored peoples" or "colored leader") to refer not necessarily to race or to skin color but to one's alignment with the Tricontinental's anti-imperialist politics. Moreover, through the use of racially coded terminology and through the repetition of images of mostly Anglo-American policemen and African American protestors, Tricontinental materials metonymically employ the colonial and Jim Crow categories of "white" and "colored," using white policemen to signify global imperial oppression and an African American identity to stand in for all "the exploited people of the world." In this way, the racial divide of the Jim Crow South functions as a metonym not for a global color line of phenotypic difference but for a Tricontinental power struggle in which all radicalized, exploited peoples, regardless of race, are implicated and thus discursively colored.

I refer to this racial abstraction as the Tricontinental's metonymic color politics. The phenotypic language used to describe the Tricontinental revolutionary is a racial abstraction, meaning the designation of "color" is dissociated from physical characteristics, signifying rather an ideological position of anti-imperialism. Rodriguez makes this very assertion when she explains that when Williams refers in his newsletter to Fidel Castro, a white descendant of a Spanish landowner, as "colored," the word is disconnected from a black nationalist insistence on ethnicity or the suggestion of a pan-Africanist cultural heritage. Rather, in the spirit of Tricontinentalism, it is used to "forge a solidarity based on a common exploitation."[136] Color, for Williams, is coded to signify the same global revolutionary subjectivity to which Guevara refers.[137] So, while the new revolutionary subject, as defined by Guevara and the OSPAAAL, finds its clearest expression in the politicization of the "colored" identity of the former slave, lending a central representative position to African American activists within the global anti-imperialist struggle, this discourse of color is transcendent of a direct relationship to physical appearance.

The rhetorical openness of the use of "color" in Williams's writings, which Rodriguez aligns with a Tricontinentalist ideology and that I call metonymic color politics, is distinct from the color-blindness for which Soviet communism was often criticized in that the Tricontinental does not reduce its project to a class struggle that will resolve racial inequality through the institution of socialism but rather places liberation from racial subjugation at the forefront of its political project.[138] In other words, it revives the Comintern's rhetoric on black liberation, which attributes a vanguard position to African Americans. However, rather than the class-over-race rhetoric of the Comintern, Tricontinentalism employs the category of color in an effort to foreground racial inequality without collapsing into racial essentialisms. Additionally, it does not engage in what Gayatri Spivak calls "a strategic use of positivist essentialism in a scrupulously visible political interest," or the homogenizing suppression of difference that is often used by marginalized peoples to forge an essentialized group identity for political purposes.[139] Rather, the common ideology that metonymically "colors" and unifies the Tricontinental's delegations creates a chain of equivalences that recognizes various experiences of oppression and exploitation. Diverse ethnic, national, and linguistic groups are linked through a shared Tricontinentalist worldview yet maintain their heterogeneity as individual movements with distinct causes and goals. This can be seen clearly in the OSPAAAL's posters, through which, most often, the OSPAAAL announces a specific day of solidarity that is to be celebrated with a specific struggle, acknowledging the unique identity of each movement but situating it within the larger structure of the organization.

Although the Tricontinental acknowledges the individual circumstances of each cause represented and although the articles in *Tricontinental Bulletin* sincerely attempt to delve into the complexities of each movement, it must be said that the Tricontinental's cultural production oversimplifies the causes that it engages. However, this oversimplification is distinct from the essentialist associations with myth, irrationality, and other colonialist tropes encapsulated in the color curtain concept. Moreover, I do not suggest that there are no instances in Tricontinental materials where "color" is indeed used to refer specifically to race and phenotypic appearance. However, the Tricontinental's materials reflect an awareness of the danger of slippage from color as political abstraction to racial determinism and, on the whole, racial determinism in Tricontinental texts is not sustained.

This understanding of Tricontinentalism's metonymic color politics provides insight into reading a text like Álvarez's *Now*. For example, John Hess criticizes the way in which Álvarez conflates multiple groups within *Now*:

> When Álvarez sets up the analogy in *Now* among Nazis, the KKK, the U.S. government, the police and guardsmen (this was before Kent State), white racists, and LBJ, what is he trying to indicate? Is he arguing that they are all Nazis, that politically the U.S. is a fascist state. . . . Or is he saying that all these men . . . repress disenfranchised people? I can't answer this question, and think that this ambiguity, which works well on an emotional level, is also Álvarez's greatest weakness as a filmmaker.[140]

However, in view of the preceding discussion, we might consider Álvarez's fusion of images of repression into the oversimplified category of "North American policemen" in a different light. By depicting the white policemen's oppression of African Americans, Álvarez exploits the colonial categories of "white" and "colored." So, while the film exhibits an attempt to incorporate African Americans into the anti-imperialist project of the Tricontinental, it also appropriates an African American identity to stand in for all "the exploited people of the world." Just as the "policías" embody imperialist oppression, the "negros" epitomize Hardt and Negri's notion of the potential revolutionary multitude.

This is made more explicit in another of Álvarez's newsreels, *El movimiento Panteras Negras* (The Black Panther Movement), a newsreel about encounters between black militants and police in the United States, which was released on August 19, 1968. Following the opening sounds of sirens and bongos, a sonic representation of the divide between the white police and the black protestors depicted in the film, a voice-over reads a quote attributed to Malcolm X: "The African American problem is not a Negro problem or a North American problem but a problem of humanity."[141] In this way, the film immediately establishes the connection between African Americans' struggle and a larger international community.

The rest of the film alternates between quotes by Martin Luther King Jr. and Huey P. Newton, coupled with images of police brutality against African Americans and images from a police manual on riot gear with a voice-over that—in a *détournement* that is typical of Tricontinental materials—sarcastically narrates the manual with an invented text that reads like an advertisement.[142] Images from the police manual instructing on the use of military-grade mace are narrated by a man's voice who states, with the bravado and rhyming wit of a radio advertisement, "Mace is a novel chemical product to spray at rioting blacks' eyes. It never fails. A sprayed black is a down black. Request a free demonstration. Use mace and laugh at what takes place."[143] While the film posits that the tear gas, mace, flame-throwers, and tanks in the police manual are designed specifically for use against black militants, the voice-over also boasts that these weapons are "economical and efficient against workers, students, blacks, whites, and against all who disturb peace and order."[144] By extending the possible victims of police oppression to whites and to the general descriptors of students and workers, the film signals the many images of bloodied black protestors as emblematic of a larger power struggle that goes beyond a simplistic black/white divide.

This point is further emphasized in the last frame of the film, which states over a map of the world that 1968 is "the year of the heroic guerrilla fighter."[145] Instead of ending the film with a statement of solidarity with the Black Panthers or African Americans in general, the film explicitly collapses their struggle into a global unity and signals African American militants as representative of all the *guerrilleros* fighting imperialism all over the world. The film is at once a reference to the African American cause and to the struggles of black people everywhere as well as an abstraction of the global struggle represented by all Tricontinental delegations. The white policeman becomes a metonym for global empire and the black protestor stands in for all "the exploited people of the world."

This same argument is made more succinctly in the 1967 OSPAAAL poster (fig. 2.3) by the Cuban graphic artist Jesús Forjans in which the alignment between the message of Álvarez's films and that of the Tricontinental is displayed quite explicitly. The poster, which states "NOW!" at the top in black block letters depicts a white policeman with his back toward the camera, using his baton to threaten a black protestor who appears to be shouting and who is facing the camera. The image, taken from a photograph of a 1964 civil rights protest in Nashville, Tennessee, is quite similar to the photograph on the cover of the second issue of *Tricontinental Bulletin* that was discussed at the beginning of this chapter as signifying the Tricontinental's politics of identification and disidentification through a black/white divide. This poster overtly references Álvarez's film but extends its revolutionary message to the entire organization of the OSPAAAL.[146] Whereas almost all other OSPAAAL posters state the organization's geographically and culturally cross-cutting solidarity in three languages with a particular cause or group of people, the image on this poster, like the photograph discussed at the beginning of this chapter, need not be assigned to a particular group. It is at once a reference to the African American cause as well as an abstraction of the global struggle with which every OSPAAAL member can identify. The white policeman signifies global empire and the black protestor embodies the global subaltern struggle.

Considering this, I return to Hess's apparent confusion with the conflation of many causes and oppressive forces in *Now*. While perhaps a fair criticism of the totalizing perspective of the film as well as the Tricontinental itself, this critique is symptomatic of both a lack of historical context in discussions of *Now* and a dearth of scholarship on the ideology of Tricontinentalism. The way in which Tricontinentalism destabilizes colonial racial categories by employing its very vocabulary as markers of ideological position rather than

FIG. 2.3 Jesús Forjans, "NOW!" (1967). COURTESY LINCOLN CUSHING / DOCS POPULI.

phenotypic appearance is parallel to the way in which it deterritorializes empire through locating its victims in the geographic North.

The Tricontinental's vision of global oppression and resistance employs a defined geographic location, the U.S. South, and a clearly demarcated racial divide as metonyms for a geographically fluid and transracial global subaltern subjectivity. This discursive move is, I would argue, a trope that is repeated in a range of anti-imperialist cultural production in the Americas, meaning that I would like to suggest a film like *Now* as more of an exemplar than simply an isolated filmic event. In looking beyond similar texts' apparently simplistic oppositions by seeing how their representations of local hegemony are actually metaphors for an immanent empire and how their racialized discourses are divorced from a one-to-one relationship to physical appearance, we may begin to outline a Tricontinentalist poetics and, in doing so, better situate our engagement with emerging concepts of transnational subalternity within the wider trajectory provided by Tricontinentalism.

THREE

The "Colored and Oppressed" in Amerikkka

Trans-Affective Solidarity in Writings by Young Lords and Nuyoricans

On December 7, 1969, a group of mostly Puerto Rican and African American men and women between the ages of eighteen and twenty-two, wearing military fatigue jackets and purple berets and calling themselves the Young Lords, attended a testimonial Sunday at the First Spanish Methodist Church in El Barrio, or East Harlem. Inside the sanctuary of the large brick church, the Lords planned to "testify" to request approval from the middle-class Puerto Rican congregation to use the church's facilities to host a free-breakfast program for children. Although the pastor, a Cuban exile named Reverend Humberto Carranza, had already denied their request several times, the Lords insisted that these facilities were unused six days a week.[1] In their view, they were offering to provide the food and manpower to ensure that the neighborhood's children could arrive to school fully fed and ready to learn; all they needed from the church was the space. During the months of October and November, the Young Lords attended several worship services and coffee hours to try to convince the congregation to allow them to use the facilities. Throughout one service, the Lords reportedly stood up when the congregation sat down and sat down when the congregation stood up. At another service, they each held up a copy of a poster depicting Jesus Christ carrying a rifle over his shoulder, a quintessential image of liberation theology intended to critique the church's isolation from the surrounding community.[2]

This particular poster, mentioned only in passing in a Methodist diocesan report, is one of the many posters distributed by the Organization of Solidarity with the Peoples of Africa, Asia, and Latin America (OSPAAAL) among its constituents around the world. It was designed for the Tricontinental alliance in Havana in 1969 by the Cuban artist Alfredo Rostgaard, and it contained the logo for the OSPAAAL in the upper right-hand corner. The Young Lords' use of this internationalist OSPAAAL poster in an otherwise local, neighborhood dispute in East Harlem should not be passed over lightly. It is not mere coincidence and is just one of many instances that speak to a transnational exchange between the Young Lords in the United States and the material production and ideology of Tricontinentalism, an exchange that is the central focus of this chapter.

The mounting tension between the Lords and the First Spanish Methodist Church during the months of October and November 1969 came to a head on December 7 when the Young Lords' chairman, Felipe Luciano, rose to speak at the testimonial Sunday and was reportedly prevented from doing so by plainclothes policemen whom the pastor had alerted of the Lords' presence. This led to a brawl between police, Young Lords, and congregation members in the sanctuary in which Luciano would eventually leave the scene with a broken arm.[3] On December 28, the Young Lords responded by taking over the church, barricading the building and famously renaming it "La iglesia del pueblo," or "the People's Church." For the duration of their eleven-day occupation that ended when the church was surrounded and overtaken by police, the Lords used its facilities to provide free-clothing drives, breakfast programs, a day-care center, health programs, political education, and nightly entertainment to the local community. During a slow news cycle, the church takeover received widespread media attention. Celebrities like Jane Fonda and Pia Lindstrom arrived on the scene to interview these young, politically conscious activists sporting afros, dark sunglasses, and berets displaying their logo (a raised fist holding a gun over the outline of a map of Puerto Rico).[4]

The entire church takeover and occupation was captured on film by Newsreel, a collective of radical filmmakers founded in New York City in 1967, which released the footage in their powerful documentary on the Young Lords, *El pueblo se levanta* (The People Are Rising) (1971).[5] This film opens with footage from inside the People's Church in which twenty-five-year-old Pedro Pietri, who would become one of the most famous poets of the burgeoning Nuyorican literary movement, delivers his now-canonized poem "Puerto Rican Obituary" for the very first time.[6] Following his spoken-word performance, the film cuts to the sound of machine guns firing while the words "THE NEWSREEL" flash in white, block letters on a black screen. Significantly, and again not coincidentally, this was a direct reference to the closing frame of Santiago Álvarez's Tricontinental newsreel *Now*—discussed at length in the previous chapter—which the New York group Newsreel was responsible for distributing throughout the United States.[7]

In its first ninety seconds thus, *El pueblo se levanta* draws a link between the literary and cultural production of the Nuyorican movement to which Pedro Pietri was central, the Young Lords' church takeover and political organizing in East Harlem, and the ideology of Tricontinentalism to which Álvarez's film alludes. The connections between these—the Young Lords, the Nuyorican movement, and the global Tricontinental alliance headquartered in Havana—will form the central coordinates of this chapter.

While it is well known that several Nuyorican poets like Pietri, Felipe Luciano, and Pablo "Yoruba" Guzmán were actively involved with the Young Lords Party, the political contextualization of the Young Lords and of Nuyorican writers within contemporary scholarship on these subjects generally does not extend beyond an association with the Black Panther Party (BPP), Puerto Rican nationalist movements, and a broadly defined notion of "Third Worldism."[8] However, although it has gone unnoticed in scholarship on the Young Lords and the Nuyorican movement thus far, I argue that these writings contain an explicit and direct engagement with the ideology of Tricontinentalism. In other words, many of these writings directly reflect the Tricontinental's deterritorialized notion of empire, its characterization of African Americans as vanguards of a global struggle, as well as its metonymic color politics in which a racial vocabulary is used to refer to a revolutionary subjectivity organized around mutual ideological affinity rather than identity categories. By overlooking the Tricontinentalist platform of the Young Lords Party and of many closely related Nuyorican writings from the late 1960s and 1970s, prior scholarship on these subjects has failed to truly understand the political ideology put forth in these writings. In fact, I would argue that any scholarly approach to the Young Lords and to closely related Nuyorican writings that does not situate them within the broader frame of Tricontinentalism is one that falls far short of a complete and informed analysis of these works.

The study of Tricontinentalism in Nuyorican writings in this chapter furnishes the scaffolding for what I will call the Tricontinental's model of trans-affective solidarity in which the ideology of Tricontinentalism is both upheld by and produces as surplus value an imagined transnational, transethnic, transracial, and translinguistic affective encounter. That is, the Tricontinental's ideal vision of a collective social subject is not forged through the social contract provided by the state or through a narrow definition of class or race but rather through a radical openness facilitated by affective encounter. The Tricontinental envisions a political subject whose becoming rests in "making solidarity itself," to use Lauren Berlant's terms, or in forging a collectivity through the "attachment to the process of maintaining attachment" and to "the pleasure of coming together."[9] The Tricontinentalist project of generating a new transnational political subject held together through affective attachment—which is articulated in a wide range of closely related artistic and literary texts and which anticipates models of resistant political subjectivities under contemporary global capitalism—presents itself as a rehearsal for the eventual realization of a new global social relation. In this sense, as I will argue in the coming pages, the means and the ends of Tricontinentalist politics are the same: the repetitive and persistent proclaiming of affective relation and community across national, linguistic, and ethnic borders is both the political act and the ultimate aspiration of Tricontinentalism.

While the Tricontinental's model of trans-affective solidarity will be addressed at length, this chapter is structured according to three primary objectives. First, after providing a brief background on the Young Lords and situating this organization within the broader "U.S. Third World Left," I use the Young Lords and Nuyorican writings as a case study for how Tricontinentalism circulated outside of Cuba and outside of materials produced by the Tricontinental alliance itself.[10] As I have argued in previous chapters, Tricontinentalism did not originate with the 1966 Tricontinental Conference; rather, the OSPAAAL became an official mouthpiece for theories of power and political subjectivity that were already in circulation. This is especially relevant when considering groups like the Young Lords, whose roots are also found in the black Atlantic négritude/negrismo/New Negro exchange, which I have defined as a foundation for the later emergence of Tricontinentalism. Whereas the previous chapter outlined the discourse of Tricontinentalism in texts produced within Cuba, the New York Puerto Rican texts analyzed here speak to the circulation of this discourse in a range of cultural production beyond materials distributed by the OSPAAAL and beyond the writings of African American Black Power activists. Through the analysis of the Young Lords' Tricontinentalist writings and especially its multiracial political vision, I introduce in this section the notion of the Tricontinental's model of trans-affective solidarity in which Tricontinentalism both produces and is dependent on affective transgressions of racial, linguistic, national, and class borders.

At the same time that a study of Tricontinentalism in New York Puerto Rican texts reveals how this discourse circulated outside of Cuba, the OSPAAAL also disseminated Young Lords' writings among its international constituency. Considering the inclusion of Young Lords' texts within the pages of *Triconti-nental Bulletin* provides a helpful lens for understanding the Tricontinental's precarious political positioning between Cuba's communist government and the diverse constituents of the alliance. Through a discussion of the Young Lords' progressive politics on gender and sexuality alongside Cuba's so-called *quinquenio gris* (five gray years) (1971–1976), a period of repression of artistic and sexual freedoms in Cuba, the second objective of this chapter is to outline the tension between the increasing Sovietization of the Cuban state in the early 1970s and the Tricontinental's role as a site of convergence for radical organizations with diverse views. The discussion of gender and sexuality in this chapter sets the stage for the chapter that follows, which addresses more fully the dissonance between the policies of the Cuban state and the rhetoric espoused in the majority of Tricontinental materials, a dissonance that is especially apparent in the realm of racial justice discourses.

Finally, after tracing the material and ideological exchange between the Young Lords and the Tricontinental and using this exchange to discuss the Tricontinental's mediation between its international constituents and the Cuban state, I then move beyond political ephemera toward a study of the circulation of Tricontinentalism in closely related literary writings. Through these literary works, I return to the Tricontinental's model of trans-affective solidarity since this Tricontinentalist vision of political collectivity is poeticized in many of these writings. Through readings of creative works by Nuyorican writers Pedro Pietri, Felipe Luciano, and Miguel Algarín, and through an extensive analysis of Piri Thomas's *Down These Mean Streets* (1967), this chapter's discussion of New York Puerto Rican literature provides an opening for future scholarship that would explore the influence of Tricontinentalism in parallel cultural movements.

At first glance, the inclusion of Piri Thomas's *Down These Mean Streets* in this analysis of literary writings may seem out of place both because Thomas was not affiliated with the Young Lords and because, although he influenced them greatly, he was considerably older than the other Nuyorican writers considered in this chapter. However, the discussion of Thomas's book—especially regarding its representation of the Jim Crow South as a microcosm of global inequities, its discussion of solidarity with African Americans, and the protagonist's identification with a Southern black subjectivity—not only reveals the presence of Tricontinentalist ideology in Nuyorican writings decades prior to the official formation of the OSPAAAL but also demonstrates how the lens of Tricontinentalism changes how we read even such an exhaustively studied text. In this sense, this chapter models a Tricontinentalist reading praxis, providing an opening for future scholarship that would engage in a reorientation of movement-era texts through the transnational lens of Tricontinentalism.

THE YOUNG LORDS AND THE U.S. THIRD WORLD LEFT

The Young Lords Organization (YLO) initially formed as a street gang in 1968 in Chicago. Through fighting the removal of Puerto Ricans from the Lincoln Park neighborhood and through the leadership of José "Cha-Cha" Jiménez, it quickly became an organization dedicated to social justice. News of the YLO reached New York when the June 7, 1969 issue of the BPP's newspaper published an article about the formation of a "Rainbow Coalition" among the Chicago BPP, the YLO, and the Young Patriots Organization (a white street gang turned leftist political activist group aimed at assisting migrants from the Appalachia region).[11] This article circulated among members of a group of undergraduate students at the State University of New York College at Old Westbury who were interested in the history of Puerto Rican national liberation movements and who had formed a reading circle called the Albizu Campos Society (SAC), named after the Puerto Rican independence leader and former president of the Puerto Rican Nationalist Party, Don Pedro Albizu Campos, whose death in 1965 sparked several student groups in the New York City area that modeled themselves after his work.[12] After an eighteen-year-old SAC member named Pablo "Yoruba" Guzmán read the article in The Black Panther about the Rainbow Coalition, Guzmán and fellow SAC members, Miguel "Mickey" Meléndez and David Pérez, drove to Chicago to meet Cha-Cha Jiménez and the YLO.[13]

Despite their shyness as young college-educated community organizers around Chicago gang members, the three returned home with permission from Jiménez to open a YLO chapter in New York. This branding came with purple berets because, as Guzmán writes, "even though they claimed to be moving away from street life, the Lords weren't giving up their colors."[14]

Immediately upon their return, on Saturday, July 26, 1969, the sixteenth anniversary of Castro's 26th of July Movement, the New York chapter announced its formation at a demonstration in the East Village's Tompkins Square Park.[15] The differences apparent from the beginning between the two chapters would eventually lead to their split in April 1970, and the New York chapter would change its name to the Young Lords Party.

The membership of the Young Lords Party would eventually reach the thousands. It was primarily made up of Puerto Rican youth, born or raised stateside, from working-class and Spanish-speaking families, but it also included African Americans, white Americans, and youth of Cuban, Dominican, Mexican, Panamanian, and Colombian descent who grew up in close proximity.[16] Twenty percent of its membership was African American, including Denise Oliver, the first woman named to the organization's Central Committee.[17] In the Young Lords Party's short existence, before the ideological shift through which it became the Puerto Rican Revolutionary Workers' Organization in 1972 and before eventually dissolving in 1975, the organization accomplished a great deal.

Within months of its founding, the Young Lords Party created its own bilingual newspaper, *Palante* (Forward), and radio show. It organized several successful community projects such as programs to provide free breakfasts and lead-poisoning detection. Through their first and highly successful initiative—the famous "Garbage Offensive"—the Lords called citywide attention to the Department of Sanitation's neglect of poor communities in the city, achieving reform and attracting more members to the organization.[18] Eventually, branches were set up in Hoboken, Newark, Jersey City, Bridgeport, New Haven, and Philadelphia. Other major successes for the Lords include the occupation of the neglected Lincoln Hospital in the South Bronx, where they called for improvements in conditions and care and for worker-community control of its operations and where they even began a successful heroin detox program inside the hospital, as well as the so-called liberation of a TB truck to vaccinate neighborhood children against tuberculosis (an action for which the young lawyer and later TV star Geraldo Rivera would intervene on behalf of the Lords).[19] In October 1970, the Young Lords Party mobilized ten thousand people for a march on the United Nations. It also created an Inmates' Liberation Front that participated in the negotiations that followed the September 1971 Attica Prison riot.[20]

The Young Lords Party emerged alongside the "Black . . . Red, Yellow, and Brown Power Movements" of the 1960s and 1970s in the United States that included such organizations as the BPP, the American Indian Movement, the Brown Berets, and the Red Guards, among others.[21] These organizations responded both to opportunities in education and community organizing provided through the governmental policies of Lyndon B. Johnson's War on Poverty and to the deficiencies of those programs in addressing the needs of urban, poor communities. They formed part of a larger trend that Laura Pulido and Cynthia A. Young have each keenly called a U.S. "Third World Left," which was composed of organizations with "a membership of at least half people of color" with varying ideological positions, such as revolutionary nationalism, Marxism-Leninism, and Maoism.[22] Many of the organizations that made up the U.S. Third World Left drew inspiration from post–World War II decolonization movements in Africa and Asia, African American civil rights in the United States, and the Cuban and Vietnamese struggles against U.S. military intervention.

In providing an alternative 1960s historiography to those of the white-dominated "New Left," both Pulido's and Young's individual studies of the U.S. Third World Left argue that an engagement with the Cuban Revolution was central to the internationalist orientations of many of these movements, and they emphasize the importance of print culture in spreading Third World leftist ideas around the globe. However, neither of their works mentions the Tricontinental alliance (OSPAAAL) despite the fact that the OSPAAAL, as I outlined in previous chapters, served as the primary infrastructure for the production and dissemination of much of Third World leftist political ephemera.

In the pages of *Tricontinental* and *Tricontinental Bulletin*, there is significant evidence of a sustained exchange between many U.S. organizations and the OSPAAAL. Moreover, Tricontinentalism as a discourse and political ideology would deeply inform the views of key activists and organizations within the U.S. Third World Left. For example, George Mariscal has challenged the lens of cultural nationalism through which the Chicano movement is often framed, pointing rather to the internationalist perspectives of key Chicano leaders, like Reies López Tijerina and Rodolfo "Corky" Gonzáles, and organizations such as the Alianza Federal de Pueblos Libres (Federal Alliance of Free City-States), the Brown Berets, and the Crusade for Justice. Mariscal devotes an entire chapter of his book, *Brown-Eyed Children of the Sun: Lessons from the Chicano Movement, 1965–1975* (2005), to Chicano participation in the Venceremos Brigades in Cuba and to the meaning of Cuba, and especially the figure of Che Guevara, within the iconography of the Chicano movement.

While he does not mention the Tricontinental or any of its cultural production, many of the examples of Chicano internationalism that he cites contain overt echoes of Tricontinentalism. For example, Mariscal discusses the work of Elizabeth "Betita" Sutherland Martínez—"perhaps the best-known Chicana with civil-rights and social-justice credentials"—as a clear example of the internationalist position of some key figures of the Chicano movement.[23] He explains that she sought to transform the ethnic nationalist Chicano category of *la familia* (the family) "into an internationalized solidarity of resistance, what she called 'the whole familia of La Raza, the whole family of oppressed peoples.'"[24] Martínez significantly began her activist career by working on behalf of Robert F. Williams, the African American activist discussed in the previous chapter who was present at the Tricontinental Conference, through "traveling to Monroe, North Carolina, in order to join the Robert Williams Defense Fund."[25] Mariscal also mentions that Martínez traveled several times to Cuba, including her attendance, along with Stokely Carmichael and members of the Student Nonviolent Coordinating Committee (SNCC), at the July 1967 meeting of the Organization of Latin American Solidarity (OLAS) after which she published her insightful analysis of postrevolutionary Cuba in *The Youngest Revolution: A Personal Report on Cuba* (1969).

However, an important point left out of this contextualization is that the OLAS was composed of the Latin American delegates of the larger OSPAAAL, and the 1967 OLAS meeting that Martínez and Carmichael attended was organized as a smaller follow-up to the 1966 Tricontinental Conference. Indeed, Martínez even wrote articles for the OSPAAAL publications *Tricontinental* and *Tricontinental Bulletin*.[26] More important, alongside the material evidence for Martínez's engagement with the OSPAAAL, her framing of *la familia* as an "internationalized solidarity of resistance" made up of "oppressed peoples" has obvious resonance with the Tricontinental notion of "the exploited people of the world" that is outlined in the previous chapter.[27]

Members of the U.S. Third World Left like Martínez engaged with the Tricontinental's transnational and transethnic vision to varying degrees. Whereas the BPP and the Los Angeles–based Asian American East Wind made major efforts to form multiracial coalitions and the BPP maintained an ongoing material exchange with the OSPAAAL, other organizations like the Chicano Center for Autonomous Social Action (CASA) were "less inclined to emphasize multiracial activism."[28] Similarly, some American Indian organizations—like the National Indian Youth Council, which first employed the term "Red Power"—demonstrated hesitance toward multiethnic civil rights organizing because these coalitions could threaten to muddle specific American Indian claims to "treaty rights, sovereignty, self-determination, and cultural preservation."[29] These differences also occurred within individual organizations themselves. For example, although some members of the Chicano organization the Brown Berets developed an internationalist position in which they "started talking about Che Guevara, the Cuban revolution . . . started forming a Third World ideology . . . started reading Mao, Fanon," their prime minister, David Sánchez, apparently never strayed from his culturally nationalist and antileftist position.[30]

In this sense, the case study on the Young Lords in this chapter is not intended to serve as a universal example. Not all activists and organizations within the broader Third World Left engaged Tricontinentalism to the level of the Young Lords or even at all. Rather, this case study on the Young Lords is intended to provide an opening for future scholarship that would create a fuller portrait of the relationship between Tricontinentalism and radical organizations within the United States, within the three continents of the Tricontinental alliance, and beyond.

The Young Lords Party's membership was made up of mostly children of economically disadvantaged individuals who migrated from Puerto Rico in the context of Operation Bootstrap, the post–World War II industrialization campaign in which U.S. companies were encouraged through tax exemptions to move their factories to the island where they could pay significantly lower wages. Operation Bootstrap caused a rapid shift from an agricultural to a manufacturing economy; despite the new manufacturing jobs, the collapse of the agricultural industry left many unemployed, resulting in an enormous surge in migration mostly to New York City. According to Lisa Sánchez González, "From the late 1940s to the 1960s, the stateside Puerto Rican population grew from about seventy thousand to almost one and a half million people strong, over half of whom took up residence in the New York City area."[31] The parents of the Young Lords came to the mainland looking for better opportunities for themselves and their children; instead, they often found a life of tenement housing, unsafe living conditions, more unemployment, and further poverty.

The Lords viewed their conditions in New York as directly resulting from forced migration due to the U.S. economic and military domination of the island.[32] In this sense, they identified closely with the island's history of nationalist struggles and with other Puerto Rican pro-independence organizations formed in the 1960s like the Pro-Independence Movement, Armed Commandos of Liberation, and the Independent Armed Revolutionary Movement. However, although the Lords saw themselves as inheritors of the legacy of the struggle for independence in Puerto Rico—organizing demonstrations to coincide with anniversaries of key moments in the nationalist struggle like El Grito de Lares, the Ponce Massacre, and the Jayuya Uprising—they were also critical of what they viewed as a bourgeois liberalism underlying earlier nationalist movements.[33]

Similar to the BPP, they described their movement as developing out of the working class and *lumpen*, which they used to refer to the sector of society that includes the chronically unemployed, drug addicts, and prostitutes.[34]

Significantly, however, the Young Lords Party did not just view their political project within a Puerto Rican nationalist frame. Rather, I argue that they envisioned their struggle through the internationalist lens of Tricontinentalism. The Tricontinentalism of the Lords' ideology can be found in their writings and propaganda, such as in the newspaper *Palante*, the film *El pueblo se levanta*, the 1972 pamphlet *Ideology of the Young Lords Party*, and a 1971 compilation of Young Lords writings called *Palante: Voices and Photographs of the Young Lords, 1969-1971*. In these materials, the Lords argue—like the Tricontinental—that African Americans hold a vanguard position in a global war against imperialism. They position themselves as fighting alongside these vanguards, contributing to the struggle from an important position that is both geographically and constituently internal to empire. Most significantly, the Lords align with Tricontinentalism by employing a radically inclusive political signifier of color to refer to a global and nonracially essentialist revolutionary subjectivity to which they consider themselves to belong.

THE YOUNG LORDS' TRICONTINENTAL STRUGGLE IN AMERIKKKA

In a photograph (fig. 3.1) by the Young Lords photographer Hiram Maristany, Minister of Education Juan González looks proudly at the camera from the doorway of the Young Lords headquarters in El Barrio.[35] The front window of the headquarters to his left is covered in political posters, many of them containing images of heroes of Puerto Rican independence like Pedro Albizu Campos and the poet Julia de Burgos. On the far right side of the window hangs the 1969 Tricontinental poster by Alfredo Rostgaard that the Lords held up in the First Spanish Methodist Church in the weeks leading up to the church takeover. It depicts Jesus Christ with a halo around his head and a gun on his back.

In the lower left corner hangs another 1969 Tricontinental poster by Rostgaard, made for the third anniversary of the Tricontinental Conference, in which a guerrilla fighter in multicolor camouflage appears with a blank face that can be filled in by any one of the three faces on the right side of the poster (at the top, an African with black skin and blue hair; in the middle, an Asian with yellow skin and purple hair; and, at the bottom, a Latin American with red skin and gray hair) that are intended to represent the three regions of the Tricontinental alliance (fig. 3.2).[36] This image draws on the Black, Yellow, and Red

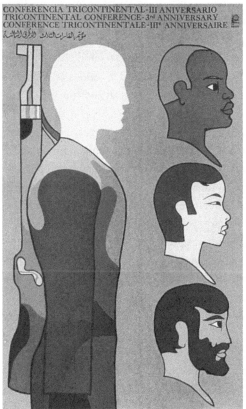

FIG. 3.1 Juan González at the Young Lords' headquarters (1969). PHOTOGRAPH BY HIRAM MARISTANY.

FIG. 3.2 Alfredo Rostgaard, poster for the third anniversary of the Tricontinental Conference (1969). COURTESY OF LINCOLN CUSHING / DOCS POPULI.

"Power" movements of the moment.[37] At first glance, it appears profoundly simplistic, adopting the language of colonialism that groups heterogeneous populations into color categories, and representing, for example, the diverse region of Latin America through a "Red" history of indigenous struggles, a representation that could be viewed as appropriating indigeneity and veiling the tenuous relationship that many Latin American leftist movements affiliated with the Tricontinental alliance had with indigenous communities.[38] However, considering the discourse of Tricontinentalism laid out in the previous chapter, this poster also captures the fluidity of the Tricontinental's use of color to describe its revolutionary subjectivity.

As outlined previously, Tricontinentalism seeks to provide an alternative to both the color-blindness for which the rhetoric of the Comintern was criticized as well as to the race-based essentialism of the black Atlantic notion of a color curtain by conceiving of a new, nonessentialist, and primarily ideological political signifier of color. Tricontinentalism foregrounds issues facing racially oppressed peoples, conceiving of global capitalism as racial capitalism, but the relationship between a Tricontinentalist revolutionary subjectivity and racial and ethnic identity categories is always unstable. Through its metonymic color politics, in which it defines the Tricontinentalist subject as "colored," color transcends racial and ethnic categorizations and functions as a signifier of a resistant ideological position shared by a transracial and transethnic political community.

While the poster does maintain three distinct racial categories to represent the three regions, its use of color—a metonym for the revolutionary unity of Tricontinentalism—is deliberately multiple; it is black, yellow, red, but also blue, purple, and green. The Tricontinental's revolutionary subject depicted in this poster is not presented as a literal depiction of solidarity between three clearly defined and static racial groups but rather is multifaceted, leaving only the Tricontinental's open political signifier of color as a marker of its resistant community. This Tricontinentalist position, which drew together a white Puerto Rican like González with other Lords members like African American Denise Oliver or black Puerto Rican Pablo "Yoruba" Guzmán, is, I argue, the intrinsic yet heretofore overlooked basis of the entire internationalist ideology of the Young Lords' early years.

As indicated by the photograph of González at the Lords' headquarters, there is ample evidence of the level of material culture for an exchange between the cultural production of the Tricontinental and the Young Lords. For example, an OSPAAAL poster that was folded up in the March–April 1970 issue of *Tricontinental* later appears in the lower right-hand corner of an article in the October 16, 1970, issue of *Palante*. The article, entitled "U.S. Out of Quisquella" (employing the Taíno name for the island of Hispaniola), decries U.S. interference in political affairs in the Dominican Republic.[39] Below the article is an image taken from a poster by OSPAAAL artist Rostgaard—intended to depict the 1965 invasion of Santo Domingo by the U.S. military—in which the profile of a white U.S. soldier holding a white machine gun is splintered by a black machine gun that emerges out of the poster's pitch-black background. Similarly, an image from an OSPAAAL poster of a raised fist in the shape of the South American continent holding a gun, which the Cuban artist Asela M. Pérez Bolado designed for the 1970 International Week of Solidarity with Latin America, appears in the center of an article on armed struggle in Puerto Rico by Juan González in a 1971 issue of *Palante*.[40]

This transnational exchange of ideas and visual culture was mutual, meaning the OSPAAAL images did not just contribute to the pages of *Palante*, but the Young Lords appear in Tricontinental materials as well. The January 1970 issue of *Tricontinental Bulletin*, for example, discusses the Lords' participation in the Rainbow Alliance in Chicago.[41] In the same year, the July–October 1970 issue of *Tricontinental* published an exclusive interview with Cha-Cha Jiménez along with the Chicano leader Corky González.[42] Most significantly perhaps, illustrations of the New York Young Lords Party's Minister of Finance Denise Oliver and Field Marshall Gloria González appear on the front and back covers of the March 1971 issue of *Tricontinental Bulletin* (figs. 3.3 and 3.4), which reprints the Lords' Thirteen-Point Platform as well as its position paper on women's roles in liberation struggles.[43]

Yet beyond this material evidence for the Young Lords' integration into the transnational political exchange facilitated by the Tricontinental, I argue that Tricontinentalism underlies the fundamental tenets of the Lords' ideology. Although these connections have not been discussed in prior scholarship, I would argue that any scholarly approach to the Lords' political platform that does not situate them within the broader frame of Tricontinentalism is one that fails to truly understand the ideological underpinnings of this highly influential and historically significant organization. Whereas—as Monica Brown has pointed out in her discussion of gangs in East Harlem—the gang model provided some members of previous generations of New York Puerto Ricans with an "individual and collective identity in ethnic and geographic (territorial) terms," the Lords would propose an opposing model constructed around a deterritorialized and ethnically fluid political community.[44] In the

FIGS. 3.3 AND 3.4 The front and back covers of *Tricontinental Bulletin* 60 (March 1971).

pages that follow, I trace this Tricontinentalist vision within Young Lords texts, eventually proposing the Young Lords as a case example of what I call the Tricontinental's model of trans-affective solidarity.

According to Minister of Education Iris Morales, who traveled to Cuba in the mid-1960s with a Venceremos Brigade, the Young Lords envisioned themselves as "part of a larger movement . . . connected with millions of people" and were moved to change a world social and economic order by the "Cuban and Chinese revolutions and by liberation struggles in African and Latin America."[45] *Palante* clearly exhibits this global vision by reporting on liberation movements on other continents, such as in Vietnam, Guinea-Bissau, and Palestine, and establishing links between those struggles and that of the Lords. In an article entitled "Free Palestine" by Felipe Luciano, for example, the Lords position their own political project as unified with that of Palestinians, stating that, "like our brothers and sisters in Palestine, the Young Lords Party is fighting the battle for the liberation of all oppressed people."[46]

Similarly, a February 19, 1971, article declares, "Puerto Ricans must realize that our fight is the fight of the Laotians, of the Vietnamese, of the Cubans, of the Brazilians, of the Guineans, of the Native American (Indian), and of Black people living in the u.s."[47] While the United States is identified as the primary enemy throughout Lords propaganda materials, *Palante* also reports on struggles with a less clearly defined link to the U.S. government. The March 5–19, 1971 issue, for example, is "devoted to checking out various struggles around the world" and includes a collage of minireports on diverse liberation struggles that visually equate police violence against African Americans in Wilmington, North Carolina, to government repression in Milan, Italy, to worker strikes in Argentina, India, and Panama.[48] Like in Tricontinental materials, here the enemy becomes delinked from the United States as a geographically defined nation-state and is presented in much broader terms.

While the Lords' writings show an openness toward and incorporation of Marxist analysis, they consistently frame their struggle not primarily in terms of class but through a political signifier of color. This Tricontinentalist positioning is reflected in the Lords' Thirteen-Point Program and Platform, originally written in 1969 and reprinted in *Tricontinental Bulletin* as well as on the final pages of every issue of *Palante*. This platform describes the Young Lords Party as a "revolutionary party fighting for the liberation" of "all colored and oppressed people," and it claims that, like anticolonial and anti-imperialist struggles around the world, "the Latin, Black, indian, and Asian people inside the u.s. are colonies fighting for liberation."[49] Here, their position reflects the internal-colony model, an open and flexible conceptualization of colonialism that many U.S. Third World Left organizations used to compare their own experiences of ghettoization, police brutality, and racialized oppression under U.S. capitalism to colonialism elsewhere.[50] However, the Lords here also suggest a confluence between the notion of "colored" and the broader term of "oppressed," an equivalence that I will discuss in more detail shortly.

In the film *El pueblo se levanta*, Pablo "Yoruba" Guzmán explains to a group of activists inside the sanctuary of the "People's Church" that the Lords' political project "ain't just East Harlem. Remember we relate to an international struggle. It may sound ridiculous, but this all links up from what's happening from Vietnam to Puerto Rico to Watts. Don't ever forget that. . . . We in the belly of the monster and people all over are waiting for us to take care of business." Guzmán frames the Lords' organizing in East Harlem as part of a global, Tricontinental struggle, in this case specifically against U.S. imperialism, that unifies Vietnamese, Puerto Rican, and African American radicals, and in a way identical to the discourse in Tricontinental materials, he emphasizes the importance of the struggle waged from within the heart of empire.

In her analysis of *El pueblo se levanta*, Cynthia A. Young points out that immediately after Guzmán's speech "the film cuts to the police raiding the People's Church. In effect, [the] editing elevates the Lords to the level of national liberators."[51] However, if we frame this moment of the film within the Tricontinentalist ideology detailed in the previous chapter, we might understand the police here as a stand-in for global empire, situating the Lords' takeover not as a nationalist movement, as Young suggests, but as part of the international struggle that Guzmán describes. This use of policemen to metonymically signify a global system of white supremacy and imperial dominance is reiterated throughout *Palante* through the image of the pig, a derogatory term for policemen. In the spirit of the representation of the "pig" in *The Black Panther*, and especially in Emory Douglas's iconic illustrations therein, in the section "Pig of the Week" in *Palante,* the pig is employed to capture the entirety of a racialized system of oppression, referring not only to policemen but also to district attorneys and judges who are presented as complicit in the attempted destruction of the Lords through trumped-up conspiracy charges. This is reiterated through illustrations of pigs in *Palante*, such as one on the back cover of a 1970 issue that discusses the deplorable conditions in Lincoln Hospital and in which two pigs in white lab coats hold money in their hands as they stab a Puerto Rican man lying on a hospital bed.[52] In this image, the pig clearly stands in for the government and private mechanisms of racial capitalism whose power permeates all aspects of life and death.

Through the figure of the pig and other forms of apparently simplistic oppositional language and imagery, the Lords attempted to capture the plural and decentralized mechanisms of power and propose an equally decentralized, Tricontinentalist vision of resistance. For example, in yet another appropriation of OSPAAAL materials, the December 23–January 9, 1971 issue of *Palante* includes a portion of the 1967 OSPAAAL poster by the Cuban artist Jesús Forjans in which a white policeman, whose back faces the camera, threatens to hit a black protestor with his baton.[53]

As I argued in chapter 2, this particular OSPAAAL poster, whose title, "NOW!," references Álvarez's eponymous film as well as the African American struggle in general, intentionally does not state its solidarity with a particular struggle as do most other OSPAAAL posters. Rather, the image is employed to demonstrate the Tricontinental's nonessentialist politics of identification and disidentification through an apparently simplistic black/white divide. Indeed, *Palante* employs this image precisely in the deterritorialized manner in which the Tricontinental intended it, using it not in a discussion of African Americans but rather in an article on government oppression in Aguadilla, Puerto Rico. Here again appears an example of the metonymic color politics of Tricontinentalist materials: the police or "pig" is a metonym for the mechanisms of power that rule life and death everywhere from New York City to Aguadilla, and the black protestor metonymically signifies a global resistance that is equally expansive in its conceptualization.

Like in Tricontinental materials, among those the Lords call "colored and oppressed people," they attribute a particularly representative position to black people, and especially to African Americans. This is indicated clearly in an article on alliances between the BPP and the Young Lords from the February 19, 1971 issue of *Palante*, which states, "The Young Lords recognizes that Black people have been and are the most oppressed group of people in amerikkka. As such, Black people will lead, the revolution, in the u.s."[54] This position is further developed in *Palante: Voices and Photographs of the Young Lords, 1969–1971*, in which Deputy Minister of Information Pablo "Yoruba" Guzmán writes, "We know that the number-one group that's leading the struggle are Black people, 'cause Black people—if we remember the rule says the most oppressed will take the vanguard role in the struggle—Black people, man, have gone through the most shit."[55] This position is frequently summarized in Young Lords materials by their consistent spelling of America as "Amerikkka." Like in the arguments made in *Tricontinental*, *Tricontinental Bulletin*, and Álvarez's *Now*, the racial oppression of the Jim Crow South, of which the Ku Klux Klan is a clear symbol, emerges as a microcosm of an unequal power structure not only in the United States but also metonymically around the globe. Just as the KKK, like the white policeman in *Now*, stands in for that global hegemony, "black people" in the United States epitomize for the Young Lords those "colored and oppressed people" around the world.[56]

Central to the Young Lords' identification with black people is a critique of the racism by some Puerto Ricans toward their African American neighbors in Harlem. In an article entitled "Racismo Borinqueño" (Puerto Rican Racism), Iris Morales discusses the myth of racial equality in Puerto Rico as well as the commonly held belief that racism on the island is due solely to U.S. influence. Morales argues that racism began in Puerto Rico with Spanish colonialism where it was used "as a justification for exploiting labor to get economic profit."[57] Morales is as critical of ideologies of whitening from the Spanish colonial legacy as she is of the more rigid racial structure in the United States, and she condemns those Puerto Ricans in the United States who attempt to "negate their blackness" and who are racist toward African Americans.[58] Both Puerto Ricans and African Americans are "victims of capitalism together," she argues, and "so we must pick up the gun and fight the racist, capitalistic pig together!"[59]

This critique of antiblack racism within Puerto Rican communities was embraced by the Young Lords leadership. In this sense, the Lords represented an alternative to other organizations of the Puerto Rican Left, such as the Puerto Rican Socialist Party, that identified more with traditional Marxism and whose leadership has been described as "being composed of upper-class Whites from Puerto Rico who looked down their noses at poor and working-class darker-skinned Puerto Ricans born in the United States" and who "adhered to a linguistic chauvinism that privileged Spanish over English and saw language, and other cultural markers, as defining nationality."[60] The Lords' racial and linguistic exclusion from leftist organizations headquartered on the island likely contributed to their identification with a broader, Triconti-nentalist solidarity and affiliation with organizations beyond Puerto Rican nationalist groups.

Regarding Puerto Rican antiblack racism, Guzmán writes,

Even in New York, we found that on a grass-roots level a high degree of racism existed between Puerto Ricans and Blacks, and between light-skinned and dark-skinned Puerto Ricans. We had to deal with this racism because it blocked any kind of growth for our people, any understanding of the things Black people had gone through. So rather than watching Rap Brown on TV, rather than learning from that and saying, "Well, that should affect me too," Puerto Ricans said, "Well yeah, those Blacks got a hard time, you know, but we ain't going through the same thing." This was especially true for the light-skinned Puerto Ricans, Puerto Ricans like myself, who are dark-skinned, who look like Afro-Americans, couldn't do that, 'cause to do that would be to escape into a kind of fantasy. Because before people called me a spic, they called me a nigger.[61]

In contrast to what Guzmán identifies as Puerto Ricans' disidentification with African Americans, Guzmán suggests that he draws from a collective memory of oppression in which he shares with African Americans the experience of being called a "nigger." The bond that is created through a shared experience of racialization links, as John Márquez writes in describing contemporary "black-brown solidarities," the "subjectivities of two racial subject positions, black and Latino/a, resulting in a compound subjectivity ... from which blacks and Latino/as can and often do collectively engage in new forms of resistance."[62]

However, whereas Márquez's notion of a "compound subjectivity" is formed through "a collective memory of similar forms of subjection," I would argue that the Lords' resistant subjectivity is even more broadly conceived in that, like the Tricontinental, it goes beyond collective experiences and circumstances and is forged around a shared ideology.[63] Perhaps we could claim that this ideology necessarily emerges from a shared experience of subjugation, but those shared experiences would have to be defined in very imprecise terms. For example, the fourth point of the Lords' Thirteen-Point Platform states, "Puerto Ricans are of all colors and we resist racism. Millions of poor white people are rising up to demand freedom and we support them.... Power to all oppressed people!"[64] The inclusion of poor whites, which is repeated throughout the Lords' writings, is striking because their inclusion is due both to the shared condition of being "poor" and "oppressed" and to their ideological affinity through which they are "rising up to demand freedom."[65]

The Lords consistently identify one of the strategies of imperial domination as "divide and conquer," which, as Education Lieutenant Iris Benítez explains, "is used in Amerikkka between blacks and Puerto Ricans, non-whites and poor whites."[66] For this reason, the Lords view themselves as fighting alongside "our African American, Latino, Asian, and oppressed white brothers and sisters."[67] Here the experience of oppression faced by some whites includes them among the "colored and oppressed people" whom the Lords claim to represent in their platform. Other times, the Lords claim that "whites must prove themselves," suggesting that for whites to belong to this global revolutionary subjectivity requires an ideological commitment rather than simply a condition of oppression.[68] Both ideological and conditional terms of inclusion are used to describe the Young Patriots Organization, which helped found the Rainbow Alliance in Chicago, and who are characterized in *Palante* as a "poor white progressive group."[69] Either way, it seems that a very broadly defined collective experience is used to determine inclusion into whom the Lords consider their "brothers and sisters," but, more important, it is the ideological position of being progressive, demanding freedom, or proving oneself that determines the terms of this amalgamated subject position.

In place of the phrase "colored and oppressed people," at times the Lords simply use "oppressed people" and at other times they employ the term "Third World people." Guzmán conflates this global subjectivity with "women, poor whites, gays, and anyone else who doesn't think or look like George Washington."[70] In other words, just as Robert F. Williams's Tricontinentalist description of Castro as "colored" situates him among Guevara's "we, the exploited people of the world"—discussed in chapter 2—the Young Lords' representation of "colored and oppressed peoples" in their platform is not necessarily meant to be a descriptor of race or phenotype. "Colored" becomes a political signifier, rather than an ethnic or racial signifier, of a global resistant subjectivity. This flexible use of color implies that whiteness too becomes a fluid category disconnected from phenotype. Whiteness emerges as a signifier of capitalistic oppression, which is summed up in the images of the policeman, the pig, and the white elite that "look like George Washington."[71]

This is not to say that there are not moments of racial and ethnic essentialism in the Lords' writings, but in general, I would argue that such essentialism is not sustained. Rather, as Tricontinentalist texts, the Lords' writings tend to push beyond a racially deterministic signifier of anti-imperialism and toward an abstract use of color that indexes an ideological position of resistance to imperialist subjugation rather than a narrowly defined race-based collectivity. The Young Lords' political subject—while not defined by race or nationality— coalesces around an ideology that is both upheld by and that produces solidarity as an affective relation. In this sense, I suggest, the Young Lords' and the Tricontinental's visions are similar to theories of political subjectivity within the context of contemporary capitalist globalization, which I will discuss in the coming pages, in which a global political subject is bound together not through the social contract provided by the state but through a radical openness facilitated through affective encounter.

TOWARD A TRANS-AFFECTIVE SOLIDARITY

In recent years, scholars are rethinking how political community is forged by examining the relationship of politics to affect, those forces beyond consciousness that drive bodies toward movement.[72] Drawing on the works of Baruch Spinoza, Gilles Deleuze, and Félix Guattari, affect in this recent scholarship generally refers to the capacity of a body to affect and to be affected, often autonomically and not necessarily through conscious decisions. While the so-called affective turn has a wide range of implications, since the mid-1990s a corpus of politically engaged scholarship within affect theory has emerged that—as characterized in the *Affect Theory Reader*—considers how disparate bodies' experiences with similar and repetitive enactments of power through global capitalism yield affective relations between those bodies that create the potential for a new form of politics.[73] For example, drawing on Michael Hardt and Antonio Negri's notion of the multitude as the emergent transnational political subject under late global capitalism, Jon Beasley-Murray has argued that the multitude, which he states "is not the traditional working class" or "the delimited identities of cultural studies' multicultural alliance," is characterized by its openness and inclusivity.[74] Its expansion, he writes, "proceeds by means of *contiguity* and contact, in resonances established through affective encounter.'"[75]

Considering that recent social movements have largely been defined by a new form of global solidarity politics—in which activists around the world express their solidarity with one another through Twitter hashtags and other digital media—we might consider this new, collective political subject to be bound together through what Clare Hemmings has called "affective solidarity."[76] Hemmings uses this term within feminist politics to indicate a move away from identity politics or even from solidarities forged through empathy and toward a political community based on affective relation. Affective solidarity refers to the political potential of affect as it is produced out of diverse bodies' mutual experience of power, as it passes from one body to another through the mutual instantiation of proclaiming solidarity, and as the affective encounter rehearses the realization of a world different from the current one. These affective politics of solidarity are, as Juliet Hooker explains, "based on fellow feeling, but . . . it is also more than just an emotion, it is also a normative orientation that moves us to action on behalf of others."[77] Tricontinentalism could be understood quite similarly in that all of its cultural production, published in four languages, is directed toward the creation of a fellow feeling that would move people to action on behalf of its constituents across the globe.

The Tricontinental's particular vision of a revolutionary subjectivity that traverses national, linguistic, racial, and ethnic categories is forged through what I would call a trans-affective solidarity, by which I mean that it is dependent on and simultaneously produces an affective transgression of borders. This is similar to Christopher Lee's conceptualization of the Bandung alliance as a communitas based on political fellow feeling and not on "locality or blood."[78] However, in the case of Tricontinentalism, this model of trans-affective solidarity does not just rest on fellow feeling; it also seeks to produce that fellow feeling through affective crossings. While affect is often used to refer to those forces below consciousness that drive us to action, Spinoza claimed that the body's actions and cognition are inseparable and develop in parallel. This is how I understand Tricontinentalism, where, as an ideological construct, it harnesses, is supported by, and produces as surplus value a political imaginary that is always situated in the envisaged affective traversing of borders.[79] As Tricontinentalism rests on and produces affective solidarity, the political action to which its trans-affective solidarity orients its constituents is intentionally fluid and undefined. Rather, the ends of Tricontinentalism, the ultimate realization of its political subject, is found in "making solidarity itself," a praxis of producing affect that both prepares for and pivots toward a new global relation.

This form of collective politics, which has primarily been studied within contemporary global capitalism but which has profound roots in Tricontinentalism, is a form of politics that, as Berlant writes, represents "an attachment to the process of maintaining attachment" where "one 'does politics' to be in the political with others, in a becoming-democratic that involves . . . the pleasure of coming together once again."[80] In this sense, we might consider that being political for the Young Lords had less to with developing a precise programmatic vision for Puerto Rico or for the U.S. urban poor and more with the act of proclaiming their belonging to a Tricontinentalist community of "colored and oppressed peoples." The repetitious proclaiming and rehearsing of a new resistant community is both the Young Lords' political ideology and political praxis.

A trans-affective solidarity that is transnational, translinguistic, transethnic, transracial, and transclass is the underlying support of and the surplus produced by a Tricontinentalist ideology in its most ideal form. The duty of the Tricontinentalist is to affect and to be affected, to participate in the process of making solidarity as it passes from one body to another and as it rehearses the emergence of a new collective body and a new global relation. This model of trans-affective solidarity will be addressed further in this chapter through its appearance in the poetics of Nuyorican writers and will be picked up again in the final chapter in relation to contemporary social movements and Black Lives Matters' concept of transformational solidarity. However, first I consider how the envisioned openness of Tricontinentalist political subjectivity and affective community had the potential within the Young Lords' Tricontinentalist praxis to transgress borders of gender and sexuality as well as how these transgressions within Tricontinentalism ran up against the limitations of the Cuban state.

REVOLUTIONARY GENDER AND SEXUAL POLITICS:
THE YOUNG LORDS, CUBA, AND THE TRICONTINENTAL

Through their expansive sense of community and solidarity with all "colored and oppressed people," the Lords operated as a markedly inclusive organization. While often understood as a solely Puerto Rican nationalist group, their diverse membership and Tricontinentalist rhetoric demonstrate a commitment to a fluid concept of community that nuances and problematizes stable national, ethnic, and racial identities. These initial zones of indistinction in regards to race, ethnicity, and nation within Young Lords ideology would eventually lead the Lords to challenge gender norms and to take on a gender and sexual political agenda that was particularly progressive in comparison to other similar groups within the Chicano and Black Liberation movements of the period.[81]

Ironically, at the same moment that the Young Lords were using their open, Tricontinentalist position on race and nation to create a more progressive gender politics, the Cuban Revolution was increasingly repressing sexual and intellectual freedoms. In this sense, Tricontinentalism contains an inherent tension—detailed in the following section—in which it attempts to mediate between its diverse constituency and the political positions of the Cuban state. This is certainly the case with gender and sexual politics, but, as detailed in chapter 4, this tension is even more apparent regarding a commitment to racial justice.

Although the YLP focused on women's oppression—such as protesting the sterilization of Puerto Rican women—and called for equality for women from the very beginning, the initial Central Committee was made up of all men: David Pérez as minister of defense, Felipe Luciano as chairman, Pablo "Yoruba" Guzmán as minister of information, Juan González as minister of education, and Juan C. Ortiz as minister of finance. Women in the YLP were assigned roles like childcare and secretarial work, and they faced sexual advances from their male counterparts.[82] In response, in 1970, the women in the organization created a women's caucus and composed a list of ten demands, including the election of a woman to the Central Committee, in order to promote the equal participation of women on all levels.

In May 1970, they lobbied for the revision of the Thirteen-Point Program and Platform, which was originally written in October 1969, to be more critical of *machismo* and more inclusive of women. Point 10 was revised from "We want equality for women. Machismo must be revolutionary, not oppressive" to "We want equality for women. Down with machismo and male chauvinism," and its position within the platform was moved to point 5.[83] They insisted that childcare be provided at meetings and that the newspaper include articles about women's liberation struggles as well as articles written by women.[84] They founded the Woman's Union, an organization focused on issues of childcare and health concerns facing Latina women, which began publishing its own newspaper, *La Luchadora*.[85]

In an early contribution to Third World feminism's analysis of the intersections between race and gender oppression, the Lords penned their "Position Paper on Women," which argues that "Third World women" face three different forms of oppression that include racial and gender oppression by the dominant culture as well as violence from "their own men."[86] They argue that women's exploitation as cheap sources of labor and sexual objects—which pushes them into the role of breadwinners—combined with a capitalistic image of manhood defined by money and status results in frustration and violence that is taken out on the bodies of Third World women by their male partners. They critique the way in which historical accounts have silenced women's roles in liberation struggles, contributing to the celebration of women for being good cooks, housewives, and mothers and the characterization of the politically engaged woman as "aggressive, castrating, hard and unwomanly" as well as "sexually accessible because what else is she doing outside of the home."[87] While they recognize that "our major enemy is capitalism rather than our own oppressed man," they insist that they are "fighting every day within our PARTY against male chauvinism."[88]

As a result of these women's call for equality and the challenge to traditional gender roles within the Party, in a 1971 collection of Lords writings, Minister of Information Guzmán would claim, "Gender is a false idea, because gender is merely traits that have been attributed through the years to a man or a woman."[89] He attributes this understanding to the influence of the "sisters" in the Party but also to that of "the Gay struggle for liberation."[90] As early as the fall of 1970 in *Palante*, Guzmán was including "gays" among those "Third World people, women, poor whites, gays, and anyone else who doesn't look or think like George Washington" that the Lords claimed to represent.[91] The Lords would eventually form a Gay and Lesbian Caucus.[92] Sylvia Rivera, a transgender woman of working-class Puerto Rican and Venezuelan background who was the cofounder of Street Transvestites Action Revolutionaries (STAR) and a member of the Gay Liberation Front and who famously participated in the Stonewall riots, marched with the STAR banner in a 1970 Young Lords demonstration against police brutality.[93] She then became a member of the Lords and brought STAR into the Young Lords as well.[94]

Denise Oliver, an African American woman whose parents were communists and who had a long history of activism in the National Association for the Advancement of Colored People, Students for a Democratic Society, and SNCC, was at the forefront of efforts to reform the Lords from within.[95] Although she had been one of the founding members and although she wrote many of the articles and drew the illustrations for *Palante* from its very inception, her role is initially listed under editorial staff in *Palante* as "communications secretary."[96] However, Oliver refused to be relegated to secretarial tasks within the organization, commenting since, "I didn't want to learn how to type because I didn't want to be typecast."[97] When the YLP agreed to elect a woman to the Central Committee, Oliver was the obvious choice, and her title was changed to minister of finance.

The leading role of women in the organization is reflected in the March 1971 issue of *Tricontinental Bulletin* in which an illustration of Oliver appears on the front cover and Oliver and Field Marshall Gloria González appear on the back cover (see figs. 3.3 and 3.4). Through these illustrations, the Lords are defined to an international community of readers by their women leaders, whose gender is stereotypically emphasized by the multiple shades of pink in the cover artwork, but whose berets—described as being "tipped in the manner of Che Guevara"—and direct gazes communicate a position of masculinist defiance and militancy.[98] While this issue includes the unrevised version of the Thirteen-Point Program and Platform, which it states was taken from an October 16, 1970 issue of *Palante,* the issue also includes the "Position Paper on Women."

The Tricontinental's focus on the women leaders of the Young Lords in this issue indicates a larger trend away from an implied male subject and toward a focus on women's activism in liberation struggles that is reflected in Tricontinental materials throughout the 1970s. Beginning in the early 1970s, women revolutionaries are often the subjects of Tricontinental posters and cover art, and articles by women authors and interviews with women revolutionaries appear with much more frequency in *Tricontinental* and *Tricontinental Bulletin*. The November–December 1974 issue of *Tricontinental*, for example, publishes the Resolution of Solidarity from the Second Congress of the Federation of Cuban Women (FMC), an organization created in 1960 in an effort to create equal opportunities for women in Cuban society. In this resolution, the nearly two thousand Cuban women delegates present at the conference express their solidarity with militant women all over the world.[99] In the pages that follow the resolution, articles on women's political organizing by revolutionaries like Fatiah Bettahar from the General Union of Algerian Women, May Sayeb y Salwa Khadia from the General Union of Palestinian Women of the Palestinian Liberation Organization, as well as Angela Davis, appear below each leader's photograph.[100]

Angela Davis in particular became an iconic figure in Tricontinental cultural production in the 1970s. Davis traveled to Cuba to attend the Second Congress of the FMC, an organization whose efforts to raise awareness of her controversial incarceration after being charged with the murder of a California judge contributed to her celebrity status within Cuba.[101] Alfredo Rostgaard designed a 1970 OSPAAAL poster in which a handcuffed Davis raises her arms over her head, breaking the chains that bind her wrists. Among other articles on Davis, a June 1971 issue of *Tricontinental Bulletin* published portions of an interview with her from her jail cell. An illustration of Davis's profile inside the mouth of a snake made to look like a U.S. flag appears alongside the article; beneath Davis's profile, Klansmen celebrate with trumpets and cymbals her consumption by the American serpent, a metaphor for her capture and imprisonment after two months in hiding.[102] In this sense, the appearance of Denise Oliver and Gloria González on the covers of the March 1971 issue of *Tricontinental Bulletin* formed part of a general trend within the Tricontinental to foreground women's central roles in liberation struggles.

The particular issue of *Tricontinental Bulletin* devoted to the Young Lords appeared during a pivotal moment in the history of the Cuban Revolution, a fact that points to an ongoing tension between Cuban national discourse and the transnational ideology of Tricontinentalism. In the late 1960s and early 1970s, Castro's Cuba was increasingly repressing sexual, artistic, and intellectual freedoms. One month after the publication of the issue of *Triconti-nental Bulletin* devoted to the Young Lords, intellectuals in Europe and Latin America wrote an open letter to Castro, published on April 9, 1971, in the Paris newspaper *Le Monde*, protesting the imprisonment of the Cuban poet Heberto Padilla who was forced to publicly repent for his book of poems, *Fuera del juego* (Out of the Game) (1968). This controversy, which would become known as the Padilla Affair, is generally viewed as the beginning of what the Cuban author Ambrosio Fornet called the quinquenio gris, a period of Stalinization of culture and repression of artistic freedoms in Cuba. Largely in response to this letter, the Castro government held the First National Conference on Education and Culture from April 23 to 30, 1971. This conference, which sought to define the Revolution's relationship to cultural and artistic activity, announced the beginning of a process of *depuración* (purification) of the nation's cultural institutions and the naming of Luis Pavón Tamayo, president of the National Council of Culture, to oversee the process.[103]

A few months after the conference, the July–August 1971 issue of *Tricontinental* reprinted the declaration of the conference in which eight hundred representatives from various organizations in Cuba provided recommendations for the country's educational and cultural politics. These statements included the condemnation of clothing styles associated with bourgeois forms of rebellion in capitalist countries and the description of homosexual activity as a "social pathology" in opposition to revolutionary militancy.[104] Among its many resolutions, the conference concluded that homosexuals would not be allowed to engage youth in artistic and cultural activities, claiming that even those with high levels of artistic talent should not be allowed to exercise influence within the state's cultural organizations. The conference thus announced the removal of homosexuals from positions of institutional influence.[105]

That this attack on gay Cubans and an implied relationship between homosexuality and intellectual activity were direct responses to the international outcry against Padilla's imprisonment was reinforced through the cover art for the *Tricontinental* issue in which these declarations appear. On the cover, the outline of a thin, angular man flies through the air embracing a book, his toes pointed gracefully behind him. His rainbow-colored wings are attached to red and blue ribbons that emerge from an American-flag, Uncle Sam top hat. The inside cover explains the artwork as the image of the "Third world intellectual disengaged from his environment, alienated from his very manner of expression by a symbiosis of colonization, and who, through the loss of contact with reality, becomes an instrument—conscious or not—of the oppressor of his own people."[106] It goes on to state that the reproduction within the magazine of the General Resolution from the First Conference on Education and Culture represents the Cuban Revolution's response to those Third World intellectuals who have criticized it. Indeed, the cover artwork characterizes these intellectuals as effeminate, tied to U.S. interests, and out of touch with reality. Notably, up until this particular issue, *Tricontinental* was distributed by Maspero Editions in Paris, France, and the Feltrinelli Bookshop in Milan, Italy. Those distributors quietly dropped out from all future Tricontinental publications in apparent protest over Cuba's growing intolerance and oppression of intellectual, artistic, and sexual freedoms.[107]

I mention this controversy because it demonstrates a tension contained within Tricontinental materials and within the organization itself. On the one hand, these materials are produced by the Cuban state and thus reflect the Cuban state's ideological positions; on the other hand, they represent a site of convergence for radical organizations with diverse views. The fact that the issue of *Tricontinental Bulletin* on the Young Lords, an inclusive organization that was far more progressive on gender and sexuality than its counterparts, appears one month before Cuba's First National Conference on Education and Culture captures this tension. Although the issue on the Young Lords does not mention their Gay and Lesbian Caucus or involvement with transgender activists, the materials published in this issue are deeply critical of gender and sexual politics within revolutionary organizations themselves. The tension between the rhetoric of the Cuban state and that espoused in the majority of Tricontinental materials will be much more apparent in the realm of racial justice discourses, which I will discuss in depth in chapter 4.

In sum, Tricontinental materials did not always directly align with Cuban politics, and, when they did, they did so at the peril of alienating the Tricontinental's transnational membership. In the same vein, the Lords' Tricontinentalism was not directly tied to the Cuban state either. Although the Lords published a series of articles on the history of the Cuban Revolution and incorporated OSPAAAL materials into *Palante*, their ideological Tricontinentalism was, in many ways, independent of any relationship to Cuba.[108] For example, an article in *Palante* on U.S. intervention in the Dominican Republic concludes with the phrase "Puerto Rico, Santo Domingo, y Vietnam—Unidos Vencerán!" (Puerto Rico, Santo Domingo, and Vietnam—united will overcome!).[109] In this quintessential articulation of a Tricontinentalist solidarity, Cuba does not figure; the Lords' Tricontinentalist alliance with struggles all over the world exists whether or not Cuba functions as mediator. This is an important point for considering the continued influence and relevance of Tricontinentalism long after the global Left's disillusionment with the Cuban Revolution. In other words, the Tricontinental's deterritorialized notion of empire, its privileging of African Americans as representative of the global struggle, as well as its use of a racial vocabulary to refer to a revolutionary subjectivity based on an ideological position of anti-imperialism all represent a discourse that does not begin or end with the Tricontinental alliance itself.

In the following pages, I suggest that this discourse appears not only in ephemera and propaganda materials produced by a political organization like the Young Lords Party, but also in closely related literary and cultural forms. I trace, thus, the thread of Tricontinentalism in the literary writings of a cultural movement very closely aligned with the Young Lords Party, the Nuyorican literary movement, and point especially to its presence in one of the most famous texts of Nuyorican literature, Piri Thomas's *Down These Mean Streets*. Through the analysis of these writings, I eventually return to the Tricontinental's trans-affective solidarity, considering how it is poeticized in these literary works. The tracing of Tricontinentalism in these literary works serves as a case study of the way in which Tricontinentalism circulates in a much broader set of Cold War radical texts, providing an entry point for further scholarship on this highly influential discourse.

NUYORICAN LITERATURE AND THE TRICONTINENTALIST TEXT

The Young Lords appeared in New York at the end of the 1960s and beginning of the 1970s alongside several Puerto Rican nationalist organizations, like the Puerto Rican Student Union and the Puerto Rican Socialist Party that made up the so-called Puerto Rican Movement of the time period.[110] Concurrent with the rise of these political organizations was a renaissance of cultural and artistic expression focused on social justice for people of Puerto Rican descent living in New York City. Through the efforts of the poet Miguel Algarín to create the Nuyorican Poets' Café in 1973 and through Algarín and Miguel Piñero's anthology *Nuyorican Poetry: An Anthology of Puerto Rican Words and Feelings* (1975), this cultural and artistic renaissance would become known as the Nuyorican literary movement.[111] Many of the writers in this movement, which includes such well-known authors as Miguel Algarín, Victor Hernández Cruz, Sandra María Esteves, Pablo "Yoruba" Guzmán, Tato Laviera, Felipe Luciano, Nicholosa Mohr, Pedro Pietri, Miguel Piñero, and Piri Thomas, among others, collaborated closely with Puerto Rican political organizations like the Lords and many were from the same age group and generation as the Lords' membership. Pietri's spoken-word performance of "Puerto Rican Obituary" from inside the People's Church, which opens the film *El pueblo se levanta*, is perhaps the most-cited example of the integration between Nuyorican politics and literature, but there is ample evidence of these artists' involvement with the Lords as well as with the Puerto Rican Socialist Party.[112]

Through their poetry and prose, Nuyorican writers of the late 1960s and early 1970s spoke to the impoverished conditions in which Puerto Ricans lived in the city and the lack of political rights for Puerto Ricans living on and off the island. Their work rejected the U.S. narrative of equality and freedom, proclaiming the emptiness of the so-called American Dream, pointing to the colonial oppression of Puerto Rico, and exposing a widespread culture of racial discrimination in the United States. Like the Lords, whose slogan "Tengo Puerto Rico en mi corazón" (I have Puerto Rico in my heart) is grammatically incorrect in standard Spanish, Nuyorican writers embraced vernacular forms of Spanish and English, using their East Harlem brand of bilingualism to create a linguistically avant-garde and community-conscious Nuyorican poetics.[113]

The political impulses of the Nuyorican literary movement are widely recognized. However, there is a tendency among some contemporary critics to oversimplify the ideological perspective expressed in these works. Juan Flores's influential and otherwise incisive *Divided Borders: Essays on Puerto Rican Identity* (1993) perhaps best embodies this position when writing of the Nuyorican literary movement: "For despite its origins in proletarian misery, and its forceful protest against abusive conditions, this art rarely suggests any specific revolutionary project. Typically, the tone is one of prolonged sarcasm, and the outcome of any emotional movement is existential desperation or individualized brooding."[114] While Flores dismisses these works as lacking an ideological project, generally the resistant politics of the Nuyorican movement tend to be summed up with a brief paragraph about the broader political context, such as the emergence of the Young Lords Party and other Puerto Rican nationalist organizations as well as civil rights and anticolonialist movements in the broad sense.

Urayoán Nöel's innovative study, *In Visible Movement: Nuyorican Poetry from the Sixties to Slam* (2014), avoids using the term "the Nuyorican movement" because he views the poetry as an "alternative to the programmatic brand of revolutionary politics" embodied by the Young Lords, which he characterizes as a "Marxist hardline approach," describing Nuyorican poetry rather as "a multiplicity of voices speaking one breath, joined by a decolonial sensibility and a commitment to a public (counter)culture of poetry."[115] While I would not deny that the Lords are programmatic in their platform and position papers or that they become increasingly ideologically rigid in later years, the analysis of the Lords' Tricontinentalism that I provide here aims to contribute to Nöel's nuancing of our understanding of Nuyorican writings from the period. The Young Lords' ideology demonstrates a flexible mobility at the limits and intersections of nationalism, internationalism, racial justice, and anticapitalist discourses that—beyond a clear commitment to militancy and a critique of the U.S. government—would be difficult to characterize as hardline and actually has more in common with the fluid sensibility of Nuyorican poetry that Nöel describes.

However, I also agree with Nöel's argument that while Nuyorican writers' work "shaped and was shaped by movement politics, it emerged not in lock-step with the movement, but as a constellation of poetic and political positions and possibilities."[116] In this vein, in what remains of this chapter, I propose to reread a few well-known texts of the early years of the Nuyorican literary movement as examples of how a critical engagement with Tricontinentalism can nuance our understanding of Nuyorican and other closely related radical writings. My intention is not to argue for a one-to-one reproduction of Tricontinentalist ideology in these texts but rather to consider how reading some Nuyorican literary works through a lens of Tricontinentalism may not only provide a more precise understanding of that "decolonial sensibility" that Nöel describes but also shed new light on the "poetic and political positions and possibilities" offered up by the texts themselves.[117]

While I eventually analyze texts by Pietri, Luciano, and Algarín—whose connections to the Young Lords are clear—and further develop there a discussion of trans-affective solidarity through their poetic representations, I devote much of the remainder of this chapter to a text that, while foundational for Nuyorican literature and highly influential to 1960s Nuyorican youth, was written by an author from a slightly earlier generation. Although Piri Thomas was the most famous and widely read Puerto Rican writer in the United States at the time and although his *Down These Mean Streets* was the first Nuyorican text to be embraced by mainstream U.S. publishers, he is not included in Algarín and Piñero's anthology, which focused on poetry, and he was somewhat peripheral to the direct political activism of many Nuyorican writers. Yet *Down These Mean Streets* could clearly be characterized as a Tricontinentalist text, especially regarding the political use of the Jim Crow South in the book, the sustained discussion on solidarity with African Americans, and the protagonist's identification with a Southern black subjectivity that eventually opens onto a broader global vision. The analysis of this text is thus intended to serve both as an example of the broad reach of Tricontinentalist discourse in writings by literary descendants of the négritude/negrismo/New Negro exchange—which I have pointed to as a root of Tricontinentalism—as well as an example of how Tricontinentalist ideology appears in texts conceived in the years before the first convening of the Tricontinental.

Down These Mean Streets is an autobiography and bildungsroman that chronicles the childhood of Piri Thomas, a Harlem-born son of a Puerto Rican mother and Cuban father, in Spanish Harlem in the 1940s; his young adulthood and involvement with drugs and gangs; and his prison time and eventual release in 1957. At the heart of *Down These Mean Streets* is the narrative of the personal transformation of the protagonist, Piri, in relation to his racial identity.[118] In this sense, Lisa Sánchez González has suggested that the novel is less a coming-of-age narrative than a coming-to-consciousness text.[119] At the beginning, Piri is resistant to being labeled as black, insisting that his Puerto Rican heritage affords him a higher status in the U.S. racial hierarchy, but by the end of the narrative, he proudly identifies as a black Puerto Rican and views his experience of racial discrimination as an impetus for political solidarity with African Americans.[120] *Down These Mean Streets* addresses the complexities of a specifically Afro-Latino experience in the United States, an experience that, both at the time and in the present day, often remains occluded in representations of Latinx communities.[121]

Because of the text's attention to Thomas's particular experience as a black Puerto Rican, Thomas is often seen as an intellectual successor of the famed Arturo Alfonso Schomburg, a black Puerto Rican writer and archivist who moved to New York in 1891 as part of a wave of Puerto Rican and Cuban political exiles who participated in the independence movements against colonial Spain in the late nineteenth century.[122] In 1892, Schomburg helped establish the Club Las Dos Antillas (Two Antilles Club), which worked for the independence of both Puerto Rico and Cuba from Spanish colonialism and which collaborated closely with the Cuban independence leader José Martí and his Cuban Revolutionary Party. Later, Schomburg became famous for his collection of historical documents related to the African diaspora in Spain and the New World, currently held at the Schomburg Center for Research in Black Culture with the New York Public Library.

Schomburg is most often known for his involvement in the Harlem Renaissance, and his commitment to the anticolonial cause and collecting of texts related to peoples of African descent throughout the Americas clearly embody the transnational exchange between the Harlem Renaissance, negrismo, and négritude. In other words, Schomburg's editorial and journalistic writings contributed to the body of work that emerged from this hemispheric dialogue and that sought to address a transnational racial hierarchy to which people of African descent were subjected throughout the Americas.[123] In Thomas's attention to the black Puerto Rican experience in Harlem, Schomburg's legacy is unavoidable, and in this sense, the Tricontinental and Piri Thomas find their roots in the same inter-American black literary and political interchange that is embodied in the figure of Schomburg himself.

While the oldest writings of mainland Puerto Rican residents are travel narratives of intellectuals organizing on behalf of independence in the mid- to late nineteenth century, generally mainland Puerto Rican literature is considered to have started at the turn of the twentieth century with the political exile of independence activists, like Schomburg, in New York in the 1890s.[124] Many of these early writings were journalistic and autobiographical and, according to Juan Flores, it was mostly during the mid-twentieth century that a Puerto Rican literature written about life in the mainland United States would truly emerge as a genre.[125] Writings that appeared during the industrialization of Puerto Rico from the late 1940s to the mid-1960s, which Flores describes as the second stage of literature about Puerto Ricans in the United States, often deal with the impoverished conditions and racial discrimination faced by Puerto Ricans in New York.[126] In general, these mid-twentieth-century New York Puerto Rican literary texts paved the way for the "third, Nuyorican stage in emigrant Puerto Rican literature."[127]

During the mid-twentieth century and beyond, African Americans and Puerto Ricans lived in close quarters in the Harlem community, but *Down These Mean Streets* was the first Puerto Rican literary text to bring these two groups together.[128] One of the major differences between the second stage of Puerto Rican migrant literature and the Nuyorican writers is the later writers' attention to the diverse language practices of the East Harlem community that resulted largely from interactions between Puerto Ricans and African Americans.[129] In this sense, *Down These Mean Streets* would be foundational for the Nuyorican literary movement in that it provides a complex linguistic mapping of Spanish Harlem in the mid-twentieth century that entails textual representations of diverse linguistic varieties, such as standard and nonstandard forms of Spanish, standard English, Puerto Rican English, Hispanized English, and African American Vernacular English (AAVE), or what Piri simply calls "a street blend of Spanish and English with a strong tone of Negro American."[130]

Much critical attention has been paid to the bilingualism of *Down These Mean Streets* and to its illuminating discussion of the problematics of ethnic identity. Prior readings examine how the text navigates both the rigid racial structure of the United States as well as the homogenizing Latin American discourse of mestizaje.[131] Studies of Piri's negotiation of these distinct but equally discriminatory discourses tend to address the text's success or failure to articulate a specifically Afro-Latino identity, and they view his identification with African Americans as aiding or hindering that goal.[132] This solidarity with

African Americans, in turn, is viewed as being based on a biological notion of race or a pan-Africanist concept of shared roots.[133] My reading builds on these previous studies but takes them in a different direction by questioning the very assumption that Thomas's examination of racial discourses is intended to resolve itself in a clear definition of an Afro-Latino identity from which a stable pan-Africanist solidarity with African Americans might be constructed.

Rather, I argue that through a close analysis of the specific moments in which Thomas textually represents AAVE, a poignant political argument emerges that transcends the apparent racial determinism generally understood as the basis for this solidarity. Through Piri's appropriation of African American speech, Thomas eventually points to a transnational power structure and proposes a political solidarity of resistance that is not bound by race or place but is, rather, equally global in its vision. In spite of the fact that Thomas defines the terms of this solidarity through a local geography and a racial vocabulary, I argue that his text ultimately aims to break completely with racial or geographic determinism and instead to propose a transnational, transracial, and transethnic subaltern, resistant subjectivity.

Prior scholarship has pointed to the autobiographical works of Black Power writers like Malcolm X or Eldridge Cleaver as clear influences on *Down These Mean Streets* and *Seven Long Times* (1974), Thomas's memoir about his seven years of incarceration, and have noted that Thomas marched for civil rights in the U.S. South with John O. Killens, with whom he was a fellow member of the Harlem Writers' Guild. However, an in-depth engagement with the political ideology of *Down These Mean Streets* has yet to emerge.[134] Although I recognize that *Down These Mean Streets* was written prior to the convening of the 1966 Tricontinental (Thomas began composing the text while in prison), and I do not suggest that Thomas had any direct contact with the alliance (such as owning copies of *Tricontinental* or its posters), I do argue that *Down These Mean Streets* engages directly with the worldview that the Tricontinental took up as its banner. By laying claim to an African American experience in the Jim Crow South, the text eventually articulates a strikingly similar vision of a deterritorialized power structure and global resistance to the one the Tricontinental would disseminate to liberation struggles around the world.

A NUYORICAN HEADING SOUTH: THE LINGUISTIC POLITICS
OF *DOWN THESE MEAN STREETS*

Down These Mean Streets's appropriation of an African American experience occurs through marked representations of AAVE. By using the term "marked," I draw from the many linguistic anthropological studies that have discussed how the social group with the most power constitutes the invisible norm from which everyone else is viewed as diverging.[135] The linguistic variety chosen by the dominant institutions and the representatives of these norms are then characterized by these institutions as superior, a phenomenon that has been called "the culture of monoglot Standard," represented in the United States by the hegemony of Standard American English.[136] The linguistic practices that diverge from this standard, and which often index other race and class divergences from white public space, are seen by these institutions as having an intrinsically negative value.[137]

Down These Mean Streets inverts this power dynamic. That is, it is not that Standard American English necessarily stands out as marked in the text but rather that, in contrast to the culture of this monoglot standard, Thomas immerses his reader in a textual linguistic landscape where the constant admixture of standard and diverse nonstandard varieties of English and Spanish establishes itself as its own internal and invisible norm, eschewing any nonstandard stigmatization by maintaining an unmarked status for this composite linguistic landscape within the text.[138] Integral to the text's linguistic landscape is the continued presence of both lexical and grammatical elements of AAVE.[139] These uses emerge out of and seek to textually represent the interactions between African Americans and Puerto Ricans in their shared Harlem community.[140] However, beyond the continuous presence of AAVE in Piri's narration, there are several exaggerated representations of African American speech that are explicitly marked in the text. These moments provide a window into the text's political thesis.

The first instance occurs when Piri's father loses his job with the Works Progress Administration, and Piri accompanies his mother to the home relief office where he serves as her translator to request food and clothing. Despite his young age, Piri perceives the humiliation his mother experiences when asking for government help. While they wait their turn to speak with the social worker, Piri overhears a woman named Mrs. Powell, whom he describes as "colored," speaking with one of the social workers: "What you-all mean, man? . . . That Ah'm taking help from you-all an' hit ain't legal? Ah tole you-all that mah man done split one helluva scene on me an' the kids. Shi-it iffen that sonavabitch evah showed his skinny ass round ouah pad, Ah'd put a foot up his ass so fast his eyebrows would swing."[141] Through such strategies as replacing the "I" with "Ah," writing "ain't," and using a hyphen to signal diphthongization in "Shi-it," Thomas marks Mrs. Powell's speech as distinct from both the norm established in the text and the Standard English with which the social worker questions the truth of Mrs. Powell's story. Piri comments that the social worker "had all our personal life put down in good English."[142] While the social worker possesses the standard ("good English") and therefore the power, Mrs. Powell, through her nonstandard speech, embodies the opposite.

By marking Mrs. Powell's speech to the point of exaggeration, Thomas creates distance between Mrs. Powell and the protagonist. Nevertheless, Piri admits that "her pleading was too close to my people's: taking with outstretched hands and resenting it in the same breath."[143] In other words, Piri recognizes that—in spite of their perceived differences—the circumstance of their poverty unites them, and in this moment, Thomas hints toward a contestatory solidarity that emerges out of a shared experience of oppression and that is defined in opposition to the dominant culture represented by the social worker. However, this suggestion of solidarity remains merely a gesture at this point in the text because of Piri's investment in differentiating himself as a Puerto Rican from African Americans.

These dynamics become more explicit in a scene that follows shortly afterward that takes place at Piri's school. Despite Piri's pleading, his teacher will not allow him to leave the class to use the restroom. Once Piri feels he cannot hold it any longer, he tries to leave and when the teacher physically prevents him from doing so, Piri hits her and runs out of the classroom with urine running down his leg. The principal of the school, looking to punish Piri for hitting a teacher, chases after Piri as he bolts out of the school toward his neighborhood, a chase that Thomas describes as an "uneven contest," emphasizing the power differential between the principal and the scared child.[144] Once Piri arrives to the building where his family lives, his neighbor, an African American woman named Miss Washington, stands in front of him to protect him from the principal. As in the earlier scene, Thomas signals a marked contrast in the linguistic varieties employed by the principal and Miss Washington.

In the scene that took place in the home relief office, Thomas did not indicate the race of the social worker, but the implication of the linguistic exchange was that he did not come from the same community as the people he was serving. This time, however, through Miss Washington, Thomas clearly indicates that the principal is white. When the principal explains to Miss Washington that Piri "punched a teacher and he's got to be chastised for it" she responds, "Now hol' on, white man. . . . There ain't nobody gonna chaz—whatever it is—this boy. I knows him an' he's a good boy—at least good for what comes outta this heah trashy neighborhood—an' you ain't gonna do nuttin' to him."[145] The contrast between the principal's and Miss Washington's words indexes not only the racial division between the characters but also their opposing views on the culture of the standard. Miss Washington's response to the principal's use of the word "chastise," saying "ain't nobody gonna chaz—whatever it is—this boy" signals a solidarity (the African American woman protecting the Puerto Rican child) against the culture of the standard represented by the principal.

Similarly, shortly afterward, the principal states, "This young man is gifted with the most wonderful talent for prevarication I've ever seen," to which Miss Washington responds, "What's that mean?," thus emphasizing the divisions between these characters once again through their vocabulary choices.[146] While the principal tries to make himself seem more benevolent by claiming that the term "prevarication" means imagination, Piri informs Miss Washington that the principal is actually calling Piri a liar. Based on the oppositional way in which Thomas presents the characters, it is not surprising that Miss Washington and the other neighbors believe Piri over the principal. Because of this community solidarity, the principal leaves and Piri remarks that "I felt like everybody there was my family."[147]

In spite of Piri's identification in this moment with Miss Washington as part of his family, I suggest that Thomas marks Miss Washington's speech with exaggeration in his text in order to communicate Piri's internalization of linguistic and racial prejudice. In other words, the linguistic representations of African American speech emblematize Piri's perception of his African American neighbors as different than, and inferior to, himself. Throughout Piri's childhood, he insists that he is not black but Puerto Rican, commenting, "It really bugged me when the paddies called us Puerto Ricans the same names they called our colored aces."[148] His insistence on his distinct identity, such that he corrects the insult "nigger" with "spic," reflects the protagonist's superiority complex over African Americans.[149]

Piri, whose brothers and mother have light skin, learns this behavior from his father. Like Piri, his father often exaggerates his Spanish accent to try to signal to white interlocutors, who he claims are less racist toward those perceived as being "Spanish," that he is not African American. Nevertheless, although Piri does not want to recognize it, Piri belongs to a society that identifies him as black. Because of his appearance, and in spite of his feelings of superiority, Piri experiences much the same discrimination that his African American neighbors do. Considering the importance of language for marking racial difference in the text, it is not surprising that the transformation that Piri experiences in relation to his racial self-perception is manifested on a linguistic level.

For example, one of the first moments in which Piri has to confront this racialization occurs in a white community on Long Island where his family has moved. When Piri tells a white girl at the school dance that he is Puerto Rican, she is surprised because he does not have a Spanish accent but rather an accent that she describes as "more like Jerry's."[150] Piri thinks to himself, "*What's she tryin' to put down?* . . . Jerry was the colored kid who recently had moved to Bayshore."[151] When Piri asks her to dance, she courteously replies that she has a boyfriend, but moments later, Piri overhears her whispering to her friends, "imagine the nerve of that black thing."[152] Her friends respond that, Puerto Rican or not, "he's still black" and therefore should not have asked a white girl to dance with him.[153] Considering that African American speech is so marked in the text, the comment that Piri has an accent like Jerry's is suggestive. It could mean that Piri's speech and that of his African American neighbors are not as different as is represented in the text or it could suggest that Piri's physical appearance, for the girl, implies an accent that the girl predetermines even before Piri begins speaking. Whatever the reason, Piri finds himself in a system in which he is identified as black in spite of whatever self-perception he may have.

The notion of a black identity that is imposed from the outside becomes especially clear when Piri returns to Harlem and becomes friends with an African American character named Brew, who speaks very similarly to Mrs. Powell and Miss Washington. Piri and Brew start a friendly game of insults that Thomas calls the "dozens."[154] In this game, Piri calls Brew an "ugly spook" to which Brew responds, "Dig this Negro calling out 'spook.'"[155] When Piri insists, like he has throughout the text, that he's not black, but Puerto Rican, Brew remarks, "You think that means anything to them James Crow paddies?"[156] For Brew, blackness is an essentializing and homogenizing category assigned by those in power, a concept akin to what Frantz Fanon has called being "overdetermined from the outside."[157] Therefore, according to Brew,

"Jus' cause you can rattle off some different kinda language don' change your skin one bit. Whatta yuh all think? That the only niggers in this world are in this fucked-up country?"[158]

This conversation with Brew begins a process of personal transformation for Piri that results in his deciding to travel to the U.S. South to see "what a *moyeto*'s worth and the paddy's weight on him."[159] In other words, he wants to experience a racial power structure to which he is subject that, while certainly present in the North, manifests itself most obviously in the Jim Crow South. Piri's growing sense that he is united with African Americans through a shared experience of oppression by white, dominant culture becomes more explicit when Piri is asked to leave a white restaurant in Mobile, Alabama. The racial divisions in the South offer a clear and honest picture of the inequalities that Piri has felt subconsciously throughout his life in which the constitutional promise of equality is "only meant for paddies. It's their national anthem, their sweet land of liberty."[160]

The image of racism and inequality with which Piri is confronted in the South is, for Thomas, only a microcosm of a larger structure. From the South, Piri decides to work for the U.S. Merchant Marine, which allows him to travel around the world delivering U.S. goods. On these travels, Piri discovers that "wherever I went—France, Italy, South America, England—it was the same. It was like Brew said: any language you talk, if you're black, you're black."[161] In this sense, like in the Young Lords' use of the term "Amerikkka," the Jim Crow South becomes a synecdoche of a global system of inequality in which blackness indexes a transnational and translinguistic subalternity that is oppositional to an equally global oppressor.

Much in the same way that Thomas employs the U.S. South as a metonym for a global system, I argue that Thomas takes up an overdetermined category of blackness to describe a transnational subaltern subjectivity that is, like that of the Tricontinental, not intended to be essentializing or racially deterministic. This becomes most clear in the two instances that occur immediately before and after Piri's trip to the South when Piri himself employs the marked variety of AAVE that Thomas previously attributed to African American characters. Before leaving for the South, Piri tells his blonde-haired, blue-eyed younger brother, José, that he has realized that he is of African descent, meaning, according to Piri, that his brother is also black on the "inside."[162] José responds indignantly, claiming that their father's dark skin color comes from "Indian blood." Piri responds to this familiar rhetoric with "Poppa's got *moyeto* blood. I got it. Sis got it. James got it. And, mah deah brudder, you-all got it!"[163] "Mah deah brudder" is the first time that Piri uses the marked variety of AAVE that, until this point, has only been used to signal difference in the text. This conversation ends in a physical fight between Piri and his brother with José screaming, "I-am-*white*! And you can go to hell!"[164]

This scene is very similar to the second and only other time that Piri imitates African American speech, which occurs shortly after Piri's return from his travels when Piri looks through his father's things and finds a picture of his father's mistress, who is white. Because of his anger against his father for having deceived his mother and for seeking out relationships with white women, Piri decides "to get back at Poppa somehow."[165] His revenge against his father takes the form of performing African American speech, saying, "Why, sho' man, if'n yuh sho' nuff willin', you can sho' nuff go wif me all," to which his father responds, "Stop that goddamn way of talking."[166] Piri continues: "'Why sho', Pops,' I said, 'if y'all doan' like the way Ah's speakin', I reckon Ah could cut it out.'"[167] This infuriates his father who attacks Piri, hitting him and screaming at him to stop "talking like you came from some goddamned cotton field."[168]

Antonio López has described this moment of the text as a kind of blackface performance, "an Afro-Latino performance of the African American."[169] Indeed, even as Piri uses this moment to express black pride and a resistance to his father's racial ideology, Piri engages here in a kind of minstrelsy, in which he parodies AAVE. These performances of African American speech provoke such anger in Piri's family members precisely because of the way that they expose the absurdity of the linguistic ideology that Piri's father and subsequently his children have used to assert their superiority over African Americans. In earlier scenes, such as in the social services office, Thomas marked the speech of African American women in order to signify, at the linguistic level, the distance between the social worker and his client and in order to suggest the perceived differences between Puerto Ricans and African Americans that underlie the protagonist's feelings of superiority. Piri's explicit performance of African American speech in these scenes represents for Piri's father and brother the inversion of this social structure.

Although Piri appropriates African American speech in order to identify himself as Afro-descendant, he does it in a marked and stereotyped way, and thus, in one sense, he maintains a difference between himself and African Americans in the very moment in which he attempts to undermine those differences. Piri describes the pronunciation he uses to emphasize his identification with black people as a "southern drawl."[170] This Southern way of speaking has little to do with Piri's actual background and experience. It is not, unlike his physical appearance or ancestry, an integral part of himself that he finally accepts and embraces, but rather a foreign caricature that he performs.

In this sense, the moments in which Piri speaks in such a marked and "southern" way suggest that what Piri wants to communicate to his family transcends skin color or blood lineage. If the Jim Crow South is a metonym of a global system, then appropriating and even performing a black, Southern identity suggests that, in addition to recognizing his own African ancestry, Piri positions himself in the place of the most oppressed. Through imitating African American speech, he aims to communicate that he, as a Puerto Rican, is subject to the same system of exploitation as those who come from the "cotton field."[171]

In both moments in which Piri imitates African American speech, although Piri does point to a racial biological essentialism that—within a U.S.-based racial framework—would make his father and his blonde brother black, what Piri articulates much more adamantly and what most infuriates his family is his identification with a Southern black subjectivity. The blackness to which Piri lays claim and that he wants to communicate to his family is not merely based on biology; it is a colonialist-cum-Jim Crow construction of blackness that he appropriates and imbues with political meaning. AAVE here functions as a dual sign through which Piri performs both his victimization to a system of exploitation and, by pointing to his solidarity with African Americans, his resistance to that system.[172] In this sense, blackness emerges in the text as a political category and tool rather than a biological one.

This analysis of the linguistic and racial hierarchies that the text exposes and that Thomas uses to communicate a politically contestatory position clarifies several issues that consistently trouble critics about this novel. Lyn Di Iorio Sandín argues that the disappearance of Brew from the text "has the effect of leaving the race question disturbingly unresolved," and many readings of *Down These Mean Streets* have struggled to understand a shift that occurs toward the end of the novel in which Piri seems to re-embrace racist stereotypes of black people.[173] For example, in a scene toward the end of the novel that takes place in the Comstock prison, Piri is approached by three inmates who he senses are planning to sexually assault him or who have "the *carcel* look of wolves digging a stone lamb."[174] Rocky, an African American inmate, asks Piri to draw a picture of him and Piri draws him as a "funny-book black cannibal, complete with a big bone through his nose," which infuriates Rocky.[175]

The racism of the drawing is unsettling because, as Richard Pérez has indicated, "the drawing captures Rocky in the same racial language Piri has struggled against throughout the novel."[176] By depicting the man who threatens to rape him as a black cannibal, Piri reproduces a fiction in which rape, dark skin color, and cannibalism are collapsed into a white, colonialist fear of blackness. While I do not deny that the drawing reifies racist stereotypes, considering the previous discussion of Piri's use of African American speech, this moment might be read differently. Through the drawing, Piri makes light of Rocky's attempted rape and indicates his lack of fear of him by configuring Rocky as an exaggerated stereotype in the colonial imaginary. The cannibal of the drawing, which is coded as a rapist, is presented as an ideological construct.[177] At this late point in the text, it has already been established that Piri accepts his African ancestry as well as his appearance, but like his appropriation of African American speech in which Piri performs blackness, Piri points in the drawing to a dissociation between phenotypic appearance and the construction of blackness within colonial discourse. Although one cannot deny the reproduction of racist images in the drawing and in his imitation of AAVE, it is important to understand that in each of these cases, Piri uses these symbols as weapons. Whereas the young Piri believed subconsciously in the ideology that gave meaning to these colonialist caricatures, such as that of the cannibal, for Piri, as an adult, this image has become nothing more than a tool that he can wield for his own ends.

However, Thomas does not just stop with a Calibanesque reclaiming of the cannibal as weapon. As the essentialist notions of blackness begin to lose their weight, Piri also begins to see whiteness as a construct that becomes destabilized from a direct relationship to physical features. This represents another area in the text that has bothered some critics. During his incarceration, Piri converts to the Nation of Islam. When the imam in prison states, "God or Jehovah is the white man's God and he's used his Christianity as a main weapon against the dark-skinned inhabitants of this world," this theology resonates with Piri because he had long been bothered by the white appearance of Jesus Christ in many representations.[178] For example, in a previous scene, Piri symbolically blows smoke in the face of a portrait of a white Jesus at Brew's apartment.

However, at the end of the book, he embraces the Christianity with which his parents raised him, saying, "If God is right, so what if he's white?"[179] Critics have struggled with this easy acceptance of a white God because the entire book up to this point is dedicated to breaking down white supremacist notions. Sandín explains this moment with the comment that "the passage in which he takes on the white God is extremely brief, facile, and unconvincing, even if we know that in real life, Piri did take on religion."[180] However, instead of dismissing Piri's comment (Thomas did not just convert to Christianity; he wrote an entire book about it called *Savior, Savior Hold My Hand* [1972]) or viewing this moment as indicative of the text's ultimate failure, I think that, when read within the context of the previous discussion, Piri's comment can be interpreted entirely differently.

If we accept that the text emphasizes a separation between phenotype and the colonialist iconography attached to that phenotype, such that the categories of black and white become unhinged from racial essentialisms, then the idea of a white God is revealed as a farce. The rhyme and playful tone of the phrase, "If God is right, so what if He's white?," certainly suggest as much. Instead of signaling a rejection of all that Piri has stated, this phrase represents the culmination of an ideology developed throughout the text that attempts, through dissociating skin color and other racialized features from colonialist stereotypes, to unhinge those essentialisms that apply color to beings as ethereal as gods.

Through Piri's ideological transformation, Thomas argues for the existence of a transnational system of oppression and proposes a resistant political solidarity that crosses ethnic and linguistic boundaries. Although at first glance, this solidarity appears to be defined through racial identification, it eventually seeks to destabilize clearly defined racial categories, proposing a resistant subjectivity that is fundamentally open, a concept to which Piri hints at the end of the novel, stating "around the world, hear this, North and South, East and West: We are all the same in our souls and spirits and there's nobody better than anybody else, only just maybe better off."[181] *Down These Mean Streets* would have significant influence on the New York Puerto Rican generation, such as the Young Lords and Nuyorican poets. As Monica Brown has noted, "The structuring ideologies of the Young Lords corroborate many of Thomas's criticisms about the U.S.-colonial relationship with Puerto Rico and the deeply entrenched and troubling racist realities of the United States."[182] That parallel "structuring ideology" that Brown sees in both Young Lords' writings and in *Down These Mean Streets* is, I would argue, an ideology of Tricontinentalism.

The open resistant subjectivity that Thomas presents in his text—like the Tricontinental that would take shape one year before the publication of *Down These Mean Streets*—is not a perfect model for international solidarity among subaltern groups. While a group like the Young Lords would attempt to expand Tricontinentalism's racially open political signifier toward gay, lesbian, and transgender activists, the politics of representation of women and nonheteronormative subjects in *Down These Mean Streets*, as well as in many other Nuyorican writings, are highly problematic and have been widely discussed.[183] However, reading *Down These Mean Streets* within the context of an ideology of Tricontinentalism sheds light on Thomas's use of a racial category as a political signifier for a global subaltern subjectivity that would be influential to a later generation of Nuyorican writers and that would continue to have relevance for contemporary notions of subaltern politics.

"TO BE CALLED *NEGRITO* MEANS TO BE CALLED LOVE": A POETICS OF TRANS-AFFECTIVE SOLIDARITY

If, after close analysis, we see an underlying Tricontinentalism in Piri Thomas's work, which was written prior to the official convening of the 1966 Tricontinental, Tricontinentalist discourse is even more apparent in the more overtly political, literary works closely aligned with the Young Lords Party and published in the years following the Tricontinental Conference. The reading I provided of *Down These Mean Streets* is intended to open the door to critical rereadings of other related radical writings, which I will attempt in the coming pages, that would address these texts' engagement with, or positioning toward, a Tricontinentalist ideology and thus better situate them within the context in which they were composed.

Like *Down These Mean Streets*, many Nuyorican writings are literary inheritors of the interwar négritude/negrismo/New Negro movements. Nöel has traced, for example, the resonance of Aimé Césaire's raw, visceral, and surrealist négritude poetics in texts like Pietri's "Puerto Rican Obituary."[184] Similarly, Algarín's "Mongo Affair," where the "mongo" serves as the overarching metaphor of oppression, recalls the "morne" of Césaire's *Notebook of a Return to the Native Land* (1939). As Tricontinentalism developed out of this interwar exchange, so too do the Nuyorican writings of the late 1960s and early 1970s demonstrate an engagement with this emergent ideology.

We might consider "Puerto Rican Obituary," first performed in the People's Church, a church that Pietri attended throughout his childhood, and first published in *Palante*, to be one such Tricontinentalist text.[185] Pietri, who was raised in a housing project in Harlem and who had been drafted to Vietnam, was intimately involved with the Young Lords.[186] He performed, for example, at a benefit to raise money for imprisoned Lords, and in a 1971 *Palante* article about Pietri entitled "Entre todo el pueblo se escribe un poema" (A Poem Is Written among the People), Pietri provides his address and phone number for any *Palante* reader who wants to get in touch or provide corrections to his poems.[187]

Pietri presents his famous poem as an obituary for the general Puerto Rican migrant population to whom Pietri gives the common names "Juan, Miguel, Milagros, Olga, Manuel," writing not just for people who have died in the past, but for those who "died yesterday today / and will die again to-morrow."[188] The poet associates this dying with the empty dreams of Puerto Rican emigration to the United States, claiming, "All died / dreaming about america."[189] In other words, the very notion of the American Dream, in which the immigrant pulls herself up out of poverty through hard work, inversely represents the death of Pietri's characters. Their dreams of social uplift "about queens / Clean-cut lily-white neighborhood," which are also their deaths, isolate them from one another.[190] They end up hating instead of helping one other because one has a "a used car . . . in better running condition . . . a color television set" or because one "made five more dollars on the same job."[191] The only way for them to "return from the dead," the poem suggests, is for their consciousness to awaken to the lies that they have been sold.[192]

The poem ends with a nostalgic vision in which the poetic voice imagines that "If only they / had turned off the television / and tune into their imagination / If only they / had used the white supremacy bibles / for toilet paper purpose," then they would have been "where beautiful people sing / and dance and work together . . . where you do not need a dictionary / to communicate with your people / Aquí Se Habla Español all the time."[193] As these lines are preceded with the statement that "PUERTO RICO IS A BEAU-TIFUL PLACE," this ending has generally been read as an idealistic, spiritual return to Puerto Rico.[194] However, the final lines of the poem take a political turn that suggests an alternative reading of this imagined, utopic space: "Aquí Que Pasa Power is what's happening / Aquí to be called negrito / means to be called LOVE."[195] While the political reference to the Black and Brown Power movements here is quite obvious, it is the final line of the poem that calls my attention.

In a move that recalls Piri's minstrel performance of AAVE, Pietri uses the term "negrito" (little black), which draws from the "racist caricature of black people by white actors" from the nineteenth- and early twentieth-century popular tradition of blackface *bufo* theater from the Hispanic Caribbean.[196] While many variations of the negrito figure appeared in bufo theatrical productions, in general, this figure was attributed with "a wide variety of largely negative characteristics, including greed, lechery, stupidity, incompetence, wanton sexuality, and deceit."[197] With the diminutive suffix "ito," negrito is often employed throughout the Hispanic Caribbean today as an affectionate term for children and partners, regardless of their race or ethnicity. Yet, as Jill Lane writes, "Its meaning—especially in the nineteenth century—is never free of the infantilizing, patronizing connotation that 'little' carries when applied to an adult black male."[198] The double meaning of negrito—both as term of endearment and racial slur—has been characterized as an effect of the central role of bufo theater, especially in eliciting communal humorous responses to the negrito figure, in cohering nationalist identities in Hispanophone Caribbean islands.[199]

With Pietri's allusion to the use of a historically racially derogatory and patronizing term in Puerto Rico to express love and endearment between people, regardless of race, the line "Aquí to be called negrito / means to be called LOVE" is often interpreted to convey an idealistic vision of Puerto Rico as a place free of the racism in the mainland United States. Certainly this reading is a valid one because the preceding lines are laden with nostalgia for the island. However, considering the context in which Pietri first performed this poem, two years after *Down These Mean Streets* was published, in the midst of the Young Lords' takeover of the First Spanish Methodist Church, and in the presence of Newsreel filmmakers who took their cues from Santiago Álvarez, I am inclined to read this line differently. I read the "Aquí" (here) as the space of the church where diverse peoples come together for a common political purpose or "where beautiful people sing / and dance and work together."[200] In this reading, "negrito," like the Young Lords' use of the term "colored," captures in a word the revolutionary subjectivity that is performed in that space.

In the lines "Aquí to be called negrito / means to be called LOVE," Pietri uses the infinitive "to be," indicating the way in which this new resistant subject is simultaneously constituted "aquí" in the present space of the church and also remains a future possibility, something "to be" realized.[201] Here, we have a clear vision of what I have called the Tricontinental's model of transaffective solidarity, a political praxis and ideology founded on the production of affective relation across national, linguistic, and ethnic borders. The affective solidarity that passes from one person to another in the space of the church performs the formation of a future transnational collective political subject. What is happening "aquí" in the church is a kind of rehearsal for that which is "to be" in the future. Here the making of solidarity, or the proclaiming of a resistant community forged through affective crossing—in which those within the community call one another negrito and call one another LOVE—is itself the political act.

By ending his poem with the phrase "Aquí to be called negrito / means to be called LOVE," I suggest that Pietri refers precisely to that trans-affective solidarity that binds together a radically open and ever-expansive revolutionary subject. This political imaginary based around trans-affective encounters is, for Pietri, the only way to prevent ongoing spiritual and political death. The emphasis here on affective ties is not, I would argue, the kind of ethnic essentialism through which négritude, for example, appropriated colonialism's "division of affective labor by which feeling was lodged with the subaltern" in order to devise a celebratory, anticolonial notion of blackness defined by its exclusive access to the world's emotion and spirituality.[202] Fanon would critique this central aspect of négritude as a mere inversion of a vision of whiteness defined by rationality. In contrast, Pietri's use of "negrito"—like the Lords' use of "colored"—pushes beyond a racist association between people of color and emotion; affective encounter here becomes an opportunity to destabilize identity categories and to imagine a new possibility for transethnic and transracial political community.

In this way, I do not read Pietri's reference to the affectionate term "negrito" as an idealized dismissal of the presence of racism in Puerto Rico or in the Hispanic Caribbean; in fact, it is quite the opposite. Reading his poem in light of its Tricontinentalist context suggests that Pietri sums up in the word "negrito" what the Lords summed up in the word "colored." In other words, Pietri captures how the presence of a deterritorialized imperial and racist power structure leads to the creation of a new revolutionary subjectivity among the exploited or among those Tricontinentalist "colored and oppressed peoples" who were gathered in love and solidarity at the People's Church.

In this sense, "negrito" in Pietri's poem functions similarly to the word "nigger" in Young Lords Chairman Felipe Luciano's poem, "Jíbaro, My Pretty Nigger," which appeared both in 1970 on the first album of the Original Last Poets (an African American and Afro-Puerto Rican performance poetry and music group that laid the groundwork for the emergence of hip hop and in which Luciano was a founding member) and in a 1968 concert film called *Right On! Poetry on Film*, directed by Herbert Danska, in which Luciano performs the poem in his Young Lords beret. He also recorded this poem a few years later at Sing Sing Correctional Facility for the salsa legend Eddie Palmieri's album *Live at Sing Sing* (1972).

"Jíbaro, My Pretty Nigger" presents the *jíbaro*—a Puerto Rican term referring to a peasant or poor farmer that emerged in the nineteenth century as a nationalist icon of traditional Puerto Rican life and customs—as a common ancestry in the Puerto Rican countryside shared between those on the island and the mainland. Coded as a rural, Hispanic peasant and a refuge of racial and moral purity for the nation, this figure was framed as a "cultural antidote" to the threat of Americanization of the island.[203] Jíbaro nationalism was further popularized in the early twentieth century as a kind of backlash to the prominence of the celebration of Afro-diasporic arts and culture in the concurrent negrismo movement.[204] Luciano pushes back on the white nationalism that surrounds this figure by appropriating the figure for himself and coding the jíbaro not as white Hispanic but as black, or as "mi negro lindo" (my pretty black man).[205] He signals a continuity of experience of migration shared by jíbaros from past and present, writing of "the bowels of the ship that vomited you up on the harbors of a cold metal city to die."[206] This description of migration to the mainland on ships like the *Marine Tiger* has, as Roberto Márquez writes, "more than just a passing resemblance to the slave ships of the Middle Passage."[207] This shared history of migration and oppression is expressed through Luciano's use of the pejorative term "nigger" in its reclaimed status among some African American users as a term of endearment.

Much in the same way that Thomas uses AAVE to communicate his solidarity with African Americans, Luciano also employs the slang word "nigga" to communicate this affective affiliation. He writes, "yea, you my cold nigga man / And I love you 'cause you're mine," a line that directly recalls Pietri's "Aquí to be called negrito / means to be called LOVE."[208] Interestingly in a poem that on its face appears to be about Puerto Rican nationalism and unity among those on and off the island, Luciano only uses the Spanish term "negro" once and does not employ Pietri's affectionate term "negrito" but rather the English pejorative "nigger" as well as the AAVE term "nigga." In both the context of his performance with the Original Last Poets as well as in Sing Sing Correctional Facility, Luciano inverts the English pejorative term and repeatedly uses "nigga" to construct a communal memory and identification between himself and his interlocutors. While this use of "nigga" has been read as a solely Afro-diasporic vision, read in the Tricontinentalist context of Luciano's membership in the Young Lords, we might come away with a reading closer to the one I have provided of Thomas's appropriation of black English and Pietri's "negrito." Luciano privileges African American experience and, in a way similar to Tricontinentalism, uses the Jim Crow vocabulary of racialization to metonymically signify a trans-affective solidarity shared perhaps not only among Puerto Ricans or with African Americans but with exploited peoples everywhere.

This same vision is provided in Thomas's *Down These Mean Streets* in which Piri's identification with others across the globe is expressed through his affective ties to his African American friend Brew. For example, the paragraph that concludes the section in which Piri travels around the world begins with "I learned more and more on my trips" and ends with "Brew, baby, you were right! . . . Where the fuck are you, baby? Damn, man, you're my ace, you're my one brother."[209] Piri's expanded understanding of global inequities and his affection for Brew are inextricable from one another. Piri's love for Brew and his claiming of him as "my one brother" clearly anticipates and mirrors Pietri's and Luciano's affective poetics. The relationship with Brew is what pushes Piri to eventually arrive at his transnational and transracial vision that "around the world . . . North and South, East and West: We are all the same in our souls and spirits."[210]

From Thomas to Pietri to Luciano, the trans-affective solidarity of Tricontinentalism undergirds some of the most foundational texts of the Nuyorican movement, and yet there are many more examples. Consider "Tangiers," written in a mix of English, French, and Spanish, by Algarín. The poem, which was included in Algarín and Piñero's *Nuyorican Poetry* anthology, is a love poem to the people of Tangier in which Algarín writes, "Tangiers yo ya te quiero" (Tangiers I already love you).[211] This love stems from a loosely parallel, shared experience of oppression in which "our inner-city jungles / match yours and they are equally / poor, dirty, misunderstood, desperate / and we are struggling, hustling men / just like your boys."[212] The poem goes on to reflect on the Nuyorican experience and in an echo of José Martí's refrain that is oft-repeated in Tricontinental materials' discussion of African Americans, Algarín writes, "we exist inside the belly of the / monster . . . we are its muscles . . . its dishwashers, its toilet cleaners, / and its revolutionaries."[213] From the poem's conflation of experiences of oppression and poverty in Tangier and "in the belly of the monster," a formulation of a transnational and translinguistic revolutionary subject begins to emerge, described in a mix of English and French in the phrase "a revolutionary is un merchand ambulant, / a revolutionary is a petit taxi."[214] In other words, a revolutionary subject that transgresses language, nationality, and race surfaces here, and the poem ends with the statement in all caps, printed in both Spanish and English, that "THE ONLY DIFFERENCE / BETWEEN AN ARAB AND A PUERTO RICAN / IS THE WAY IN WHICH THE

WIND BLOWS."[215] Here again, we see a vision of Tricontinentalism where any Tricontinentalist revolutionary could stand in for the other, no matter how geographically, linguistically, racially, or nationally distant.

It must be noted that the trans-affective solidarity of Tricontinentalism found in these texts is expressed through an exclusionary heteromasculinist fraternity. The boys of Tangier provoke Algarín's expression of love. Piri and Brew's relationship is bonded through their mutual exploitation and objectification of women.[216] Luciano uses the jíbaro, a historically masculine figure, to express his poetic image of solidarity and affection. All these articulations of the trans-affective solidarity of Tricontinentalism are promising yet limited. However, as we saw in the case of the Young Lords, some initially limited instantiations of Tricontinentalism contained the potential for opening onto a much larger and more inclusive revolutionary collectivity.

The texts analyzed in this chapter are intended to serve as examples for reading some Nuyorican, as well as other related radical writings from within the United States and beyond, through the lens of Tricontinentalism. In producing these Tricontinentalist readings, I suggest these texts as part of a much larger international body of cultural production that reflect the influence of Tricontinentalism. Although Nuyorican cultural production is not commonly studied alongside Cuban films or the Tricontinental's political ephemera, these writers viewed their local struggles as part of a transnational movement that transcended the linguistic and national boundaries that have generally determined the study of cultural production. Reading these texts within the light of Tricontinentalism not only helps us understand them better but also allows us to consider the impact that these writers have had on a contemporary political imaginary in which movements of political solidarity spanning national, linguistic, racial, and ethnic boundaries are becoming increasingly commonplace.

CODA: THE NUYORICAN MOVEMENT IN THE CONTEMPORARY POLITICAL SCENE

While Piri Thomas and many of the foundational writers of the Nuyorican movement remain widely read to this day, the closely affiliated Young Lords Party has received little scholarly attention. However, from July to December 2015, the Bronx Museum of the Arts, El Museo del Barrio, and Loisaida, Inc., partnered on a multivenue exhibit on the Young Lords Party that included cultural and educational programs intended to inform people about the Lords' contribution to "the struggle for civil rights" and "to spark conversations about grassroots community activism today."[217] According to the Bronx Museum's executive director, these exhibits were motivated by a recognition of the significance of the Young Lords Party and the timeliness of the issues around which they organized as well as by the fact that "the lasting significance of their achievements has rarely been examined."[218]

Despite all they accomplished, the Young Lords Party was in existence for only a brief period, meeting its demise six years after its inception. Over the course of its first few years, the Lords became increasingly focused on the liberation of Puerto Rico, launching its "ofensiva rompecadenas" (break chains offensive) in March 1971, which directed the organization's resources and attention away from New York Puerto Rican communities and toward the island. This would have a negative impact on its appeal to non–Puerto Rican members.[219] Then, under the leadership of Gloria Fontáñez, it moved away from a Tricontinentalist view of resistance—in which the Lords envisioned a global revolutionary subjectivity through a discursively open category of color and through a trans-affective solidarity—toward an increasingly dogmatic, class-based analysis of political struggle, changing its name to the Puerto Rican Revolutionary Worker's Organization in 1972 and defining itself "as a multinational communist organization."[220]

Like many other similar groups, the Lords were victims of the FBI's COINTELPRO program, which sought to exploit factionalism within revolutionary organizations in the United States, and the organization became increasingly violent toward its own membership. By 1975, the Young Lords Party was essentially defunct.[221] The New York City secret police surveillance unit's files from 1955 to 1972 that cover the Young Lords, as well as other groups like the Black Panthers and the Nation of Islam, have been missing for decades, leaving many of the details of the Lords' demise unclear. Johanna Fernández, a historian and expert on the Young Lords Party, sued the city for the documents in 2014. The lawsuit was dismissed in May 2016 when the New York City Police Department provided sworn affidavits that it was unable to locate any of the documents. But the following month, 520 boxes of these surveillance records (an estimated one million pages) turned up in a warehouse in Queens. As of this writing, the documents will soon be made available to the public and more will be revealed on the final years of the Young Lords Party.[222]

While the Lords eventually faded into nonexistence, their central concerns, especially in their earliest years—like healthcare access, gender equality, police violence, and prison conditions—continue to be at the forefront of political dialogue in the United States today. Moreover, the issue of Puerto Rico's colonial status—which was so central to the Nuyorican writers discussed in this chapter—is becoming increasingly urgent. On August 1, 2015, twelve days after the U.S. embassy opened in Havana for the first time in over a half century, Puerto Rico defaulted on some of its debt in an ongoing and crippling debt crisis due to U.S. economic policies toward the island that, once again, have forced staggering numbers of Puerto Ricans to migrate stateside. As Maritza Stanchich wrote in a July 31, 2015, article for the *Huffington Post*, "President Obama stated that it was time to acknowledge U.S. policy toward Cuba had failed. Shouldn't he now also be admitting the same about Puerto Rico?"[223]

One year later, in August 2016, President Obama appointed a seven-member financial control board through the Puerto Rico Oversight, Management, and Economic Stability Act (PROMESA) to oversee Puerto Rico's economy and the restructuring of its debt. The unelected board and its austerity measures generated an eruption of protests on the island. While Puerto Rico's fiscal crisis is due to a diverse set of factors that includes mismanagement by local government, it is largely attributable to the predatory economic policies inherent to the colonial relationship of the United States to Puerto Rico, such as the U.S. monopoly over all trading ships (in place since the 1917 Jones Act), which has a considerable impact on the price of all imported goods, as well as the enormous disparity in federal funding provided to Puerto Rican entitlements in comparison to those in the continental United States. Beyond the reasons unique to the Puerto Rican case—it has historically not been authorized to file for bankruptcy or seek assistance from the International Monetary Fund, for example—the crisis is also the fallout of the kinds of neoliberal economic policies that have resulted in similar economic collapses throughout the continent such as the post-NAFTA exodus of multinational corporations seeking lower wages, the exorbitant fees imposed by Wall Street as Puerto Rico's credit was downgraded, as well as the tax-free haven that Puerto Rico provides to speculators specializing in high-risk bonds.[224]

As Puerto Rico's colonial status has been at center stage in the U.S. media, protests have continued throughout the United States against the white-on-black police violence that so often was the focus of the Young Lords' and Tricontinental materials. Similar to the massive protests against neoliberal economic policies in 2011, these protests use social media to garner solidarity and to bring people out into the streets. However, while the methods are similar, there are not currently overwhelming links between the antiglobaliza-tion movement, which aims to contest the unchecked power of multinational corporations and the liberalization of trade and financial markets, and this surge in racial justice activism. In this sense, perhaps we could view one of the greatest contributions of the Young Lords and the writers of the Nuyori-can movement as their participation in envisioning a Tricontinentalist model for transnational anticapitalist activism organized through a focus on racial justice. This image of revolutionary activism that the Tricontinental helped to devise was as broadly inclusive as the current alter-globalization movement aims to be, but racial inequality was always held at the forefront of its critique. The contemporary disjuncture between alter-globalization and racial justice discourses will be discussed at length in the final chapter of this book. For now, suffice it to say that the Young Lords' participation in the constitution and dissemination of a Tricontinentalist model for a global struggle against racial capitalism forged through a trans-affective solidarity is, I believe, at the heart of their ideology and is a model from which we still have much to learn.

FOUR

"Todos los negros y todos los blancos y todos tomamos café"

Racial Politics in the "Latin, African" Nation

On May 2, 2013, Assata Shakur—the former Black Panther who escaped the maximum-security wing of the Clinton Correctional Facility for Women in New Jersey in 1979 and who received political asylum in Cuba in 1984—became the first woman to be placed on the FBI's list of Most Wanted Terrorists. This announcement, made on the fortieth anniversary of the death of the New Jersey state trooper whom Shakur was convicted of killing, has been highly controversial. Shakur maintains her innocence, pointing to the many holes in the prosecution's case and explaining that she is a victim of an FBI counter-intelligence program (COINTELPRO) that specifically targeted domestic black militant groups.

With the process toward normalization of relations between the United States and Cuba that began in December 2014, many of Shakur's supporters in the United States expressed their objection to the possibility that Shakur could be extradited to the United States to face imprisonment. Due to the controversy over her terrorist status and the possibility of extradition, countless articles have appeared about Shakur in the global media, and public interest has been renewed in Cuba's Tricontinentalist commitment to the African American freedom struggle and its role in protecting African American militants from capture by the U.S. government.

Only six weeks prior to the FBI's announcement of Shakur's terrorist status, Roberto Zurbano Torres, an Afro-Cuban scholar and former editor-in-chief for Cuba's famed cultural organization Casa de las Américas, published an article in the *New York Times* entitled "For Blacks in Cuba, the Revolution Hasn't Begun."[1] In this article, Zurbano claims that the economic reforms in Cuba over the last decade, which reflect an increasing trend toward private enterprise, have disproportionately benefited white Cubans who use funds provided by their families in Miami to convert their houses into private restaurants and bed-and-breakfasts. Racial inequality in Cuba is nothing new, Zurbano explains, "and a half century of revolution since 1959 has been unable to overcome it."[2]

Zurbano attributes this lack of progress to the official silence surrounding the problem of racism in Cuba. He explains that the Cuban government's claim in 1962 to have ended racial discrimination on the island has meant that, for many years, it has been seen as counterrevolutionary to publicly raise the issue of black Cubans' restricted social mobility. The official silence regarding the nation's racial inequalities only reinforced the problem, he explains, and his article seeks to open up dialogue so as to "bring about solutions that have for so long been promised, and awaited, by black Cubans."[3]

In the week that followed the publication of his article, Zurbano experienced a tremendous backlash in the Cuban press. *La Jiribilla*, a weekly digital arts and culture magazine, published seven rebuttals, all written by leading Afro-Cuban intellectuals, in its March 30–April 5, 2013, issue. Much of the protest responded to the article's title (which Zurbano later claimed was mistranslated by the *New York Times*) because the phrase "the Revolution hasn't begun" seemed to imply that the Cuban Revolution had done nothing to improve the lives of black Cubans.[4] Others acknowledged that there was truth to what Zurbano wrote but claimed that these debates needed to remain "entre nosotros" (between us) and critiqued him for publishing the article in the *New York Times*.[5]

According to Desiderio Navarro's analysis of the role of the intellectual in communist Cuba in "In Medias Res Publicas: On Intellectuals and Social Criticism in the Cuban Public Sphere" (2002), the notion that Cuban intellectuals should not provide the Cuban Revolution's enemies with any critique that would further the negative propaganda against it, as well as the insistence that a critique of any negative element of Cuban society is only legitimate when it notes the positives that exist alongside it, is a common rhetorical strategy that has been used over the last fifty years to limit social criticism in the public sphere in Cuba. This has especially been the case with taboo subjects such as prostitution and racism. Equally common, Navarro notes, are the reprisals through which the Cuban government disciplines intellectuals who step out of bounds. Indeed, the day after *La Jiribilla* published its seven responses to Zurbano's article, he was demoted from his position as editor-in-chief at Casa de las Américas to that of researcher.

Zurbano responded to the controversy in an article entitled "Mañana será tarde: Escucho, aprendo, y sigo en la pelea" (Tomorrow will be too late: I listen, I learn, and I continue in the struggle), published one week later in the April 13–19, 2013, issue of *La Jiribilla*, in which he claims that his commitment to fighting racial discrimination is in line with the Revolution's own goals. He defends his decision to publish in a U.S. press instead of in a Cuban publication, because racism is "a globalized phenomenon and the fight against it goes beyond any border" and because that venue allowed him to expand the discussion to a global audience.[6]

I introduce these two instances, Shakur's exile and Zurbano's efforts to increase the visibility of racial inequalities in Cuba, because of the way in which their juxtaposition points to a dissonance between Cuba's integral participation in a Tricontinental discourse on racial inequality, through which Cuba has long positioned itself as an outspoken supporter of black liberation movements, and its domestic one, in which people have had to struggle, often risking their careers and well-being, in order to further public dialogue on racism.[7] Zurbano's argument in "Mañana será tarde" that racial discrimination is a global problem allows him to defend publishing his piece within the U.S. media and to claim that exposing racism anywhere, even within Cuba itself, is an act aligned with the Revolution's goals. In other words, Zurbano uses the Cuban government's own rhetoric on global racial inequality, which it articulated most clearly through its leading role in the Tricontinental, to justify writing about the existence of racial inequality in Cuba.

This rhetorical strategy is not new. The Tricontinental's critique of a global system of racial inequality tied to the expansion of a deterritorialized empire should have, in theory, provided a ready-made platform for discussing the ongoing struggle to eliminate all vestiges of racism within Cuba's domestic sphere. In other words, to call attention to the presence of racial discrimination domestically would be to call attention to the way in which the Revolution was not living up to its ideals, and thus could be posited as a critique of the communist government that was still pro-revolutionary. Indeed, especially in the mid-1960s around the time of the Tricontinental Conference, some Cuban activists and artists would attempt to position their critique of racial inequality precisely in this way.

As we have seen in previous chapters, the Tricontinental's ideology circulated widely among radicals in the Americas and around the world. Through the Tricontinental's focus on the African American freedom struggle and through Cuba's primary role in producing the Tricontinental's cultural production, Cuba presented itself to the world as a society deeply committed to the struggle for racial equality. This image of Cuba allowed organizations like the Young Lords and the Black Panthers to view their struggle as aligned with the Cuban Revolution and to envision their local movement as part of a global, Tricontinental one, and it even encouraged some U.S. black militants to see Cuba as a safe haven in which to seek asylum. Yet the racial realities those militants faced on the island would often sharply contradict Cuba's internationalist image as a champion of racial justice.

Whereas previous chapters detailed the formation of the discourse of Tricontinentalism and the dissemination of that discourse through both the wide-reaching cultural production of the Organization of Solidarity with the Peoples of Africa, Asia, and Latin America (OSPAAAL) and closely related radical texts, this chapter has two primary interventions. First, it considers the inherent contradiction in Cuba's primary role in producing the Tricontinental's antiracist material. Within this discussion, I consider both the Cuban government's fraught relationship with African American and Afro-Cuban activists in the late 1960s and 1970s as well as how the dissonance between Cuba's domestic and internationalist racial discourses is clearly demonstrated in state rhetoric surrounding Cuba's involvement in the Angolan Civil War beginning in the late 1970s.

While some U.S. black activists like Assata Shakur, Angela Davis, and William Lee Brent consistently expressed their support for the Cuban government, others like Robert F. Williams, Stokely Carmichael, and Eldridge Cleaver would distance themselves from Cuba as they became more aware of the repression of black political organizing on the island. Additionally, at the same time that U.S. black radical groups like the Black Panthers faced ongoing political persecution and factionalism in the 1970s, Cuba was becoming further entrenched in the conflict in Angola. This contributed to a shift in Tricontinental materials from a focus on the U.S. South, which was used as a microcosm for an expansive global empire characterized by racial capitalism, toward a focus on apartheid South Africa. In this process, the Tricontinentalist concept of the "South"—through which a stark racial division is used metonymically to signify a transnational power structure and transracial resistant solidarity—becomes further deterritorialized and global in scope. The U.S. South, for example, becomes compared to South Africa, which is then compared to political relations in the Southern Cone of Latin America. In other words, a Tricontinentalist vision of the South as indexing spaces of inequity around the globe—which anticipates the contemporary usage of the term "Global South"—is even more fully articulated in Tricontinental materials in the late 1970s.

Second, through pointing to a disconnect between Cuba's domestic and internationalist racial discourses, I trace the way that Tricontinentalism, grounded in black Atlantic thought, has been employed by some black Cuban intellectuals to shine a light on the Cuban Revolution's duplicitous racial politics. Specifically, I examine this critique through the filmic work of Nicolás Guillén Landrián, a direct descendant of the négritude/negrismo/New Negro exchange from which Tricontinentalism emerged. After using the censored film *P.M.* (1961) to argue for the central role of documentary in early critiques of the Cuban Revolution's racial politics, I move to a close analysis of the work of Guillén Landrián, an Afro-Cuban filmmaker, the nephew of the famed negrista poet Nicolás Guillén and a student of Santiago Álvarez. Through Guillén-Landrián's work, I consider how Tricontinentalist discourse provides a platform from which some intellectuals have launched critiques of the Cuban government's hypocritical dismissal of domestic racial inequalities.

While Guillén Landrián's work does not primarily focus on forging transnational solidarity (and thus the metonymic color politics and trans-affective solidarities that I have identified as core elements of Tricontinentalist discourse are not immediately apparent in his work), I argue that Guillén Landrián appropriates a Tricontinentalist critique and filmic aesthetic, used to condemn racial inequality abroad, in order to expose racial discrimination within Cuba. More specifically, Guillén Landrián appropriates the hard-hitting aesthetic of Álvarez's Tricontinental newsreels to shed light on racial inequities within the Castro government's policies and thus to expose the hypocrisy of its internationalist commitment to black freedom. In this sense, Guillén Landrián's work—as an example of an understudied Afro-Cuban response to Tricontinentalist ideology—is a testament to an inherent contradiction and lack of self-criticism within the Tricontinental's focus on racism in the imperialist North. However, it also reveals the way in which Tricontinentalism as a discourse and set of aesthetic praxes transcends the Cuban Revolution's own politics and rhetoric, and has even been employed as a critique of it.

GUILLÉN-LANDRIÁN IN CONTEXT: THE SOVIET PERIOD
AND THE 1960S NEGRISTA MOVEMENT

In the early years of the Cuban Revolution, Cuba's film industry rapidly expanded its documentary output. Between 1959 and 1960, documentary films produced per year increased from four to twenty-one, and by 1965, the Cuban Film Institute (ICAIC) was making forty documentaries annually.[8] Guillén Landrián was one of three black filmmakers at the ICAIC during this period and was a student of the renowned Cuban filmmaker Santiago Álvarez, who, as I discussed in chapter 2, made nearly all of the newsreels that formed part of the Tricontinental's propaganda apparatus.[9] In 1968, Guillén Landrián was commissioned by the ICAIC to make a documentary on the Cordón de la Habana (Havana greenbelt), an ambitious agricultural campaign by the Cuban Revolution to plant fruit trees, coffee, and peas in the peripheral zones of Havana.[10] This twenty-minute short, *Coffea arábiga* (1968), would face censorship and would contribute to the filmmaker's branding as a political dissident and his eventual expulsion from the ICAIC in 1972.[11] Although this backlash is generally attributed to *Coffea arábiga*'s irreverent pairing of images of Fidel Castro with the Beatles' song "The Fool on the Hill," as well as to the coincidence that the Cordón de la Habana ended in failure, I maintain that Guillén Landrián's critique cuts much deeper, arguing that the racial hierarchies of Cuba's colonial legacy are perpetuated within the Revolution's agricultural policies.

Coffea arábiga is especially significant because its critique appears during the early years of Cuba's Soviet period (1961–1991), which produced a general textual silence on post-1959 racial inequalities within Cuba.[12] While ample symposia, conferences, and artistic works on this subject were produced in the Castro government's first three years, in April 1961, the day before the Bay of Pigs invasion, Castro publicly declared the socialist nature of the Revolution. As early as 1962, official discourse held that the color-blind economic and social reforms made in its first three years served to fully eliminate systemic racial inequalities in communist Cuba.[13]

Scholarship, public activism, and artistic production that countered this position were henceforth systematically discouraged, censored, and repressed.[14] For this reason, prior to the capitalist reforms and dollarization of the economy in the 1990s, the limited scholarly writings published on this subject were generally authored by writers living abroad. The harshest condemnations of the Castro government's position on race came from black militants who spent brief periods in Cuba and wrote about their experiences upon leaving.[15]

However, most scholarship on racial inequality produced abroad during this period fell somewhere between an outright rejection or a total embrace of the government's rhetoric, recognizing how reforms benefited black Cubans but also acknowledging to various degrees the persistence of inequalities.[16] One notable exception to this trend is the Afro-Cuban historian Walterio Carbonell's *Crítica: Como surgió la cultura nacional* (Critique: How the National Culture Emerged) (1961), censored until 2005, which denounced the government's color-blind discourse for reproducing the very nationalist rhetoric that had legitimized the continuation of white power in the early republic.[17] However, generally, domestic Cuban scholars tended toward silence on contemporary racial issues, focusing their efforts retrospectively on subjects like the heroic leadership of Afro-Cubans in the wars of independence, the country's history of plantation slavery, or the exploitation of black labor by U.S. companies prior to their nationalization.[18]

Despite this general climate of repression and censorship, some Cuban writers and artists continued to produce texts that challenged this triumphalist position toward racial equality. One significant example is the emergence in the mid-1960s of a loosely affiliated group of young black intellectuals and artists, which has been characterized as a negrista movement by Lillian Guerra and as a Black Power movement by Juan Felipe Benemelis, and which included Guillén Landrián, Walterio Carbonell, the writer Juan René Betancourt, the filmmaker Sara Gómez, the playwright Eugenio Hernández Espinosa, the ethnographer Rogelio Martínez Furé, and the poet Nancy Morejón, among others.[19] Members of this black intelligentsia would face various forms of censorship and persecution in the early Soviet period as they tried to call attention to ongoing racial inequalities within Cuba. In 1967, for example, some of these intellectuals reportedly prepared a statement on race in Cuba that they submitted for presentation at the 1968 World Cultural Congress, a meeting of intellectuals and artists from seventy countries on cultural issues facing the so-called Third World that was largely a cultural follow-up to the political meeting of the Tricontinental.[20] This cooperation among Afro-Cuban intellectuals and their comments on race were labeled by then Minister of Education José Llanusa Gobels as seditious, and the writers and artists involved were branded as troublemakers. Although this document is often referenced in accounts of Afro-Cubans' attempted participation in the 1968 World Cultural Congress, the contents contained therein are not detailed and remain unavailable. Similar to scholarship from this period, works by these intellectuals that focused on pre-1959 race relations or that dealt with individual prejudices and attitudes were more likely to be published while those focused on discriminatory policies and systemic racial inequalities tended to be censored.[21]

Black Cuban intellectuals were not the only people to face repression and censorship during the Soviet period; indeed, artists and intellectuals perceived as veering from official positions or as representing any nonstate entity were systematically marginalized. However, Cuba's racial discourse represented a particularly sensitive subject because Cuba's support of black liberation movements abroad formed an integral part of its foreign policy and global political position. In this sense, although Guillén Landrián's *Coffea arábiga* is not the only text from the period to suggest that the Cuban government's racial discourse may contribute to the continuation of racial inequalities, his critique of discrimination within its agricultural policies is unique and profoundly important because of the way it explicitly attempts to intervene into the international dialogue on racial justice in which the Castro government was engaged in the late 1960s. Guillén Landrián appropriates what I have called a Tricontinentalist rhetoric and aesthetic, which the government used to critique racism in places like the United States and South Africa, to argue that the racial hierarchies of Cuba's colonial past continue within the Revolution's agricultural campaign. Through attempting to undermine the state's racial discourse at its very core, *Coffea arábiga* opens a window to a counterposition and critique of racial inequality articulated from within Cuba during the first decade of its Revolution.

THE ERASURE AND REVIVAL OF NICOLÁS GUILLÉN LANDRIÁN

Despite his status as one of Cuba's only black filmmakers and despite his blood relation to revolutionary Cuba's poet laureate, Nicolás Guillén Batista, until very recently, Guillén Landrián has been largely absent from Cuban film historiography. Michael Chanan's *The Cuban Image* (1985) and his later *Cuban Cinema* (2004), which are considered the disciplinary standard on Cuban film, discuss in detail both the released and unreleased work of Sara Gómez and Sergio Giral, the other two black filmmakers at ICAIC in the 1960s. However, neither of these texts even mention Guillén Landrián.[22] Prior to 2002, only four of the eighteen documentaries that he directed before the age of thirty-four were ever shown publicly, and six of his films have been completely lost.[23]

Guillén Landrián claimed to have suffered decades of political persecution at the hands of the Cuban government before eventually moving to Miami in 1989, where, prior to his first exhibit at the Cuban Museum of Arts and Culture in 1990, he sold his extraordinary cubist paintings for very little and where he eventually made his final film, a portrait of downtown Miami called *Inside Downtown* (2001). After his death of pancreatic cancer in a Miami hospital in July 2003, his widow returned to Havana, burying him in the Colón Cemetery and resettling in an apartment filled with her late husband's paintings.[24]

The censorship of Guillén Landrián's films has resulted in a dearth of scholarship on his work. However, with the loosening of restrictions in Cuba in recent years toward previously censored artists and intellectuals, this has begun to change dramatically. Several of his films were publicly screened in Cuba in 2002.[25] In 2003, the Cuban director Manuel Zayas released a documentary on Guillén Landrián called *Café con leche* (Coffee with Milk). *Café con leche*, along with two other recent documentaries on Guillén Landrián, has been instrumental in the revival of the censored filmmaker's work both in Cuba and abroad.[26] In recent years, Guillén Landrián's films have been shown at film festivals around the world, and many of his films are now available on YouTube. Within Cuba, Guillén Landrián has developed a cult following among filmmakers, film critics, and scholars of Afro-Cuba, and his work is taught at Cuba's International Film and Television School (EICTV). In the spring of 2013, a Chilean journal of film criticism, *La Fuga*, devoted an entire issue to this long-elided director, publishing articles by film critics living in Cuba and abroad.

Many of Guillén Landrián's films touch on subjects other than race, and the criticism that has emerged on his work generally focuses on his experimental aesthetics, the dialogue between his films and his poetry, and his divergence from the ICAIC's propagandistic cinema through depicting a complex reality in which the Revolution's projects and goals remained unfinished and through delivering critiques of the government's official discourse surrounding labor and productivity.[27] Much less has been written on his treatment of race, and studies of films such as *En un barrio viejo* (In an Old Neighborhood) (1963), which ends with a Santería ceremony held under the watchful gaze of portraits of Fidel Castro and Camilo Cienfuegos, or *Los del baile* (Those of the Dance) (1965), which shows Afro-Cubans dancing and partying, have focused on these films' ironic commentary on the government's sober socialist discourse and pejorative attitude toward Afro-Cuban religions as well as on the films' attempts to bring Afro-Cuban identity and history into the center of the national imaginary.[28]

Coffea arábiga's critique is much further reaching in its implications because, in my reading, it appropriates the aesthetic of Álvarez's Tricontinental films to launch a pointed critique not of racial discrimination in the United States but of the Revolution's perpetuation of racial inequalities through its agricultural policies. However, prior readings of *Coffea arábiga* have completely overlooked the film's central argument.[29] Lillian Guerra, whose groundbreaking *Visions of Power in Cuba: Revolution, Redemption and Resistance, 1959–1971* (2012) has largely informed my understanding of the political climate in which Guillén Landrián made his films, suggests that *Coffea arábiga* was intended not as a critique but as an "ode to Cuba's idealism" that was later misread following the failure of the Cordón de la Habana such that "once innocuous scenes became subversive."[30] As I will detail, I do not view this film as innocuous in any sense but rather as a keen and unique commentary on racial inequality that speaks boldly into a moment in which this subject matter was repeatedly silenced. However, in order to explain the weight of Guillén Landrián's critique, it is first necessary to further outline the complex racial politics to which his film responds.

SOWING THE SEEDS FOR *COFFEA ARÁBIGA*: RACIAL DISCOURSE IN REVOLUTIONARY CUBA

Through narrative, media spectacle, film, and political propaganda, the Cuban Revolution has long presented itself as the culmination of the nation's history of black political activism or as the final realization of the struggle for freedom begun by insurrectionists and *cimarrones* (maroons) during slavery and by black *mambises* (independence fighters) in the wars for independence. As discussed in chapter 1, Cuba's long struggle for national independence in the nineteenth century increasingly commingled with the cause for black freedom. This both served as a boon to the independence movement, which depended on growing black participation, and became its biggest roadblock since the first two wars—the Ten Years' War (1868–1878) and the Little War (1879–1880)—ended largely due to white Cuban fears that, absent Spanish rule, the island would become a black republic like neighboring Haiti.[31] In the period of peace that followed the Little War, independence activists, who had seen their cause dismantled through this fear of a race war, constructed a new rhetoric of independence that would attempt to undermine this fear at its core.[32] They reconceived the relationship between race and nation in Cuba, promoting racial equality as the foundation of the future Cuban nation. Building on the antiracist rhetoric of insurgents from the previous two wars, Cuban pro-independence intellectuals like Juan Gualberto Gómez, Martín

Morúa Delgado, José Martí, Manuel Sanguily, and Rafael Serra y Montalvo reflected back on the first two independence wars and argued that the experience of fighting alongside one another against colonialism and slavery had allowed Cubans to overcome racial divisions. Racial inequities were conflated with the island's history of Spanish colonialism, and they envisioned a future independent Cuba founded on inclusivity and the transcendence of race.

This vision of racial fraternity—profoundly progressive for its time—helped to unify Cubans for the final Cuban War of Independence. However, it also had a silencing effect on black Cubans organizing for racial equity because it framed a focus on racial divisions as undermining the value of race-blind nationalism at the heart of Cuba Libre. With the U.S. occupation that followed the Spanish-American War, which imposed a white supremacist ideology that framed black and mixed-raced Cubans as unfit for self-government, black Cubans organizing for their political rights under the new republic—such as in the Partido Independiente de Color—faced a double bind of Jim Crow racial oppression and Cuban race-blind nationalism.[33] The effects of these overlapping racial discourses were devastating for black political organizing, culminating in the May 1912 massacre and mass arrest of thousands of Afro-Cubans in the Oriente Province.[34]

The Cuban Revolution of 1959 would be presented as the completion of the founding fathers' vision for a raceless Cuba, curtailed by U.S. intervention. In this vein, the Cuban Revolution rhetorically positioned itself as building on the island's history of black struggle and as finally achieving the racial equity at the heart of Cuban nationalism. It would also largely continue the white paternalism and color-blind nationalism inherent to the founding fathers' vision of racial fraternity from the independence period.

Countless Cuban texts produced since 1959 have contributed to the image of the Revolution as the final stage of the nation's long tradition of black political resistance. One obvious example of this rhetoric is the well-known *Biografía de un cimarrón* (Biography of a Runaway Slave) (1966) by Miguel Barnet, president of the National Union of Writers and Artists of Cuba (UNEAC) and a former student of the negrista anthropologist and writer Fernando Ortiz. This text presents the island's history through the testimonial narrative of Esteban Montejo, a cimarrón who fought in the wars for independence against Spain and whose voice serves, in the *testimonio* style that would become popularized throughout Latin America in the 1970s and '80s, as a stand-in for the voice of the Cuban people itself. Montejo's narrative focuses on the eras of slavery and independence and never mentions the Cuban Revolution, but the Revolution's rhetoric is implicit throughout the text, permeating Montejo's constant struggle for freedom and self-determination.

While *Biografía de un cimarrón* is widely recognized as a foundational text of the Cuban Revolution, other examples of this rhetoric in widely celebrated Cuban texts include Nicolás Guillén's poem "Tengo" (I Have) (1964), which reflects on the long-awaited material and spiritual gains that the Revolution has provided for black Cubans, or the ICAIC's many films on slave insurrection and resistance, such as the trilogy by Sergio Giral or Tomás Gutiérrez Alea's *La última cena* (The Last Supper) (1976).[35] Similarly, Humberto Solás's film *Lucía* (1968), an epic of Cuba's history of political struggles, is composed of vignettes of women activists, all named Lucía, in three historical contexts: the independence period, the Machado dictatorship of the 1930s, and the postrevolutionary period. Whereas the Lucías of the first two sections are white, the Lucía of the final section is played by the multiracial actress Adela Legrá. The struggle of the final Lucía is narratively positioned as building on the courageous actions of the women who came before her as she fights back against her white husband's abusive and controlling behavior in order to participate in the state's literacy campaign.

Her desire to learn to read and write is supported by the black Cuban couple who run the local union and who try to convince her husband, Tomás, that it is his revolutionary duty to allow his wife to be tutored by the volunteer teacher from Havana, despite his jealous misgivings about his wife spending time with another man. The racial makeup of the characters subtly contributes to the notion that to be a true revolutionary, one must support the agency and full participation in revolutionary society not only of women but also of black Cubans. While, unlike other texts mentioned above, the film does not examine in depth the contribution of black Cubans to the nation's earlier resistance struggles, it suggests that these prior struggles have led to the culminating moment of the Revolution in which those who have been most oppressed (including Afro-Cubans and women) in Cuban society are now finally obtaining the rights they have long deserved.[36]

Perhaps the most famous text to situate the Cuban Revolution within a history of specifically black political struggles is "Caliban: Notes Towards a Discussion of Culture in Our America" (1971), written by Roberto Fernández Retamar, president of Casa de las Américas, in response to the outcry by European and Latin American members of the leftist intelligentsia regarding the 1971 imprisonment of the poet Heberto Padilla. In this essay, which is often celebrated as an anticolonial anthem and is frequently cited out of context of the repressive intellectual politics within Cuba in which it was published, Retamar characterizes Latin America's history of anticolonial resistance as embodied in the figure of Caliban, the monstrous island inhabitant who rebels against his master Prospero, from Shakespeare's *The Tempest*. Caliban, Retamar claims, is an anagram for "cannibal," the symbol of barbarity that Spanish colonizers attributed to Amerindians and later to Africans. Similar to this racialized othering, Retamar notes, the Spanish soldiers in Cuba's wars of independence described the insurrectionaries with the racial epithet "mambí."[37] Cubans, he argues, now see the term "mambí" "as a mark of glory the honor of considering ourselves descendants of the *mambí*, descendants of the rebel, runaway, *independentista* black—*never* descendants of the slave holder."[38] He presents the Cuban Revolution as the logical descendant of the island's history of black resistance and Caliban as the symbol of this insurrectionary history within Cuba, the Caribbean, and Latin America more broadly. According to Retamar, the Latin American intellectual has a choice between allying himself with Caliban or serving Prospero. In other words, he argues, Latin American intellectuals, and especially those who appear to be troubled over the Revolution's relationship to freedom of expression, can choose between supporting Cuba's "black" revolution (embodied in the figure of Caliban) or furthering imperialism through their bourgeois sensibilities and their distance from the realities faced by the common man.

By 1975, when Nancy Morejón published "Mujer negra" (Black Woman), which charts the history of black women's struggles on the island, culminating in a celebratory representation of the revolutionary present, this narrative of the island's history of black struggle that culminates in the Revolution had arguably become somewhat of a cliché. Some have even suggested that Morejón's poem is an ironic response to the government's rhetoric on black political resistance, because it delivers the rhetoric flawlessly but flatly and without emotional conviction.[39] All of these widely recognized texts were funded and promoted by the Cuban Revolution's strictly regulated cultural apparatus and have served to further its self-fashioning as a black political movement.[40]

This rhetoric has helped the Cuban government garner popular support for its commitment to black liberation movements abroad, most famously demonstrated years prior to the 1966 Tricontinental when Castro dramatically moved his entire UN delegation to the Hotel Theresa in Harlem in September 1960. There, thousands surrounded the hotel, day and night, while Castro met with Malcolm X, Langston Hughes, LeRoi Jones (a.k.a. Amiri Baraka), and other civil rights leaders inside. One of the activists working the crowd was a young Carlos Moore. Born in Cuba as the son of Jamaican im-migrants, Moore and his family had moved from Cuba to Harlem only a few years before. As a teenager in Harlem, Moore became involved in the Fair Play for Cuba Committee, and, as a black Cuban, he played a pivotal role in work-ing up support for the Cuban Revolution among African Americans.

In his memoir, *Pichón: Race and Revolution in Castro's Cuba* (2008), Moore describes the euphoria he experienced when he was invited to attend a private reception at the Hotel Theresa in Castro's honor. His unflinching support for the Cuban Revolution and for Castro, he explains, grew out of his wholehearted belief in the Revolution's posturing as a black movement, writing, "Africa was everything to me, and the Cuban Revolution was but an extension of Africa, and Fidel an extension of Lumumba."[41] At the reception, he was surprised to see that, with the exception of General Juan Almeida Bosque, all of the mem-bers of Castro's delegation were what he calls "lily-white."[42] As he listened to Castro express solidarity with his black brothers in a common struggle against imperialism before the UN General Assembly on September 26, 1960, Moore dismissed any notion of General Almeida's appointment as mere tokenism. However, a seed of doubt regarding the Cuban government's commitment to racial equality was planted in Moore, and once he returned to Cuba in June 1961 in support of the Revolution, his apprehension would slowly grow into full-blown dissidence against the regime's racial politics. Because Moore spoke out against racism in Cuba, he suffered imprisonment and persecution on the island, and by November 1963, he would flee Cuba, reportedly fearful for his life.

The change of heart that Moore experienced toward the Castro government in the early years of the Revolution is not unique among black intellectuals who defected to Cuba or who otherwise supported the regime. While Shakur, Davis, and Brent consistently expressed their support for the Cuban govern-ment, Robert F. Williams, Carmichael, and Cleaver all had similar stories of growing distrust and eventual outright dissidence toward Castro's govern-ment.[43] Williams's Radio Free Dixie, where Moore worked as a newscaster and which broadcast to the United States, faced criticism from the Cuban govern-ment for its promotion of black militancy.[44] After four years in Cuba, Williams would leave for China, writing an open letter to Castro criticizing his hypocriti-cal racial discourse and stating that "Cuba was in the hands of a white petite bourgeoisie."[45] Carmichael, who was initially warmly welcomed in Cuba, later spoke out against the Cuban government, claiming that socialism does not nec-essarily imply the elimination of racism.[46] Similarly, after Cleaver attempted to start a Black Panther Party in Cuba, he fell out of favor with the regime and left Cuba for Algeria, characterizing Cuba's government as "the white, racist Castro dictatorship."[47] In short, according to these activists, Cuba was not the racism-free promised land that it claimed to be. Ruth Reitan has described the relationship between African American activists and the Cuban Revolution in the late 1960s as "the decline of an alliance," which she argues was due to the rising influence of the more conservative communist faction and the decreasing influence of the more internationalist Guevarist faction within the Cuban government.[48] This interpretation is helpful in considering the experience of those like Williams, whose vision for armed struggle in the United States would have been subject to this factionalism, but it does not take into account that African American activists continued to forge relationships with Cuba in the 1970s and 1980s or that many activists' support of and/or dissent from the Revolution was based on their individual experiences within Cuban society.

In its earliest years, the Castro government made major strides in turning the tide of racial inequity, especially in the area of segregation. In 1959, Castro addressed the issue in numerous speeches and interviews: private beaches were made public, ending their de facto segregation; public parks were remodeled to encourage further integration; countless seminars and conferences were held to discuss the problem; and by 1960, private clubs that had been segregated were nationalized and open for public use.[49] While a true commitment to desegregation arguably would have been reflected at the highest levels of government, when Castro visited the Hotel Theresa in Harlem, his antiracist rhetoric in the international sphere lined up at least on the surface with his domestic policies.

However, in April 1961, the day before the Bay of Pigs invasion, Castro publicly declared the socialist nature of the Revolution, and as early as 1962 official discourse held that racial discrimination had been eliminated by the economic and social reforms in communist Cuba.[50] Anyone who critiqued that notion or who tried to organize around racial identity was subsequently characterized as divisive and counterrevolutionary. In September 1961, more than 170 black organizations were shut down under the auspices of desegregation and further incorporation into revolutionary society.[51] Members of several black movements that emerged in the late 1960s and 1970s, such as Movimiento Liberación Nacional, Movimiento Black Power (1971), and the Afro-Cuban Study Group (1974), are reported to have suffered various forms of political persecution, such as imprisonment, forced renunciation of their beliefs, and forced exile.[52] Because of its large Afro-Cuban membership, the publishing house El Puente was accused of being a Black Power organization and was closed in 1965.[53]

This suppression of black political organizing in Cuba is not unique to the postrevolutionary period. The most infamous example of similar policies is Cuba's 1909 Morúa Law, which outlawed political parties based on race and which was eventually brutally enforced with the 1912 massacre of members and suspected sympathizers of the Partido Independiente de Color. As David Luis-Brown has pointed out, "This slaughter of Afro-Cubans was justified in part through an appeal to the very race-blind discourses that Martí and other *independentistas* used as the bedrock of their nationalism."[54] In the decade following the 1912 massacre, in which race-blind nationalism and Jim Crow white supremacy combined to justify a massive political and racial lynching, the cultural movement of *afrocubanismo* (a.k.a. negrismo) would emerge. Afrocubanismo rejected the racial logics of U.S. imperialism by valorizing black cultural contributions to national identity and by celebrating the cultural and racial mixing at the heart of *cubanidad* (Cubanness).[55] Whereas the earlier vision of a raceless Cuba Libre in the independence movements was more concerned with racial fraternity than racial mixing, the nationalism of the early Cuban republic would frame the unity of cubanidad through a vision of a mixed-race nation. Although afrocubanismo would provide professional advancement for some Afro-Cuban artists, it would also consist of the "commodification and folklorization of afro-cuban secular and religious culture" by white artists and was often used to promote national consolidation while disavowing racial inequalities.[56]

The disillusionment experienced by U.S. black activists in postrevolutionary Cuba decades later is thus a symptom of the way in which the state's domestic discourse on race continued these prerevolutionary traditions and did not line up with the internationalist discourse of Tricontinentalism that Cuba played an active role in creating.[57] As I have established, Tricontinentalism, a movement and worldview of an international group of radicals in which the Cuban Revolution was one—albeit major—player, is characterized by a committedly antiracist rhetoric in which the exploitation of black people is viewed as the foundation of an imperial power that oppresses Cubans, African Americans, and other exploited peoples. In contrast, the Cuban Revolution's domestic racial discourse has been characterized as one of "inclusionary discrimination," which Mark Sawyer describes as a mix of Latin American exceptionalism, in which the prerevolutionary framing of Cuba as a raceless nation and the later celebration of *mulato* and *mestizo* figures (through such movements as negrismo) is used to support a myth of racial democracy, as well as Marxist exceptionalism, in which socialist reforms are purported to have eliminated racial inequalities.[58]

Whereas Tricontinentalism would attempt to revise the racial essentialisms and stereotypical representations of negrismo, the Castro government often unquestioningly continued this prerevolutionary racial discourse domestically. The Revolution's celebration of black resistance, often through negrista tropes like Retamar's use of the cannibal figure to define the Cuban Revolution as the symbol of a resistant Latin American politics, dovetailed from prerevolutionary racial discourses and arguably had little relevance to the reality of black political mobilization in Cuba. The Revolution's domestic racial discourse combined the prerevolutionary myths of racial democracy with its postrevolutionary Marxist ideology to argue that racism did not exist in Cuba and that, as Sawyer has noted, racial inequalities in Cuba are not systemic but are the "result of the individual incapacities of blacks."[59] In this sense, Cuba's role in producing the many texts within Tricontinental cultural production that dealt with racial discrimination abroad allowed the communist government to externalize its racial problems, pointing to racism as an expression of U.S. imperialism to which both Cubans and African Americans were subject and denying the presence of racial inequalities within Cuba itself.

Cuba's two-pronged racial discourse—inclusionary discrimination in the domestic sphere and radical antiracism in the international context—has at times converged in remarkable ways, such as when Castro famously described Cuba for the first time as a "pueblo latinoafricano" (Latin African people) when discussing Cuba's military backing of the People's Movement for the Liberation of Angola (MPLA).[60] Cuba's support of the MPLA occurred in the wake of Angola's independence from Portugal during the power struggle between the MPLA and the two militant organizations backed by the United States and South Africa: the National Liberation Front of Angola, and the National Union for the Total Independence of Angola (UNITA). In previous years, Cuba helped fund liberation struggles in other African countries like Algeria, Guinea-Bissau, and the Congo through sending weapons, clandestine military instructors, and contingents of medical professionals, such as Che Guevara's oft-cited covert operation to train Congolese rebels in 1965. However, the intervention in Angola in 1975 required a much larger financial and military commitment from the Cuban people.

Although Cuba had backed the MPLA for some time with military training and weapons, when South African regular troops invaded Angola on October 23, 1975, Cuba increased its support to Angola on an unprecedented scale.

Between 1961 and 1974, fewer than two thousand Cubans had been sent to Africa, but with the initiation of Operation Carlota—named after an enslaved woman who led a revolt on a sugar mill in Matanzas, Cuba, in 1843—thirty thousand Cuban troops would arrive to Angola between October 1975 and April 1976.[61] As Gabriel García Márquez explained in his short and triumphalist account, "Operation Carlota" (1977), this time the Cubans were not simply sending aid, but rather "undertaking large-scale regular warfare 10,000 kilometers away from home at an incalculable economic and human cost and with unforeseen political consequences."[62]

The extent of Cuba's military support to Angola, initiated without the approval of the Soviet Union and against the Soviet policy of peaceful coexistence, was unprecedented and is said to have "stunned" the U.S. government since "extracontinental interventions were the preserve of the superpowers, of a few West European countries, and of China."[63] In a speech delivered on April 19, 1976, on the fifteenth anniversary of the Bay of Pigs invasion, Castro would explain this unprecedented mobilization in Angola to the people of Cuba through appealing both to a Tricontinentalist solidarity based on a shared struggle against imperialism, calling the first end to the Angolan Civil War in 1976 the "twin sister of the victory at Girón," but relying much more emphatically on a racial discourse at the heart of Cuban nationalism.[64] He states, "At Girón, African blood was shed, that of the selfless descendants of a people who were slaves before they became workers, and who were exploited workers before they became masters of their homeland. And in Africa, alongside that of the heroic fighters of Angola, Cuban blood . . . also flowed. Those who once enslaved man and sent him to America perhaps never imagined that one of those peoples who received the slaves would one day send their fighters to struggle for freedom in Africa."[65] He goes on to emphasize that this "African blood" that was shed at Girón (the Bay of Pigs) gives Cuba its identity as a mixed-race "Latin-African people." Using the logic of Cuba's myth of racial democracy, he argues that this mixed-race identity automatically makes Cuba an enemy both of racism in general and of the expansion of apartheid into Angola specifically. To this identity-based rationale, he adds the familiar appeal within revolutionary nationalist discourse—clearly indicated in the naming of the operation after a slave revolt—to a long history of black resistance on the island, comparing Cuban and Angolan defiance of the United States to that of a slave who has broken his chains.

While this speech on the anniversary of the Bay of Pigs invasion is commonly cited as the first time that Castro famously referred to Cubans as a

"Latin African people," he actually used this term one month earlier in a speech given on March 14, 1976, alongside the political leaders Ahmed Sékou Touré of Guinea, Agostinho Neto of Angola, and Luís Cabral of Guinea-Bissau at a mass rally celebrating African independence in a stadium in Conakry, Guinea.[66] In that speech, republished in *Tricontinental*, Castro's use of the term marks important similarities and differences with the one given a month later before a Cuban audience. In Guinea, he states,

> We Cubans helped our Angolan brothers and sisters, first and foremost on principle, because we are internationalists and secondly, because our people are both Latin-American people and Latin-African people. Millions of Africans were shipped to Cuba as slaves by the colonialists and a good part of Cuban blood is African blood. And today our people are a revolutionary people, a free people and an internationalist people who know how to fulfill their revolutionary duties and their duty toward their brothers and sisters in Angola.[67]

A comparison of this speech with the one delivered in Cuba one month later is particularly revealing of the Cuban state's dual racial discourse. In the speech in Guinea that is reprinted in *Tricontinental*, Castro emphasizes that Cuba's support of Angola is "first and foremost" an ideological, Tricontinentalist or "internationalist" project, and, second, is motivated by an African blood lineage shared by a "good part" of Cubans.[68] However, in the speech offered to the Cuban people, the logic for this support is inverted. The ideological rationale in which he compares the Bay of Pigs and the victory in Angola is only an implicit ideological argument for Tricontinentalism. Rather, he emphasizes much more emphatically a blood-based solidarity and a lineage of black resistance within the nation's history on which the Revolution's policy in Africa capitalizes.

Because such a high percentage of the Cubans who left the island after 1959 were white, by the time of these 1976 speeches, Cuba's concentration of Afro-descendant people had indeed steadily increased.[69] Additionally, there is evidence that by 1980 Cuba had made significant gains in measures of racial equality such as life expectancy, educational achievement, and representation in political leadership at lower and middle levels of government.[70] However, a survey of the racial makeup of the executive committee of the Communist Party of Cuba (which contained 7 percent black representation in 1975) as well as the awareness of the restrictions that existed in the mid-1970s against African-derived religious and cultural practices call into question an easy acceptance of this presentation of the revolutionary nation as one founded in black empowerment.[71] In his speech to the Cuban people, Castro deftly maneuvers both Cuba's internationalist and domestic racial discourses, calling Cubans to an identification with Angolans that goes beyond an affiliation with a Tricontinentalist ideology and emphasizing a duty based in blood ties and a shared history of black oppression and resistance.

At the same time that Cuba's intervention in Angola could be cast as the height of Tricontinentalism, the subtle difference between the speech given in Guinea and that given in Cuba also points to the limits of Tricontinentalist solidarity. Not discounting the major financial sacrifice and loss of Cuban lives in Angola, one could argue that whereas Tricontinentalism may have been rationale enough for Cuba to send weapons and doctors abroad, the level of engagement required of Cubans in Angola would necessitate a justification that appealed to nationalist mythology and prerevolutionary racial discourses at the core of Cuban national identity. In other words, Castro posed the war in Angola as an extension of the Cuban struggle that grew directly out of Cuba's own black resistant history. The difference between the two speeches points to the way that the Cuban state often simultaneously navigated its dual racial discourses, at times more successfully than others. In the case of the Angolan Civil War, Castro engineers a defense of Cuban intervention in Angola in which he concurrently brandishes Cuba's domestic and internationalist racial narratives in ways that rhetorically appear to strengthen rather than contradict one another.

Cuba's backing of the MPLA in the Angolan Civil War would eventually require sixteen years, from 1975 to 1991, and hundreds of thousands of troops.[72] After a prolonged struggle, the Cuban-Angolan victory against UNITA and South African Defense Forces at the famous battle of Cuito Cuanavale from November 1987 to March 1988 would have a profound and lasting impact. The Cuban government was able to negotiate for the independence of Namibia from South Africa in exchange for the removal of Cuban troops from Angola, which took place in June 1991.[73] In general, this victory is seen as the major turning point toward the fall of the apartheid regime. Nelson Mandela acknowledged this one month after Cuba's withdrawal from Angola, traveling to Havana where he embraced Castro, stating, "The Cuban internationalists have made a contribution to African independence, freedom and justice unparalleled for its principled and selfless character. . . . Cuito Cuanavale was a milestone in the history of the struggle for southern African liberation!"[74] With Cuba's role in the defeat of apartheid in South Africa, Tricontinentalism achieved perhaps its most profound and lasting impact.

Although the African American struggle continued to feature in Triconti-nental materials throughout the late 1970s and 1980s, and although the Tricon-tinental expressed a commitment to antiapartheid in South Africa from its very inception, as Cuba ramped up its involvement in the late 1970s in the Angolan Civil War, Tricontinental materials turned their focus from the U.S. South toward South Africa. This shift is likely due to several factors, such as an in-creased international focus on South Africa and on the civil war in Angola in general, as well as the debilitating effect that political persecution and faction-alism had on U.S. black radical groups like the Black Panther Party throughout the 1970s. While I have argued for an understanding of Tricontinentalism as a transnational movement in which the OSPAAAL's materials often reflected concerns and issues beyond those of the Cuban state's foreign policy, it is also important to remember that Cuba funded and provided the bureaucracy for all Tricontinental cultural production, meaning that as many prominent African American activists distanced themselves from Cuba in the late 1960s and as Cuba ramped up involvement in Africa in the 1970s, it was likely more con-ducive to Cuba's internationalist reputation for these materials to focus on the antiapartheid cause. Whereas initially Tricontinental materials consistently represented the U.S. South as a microcosm of an expansive global empire char-acterized by racial capitalism, from the mid-1970s forward, apartheid South Africa became the fulcrum on which this Tricontinentalist understanding of power and resistant solidarity was forged. Despite this shift, the key elements of the rhetoric and ideology of Tricontinentalism remained the same.

Tricontinental cultural production from the late 1970s and 1980s shined a spotlight on South Africa through such avenues as posters devoted to the con-demnation of apartheid and to solidarity with South African liberation strug-gles; articles about the antiapartheid struggle by Oliver Tambo, the leader of the African National Congress, and the Namibian antiapartheid politician Sam Nujoma; proclamations calling for the release of Nelson Mandela; analy-ses of South African military strategy in Angola; and reporting on antiapart-heid organizing around the globe. A *Tricontinental* article entitled "United States and Apartheid" bridges the earlier focus on African American activism with the increased emphasis on South Africa by articulating the relationship between devices of racialization within the United States and those in South Africa. This article was written by Jane McManus, a U.S. citizen living in Cuba who was the English translator for *Tricontinental* and the long-term partner of the Black Panther William Lee Brent, who hijacked a passenger jet to Cuba in 1969 where he remained in exile until his death in 2006.[75] McManus writes,

A whole range of devices is employed within the United States to maintain vast numbers of blacks, Native Americans, Chicanos, Puerto Ricans, and other groups in the position of second-class citizens subject to many of the same restrictions that blacks in South Africa face: educational, job, and housing restrictions; imprisonment in numbers far greater than their proportion to the population; lack of medical and child care facilities; massive unemployment; genocidal efforts at mass sterilization; and human indignities that range from verbal attacks to police brutality.[76]

In sum, according to McManus, apartheid as a system of racialized, biopolitical oppression is not limited to South Africa but is integral to the imperialistic nature of both the United States and its South African ally.

This vision of transnational apartheid that appears in later Tricontinental cultural production is similar to the symbology of the Jim Crow South used in earlier Tricontinental materials to metonymically signify a global struggle against imperialism. Apartheid as representative of a deterritorialized configuration of global dominance is further emphasized in an article, which follows McManus's essay and is entitled "The Export of Apartheid to Latin America," which discusses economic and military ties between the apartheid regime and right-wing military dictatorships in the Southern Cone of Latin America. While it points to the Chilean military's participation in operations against the South West African People's Organization and instances of South African assistance to Southern Cone Latin American military governments, it emphasizes that these Latin American countries have a similar "fascist and racist government" that "is allied with US imperialism and the transnational enterprises" and that, like South Africa's treatment of the native black population, "in the name of progress and civilization, commit[s] the most barbarous crimes against the people."[77] Here, apartheid South Africa's racial divisions operate very similarly to the metonymic color politics that I have analyzed in earlier chapters. In the same way that African Americans were posed as representative of all peoples victimized by and resistant to imperialism, black South Africans become compared here to the largely white and mestizo leftist and student populations who were tortured and "disappeared" in the Southern Cone. In the same vein, the article goes on to compare South African apartheid to the United States' colonial relationship with Puerto Rico, arguing that "Puerto Rico and South Africa become simply two aspects of one single racist and imperialist philosophy practice."[78] While the U.S. South in prior Tricontinental materials was consistently used as a microcosm of a global system—meaning the Tricontinental always conceived of the South in global terms—as the role of the U.S. South within Tricontinentalism becomes replaced with South Africa (which is then compared to Southern Cone Latin America), an even clearer portrait of a Global South emerges. The Souths referenced here capture a loosely defined geographic region, but more importantly they operate together as a signifier of global inequity. The author claims, "Relations between the racist regimes of southern Africa and those of the Southern Cone of Latin America must be understood on the basis of the role they play in imperialism's global strategy, particularly the part of it concerned with the South Atlantic."[79] Here, the "global strategy" of imperialism—much like Glenda Gilmore's description of the racial hierarchy of "Dixie" that traveled in the early twentieth century through U.S. expansion—is carried out through "racist regimes" in a region the author calls the "South Atlantic." This vision of a Global South, or perhaps in this case more precisely a "Global South Atlantic" to use a term coined by the critics Kerry Bystrom and Joseph Slaughter, anticipates an increasingly relevant critical apparatus for the study of contemporary capitalist globalization, a subject that will be at the center of chapter 5.[80]

Cuba's involvement in ending the apartheid regime as well as its pro-black rhetoric surrounding its intervention in Angola would eventually contribute to some gains for Afro-Cubans at home. For example, in 1986, in the third congress of the Communist Party of Cuba (PCC), Castro "broke the long-standing official silence on race," acknowledging that racism and racial discrimination continued to be a troubling part of Cuban society.[81] This resulted in the election of a Central Committee to the PCC in which members of African descent made up 28 percent of the total.[82] Additionally, restrictions against African-derived religious practices were lifted in 1987.[83] However, despite other gains since 1959 in education and healthcare, racial inequalities in housing and overrepresentation in the prison population persisted.[84] Overall, despite its central participation in conceiving a Tricontinentalist critique of racism in places like the United States and South Africa, arguably the Cuban Revolution's domestic discourse of inclusionary discrimination has remained relatively static since 1961.

In sum, the Tricontinental helped to foment solidarity among liberation struggles around the world, supporting the creation of an impactful global revolutionary subjectivity and providing an ideological frame for Cuba's military and financial support for struggles abroad. Yet Cuba's central role in Tricontinentalism also allowed it to externalize its own racial problems, attributing racial discrimination to the imperialists and denying its presence in Cuba.[85] While the Castro government supported black liberation abroad through Tricontinentalism, in the domestic realm, it consistently claimed that its redistribution of wealth had ended racial inequality. Subsequently the government sought to silence those who critiqued that notion or who tried to organize around racial identity.

However, the model of transnational revolution devised through the Tricontinental also provided critics of the regime's racial politics with a readily available and easily recognizable platform from which to launch their critique. The very ideological framework through which Cuba expressed solidarity with liberation movements abroad and externalized racial issues to the imperialist North would be used to call attention to racial discrimination under the revolutionary government. Some who criticized the Cuban Revolution's claim to have ended racism would take up the Tricontinentalist argument that black exploitation is foundational to a deterritorialized imperialist power structure and, by pointing to continuities between Cuba's past and its revolutionary present, would use a Tricontinentalist argument to argue for the continuation of racial inequality under the Castro regime. Since empire was theorized as transcendent of any one particular nation or power and since the Tricontinental did not necessarily propose socialism as the solution for dismantling global empire, then it was logical (and still in line with this rhetoric) to argue that imperialism and thus racial inequality might still have a hold in Cuba.

This argument, which has largely driven critiques of the Cuban Revolution's color-blind racial discourse, has been articulated in varying ways. Some have claimed that while the Revolution has done much to challenge racial discrimination, the legacy of prerevolutionary colonialism and slavery is still firmly entrenched in communist Cuba, and the government must be more aggressive in its policies to overcome it. For others, like Guillén Landrián in *Coffea arábiga*, this critique is more strident, claiming that the Revolution, through its very actions and rhetoric, furthers both the discriminatory practices and exoticizing racism of the prerevolutionary period and therefore does not follow through on its Tricontinentalist rhetoric.

The use of Tricontinentalist discourse to critique the Revolution can be found in texts by U.S. black activists who played a central role in envisioning Tricontinentalism and who employed their internationalist and antiracist stance of Tricontinentalism in order to critique the Cuban government. Much of the scholarly work on writers' dissidence with Cuba's racial politics has focused on these non-Cuban perspectives. However, because the OSPAAAL's propaganda apparatus was the organizing structure of Tricontinentalism, I find the cultural production closely associated with it to be the most fitting starting point from which to outline how Tricontinentalism could be used to critique the regime itself.

As noted in chapter 2, the Tricontinental had several propaganda outlets through which it disseminated its ideology: the pages of *Tricontinental Bulletin*, the magazine *Tricontinental*, the now-famous posters that were folded up inside of *Tricontinental*, pamphlets and ephemera, the ICAIC Latin American Newsreel, and radio programs. Because the posters and publications were overseen by the OSPAAAL, which was led by high-ranking government officials like its general secretary, Osmany Cienfuegos, critiques of the government in these texts are not readily apparent. However, the ICAIC Latin American Newsreel, overseen by the Cuban Film Institute, could be viewed as providing more artistic license.

This is not to say that the ICAIC did not strictly control its output or was not involved in censorship, the most famous example being its denial of permission for the public screening of *P.M.*, a documentary by Sabá Cabrera Infante (the brother of Guillermo Cabrera Infante, the famed writer and editor of *Lunes de Revolución*) and Orlando Jiménez Leal.[86] Indeed, a discussion of the censure of this film will provide further context for analyzing Guillén Landrián's argument and the official reaction to it.

CUBAN DOCUMENTARY AT THE INTERSECTION OF RACIAL AND AESTHETIC POLITICS

P.M., a fifteen-minute film that depicts Cubans, especially black Cubans, drinking and dancing at bars, was banned from public exhibition six weeks after the Bay of Pigs invasion and six weeks after Castro declared the Revolution to be socialist. The reasoning for the film's censure has been explained in various ways. Guillermo Cabrera Infante, the editor of *Lunes de Revolución*, the arts and culture supplement of the newspaper *Revolución* that independently provided the funds for the film, described the issue as a turf war in which *Lunes de Revolución*, by making its first-ever film, was thereby staging an incursion on the ICAIC's control over the film industry.[87] In William Luis's reading, the conflict goes much deeper in that the film's censure represented the culmination of ongoing aesthetic and political differences between the ICAIC and *Lunes de Revolución*.

Whereas the members of *Lunes de Revolución* aligned themselves with the 26th of July Movement, the Castro government gave control of its new film institute to the communist Cine Club Marxista (Marxist Film Club), which had long maintained a close relationship with the Popular Socialist Party (PSP).[88] According to Luis, the ICAIC's censure of *P.M.*, and the closure of *Lunes de Revolución* that would follow the controversy, is the result of the communists' increasing power in the immediate wake of the Revolution's public alignment with the Soviets and is an early example of the growing tendency toward centralizing the country's cultural apparatus.[89] In response to the ICAIC's refusal to show the film, *Lunes de Revolución* compiled a protest document with the signatures of two hundred artists and intellectuals. Castro arranged three meetings in the José Martí National Library in June 1961 in which representatives from the PSP and from both the ICAIC and *Lunes* were in attendance. In these meetings, the ICAIC's director, Alfredo Guevara, would accuse *Lunes* of being anti–Soviet Union and antirevolutionary, seeming to use the controversy to centralize the country's film industry under his leadership and to confirm Luis's interpretation of bitter political differences between the two groups.

In addition to these political disagreements, *Lunes* and the ICAIC differed in aesthetic preference as well. *P.M.* was highly influenced by English Free Cinema, which emphasized an observational use of the camera rather than an interventionist or propagandistic one, whereas the ICAIC found Italian Neorealism, and later the Soviet-inspired montage of Santiago Álvarez, in which the filmic image becomes a tool for communicating a clear political message, to be more conducive to a militant, revolutionary cinema. Directors of *Lunes,* like Carlos Franqui and Guillermo Cabrera Infante, maintained a more open posture in their cinematic appreciation and, in response to the censure of *P.M.*, published the February 1961 issue *"Lunes* va al cine" (*Lunes* Goes to the Movies), which included a debate on Italian Neorealism versus Free Cinema and a section on eroticism in film. The section on eroticism included photographs of the sexiest actresses of the moment, including several U.S. actresses, which was viewed as a direct affront to the official positions represented by the ICAIC.[90]

The two organizations' differing ideological postures can be seen in the difference between *P.M.* and *Cuba baila* (Cuba Dances) (1963), an ICAIC film to which Luis mentions that *P.M.* was responding. *Cuba baila,* by the Cuban film screenwriter, director, and theorist Julio García Espinosa, was the first feature film to be completed by the ICAIC.[91] However, because it dealt with the prerevolutionary bourgeoisie and the ICAIC intended to make its debut with a film about the revolutionary struggle, *Cuba baila* was not released until 1963.[92] It narrates a father's attempt to give his daughter a *quinceañera* party based on bourgeois ideals of decorum and propriety, exposing the race and class divisions that dictate where and how Cubans dance. The weak and taciturn father, Ramón, emerges as the hero in the end when he admits that he does not have the money to throw his daughter's party at the salon where wealthy white people host their events and instead invites guests to a public concert and dance that is often attended by lower classes and especially by black Cubans. The film ends with a display of unity as the community, previously divided by race and class differences, comes together to dance and celebrate.

The film opens with footage of a public dance, attended largely by Afro-Cubans, in the location where Ramón will eventually host his daughter's party. Ramón and his wife stand by, watching disapprovingly as women shake their hips in tight-fitting hourglass dresses. In overlay appears the phrase "This story could have occurred in Cuba in any past period of its republican life. Now, the middle class awakens and cronyism has been eliminated."[93] Thus, the film asserts from the very beginning that the race and class divisions that the film attempts to address are decidedly prerevolutionary and have been resolved by the Castro government. According to *Cuba baila*, segregation in the Cuban social scene is a thing of the past. This claim is the central issue, I believe, in the controversy over *P.M.*

While I certainly agree with Luis's arguments that these two films represent organizations with differing political affiliations at a time when Cuba was becoming increasingly intolerant of political difference and while I also agree that *Cuba baila*, overseen by the father of Italian Neorealism, Cesare Zavattini, takes a decidedly different approach than *P.M.*'s Free Cinema–inspired refusal to impose an interpretation on its viewers, I suggest that these two films' treatment of racial segregation is central to the discussion. *P.M.*'s treatment of race has not gone without comment. Only six weeks after the Bay of Pigs invasion, the ICAIC viewed the film as "aesthetically and politically irresponsible," because, according to Chanan, "it presented black people in roles associated with the state of oppression from which they were in the process of liberation."[94] In other words, in a time when the state desperately needed national unity in the face of the external threat epitomized in the Bay of Pigs invasion, and in a time when the Revolution was making major efforts to desegregate public spaces, these images of drunkenness and dance were viewed as reifying racist stereotypes and were offensive to the severe sobriety of the political moment.

Yet many of the images in *P.M.*, such as the films' lingering focus on black women's hips and buttocks, are so similar to those of *Cuba baila* that it seems that the issue at hand is not necessarily regarding the oversexualized and frivolous representations of black subjects. In other words, based on the lack of censorship of *Cuba baila* as well as the Revolution's willingness to take up other stereotypical representations, it is unlikely that the negative response to *P.M.* emerged out of the government's critical stance toward the film's representations of black people. Rather, whereas *Cuba baila* asserts that segregation in Cuban popular culture is a thing of the past, *P.M.* shows a specifically Afro-Cuban nightlife in a specifically postrevolutionary context.

In this sense, I understand the conflict between Italian Neorealism and Free Cinema, or the conflict regarding whether the camera should be used to observe or to intervene, to be an underlying discomfort with *P.M.*'s refusal to impose a prerevolutionary timeline on the behaviors that it attempts to capture. It presents a postrevolutionary reality and does not attempt to fit that reality neatly into the Castro government's discourse on race. *P.M.* implicitly attests to the fact that what *Cuba baila* wants to present as a thing of the past continues in postrevolutionary Cuba, despite the rhetoric of Marxist exceptionalism that claims that socialist reforms have eliminated these kinds of race and class divisions.

In the final meeting on June 30, 1961, one month before all political parties would be consolidated under the Integrated Revolutionary Organizations (ORI), which would later become the Communist Party of Cuba, Castro would give his famous "Palabras a los intelectuales" (Words to the Intellectuals) speech, in which he defined the Revolution's cultural politics with the phrase "Dentro de la Revolución, todo; contra la Revolución, nada" (Within the Revolution, everything; against the Revolution, nothing). Neither *P.M.* nor *Lunes de Revolución* would be deemed to fit "within the Revolution," and within a few months (November 1961), *Lunes de Revolución* would close.[95]

As demonstrated by *P.M.*, the authoritarian control over cultural production that would become the norm in Cuba in the 1970s was already being experienced by artists in the early 1960s. Yet the conversation that *P.M.* began would not end there. *P.M.* set a precedent within Cuban cinema for the filmic image as an effective and deeply cutting mode of critique against the Revolution's rhetoric on racial equality and, as I will argue in the pages that follow, film continues to be used in this capacity.[96] While the closure of newspapers and radio stations that opposed the Castro government began earlier than 1961, following the censorship of *P.M.*, independent magazines and presses that supported the Revolution were shut down as the country's intellectual institutions were centralized. The controls placed on intellectuals that began in the early 1960s culminated in the 1971 Padilla Affair, in which Heberto Padilla was imprisoned and forced to publicly repent for his book of poetry, *Fuera del juego* (Out of the game) (1968), an event that is generally viewed as the beginning of what Ambrosio Fornet has termed the *quinquenio gris* (five gray years) (1971–1976), a period of intensified Stalinization of culture and repression of artistic freedoms in Cuba. According to Desiderio Navarro, the quinquenio gris is a euphemism because, on one hand, it "in fact lasted for about fifteen years (approximately from 1968 until 1983), and, on the other, was in fact not gray but black for many intellectual lives and works."[97]

Guillén Landrián made *Coffea arábiga* during this highly repressive period. Before directing the film, the filmmaker was reportedly sentenced to two years of hard labor on the Isle of Youth for what he described as ideological differences with the Cuban government.[98] He does not elaborate on what those ideological differences were, but beginning in the mid-1960s, in an effort to achieve greater productivity through a highly disciplined labor force, the Cuban government began policing everything from fashion and music tastes to sexual preference and adherence to gender norms. Those who were perceived as conforming to capitalism and U.S. culture through, for example, wearing one's hair long, listening to Beatles music, or critiquing the actions of the government, even from a position of Marxism, were accused of "ideological diversionism" and were often sent to labor prison camps that were euphemistically called Military Units of Assistance to Production (UMAPS).[99]

Due to psychological distress (apparently he set a group of chickens on fire at the labor camp), Guillén Landrián was released from prison, treated with electroshock therapy at a military hospital in Havana, and placed under house arrest in Havana where he requested to either continue making films or leave the country.[100] He was returned to the ICAIC but was moved from the Artistic Department to the Department of Scientific and Technical Documentaries, which Guillén Landrián has explained as a concession to the ICAIC's management that reluctantly took him back.[101] *Coffea arábiga*, perhaps the most politically controversial of his films, would be his first film in the Scientific and Technical Department.

The film was commissioned to promote the Cordón de La Habana, which aimed to supply food to Havana, allowing it to become self-sufficient while redirecting labor from the state's offensive against private businesses.[102] It formed part of a larger de-urbanization effort in this period, which posited rural communities as a moral alternative to corrupt urban lifestyles.[103] In this sense the Cordón de La Habana aimed to integrate *habaneros* into the spirit of La Gran Zafra (the ten-million-ton sugar harvest), a national campaign to drastically increase sugar production throughout the late 1960s, culminating in a ten-million-ton crop in 1970. La Gran Zafra emphasized the volunteerism required to produce this massive crop as the moral prerogative of the Revolution's hardworking and disciplined *nuevo hombre* (new man). In other words, the campaign epitomized the very state discourse around labor, productivity, and discipline against which Guillén Landrián and many others' "ideological diversionism" was severely punished in the UMAPs. The Cordón de La Habana was eventually largely unsuccessful, resulting in a small agricultural yield disproportionate to the publicity surrounding it. More important, La Gran Zafra of 1970 fell far short of its goal, leaving behind economic difficulties and a blow to national morale.

While *Coffea arábiga* was commissioned as part of the promotional materials for this campaign, the didactic portions of the film, although aesthetically experimental and sophisticated, do little to clearly explain to the Havana public how to plant and grow coffee and conspicuously do not contribute to the production of the new disciplined labor force. Guillén Landrián makes his lack of interest in this area known in the section of the film on fertilization that simply states "fertilización, ¿está claro?" (fertilization, is it clear?). Instead, as I will detail, the film uses the steps for planting and growing coffee to structure a much further-reaching political statement on Cuba's racial discourse, responding directly to the state's hypocritical position toward racial equality.

A TRICONTINENTALIST READING OF *COFFEA ARÁBIGA*

Considering the controversy over *P.M.*, the importance of the ICAIC newsreels to the Tricontinental's propaganda, as well as the gap between the Revolution's international face of Tricontinentalism and its domestic one of inclusionary discrimination, it is not surprising that there would be heightened sensitivity directed at a film like *Coffea arábiga* that exposed Cuba's inconsistent treatment of racial discrimination. *Coffea arábiga* uses the Tricontinentalist view of the exploitation of black labor as foundational to imperialism to critique the continuation of prerevolutionary race relations in postrevolutionary Cuba. *Coffea arábiga* delivers its Tricontinentalist argument through employing the aesthetics of Álvarez's newsreels, used to condemn racial discrimination in places like the United States but significantly never used to discuss domestic racial inequalities, in order to denounce the perpetuation of the exploitation of black labor within the state's agricultural campaign.

The influence of Álvarez, whose newsreels largely defined the Tricontinental's anti-imperialist filmic aesthetic, can be seen in some of Guillén Landrián's earlier films. For example, *Retornar a Baracoa* (Returning to Baracoa) (1966), a film that depicts life in the remote and rural town of Baracoa and that skeptically presents state development projects there, engages in some of the experimentation with montage for which Álvarez would become known, such as animation of photographs, ironic pairings of soundtrack and image, and captions that critically narrate and evaluate the presented materials. However, in general, Guillén Landrián's prior work consists of long takes set to instrumental music that lend a slow-moving and pensive quality to the films. They do not engage in the hyper-editing through which Álvarez communicates his hard-hitting political arguments.

Guillén Landrián's aesthetic choices change dramatically with *Coffea arábiga*, which clearly draws from Álvarez's emphasis on quick cuts and zooms, found material, and montage. Through the often-ironic interaction between image, sound, and graphic text, Guillén Landrián delivers his argument through creating associations and revealing fissures between sound and image, discourse and reality. The choice of this Tricontinentalist medium is integrally tied to the message of the film. Through a *détournement* of Cuba's Tricontinentalist discourse, Guillén Landrián appropriates the aesthetic of Álvarez's newsreels to shed light on racial inequities within the Castro government's policies and thus to expose the hypocrisy of its internationalist commitment to black freedom.

Coffea arábiga alternates between instructional material on how to plant coffee and commentary on the history of Cuba's coffee industry. At first glance, this historical commentary appears to present a tidy narrative in which the Cordón de La Habana campaign represents a revolutionary form of coffee production that liberates Cuba's proletariat from the oppressive, capitalistic coffee plantations of the past. For example, Guerra argues that, through the film, "Guillén Landrián portrayed the Revolution as an inversion of the historical exploitation and marginality of blacks, depicting slaves as the intellectual authors and heroes of Fidel's contemporary *Plan Café*."[104] However, I will argue that at the same time that Guillén Landrián presents this triumphalist narrative, he subtly undermines it as well by pointing to the continuation of the racial hierarchies of the colonial past under the Revolution's present agricultural model. In this way, he launches the same critique against the Castro regime's racial politics that the Tricontinental makes of imperialist nations. He achieves this critique by arguing for the continuities and similarities between three historical moments of Cuban coffee production: nineteenth-century slavery, postindependence U.S. occupation, and postrevolutionary Cuba, positing that the revolutionary era has only supposed a continuation—rather than a heroic reversal—of the racial politics of slavery and U.S. occupation.

The opening sequence suggests the ironic skepticism that will endure throughout the film. Guillén Landrián opens his film with the voice of his uncle, Nicolás Guillén, reading the final stanza of a poem, "Un largo lagarto verde" (A long green lizard) (1958), in which the poet presents the island as an alligator, once sad and enslaved, who has woken up from his slumber. The film then reiterates this transition from slavery to awakening by recalling the history of slavery within coffee production, stating that coffee was first cultivated in Wajay, a municipality of Havana. Guillén Landrián further emphasizes the historical connection between coffee production and slavery by showing images from the Museo de la Gran Piedra, a nineteenth-century coffee plantation that was originally the property of French immigrants who left Haiti in the wake of the Haitian Revolution. It then cuts to a black screen with white text that states "los negros en el cafetal como mano de obra" (blacks in the coffee plantation as hard labor). It reverts back to images of the plantation and then cuts to another black screen with white letters that ask the seemingly sarcastic question "¿cómo? ¿los negros?" (what? blacks?) and then the answer "sí, los negros" (yes, blacks). As drums begin to play in the background, a photograph of broken chains appears, followed by footage of drums and black Cubans dancing in traditional dress.

The juxtaposition of the dancing with broken shackles suggests dance as symbolic of a liberation from slavery that is parallel to the poetic image of the island as a formerly enslaved alligator that has awoken. However, the ironic tone with which the film asks the obvious question "¿los negros?" destabilizes a facile analysis of this moment of the film, introducing a subtle irony that will become more explicit when this same dance footage, to which I will return in the coming pages, appears again later in the film.

Guillén Landrián then builds on this irony by using the sequence that follows to suggest the film's discourse as alternative to the one provided by the state and thus to metaphorically plant the seeds for his argument. After the commentary on the history of slave labor within coffee production in Cuba, the credits roll, and a black screen with white letters announces a new section entitled "preparación de la tierra" (soil preparation). Following a still image of a propaganda poster that equates working in agriculture to the revolutionary struggle, a voiceover of an engineer explains the process of planting coffee. The engineer speaks over the sound of typewriters while typeset letters flash onscreen, forming political slogans like "seguro, seguro, a los yankis dales duro" (for sure, for sure, hit the Yankees hard). In this way Guillén Landrián sets up the Revolution's official discourse, which presents agricultural labor as a patriotic act.

In the scenes that follow, he suggests that his film's argument will not follow this official line. After the engineer's report, photographs of Havana's cityscape appear as the Cordón de la Habana radio program plays in the background. An interviewer then asks a fashionably dressed woman (wearing large sunglasses, a pixie haircut, and a pattern shift dress), who appears to be standing on Calle 23 in the busy Vedado district of Havana, her opinion on the Cordón de La Habana.[105] Instead of giving an opinion, she begins to explain the process of planting shade-grown coffee in the outskirts of the city, repeating nearly word for word the sound bite from the Cordón de La Habana program that played immediately before this scene. During her explanation, she switches into Bulgarian, a moment that has been read as an allusion to the increasing Soviet influence over Cuba's official discourse.[106] As she is still speaking, the Supremes' "You Keep Me Hanging On" begins to steadily increase in volume in the background. With a technique strikingly similar to Álvarez in *Now*, the camera zooms in and out on different parts of the woman's face to the rhythm of the lyrics "set me free, why don't you, baby," suggesting that this woman needs to be freed from her rote understanding of the campaign and repetition of state propaganda. While this scene reiterates the antibourgeois and anti-urban rhetoric that helped motivate volunteerism in the Revolution's agricultural campaigns, it simultaneously suggests that the liberation the film will provide will be an alternative discourse to the official one indicated by the radio program.

The film goes on to further undermine the supposed patriotism of the agricultural campaign and nuevo hombre discourse that views agricultural labor as liberating. It presents limited information on fertilization and on the parasites and diseases that can damage the plants, explaining that plants catch diseases just like humans do. Through anthropomorphizing the plants' suffering, showing the *pata prieta* (an illness, literally translated as "black leg," that especially affects tobacco and that turns the roots of plants a dark color) as feet with dark plantar warts on the heels, the caption that follows with the word "control" acquires multiple meanings. "Control" here seems to refer to the need to control the diseases that affect the crops before they become unmanageable, the control over the human body implicated by the opening section on slavery, and the control over the mind expressed by the woman's rote repetition of state propaganda.

This suggestion of the control over mind and body inherent within the history of the coffee industry links the opening section on slavery to the second chapter of historical commentary, which introduces the three main coffee companies that were nationalized by the state and whose owners would relocate their headquarters to the United States.[107] After the caption that states "Los café Tu-Py, Pilón, Regil presentan" (Tupy, Pilón, Regil Coffee present), photographs of upper-class, white women are juxtaposed with images of one-room shacks and the calloused and cut hands of a worker. These photographs as well as images of white-on-black oppression, such as a photograph of three smiling white women holding a black woman by her arms as she appears to attempt to struggle free, are paired with a recording of an English lesson read by a woman in an eerie and echoing whisper. "Do you believe in Santa Claus?" the woman on the audio track asks as bombs drop, creating a direct association between the history of U.S. occupation signaled by the English lesson, the continued threat of U.S. invasion indicated by the bombs, the oppressive racial hierarchy of the island's history of coffee production seen in the photographs, and the coffee companies that have now established themselves in Florida. In this way, the coffee companies come to embody a host of signifiers of colonial hegemony from Cuba's past and present. The film asks its viewers, "Quieren Uds. tomar Café Regil, o Pilón, o Tupy?" (Do you want to drink Regil, Pilón, or Tupy Coffee?). "No!" it replies, with guns pointed in the air, presenting yet again, as in the section on slavery, a narrative in which the Revolution's new agricultural model liberates Cuba's people from its oppressive past. As indicated through the suggestion that the woman in Havana needs to be "set free" from revolutionary propaganda, the final section of the film destabilizes this celebratory representation of the agricultural campaign.

The last half of the film is devoted to the Cordón de La Habana and to coffee production under the Revolution. Based on the repetition throughout the film of the transformation of Cuba's enslaved past to a liberatory present, one would expect this final section to be a triumphant celebration of the new agricultural model. Instead—and here is where the film takes a turn markedly critical of the Revolution—Guillén Landrián insists on the similarities between the island's history of coffee production and the revolutionary present.

The section begins with a celebratory tone that equates the rise of Castro with the blooming hope embodied in the agricultural campaign: the sound of marching snare drums is coupled with a black screen containing "26 DE JULIO" (referring to Castro's 26th of July Movement) in white block letters and then footage of Castro ascending a platform to chants of "Fidel." A photograph of Castro's bearded smile appears and then dissolves into images of coffee flowers blooming.

Next, however, the film takes an unusual turn that automatically destabilizes this celebratory reading. The camera fades in and out, lending an animated quality to the subject's actions, between a series of photographs of a seated black woman styling her straightened hair with rollers while she listens to the nightly romantic poetry reading of the Radio Baracoa station. The sequence of the woman rolling her hair is recycled from one of Guillén Landrián's previous films, *Retornar a Baracoa*, a film that splices images of the poverty of rural Baracoa with footage of new development projects there, capturing thus the tension of these transitions and questioning the extent of the government's commitment to not only build factories in this region but also truly revolutionize the Baracoa community.[108] In *Retornar a Baracoa*, the images of the woman curling her hair are followed by a photograph of a young man leaning on his arm and looking back toward the camera and then by several photographs of him sitting on a bench in the street. In this way, Guillén Landrián suggests that the woman rolls her hair in the privacy of her home in order to satisfy the male gaze that she meets in the street. In fact, in the mid-1960s, it became common for women to wear their hair in rollers out in the fields and in public in general. This fashion statement has been viewed as part of a general emphasis on women's new status as a substantial part of the workforce and thus liberated from a patriarchal public/private divide.[109] In the context of *Retornar a Baracoa*, this sequence suggests that the radical changes that had taken place throughout the country in the relationships between men and women had not occurred in the remote and impoverished Baracoa.

Yet when this sequence reappears in *Coffea arábiga*, it takes on a different meaning, adding to its critique of societal, patriarchal norms a critique of racial inequality directed at state policies. Aisha Cort provides an insightful reading of the images of the woman styling her hair by reflecting on the way that natural hairstyles, popular among African Americans in the late 1960s as a politically charged rejection of white cultural standards of beauty, were frowned upon during this period in Cuba. Black Cubans who wore their hair naturally were associated with the Black Power movement and were persecuted.[110] This was consistent with the Cuban government's general rejection of countercultural influences imported from the North. However, even considering this general trend, it is noteworthy that at the same time that Cuba, through the Tricontinental, was producing celebratory films and propaganda materials on U.S. black activism that featured photographs and film footage of activists who wore their hair naturally in afros, the appropriation of this symbology by Afro-Cubans would be suppressed. Cort writes, "Landrián challenges the authenticity and revolutionary value of straightened hair and also reevaluates the stigma and negative connotations of the natural characteristics of black hair."[111]

Building on Cort's reading of the film's commentary on the stigma against natural hairstyles in 1960s Cuba, I would suggest this moment of the film as encapsulating what will be its central critique of the state's hypocrisy regarding its commitment to black freedom. Hair here signals the distance between the rhetoric of Tricontinentalism and Cuba's domestic racial discourse and suppression of black organizing. Like in *Retornar a Baracoa*, *Coffea arábiga* cuts briefly to the photograph of the young man looking at the camera, thus maintaining the association between her hairstyle and the male gaze. However, in *Coffea arábiga*, this photograph is followed by magazine clippings reporting on women's heroic role in the agricultural project coupled with choral voices singing "libertad" (freedom). Significantly, the film then cuts to footage of white women wearing their hair in rollers and working in the fields. This juxtaposition drives home the incongruity between the societal control over black women's hairstyles and the rhetoric of the agricultural campaign that encourages these same women to be active participants in revolutionary society. Only white women, it seems, have been allowed to achieve this libertad that is embodied in wearing their curlers out to the fields, while black women are forced to continue to meet patriarchal and racist standards of beauty.

Guillén Landrián makes this critique of racial inequality much more explicit in the footage that follows in which he presents the viewer with a racial hierarchy within the division of labor in the agricultural campaign. For example, he shows the *secaderos* (dryers) as white women talking and laughing while they leisurely dry the coffee beans with their shovels (fig. 4.1). Minutes later, he presents black women working in a loud, threshing factory. This subtle representation of the division of labor along racial lines ironizes the film's statement that in order to work in the threshing room, one has to have good sight and "buenos ojos" (good eyes) (fig. 4.2). As Guillén Landrián cuts to a close-up of a black woman's eyes, he imbues this supposed requirement of good eyesight with racial connotations (fig. 4.3).

The film's commentary on the racial division of labor is then followed by footage of black and white Cubans drinking coffee, a cheering crowd, Castro ascending a platform again to give a speech, and then, significantly, the same footage of drumming and dancing that appeared toward the beginning of the film in association with the history of coffee-plantation slavery. While one might view this dancing as parallel to the celebratory tone expressed by the cheering crowd waiting for Castro's speech, considering the racial divisions in Guillén

FIG. 4.1 Drying coffee beans with shovels. Film still from *Coffea arábiga* (Havana, Cuba: ICAIC, 1968).

FIG. 4.2 Threshing requires "buenos ojos." Film still from *Coffea arábiga* (Havana, Cuba: ICAIC, 1968).

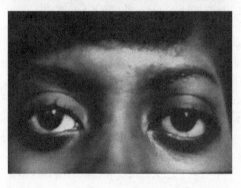

FIG. 4.3 A black woman's eyes. Film still from *Coffea arábiga* (Havana, Cuba: ICAIC, 1968).

Landrián's representation of the Cuban government's agricultural project, the reappearance of this footage from the section on slavery suggests the continuity of racial hierarchies that divide labor under the Revolution.

This ambiguous moment in the film is then paired with the statement "En Cuba, todos los negros y todos los blancos y todos tomamos café" (In Cuba, all blacks and all whites and everyone drinks coffee), a phrase that revises the famous lyrics "Ay Mamá Inés, todos los negros tomamos café" (Ay Mama Inés, all us blacks drink coffee) from a song that was originally composed by planta-tion slaves, then used in the caricaturesque blackface *bufo* theater, and made internationally famous by the Afro-Cuban musician Ignacio Villa during the negrismo movement.[112] Although one could view this revision of the slave song as according with the more egalitarian concept that "everyone" drinks coffee and, more important, harvests coffee, and thus as a triumphant portrayal of the Revolution's achievements, both the dance footage that precedes this statement and the images that come afterward will call this reading into question.

As the Beatles song "The Fool on the Hill" begins to play—which is al-ready suggestive of the contestatory nature of the film, because the Beatles were banned on the radio in the mid-1960s—the photograph of the worker's calloused hands from the section on U.S. imperialism appears, suggesting yet again the continuity between the inequality of Cuba's prerevolution-ary past and its present. In this sense, the seemingly guileless celebratory phrase that all whites and all blacks drink coffee becomes permeated with an irony that works to undermine the state's celebratory rhetoric and that connects, rather than divorces, that rhetoric to the oppressive history of Cuban agriculture.

"FIN PERO NO ES EL FIN"

Through presenting the racial hierarchies of coffee production within three dis-tinct moments of Cuban history (nineteenth-century slavery, postindependence U.S. imperialism, and postrevolutionary Cuba), *Coffea arábiga* makes an argu-ment that is very similar to the one presented in the Afro-Cuban writer Walterio Carbonell's censored 1961 text, *Crítica: Como surgió la cultura nacional.* In this text Carbonell, who in 1959 originally proposed the idea for the Tricontinental Conference, argues that the exploitation of black labor has characterized Cuban history. He states that the republic's egalitarian banner of "con todos y para todos" (with all and for all) served as a legitimizing rhetoric for the continuation of white domination postindependence.[113] He warns that this ideology is being perpetuated within the Castro government's rhetoric and urges a revision of what he calls "the ideological power of the bourgeoisie."[114] Guillén Landrián and Carbonell had previously collaborated on the statement on race in Cuba that was prohibited from being presented at the 1968 World Cultural Congress. When we view *Coffea arábiga* within the context of Carbonell's argument, the celebratory phrase "in Cuba, all blacks and all whites and everyone drinks coffee" obtains yet another layer of skepticism toward this simplistic image of racial harmony.

In addition to echoing Carbonell, the film's discussion of the continuation of prerevolutionary labor relations within coffee production engages, and provides an alternative to, the well-known sugar-based critique most closely associated with Fernando Ortiz's *Cuban Counterpoint: Tobacco and Sugar* (1940). Ortiz, whose anthropological writings would undergird negrismo's mythic construction of Afro-Cuban culture as a talisman against U.S. military and economic interventionism, famously argued in *Cuban Counterpoint* that the sugar industry in Cuba, mostly owned by North American companies at the time of Ortiz's writing, had produced the economic conditions for the continuation of U.S. imperialist domination on the island. While Ortiz's argument clearly resonates within the Tricontinental's view of plantation slavery as foundational to imperialism, Ortiz's critique of the sugar industry has been inextricably tied up in negrismo's colonialist tropes.

A clear example of this link is found in Antonio Benítez-Rojo's influential *The Repeating Island: The Caribbean and the Postmodern Perspective* (1989). Benítez-Rojo rewrites Ortiz's pan-Caribbeanist argument for the similarities of plantation-based economies, using the "plantation machine" and the racial hierarchies it implies, to refer not only to the division of labor and resources within individual plantation economies but also to a socioeconomic structure that repeats itself continuously throughout Caribbean history, turning out "mercantile capitalism, industrial capitalism," and "imperialism."[115] He defines the plantation system, the quintessential "Caribbean machine," as being that "certain way" that the Antilles connect North and South America.[116] He associates this "certain way" of the Caribbean to an Afro-Caribbean, and specifically Afro-Cuban, body by relating how he was consoled during the 1962 Cuban Missile Crisis and realized that there would not be nuclear war when "two old black women passed 'in a certain kind of way' beneath my balcony. I cannot describe this 'certain kind of way'; I will say only that there was a kind of ancient and golden power between their gnarled legs . . . a symbolic, ritual wisdom in their gesture."[117] Later he adds that the "certain" thing that makes Martin Luther King Jr. a Caribbean person is not only "his African ancestry" but also "the ancient wisdom embodied in his pronouncements."[118]

In these moments of the text, especially through his metaphor of the "old black women" whose way of walking reminds the writer of the permanence and continuity of the Caribbean world, Benítez-Rojo represents that "certain way" of being Caribbean through the very essentialist tropes for which negrismo and writers like Ortiz have been criticized. For him, Caribbeanness, which is inextricably tied to blackness through the history of the plantation machine, also means being linked to that "symbolic, ritual wisdom" that ne-grista and other afrocriollo writers often attributed to black Caribbeans.

In contrast to a writer like Benítez-Rojo, Guillén Landrián takes up Ortiz's commentary on the plantation and its links to imperialism but does not blunt the sharp edges of his argument by slipping into racial essentialisms. In the spirit of Tricontinentalism, *Coffea arábiga* moves beyond the tropes of negrismo, using the folkloric dance footage at the beginning and the end of the film and the song from bufo theater not to further the Cuban Revolution's empty celebration of black culture but to critique the Revolution's half-hearted commitment to actual racial equality.

Additionally, the film points to the state's hypocrisy, in which it supports black struggles abroad while furthering inequalities at home, through employing the very aesthetic form of Álvarez's newsreels that was used by the Tricontinental to critique racial discrimination abroad. Guillén Landrián appropriates a Tricontinentalist ideology (in which a struggle against racial discrimination is integral to a struggle against a deterritorialized empire) and a Tricontinentalist aesthetic (Álvarez's newsreels) to argue that the Revolution does not measure up to its Tricontinentalist ideals. In this way, he exposes an inherent contradiction in the relationship between Cuba and the antiracist Tricontinental movement. Conversely, although the Cuban Revolution was largely responsible for the publication and dissemination of the Tricontinental's posters, films, and journal, through which it would externalize racism to the imperialist North, the film is also a testament to the way in which Tricontinentalism as a discourse transcends the Cuban state and could even be employed as a critique of it. This discourse would continue to circulate within radicalist circles inside and outside of Cuba, maintaining its influence even in contemporary notions of transnational subaltern resistance.

Guillén Landrián ended most of his films with the phrase "Fin pero no es el fin" (The end, but it is not the end), thus suggesting the work of art as an incomplete process intended to foster further debate and reflection. After many years of erasure, *Coffea arábiga* is still the powerful and provocative film that Guillén Landrián intended. It gives voice to a largely silenced Afro-Cuban counterdiscourse formulated during the first decade of the Revolution and during the early years of Cuba's Soviet period and reveals an Afro-Cuban response to the discourse of Tricontinentalism. In this way, it remains an enduring and bold critical statement on the Castro government's complex racial politics at the height of the influence of Tricontinentalism around the globe.

FIVE

The (New) Global South in the Age of Global Capitalism

A Return to the Tricontinental

Previous chapters discussed the roots of Tricontinentalism in interwar black Atlantic anti-imperialisms, outlined how Tricontinentalism attempted to revise these prior anti-imperialisms into a global vision of resistance, tracked the circulation of this discourse in a diverse set of Cold War radical texts, and examined its complex relationship to Cuba's domestic gender and racial politics. In this chapter, I trace the reemergence of key aesthetic and ideological elements of Tricontinentalism within contemporary social movements. This tracing reveals how an understanding of Tricontinentalism leads to a more informed and critical engagement with our contemporary political landscape. Using digital media from the World Social Forum, such as its "Bamako Appeal," which explicitly calls for a revival of the Tricontinental, the Occupy Wall Street (OWS) movement, and the Black Lives Matter (BLM) movement, I argue that, aesthetically, recent social movements draw from Tricontinentalist cultural production in the proliferation of "political remix videos," in the creation of political posters that are at times direct copies of Tricontinental screenprints, and in the use of "culture jamming" to subvert media culture. These aesthetic returns, I suggest, are surface indicators of a much deeper ideological return to Tricontinentalism in which contemporary theoretical categories like the Global South that have emerged to describe the transnational imaginary of alter-globalization movements are reviving core components of Triconti-nentalism's ideology and global concept of power and resistance.

This contemporary revival of Tricontinentalism is, however, only par-tial. Whereas Tricontinentalism framed its global, anticapitalist movement through a spotlight on racial justice, currently there is a divergence between alter-globalization and racial justice organizing in the American hemisphere. That is, contemporary alter-globalization discourses suffer from a color-blind multiculturalism, and racial justice discourses tend to reflect a narrow focus on reforming the state. Thus, after reflecting on the resurgence of key aspects of Tricontinentalism in political aesthetics and theory, this chapter addresses how the praxis of contemporary social movements in the American hemisphere draws on the global vision of power and resistance found in Tricontinentalism but generally elides the metonymic color politics that allowed this discourse to center a struggle against racial inequity within its global anti-imperialist cri-tique. I conclude this chapter by considering how one strain of thought within the larger Movement for Black Lives—which promotes an internationalist vi-sion of "transformational solidarity" that has striking similarities to the Tri-continental's trans-affective framing of solidarity—may represent a step toward envisioning anew a global movement against racial capitalism.

In order to address how an analysis of Tricontinentalism's partial revival helps to illuminate this disjuncture between anticapitalist and racial justice organizing, I begin perhaps in an unlikely place: with a campaign poster for Barack Obama. In January 2008, in the run-up to the U.S. presidential elec-tions, the street artist and political activist Shepard Fairey created the iconic portrait that would become known as the Barack Obama "Hope" poster. Fairey printed the stenciled portrait onto posters to be distributed at politi-cal rallies and posted the image on his website.[1] This poster, which has been called "the most efficacious American political illustration since 'Uncle Sam Wants You'" and which now hangs in the Smithsonian's National Portrait Gallery, has since been copied and parodied countless times.[2] Its influences have been attributed to Andy Warhol's screenprints, the Irish artist Jim Fitz-patrick's well-known 1968 image of Che Guevara, and posters produced by the Works Progress Administration. *Interview* magazine described it as a "vaguely Russian-propagandistic-looking portrait."[3] However, although it has gone unmentioned thus far, the influence of the Tricontinental's propaganda posters that privileged the African American struggle as the vanguard of a new collective political subject and as the hope for a new global future would be hard to miss.

In fact, several of Fairey's other screenprints are almost direct copies of Tricontinental posters. A 1999 image made for his Obey Giant graphic design company appropriates a 1968 Tricontinental poster created in solidarity with Korea by the Cuban artist Gladys Acosta Ávila, changing only the background and adding the Obey logo.[4] Other Fairey images, like his 2003 poster of Angela Davis called "Angela Rough" and his "Cuban Rider" image, reproduce works done by Organization of Solidarity with the Peoples of Africa, Asia, and Latin America (OSPAAAL) artists for other Cuban organizations.[5] The Obama "Hope" poster is closely reminiscent of several 1970s Tricontinental posters that were dedicated to heroes of African liberation movements like Patrice Lumumba and Amílcar Cabral in which the subject, who is stylized in the OSPAAAL's signature simple design and bright spot colors, similarly gazes upward and to the left of the frame.[6]

While this Tricontinental influence has gone largely unnoticed, Fairey's "Hope" poster, which came to represent Obama's 2008 presidential campaign, was powerful precisely because it capitalized on a collective, subconscious memory of Cold War Tricontinentalism. The poster's reliance on the iconography of "Third World" liberation movements was reinforced by the Obama campaign slogan "Yes We Can," commonly associated with the United Farm Workers' slogan in the 1970s, "Sí se puede" (Yes, it can be done), but less commonly so with the Cuban Revolution's literacy campaign, "Yo, sí puedo" (Yes, I can). Fairey's image and the campaign slogan captured the optimism of an international Left that the election of an African American president with a background in social advocacy would represent a sea change from the neoconservatism of the George W. Bush administration.

Yet while the image played on traditions associated with social justice and populism to represent Obama's global appeal, it also inflamed the fears of the far Right in the United States, which attempted to portray him as a radical.[7] In this sense, the poster drew on a subconscious collective memory, from both the Left and the Right, of the Tricontinental's anti-imperialist message. Obama's African American identity, his birth in Hawaii, and his father's Kenyan background suggested a possible destabilization—for both sides—of the traditional relationship between the United States government and those whom the Tricontinental called the "exploited peoples of the world."

Considering the poster's message and aesthetic within a Tricontinental legacy could be read as an indication of the increasing irrelevance of this history within our contemporary context. In this view, the poster would bear witness to the end of history, the supposed triumph and inevitability of neoliberalism that was ushered in with the collapse of Soviet communism.[8] It would announce, in this way, the dissolution of Cold War transnational anti-imperialisms into the mere "hope" of a kinder, gentler, and fundamentally inevitable neoliberal empire. In this reading, one would argue that the Tricontinentalist aesthetics seen in the "Hope" poster have become delinked entirely from their radical antiracist and anticapitalist content and are now merely a tool of neoliberal multiculturalism, a term that Jodi Melamed describes as "a market ideology turned social philosophy" that posits an equivalence between neoliberal market structuring and postracial opportunity around the globe.[9] However, I would suggest a more nuanced reading in which the "Hope" poster captures a tension between the resurgence of Cold War Tricontinentalist radicalism and the predominance of neoliberal multiculturalism in our contemporary context. The tension captured in the poster is symptomatic, I would argue, of a larger trend at the heart of progressive social movements in the American region today.

In recent years, we have seen the rise of a new era of social activism, and particularly of solidarity politics, which are facilitated by innovations in information and communication technologies that allow grassroots movements to connect with sympathizers around the globe. The American continent has experienced a remarkable outpouring of protests against both economic inequities and state brutality toward racially oppressed peoples. This chapter proposes that these contemporary solidarity politics in the Americas exhibit a revival of Tricontinentalism in both aesthetics and ideology. At the same time that recent movements directed against multinational financial institutions and corporations—such as OWS or the World Social Forum—revive elements of Tricontinentalism, these movements, in contrast to the Tricontinental, tend toward color-blind discourses of solidarity that silence issues of racial inequality and that reflect the logic of neoliberal multiculturalism.

Here I am referring to the progressive organizing of the so-called alter-globalization movement, which values transnational cooperation and exchange but which is seeking radically more equitable forms of globalization than that offered by neoliberal capitalism. This form of organizing is distinct from the populist, antineoliberal stance of the far Right (and some on the far Left) that responds to capitalist globalization's decentralized power structure and multiculturalist discourse through ethnonationalism, immigrant scapegoating, and xenophobia. While it would be easy to praise the inclusiveness of the alter-globalization movement while critiquing the racial logics of the far Right's antineoliberal populism, the reality is more complicated. Alter-globalization movements do not necessarily engage in the overt racism of ethnonationalist critiques of neoliberalism, but these movements are generally still largely silent on racial inequities. As I will discuss, the alter-globalization movement has frequently suffered from its reproduction of, and complicity with, a color-blind neoliberal multiculturalism.

While alter-globalization movements often exhibit a troubling color-blindness, the struggle against violence toward racially oppressed populations—which has been gaining visibility on the world stage in the United States and Latin America—tends to be framed through critiques of the state security apparatus and often does not necessarily address how global capitalism perpetuates racial violence. In other words, within a contemporary revival of Tricontinentalism in social movements, the Tricontinental legacy has been stripped of its most valuable contribution, its metonymic color politics, which allowed for an inclusionary and nonracially deterministic resistant subjectivity while still keeping the image of global capitalism as a racializing apparatus in the spotlight. But in order to illuminate this contemporary, albeit partial revival of Tricontinentalism, it is first necessary to address the processes of erasure that have resulted in sparse scholarship and a lack of general knowledge of this influential movement.

THE TRICONTINENTAL'S ERASURE

Although its materials continue to be produced and disseminated to this day and although—as the "Hope" poster indicates—there may be a subconscious memory of the movement, the Tricontinental has been largely elided in contemporary scholarship.[10] This is due to a combination of several factors that began with events in the early 1970s. First, as discussed in previous chapters, as the Cuban Revolution became more closely allied with the Soviet Union, it began to alienate many of its international supporters; this had a negative impact on the distribution of Tricontinental materials. Beyond the Cuban Revolution's contradictory racial discourse, which is addressed at length in chapter 4, several events caused a tempering in the 1970s of the unequivocal support that the Cuban Revolution had received from many leftists. These events include Cuba's endorsement of the 1968 Soviet invasion of Czechoslovakia, which was intended to repress the Prague Spring and in which Cuba displayed a profound blind spot in regards to Soviet imperialism; the 1968 Padilla Affair in which the poet Heberto Padilla was imprisoned, sparking an outcry among leftist intellectuals around the globe; and the subsequent 1971

Cuban Educational and Cultural Congress, which outlined the Revolution's intolerance toward homosexuality, religious groups, and Western fashions.

Tellingly, *Tricontinental* was distributed in Havana as well as in Paris by Maspero Editions and in Milan by the Feltrinelli Bookshop up until the July–August 1971 issue, which included thirty-three pages of resolutions by the Cuban Educational and Cultural Congress and in which "homosexual deviations were defined as social pathology."[11] With this issue, which laid out the controversial policies that would characterize the Revolution's *quinquenio gris* (five gray years), the Paris and Milan distributors pulled out, cutting off the primary pipeline to *Tricontinental*'s European readership. Within a few years, *Tricontinental* would list other distributors in Canada, Lebanon, and Panama, and, as I have argued in other chapters, it would continue to have influence abroad. However, growing disillusionment with the Cuban Revolution arguably had a negative impact on the distribution of its materials in Europe and in other metropolitan centers.

Second, at the same time that disillusionment was increasing among the Cuban Revolution's international network, the radical Left was significantly weakened on the American continent in the 1970s and 1980s. The 1973 Chilean coup against the democratically elected socialist president Salvador Allende, who was in attendance at the Tricontinental Conference and who was a major figurehead in the OSPAAAL, announced a wave of right-wing dictatorships that would install a reign of terror against leftist activists in Latin America for the next two decades. The 1973 coup marks the beginning of the economic experiment in neoliberal policies of financial and market liberalization and privatization, which Milton Friedman termed the "Miracle of Chile," that would later characterize the economic policies of Ronald Reagan and Margaret Thatcher during the 1980s.[12] Due to the Latin American debt crisis of the early 1980s, these free-market policies begun in Chile would be extended to virtually all Latin American countries that, in return for debt restructuring, would accept the package of neoliberal reforms (austerity, privatization, trade and finance liberalization) that would become known as the Washington Consensus.[13]

During the 1970s and 1980s, the OSPAAAL maintained close ties with Latin American leftist guerrilla groups like the *montoneros* in Argentina and the Revolutionary Armed Forces of Colombia. Its materials focused much of its reporting on resistant organizing in the Southern Cone dictatorships, the activities of the Sandinista National Liberation Front in Nicaragua, and on the 1983 U.S.-led invasion of Grenada. At the same time, the sheer strength of the right wing in the Latin American region in the decades immediately following the founding of the OSPAAAL has likely contributed to the silence around this movement.

Moreover, as neoliberalism expanded its influence throughout the American continent in the 1980s, it would appropriate the antiracisms of Cold War social movements, forging an "ethic of multiculturalism" that frames capitalist development and free markets in the language of a multicultural right that is purportedly color-blind in its spreading of economic equality.[14] While Tricontinental materials would use the South African case throughout the 1980s to insist on the complicity of neoliberalism with racial inequities, the discourse of multiculturalism, in which "diversity has been cast as the essence of neoliberal exchange," would have a powerfully disarming effect on the perceived relevance of antiracist, Cold War ideologies.[15]

One domain, however, in which Cold War decolonization discourses would be thoroughly preserved is within the academy, specifically in the field of postcolonial studies. This brings me to the third and arguably most important reason for the general erasure of the Tricontinental's legacy from much of the scholarly and public memory alike. According to Robert J. C. Young, the international student protests that erupted in May 1968 began an exchange between poststructuralist theory and the intellectual work of the "Third-World radical left," which would eventually become postcolonial studies.[16] Postcolonialism was not formally articulated as a critical category of literary analysis until the 1980s, such as in *The Empire Writes Back: Theory and Practice in Post-colonial Literatures* (1989), in which postcolonial literatures are broadly defined as "all the culture affected by the imperial process from the moment of colonization to the present-day."[17] Despite this panoramic approach, in practice, the study of postcolonial literature has tended to focus on the former African and Asian colonies represented at Bandung, dismissing the Latin American region and the contribution of the Tricontinental almost entirely.[18]

Some Latin Americanist scholars, in turn, have been resistant to identify with postcolonial studies, seeing it as a sweeping categorization articulated from the North American and Western European academies and as a misappropriation of concepts long rooted in Latin Americanist traditions.[19] John Beverley, perhaps the most recognizable champion of postcolonial studies in Latin Americanist criticism, characterizes this resistance to postcolonial studies among some Latin Americanist scholars as a *neo-arielista* position, meaning that—similar to the position of the Latin American intellectual presented in José Enrique Rodó's *Ariel* (1900)—its anti-imperialist rejection of the Western academy is founded in an elitist self-distancing from Latin America's marginalized populations.[20] In contrast, scholars of literature of the Southern United States, in their innovative uses of postcolonial theory, often have had to defend its use by arguing for parallels between the histories of the U.S. South and other postcolonial contexts.[21]

Perhaps more important than this tendency to elide the Americas, however, is the way in which postcoloniality as a concept has emphasized the circumstantial, in which a conceptual premium is placed on nonwhiteness and homologized with a narrowly defined experience of former colonization, rather than the ideological basis for the Tricontinental's global revolutionary subjectivity.[22] This is precisely what Bill Ashcroft—one of the coauthors of *The Empire Writes Back*—argued when he claimed that postcolonial discourse is the discourse of the colonized and is not necessarily anticolonial in sentiment.[23] In contrast, the Tricontinental organized its global solidarity around ideological, anti-imperialist affinities. While it recognized similarities between experiences of oppression, the basis of its solidarity was not dependent on those similarities nor was it dependent on trait-based characteristics, such as race, geographical location, or the social class of a person's family background. In other words, even though Tricontinentalism has been recognized by Robert J. C. Young as a foundational moment for postcolonial studies, not only has the history of this movement been almost completely absent from the canon of postcolonial studies, Tricontinentalism and postcolonial theory are actually quite distinct in their perspectives.[24] However, over time, focus has shifted from the experience of colonization to a shared experience of the negative effects of globalization, and in these theorizations—such as in critical categories like the Global South—we are seeing a return to the nuanced geography and conceptualization of resistance found in Tricontinentalism.

THE TRICONTINENTAL'S REVIVAL

Disillusionment with the Cuban Revolution, the severe weakening of the Left in the Americas, and the canonical limitations of postcolonial studies have all led to a dearth of scholarship and lack of awareness (outside Latin American leftist circles) of the Tricontinental movement. Studies of Third World leftism often fail to even mention the OSPAAAL or the Tricontinental Conference.[25] Other similar studies use the term Tricontinental in exchange with the term "Third World" and, at times, draw an equivalence between Tricontinentalism and "Third Worldism."[26] Yet "Third Worldism" has generally been understood in the way that Michael Hardt and Antonio Negri define it here: "the notion that the primary contradictions and antagonism of the international capitalist system is between the capital of the First World and the labor of the Third. The potential for revolution thus resides squarely and exclusively in the Third World ... the Third Worldist perspective is blind to the real convergence of struggles across the world in the dominant and subordinate countries alike."[27] This conceptualization of Third Worldism clearly fails to capture Tricontinentalism's highly fluid geography and privileging of struggles located precisely within the First World. As I will suggest in the coming pages, the contemporary networked political imaginary, or what Hardt and Negri describe as the "convergence of struggles across the world," has much more in common with Tricontinentalism than has heretofore been recognized.

Despite a general erasure of the Tricontinental legacy, in recent years the Americas witnessed a return of the Left (now in decline) and with that return came a revival of Tricontinentalism. Although the alter-globalization protests that would manifest throughout the continent in the 2011 Occupy movement had precedents in Spain's Indignados and in the Arab Spring, as well as in prior social movements in the United States like the 1999 Seattle World Trade Organization protests, the Occupy protests also had profound roots in Latin America, such as the 1994 Zapatista uprising against NAFTA, the rise of *chavismo* in Venezuela in the late 1990s, the 2000 Cochabamba Water War in Bolivia, the World Social Forums held in Porto Alegre, Brazil, and the 2001 economic crisis and riots in Argentina.[28] The 2001 protests in Argentina, for example—where the term *horizontalidad* (horizontalism) was first used to refer to the prefigurative politics of antineoliberal protests in which equitable social relationships within the movement strive to "prefigure" a potential future society—largely anticipated the discourse of the later OWS movement.

At the turn of the twenty-first century, Latin America experienced a wave of leftism that became known as the *marea rosada* (pink tide), which refers to the elections of leftist governments in Latin America over the last two decades through the presidencies of Hugo Chávez in Venezuela, Evo Morales in Bolivia, Rafael Correa in Ecuador, Fernando Lugo in Paraguay, and Luiz Inácio Lula da Silva in Brazil.[29] These "pink"—meaning moderate communist and socialist—presidents distanced themselves from the Washington Consensus, concentrating rather on regional economic cooperation.[30] With the marea rosada came a resurgence of alliance politics among leftist governments in Latin America, such as the highly publicized friendship between the Cuban and Venezuelan governments and the Bolivarian Alliance for the Peoples of Our

America, and, in general, it signaled the increasing relevance of antineoliberalism for the continent at large. The pink tide resulted in a series of constitutional reforms intended to improve the rights of minority groups. These reforms primarily addressed indigenous collective rights and were largely silent on issues facing people of African descent. However, black social movements in Latin America have been able to use the recognition of the ethnic and racial diversity of national populations that is contained within these new constitutions to gain visibility and greater participation in state structures.[31]

Since roughly 2012, the so-called pink tide has been in crisis, and politics in Latin America has more recently followed the global swing to the right in electoral politics that is responding to the slow economic recovery since 2008. Beyond these larger trends, however, the crisis of the pink tide is also due to its own internal contradictions in which its social welfare programs have depended on extractivist economic-growth models that exacerbate social inequities and that radically fluctuate with the commodities market.[32] Protests in Latin America of late—such as in Brazil, Nicaragua, and Venezuela—have directed their critiques at these governments' corruption, investor-friendly policies, authoritarianism, and general failure to deliver on the demands of the very movements that put them in power.[33] In this sense, although the region's pink-tide governments are in decline, the grassroots social movements that have called for increased social equity and that have rejected privatization of state services, trade liberalization, and other key components of the neoliberal economy are still expanding.[34]

Although the rise of progressive social movements generally began about a decade earlier in Latin America, the series of bank failures that collapsed the U.S. financial system in 2008 and created the Great Recession would provoke a global financial crisis and subsequent popular backlash against neoliberal economics that, inspired by the demonstrations of the 2010 Arab Spring, manifested in protests around the world. From anti-austerity demonstrations in Spain and Greece, to student protests against inequality and profiteering in education in the United Kingdom, Chile, and the United States, to Brazilian unrest over lack of social services in the Bus and FIFA World Cup riots, to the U.S. ows movement and similar Occupy protests around the globe, the financial crisis led to mass mobilizations around world facilitated through digital social media. Through communications technologies, activists in these movements create solidarity networks with peoples of diverse nationalities, ethnicities, and languages, and with widely varying experiences of gains and losses within the neoliberal economy. Similarly, the slogans that have defined the ongoing U.S. protests against racialized police brutality, such as "black lives matter," "hands up, don't shoot," and "I can't breathe," have been used by protestors in cities like São Paolo, London, and Berlin to draw attention to police brutality toward populations of color.[35] In these new social movements, especially those in the American region, we have seen a return to Tricontinentalism both aesthetically and ideologically. By referring to a return to Tricontinentalism, I do not mean to imply that the OSPAAAL is once again becoming the central voice of the radical Left. Rather, I argue that contemporary social movements in the Americas are profoundly indebted to, and shaped by, a largely unacknowledged Tricontinentalist past.

Although the OSPAAAL continues to produce materials and maintains an active political role in fostering contact and mutual support with Cuba's allies abroad, the Tricontinental has primarily become a symbolic organization, a monument to the height of the Cuban Revolution's influence in the world. After paper shortages halted the production of Tricontinental materials during Cuba's so-called Special Period—the extended period of economic crisis in the 1990s that resulted from the impact on Cuba's economy of the dissolution of the Soviet Union—the OSPAAAL did resume production of its magazine and bulletin in 1995 and its posters in 2000. Due to continued financial pressure suffered by Cuba's institutions, the journal is currently published electronically, and printed copies are arranged by individual delegations when an issue contains articles particularly relevant to the home country.[36] Since 1995, its materials have moved away from the bold, colorful, screenprinted designs of the past, and the artwork is now produced through digital software. The themes of its posters have also changed to focus on critiques of neoliberal, multinational entities like the International Monetary Fund and the Free Trade Area of the Americas. Despite the financial difficulties of production and distribution, the OSPAAAL's materials continue to circulate in Latin America and the United States.[37]

The OSPAAAL frames its current project as an effort to "globalizar la solidaridad" (globalize solidarity) and often refers to its constituency as representing the "Sur" (South).[38] In recent years, it has supported alter-globalization movements such as the 1999 Seattle World Trade Organization protests and the World Social Forum. It currently champions South-South economic cooperation—economic integration that on its face is counter to exploitative economic relations—and it has expressed strong support for leftist civil governments in Latin America. While it continues to voice solidarity with the militant liberation struggle in Palestine, the OSPAAAL has become much less focused on militancy. It does not identify with militant, religious fundamentalist groups, and it condemned the September 11, 2001, attack on the United States.[39] However, its materials have made a concerted effort to frame U.S.-backed military aggressions and interventions, such as sending arms to Israel or the military invasion of Iraq, as acts of terror, intending thus to question apparently naturalized associations between terrorism and Islamic fundamentalism.[40]

With some exceptions (such as the unwavering support the OSPAAAL continues to express for the Maduro regime in Venezuela), the pages of the contemporary *Tricontinental* are generally in line with mainstream leftist media outlets, often including articles from publications like *La Jornada* and *Democracy Now* and reprinting articles by such well-known figures as Evo Morales and Edward Said. Overall the quality of the journalism and editorials included in its pages is as strong as it was in previous decades. Generally, although the OSPAAAL is critical of Cuban dissidents and often defends the positions of the Cuban government in its publications, it continues to strive to provide sites of transnational leftist exchange rather than simply to operate as a megaphone for the Cuban state.[41]

The OSPAAAL still supports and reports on leftist struggles in the United States. Especially under the directorship in 2001 and 2002 of Ulises Estrada Lescaille—the Afro-Cuban former ambassador to Jamaica and a former *guerrillero* in the Congo and Guinea-Bissau—some of the more recent issues of *Tricontinental* have maintained a focus on antiracist struggles in the United States. It has published, for example, several articles by the former Black Panther Mumia Abu-Jamal (who has been serving a life sentence in a Philadelphia prison since 1982) and has reported on the overrepresentation of African Americans in U.S. prisons.[42] Additionally, while *Tricontinental* generally endorsed the 2011 OWS movement, it also called attention to the underrepresentation of U.S. Latinos and African Americans within this movement.[43] Yet, despite the continued spotlight on race relations in the United States, much like in the past, *Tricontinental* has remained overwhelmingly silent on issues of discrimination and inequality faced by Afro-Cubans on the island.

The OSPAAAL continues to produce materials that are highly critical both of the United States government and, from 2008 to 2016, of President Barack Obama. The cover of a 2010 issue of *Tricontinental*, for example, designed by the Cuban artist Rafael Enríquez, critiques the 2009 awarding of the Nobel Peace Prize to Obama, surrounding a photograph of Obama with names of countries where the U.S. military is engaged and with words such as "bloqueo contra Cuba" (Cuban embargo) and "bases militares en Colombia" (military bases in Colombia) that condemn U.S. foreign policy and military interventionism. In this image, Obama holds in his hand not the Nobel Peace Prize medal but a gold coin with a dollar sign, thus undercutting the relationship of the prize to peacemaking and tying it instead to the militaristic expansion of U.S. economic interests around the world.

In most OSPAAAL materials, Obama represented merely a continuation of the same policies of the prior Bush administration. This position is captured succinctly in an image by the British cartoonist Leon Kuhn, included in a 2009 *Tricontinental* in which a skeleton in a suit with the nametag "imperialism" takes off a mask of George W. Bush and puts on a mask with the face of Barack Obama.[44] Similarly, a 2010 article called "Obama y el Oriente Medio" (Obama and the Middle East) argues that the U.S. president's policies are "more of the same: a continuation of the imperialist politics of the past, although applied with a black face."[45] A 2014 article on Obama's appearance at Nelson Mandela's funeral by the Cuban journalist Ángel Guerra Cabrera, which was originally published in the Mexican newspaper *La Jornada*, reiterates this point, stating, "although he is black, he suffers the same typical imperial arrogance of the privileged and messianic U.S. leadership. Who but the repressive bodies of that country gave a beating to the members of *Occupy Wall Street*?"[46]

In these articles, by pointing to the seeming irony of imperialist politics applied "with a black face," the authors appear to acknowledge the complication that Obama poses to the Tricontinentalist tradition of positioning African Americans as vanguards of the global movement and using the images of African Americans and later of black South Africans to metonymically signify the Tricontinental's transnational and transracial revolutionary subjectivity. While these newer *Tricontinental* materials do not necessarily employ the metonymic color politics of the past, in which a Jim Crow category of color is used as a political signifier of a Tricontinentalist ideology, they continue the tradition of delinking the essentialist relation found in earlier anti-imperialist movements between phenotype and ideological position, and they continue to express solidarity through ideological affiliations rather than racial or national ones.

With the December 2014 announcement of the stabilization of U.S.-Cuba relations, the tone of Tricontinental materials toward the U.S. government changed briefly. The OSPAAAL continued to call for the end of the embargo, the return of Guantanamo to Cuba, and the independence of Puerto Rico. It also critiqued, for example, U.S. military support of Israel. However, there was a notable softening in the rhetoric used toward the U.S. government in, for example, a July 24, 2015, article entitled "Bienvenido, Mr. Kerry" (Welcome, Mr. Kerry), published on the OSPAAAL's website in the lead-up to the visit of U.S. Secretary of State John Kerry to Cuba. This article praises the political trajectory of Kerry and gives him credit for stabilizing relations between the two countries.[47] However, regarding the March 2016 historic visit of President Obama to Cuba, *Tricontinental* republished Fidel Castro's essay "El hermano Obama" (Brother Obama), which expressed much more skepticism about the intentions of the U.S. government in Cuba.[48] Since the election of Donald Trump, Tricontinental materials have been highly critical of U.S. foreign policy toward Syria and North Korea.

Although the OSPAAAL remains a site of transnational convergence among radical movements and although it began producing materials again in 1995, the return to Tricontinentalism to which I point in this chapter actually has little connection to the continued existence and operations of the OSPAAAL itself. Just as the discourse of Tricontinentalism preceded the formation of the Tricontinental alliance, it has also superseded it. In fact, I argue that in recent social movements throughout the American continent, the aesthetics and ideology of Tricontinentalism are becoming increasingly visible.

THE TRICONTINENTAL'S AESTHETIC RETURNS

The return to Tricontinentalism aesthetically can be found in three primary aesthetic praxes of contemporary social movements: (1) posters that are reminiscent of OSPAAAL posters; (2) "political remix videos" and protest films similar to Tricontinentalist filmic production; and (3) practices of "culture jamming" and "subvertising." I do not suggest that all these aesthetic forms originated with the Tricontinental; rather, they have multiple roots that can be traced to diverse strains of modernism in the early twentieth century. At the same time that I do not mean to imply that all these cultural forms begin with the Tricontinental, I do contend that the Tricontinental played an important role in bringing all these aesthetic devices into contact with its particular anti-imperialist political ideology and in disseminating these cultural forms in materials printed in four languages. In other words, through its propaganda apparatus, the Tricontinental defined a set of radical, anticapitalist, and antiracist aesthetic practices for a broadly diverse group of social movements. These aesthetic practices are currently being revitalized in social movements in relatively obvious ways.

Beyond the work of Fairey—who, in addition to the "Hope" poster, also created the widely circulated "Trayvon Martin" portrait of the African American Florida teen who was fatally shot in February 2012 by a neighborhood watch volunteer, George Zimmerman—recent political-poster production by social activists and grassroots movements tends to reflect the influence of the OSPAAAL's famous posters. Here, I do not suggest—as I have with some of Fairey's work—that recent political posters, like those used in OWS, are actual copies of Tricontinental works but rather that they tend to employ a similar graphic language. Like OSPAAAL posters, much of contemporary political-poster production tends to avoid the sleek imagery of Western advertising, choosing instead flat, brilliant colors and bold, blocky designs. These posters similarly communicate complex concepts like inequality, globalization, and racism in simple visual terms, and the textual content of these posters is also similarly secondary to the image, creating political arguments through immediate visual impact.

There are countless instances of OSPAAAL influence in the political graphics used within recent student movements, Occupy protests, and racial justice organizing. However, one recent example is the composition of a portrait of Michael Brown, the black teenager who was fatally shot on August 9, 2014, in Ferguson, Missouri, by a white police officer, Darren Wilson. This red, yellow, and black poster by then seventeen-year-old Irish underground artist Michael McBride (fig. 5.1) was disseminated widely through the BLM Tumblr and is strikingly similar to two OSPAAAL posters: a 1976 red, brown, orange, and black portrait of Amílcar Cabral (fig. 5.2); and a 1980 red, yellow, and black image of Patrice Lumumba (fig. 5.3).[49] The latter two posters were made to commemorate the leaders' assassinations. Similar to the poster of Michael Brown, the subjects in these posters purse their lips in what could be read as a look of contempt, and their gaze, directed slightly away from the viewer, seems to point to a nearby enemy, a subtle reminder of the injustice of their deaths and of their assassins' continued impunity.

Beyond the resurgence of a Tricontinentalist graphic language in political-poster art, we have also seen the popularization of Tricontinentalist filmic aesthetics in the contemporary "political remix video" or the "political mash-up" that, similar to the newsreels of the Tricontinental filmmaker Santiago Álvarez, relies on the anti-authoritarian tradition of Soviet montage where meaning is constructed through the collision of disparate shots and through the ironic interplay of sound and image. In ways that harken to Álvarez's ironic appropriation of television footage, popular music, and visual material

FIG. 5.1 (Above left) Michael McBride, "Michael Brown: Victim of Police Brutality" (2014). COURTESY MICHAEL MCBRIDE.

FIG. 5.2 (Above right) Enrique Martínez Blanco, poster to commemorate third anniversary (January 20, 1976) of Cabral's assassination (1976). COURTESY LINCOLN CUSHING / DOCS POPULI.

FIG. 5.3 (left) Rafael Enríquez Vega, poster to commemorate twentieth anniversary of Lumumba's assassination (1980). COURTESY LINCOLN CUSHING / DOCS POPULI.

from newspapers and magazines, contemporary activist filmmakers, often in defiance of copyright laws, cut and remix preexisting audiovisual material like news and advertising footage to create satirical and political counternarratives.[50] Like Álvarez's newsreels, they draw from the tradition of détournement that subverts capitalist mass media to create meaning that is counter to the original.

Currently, there are hundreds of thousands of political remix videos on YouTube in many languages. These films represent a contemporary form of political activism in which mostly amateur but some professional filmmakers splice together music, political speeches, and clips of news anchors and TV advertisements into montages that make coherent political critiques of (most often) corporate power and economic inequality. An hour-long compilation of "political re-mix shorts" made on the Occupy movement, entitled *Occupation Nation* and created by the B Media Collective—a radical film community in Portland, Oregon, that makes films for social justice organizations and that offers workshops to the public on remixing videos—is a quintessential example.[51] The film makes its critique of the abuses of the global financial system through ironic juxtapositions of clips from Fox News and speeches by George W. Bush with scenes from *The Wizard of Oz, Pee-wee's Playhouse*, and *Monty Python*; archival footage from the 1929 stock market crash; and protest footage from OWS.

The popularization of the political remix video and its debt to Álvarez is part of a general revival of the aesthetics of 1960s radical filmmaking in contemporary political documentary film on the American continent. In Latin America, concurrent with the rise of the new Left came a revisiting of the anticapitalist aesthetics and ideals of mass amateurization that characterized the 1960s New Latin American Cinema, a movement in which Álvarez's films and films of the Cuban Revolution played a major part.[52] New Latin American Cinema—which broadly refers to the socially engaged filmmaking that emerged in Latin America in the 1960s—sought to create a cinema of liberation in which social and political films were made in an anti-Hollywood, militant style that, through the technical imperfections of low-budget filmmaking, emphasized the revolutionary process and aimed to provoke viewers to collective action.[53]

The work of the Argentine director Fernando Solanas, who originally published along with Octavio Getino the seminal film manifesto "Towards a Third Cinema" in a 1969 issue of *Tricontinental*, is perhaps the most obvious example of this trend.[54] In "Towards a Third Cinema," Getino and Solanas offer their documentary *La hora de los hornos* (The Hour of the Furnaces)

(1968)—which condemns the role of Argentina's internal elite in the ongoing foreign exploitation of the country's raw materials—as a model for a new activist filmmaking not only for Latin America but for the entire Tricontinental alliance. Recently, in 2004, Solanas finally created a sequel to this film, *Memoria del saqueo* (Social Genocide), which similarly edits found images and footage into a hard-hitting, militant montage that brings his initial argument up to date. *Memoria del saqueo* outlines how the leadership of the right-wing elite in Argentina's military dictatorship of the 1970s paved the way for the aggressive privatization and deregulation that would characterize the 1980s and 1990s, leading to the financial collapse and popular revolt in Argentina in 2001.

While Solanas's recent work is perhaps the most obvious example of this revival of New Latin American Cinema, other antineoliberal struggles in Latin America, such as the campaign in Costa Rica against the Central American Free Trade Agreement has given rise to similar films, like the protest documentary *Costa Rica s.a.* by Pablo Ortega (2006). Through the use of ironic juxtapositions, the incorporation of footage and images from a variety of sources, and especially through the ironic and humorous "nervous" montages often associated with Santiago Álvarez's films, *Costa Rica s.a.* delivers a poignant critique of those in favor of the free trade agreement.

Beyond these filmic returns, there are other aesthetic resonances of Tricontinentalism in contemporary social movements, such as in the use of so-called culture jamming or subvertising, which intends to expose and subvert hegemonic discourses within contemporary media culture and especially within corporate advertising. Although used frequently in Álvarez's films, Tricontinental materials often employed this technique in other forms, such as including fake advertisements within the pages of *Tricontinental* and *Tricontinental Bulletin* that reproduce the original advertisement but replace the text with inverted, anticapitalist messages. The final page of the November–December 1967 issue of *Tricontinental*, for example, is, at first glance, an advertisement for a 1967 Ford Mustang.[55] However, surrounding the photograph of the red Mustang are the names of the raw materials used to make the car (aluminum, copper, petroleum, and derivatives) as well as the African, Asian, and Latin American countries from which those raw materials are extracted. In essence, the advertisement suggests the Ford Motor Company as a vehicle of imperialist exploitation against the Tricontinental's delegations.

Similarly, the last page of a September–October 1968 issue of *Tricontinental* is presented as an advertisement for Bank of America. A white man in a suit with a briefcase walks down a sidewalk in La Paz, Bolivia; a bright red circle surrounds his feet. The advertisement states that he is the "man-on-the-spot" that Bank of America can put to work in any city in the world.[56] He is "a commodities expert, a foreign exchange specialist, an economist . . . in short, an imperialist agent, a good man to know to give him the punishment he deserves."[57] In other words, the message that accompanies the graphic inverts the rhetoric of capitalistic readiness and entrepreneurship, turning the red circle that surrounds the feet of the "man-on-the-spot" into a target for anticapitalist revenge.

While the term "culture jamming" was originally coined through the punk movement's disruption of corporate radio frequencies in the 1980s, it has become a major source of aesthetic expression for more recent social movements.[58] The beginning of ows, for example, is largely attributed to the Vancouver-based Adbusters Media Foundation that is best known for its not-for-profit, reader-supported magazine *Adbusters*. This magazine, which aims to "advance the new social activist movement of the information age," is particularly famous for employing culture jamming to appropriate advertisements in order to subvert and critique capitalist discourse much in the same way that *Tricontinental* did in its publications.[59] *Adbusters*, inspired by the 2011 protests in Egypt and Spain, created the original call for the September 17, 2011, occupation of Lower Manhattan and started the #OccupyWallStreet hashtag. This magazine's aesthetic praxis of appropriating brands and corporate symbols to formulate anticonsumerist and anticapitalist critiques has been theorized as helping to develop "internal social movement cohesion" based on a "deep critical solidarity," or a solidarity organized around an anticonsumerist praxis.[60] The integral role of this culture-jamming magazine in forging the cohesion and solidarity engendered within the Occupy movement is, I would suggest, yet another way that alter-globalization movements are reviving the aesthetic devices that originally helped to forge the Tricontinental's transnational solidarity. Most important, however, as I will argue in the next section, these aesthetic returns of the 1960s transnational radicalism that the Tricontinental embodied represent surface indicators of a deeper, ideological revival of Tricontinentalism.

THE TRICONTINENTAL'S IDEOLOGICAL RETURNS

Since the dissolution of the Soviet Union, power and resistance have been theorized anew within the light of contemporary capitalist globalization. Despite the elision of Tricontinentalism in contemporary scholarship, these new theories have important points of convergence with the Tricontinental's Cold War discourse. Specifically, recent theories of power and resistance share with Tricontinentalism three major similarities: (1) they conceive of power as deterritorialized and transcendent of individual nation-states, such that those located in the geographic North also suffer the negative aspects of neoliberal globalization; (2) potential resistance to power is theorized as occurring through global, lateral networks that similarly transcend geographical, national, linguistic, or racial boundaries; and (3) because power is global, it is argued that there is no outside to it, and thus resistance must occur from within. Among these recent theories, I find the Global South to have striking resonances with Tricontinentalism in that it uses the South to refer to a global system of inequity that affects diverse peoples across a fluid geography, and it theorizes transnational resistance to a decentralized power structure through ideological rather than trait-based terms.

In 2000, Michael Hardt and Antonio Negri outlined a contemporary empire facilitated through global capital and founded on the U.S. model of networked, constituent power that expands continuously outward toward an unbounded terrain. Hardt and Negri's empire expands not through destroying and replacing the structures in place but rather through an inclusive incorporation of those powers into a global network.[61] In this deterritorialized empire, which—much like the Tricontinental's view of imperialism—is not bound by national borders or controlled by any single nation-state, "there is no more outside," meaning that although there are margins and centers, within empire everyone becomes part of the systemic inside.[62] This lack of boundaries, Hardt and Negri argue, creates more revolutionary potential because it yields an international "set of all the exploited and the subjugated, a multitude that is directly opposed to Empire."[63] This concept, radically similar to Guevara's Tricontinental notion of "we, the exploited people of the world," attempts to capture the way in which the global networks of contemporary capitalism create the conditions for an equally global emancipatory politics.

Hardt and Negri's empire is one of the more recognizable contributions to a growing body of theoretical work on the networked nature of power and resistance within globalization. Scholars like Jon Beasley-Murray, Manuel Castells, Alexander Galloway, David Grewal, and Eugene Thacker argue that the source of power within the networked society of globalization cannot be located in any one place or in any one nation. Power is decentralized, existing rather in the overlapping and transnational realms of multiple networked actors that include the global media, the financial sector, national governments and military, multinational corporations, special interest groups, and consumers.[64] Sovereignty is distributed and immanent, and social control is manifested through protocols that regulate the terms of society.[65] Subjects are not necessarily forged through interpellation by an institution or by state discourse but are individuated through their function as nodes in the network and adherence to the protocols that allow power to operate.[66]

The deterritorialized and immanent sovereignty of the networked society, some have argued, results in a permanent state of exception, or an omnicrisis, in which war and conflict are framed as internal police actions, and the line separating traditional military and police is increasingly vague.[67] Power in the networked society is thus, in a way similar to Tricontinentalism, epitomized in the image of a global police that ensures capital flows and network protocols and that represents the networked society's control over all aspects of social life. Any resistance to power as embodied in this global police must then be forged at "an equally global level."[68]

Resistance, or possible challenges to power within the networked society of global capitalism, is thus conceived in diverse ways; however, there is a general consensus that counterpower emerges from within the networked society itself. Some argue that resistance is formed through swarms within the network that can shift the protocols through which power operates (for example, when mass self-communication overtakes and subverts the agenda set by corporate media) or that can put new protocols in place that prevent the convergence of parts of the network (such as protests leading to the passage of laws against collusion between the finance and political elite).[69] Others have perhaps a more radical view of the potential of counterpower, conceiving of alternative resistant networks that form from within empire and that threaten to destabilize it completely from the inside.[70]

Hardt and Negri's "multitude" that is created precisely from within global capitalism is, in this sense, one category among several models of analysis that conceive of subaltern political collectivities not through a focus on the transnational experience and legacy of European colonization (as in postcolonial theory) but through a shared experience of the negative effects of capitalist globalization. Similar categories like subaltern cosmopolitanism, grassroots globalization, counterhegemonic globalization, alternative Southern cosmopolitanism, and the Global South have arisen over the last ten years as attempts to describe how capitalist globalization facilitates the creation of horizontalist networks among grassroots movements, yielding a new transnational political imaginary and global resistant subjectivity.[71]

Among these concepts, the Global South has gained the most currency, a term that Alfred J. López, the founding editor of *The Global South* journal, describes as the "mutual recognition among the world's subalterns of their shared conditions at the margins of the brave new neoliberal world of globalization."[72] Vijay Prashad defines the concept similarly but adds an implication of political action provoked by this shared consciousness: "this concatenation of protests against the theft of the commons. . . . The global South is this: a world of protest, a whirlwind of creative activity."[73] While these definitions focus on an experience of exploitation, and thus can imply a very broadly defined circumstantial condition, López's reference to a "mutual recognition among the world's subalterns" and Prashad's insistence on the role of political protest activity imply that the Global South represents a subjectivity forged through a mutual worldview and resistant ideology.

In this way, the Global South is closely parallel to the Tricontinentalist vision of a transnational revolutionary subjectivity forged through an ideological stance of anti-imperialism. Like Tricontinentalism, the Global South as a critical category aims to transcend regional and ethnic identities and a narrowly defined historical condition of postcoloniality, and it recognizes the negative effects of contemporary global capitalism on groups located in the so-called First World. While I do not suggest that there is an exact one-to-one relationship between Global South theory and Tricontinentalism, we might view the Global South and similar critical categories as attempts to move away from postcolonial theory (in which Tricontinentalism has been consistently elided) and from other models of comparatist analysis organized around postcolonial nation-states in order to describe a contemporary revival of key elements of the ideology of Tricontinentalism.

The Global South and other similar concepts attempt to name the networked nature of political organizing today in which technologies of mass self-communication allow grassroots activists to forge relationships with allies around the globe. Today's activists commonly appropriate digital spaces to form transnational solidarities, meaning that the global marketplace also becomes the site of resistant organizing. While the Tricontinental forged its union through its magazines and posters, this contemporary Global South imaginary is facilitated through digital social media venues like Facebook, Twitter, blogs, and YouTube. The apparent contradiction of this use of social media for movements directed specifically against corporatism, deregulation, and free trade is resolved through the insider position that this form of protest takes. In other words, through the use of social media to communicate with sympathizers around the world, these grassroots movements appropriate the tools of the very system they protest, using them to spread their political messages and to fight empire from within. The "hacktivist" and the "Twitter Revolutionary" appear to occupy that space that African Americans came to signify for the Tricontinental that is resisting empire from the inside.

The systemic inside of Global South resistance today is indeed distinct from the Tricontinentalist notion of the inside. African Americans' occupation of private and public spaces to challenge a system of apartheid—a struggle that Tricontinentalism viewed as a microcosm of a global one—is disparate from the contemporary use of physical and digital spaces to produce counterpower within global capitalism. However, it is Tricontinentalism's horizontalist solidarity among liberation struggles, destabilization of trait-based political identities, privileging of an anti-imperialist struggle that is internal to empire, and a global concept of power in which victims of empire include peoples located in the geographic North that make the Tricontinental fundamentally relevant to these emergent theories. As I will suggest in the coming pages, considering the new Global South within the legacy of the Tricontinental and its black internationalist foundations has important implications for our contemporary context.

THE GLOBAL SOUTH IN PRACTICE

The revival of the ideology of Tricontinentalism in the contemporary sphere is not simply a theoretical one. Rather, it is advanced on the ground in the contemporary alter-globalization movement of which perhaps the most obvious referents are the annual World Social Forums that have taken place since 2001. Begun in Porto Alegre, Brazil, as a counter to the World Economic Forum held annually in Davos, Switzerland, the World Social Forum (WSF) is an annual meeting of civil society organizations, social justice movements, artists, intellectuals, and members of the general public who are in opposition to contemporary global capitalism. While the WSF does not include armed groups, similar to the Tricontinental, it aims to build a new political, networked subjectivity, which it calls "planetary civil society," and inclusion into the forum is nominally based on a loose ideological affinity defined around resistance to neoliberal globalization. The WSF prefers to be defined not as a movement per se but as an open space that facilitates horizontal organizing among transnational antineoliberal entities.[74] Similar to the role of the Tricontinental in bringing diverse social and political movements together, the central role of the WSF is what Boaventura de Sousa Santos has called "the work of translation," in which movements are made intelligible to one another within the larger frame of alter-globalization.[75] While it has held five of the forums in India, Kenya, Senegal, and Tunisia, and the 2006 polycentric forum was held in three locations (Venezuela, Mali, and Pakistan), over half of the forums thus far have been held in Latin America and generally the WSF has been dominated by Latin American leftist organizations.[76]

Because of its insistence on horizontal networks rather than a centralized hierarchy, the WSF does not issue statements or manifestos except for its annual call to social movements to participate. This has not prevented intellectuals and organizations involved from writing their own statements, however, although often these have caused much controversy for the ways in which these documents are perceived as attempting to move the WSF away from open dialogue and toward a set political agenda. Among several manifestos associated with the WSF—such as the 2001 "Call of Porto Alegre for the Coming Mobilization" signed by mostly human rights, land reform, and labor organizations or the 2005 "Porto Alegre Manifesto" signed by nineteen prominent intellectuals in attendance—the most famous, the Bamako Appeal, is also the one that most clearly situates the ideologies of the WSF within a Cold War historical context of Tricontinentalism.[77]

The Bamako Appeal (BA), which offers a ten-point program toward the stated aim of contributing to "the emergence of a new popular and historical subject," was created on the eve of the 2006 WSF in Bamako, Mali, at the Conference of the Peoples of Bandung, held to commemorate the fiftieth anniversary of the Bandung Conference.[78] Largely led by the French-Egyptian Marxist economist Samir Amin and the Belgian Marxist sociologist and Catholic priest François Houtart (who founded the Belgian organization on North-South relations called Centre Tricontinental), the BA aims to take the "collective consciousness" that has arisen out of the WSF gatherings and articulate this into a plan of action for a more organized mobilization against global capitalism.[79] Its emergence reflects a concern among some participants that, because of its lack of a clear ideological position, the WSF was becoming compromised by the presence of nongovernmental associations allied with the United Nations, the World Bank, and other civil society organizations not necessarily opposed to neoliberalism. In this sense, the BA does not represent the WSF as a whole but rather is a sect within it, and it was criticized for the way in which it was produced by a small group of intellectuals, distributed and commented on at the 2006 Bandung Conference by a group of invitees, and then edited by the original group.[80]

However, despite these critiques, the BA was signed by twenty-one organizations, including members of the WSF's founding secretariat and international council, such as Brazil's Unified Workers' Central and its Landless Rural Workers' Movement, as well as sixty-six high-profile journalists and activists.[81] For this reason, Peter Waterman has asserted, "these endorsements . . . suggest that the BA already *has* an international appeal to left intellectuals, social movements, and NGOs and one that could be predicted to grow."[82] While the BA is just one part of the WSF and the WSF is just one, albeit major, part of the larger alter-globalization movement, I use the BA as a case example of the return to an ideology of Tricontinentalism within contemporary antineoliberal organizing on the American continent. Similar to the Tricontinental's attempt to connect struggles in Africa, Asia, and Latin America with those inside imperial centers, the BA calls for a "reconstruction of a peoples' front of the South that is capable of defeating the imperialism of the dominant economic powers and the military hegemony of the United States."[83] This Global South would not exclude peoples in the geographic North: "on the contrary, it is a foundation for the construction of a global internationalism that would involve everyone in the building of a common civilization in its diversity."[84]

As in Tricontinentalism, the "peoples' front of the South" that is envisioned by the BA is not merely based around an internationalist proletariat but rather refers to a global subaltern subjectivity that transcends class, nationality, race, and ethnicity.[85] For example, Samir Amin has characterized the BA as intending to "contribute to the construction of the internationalism of the peoples. Note that the phrase refers to all peoples, North and South, just as it refers not only to the proletariat but to all working classes and strata that are victims of the system, to humanity as a whole, threatened in its survival."[86] If this attempt to unify the geographic North and South through an internationalist resistant front of exploited peoples was not clear enough evidence of the BA's indebtedness to Tricontinentalism, the BA—although planned to commemorate the 1955 Bandung Conference—explicitly calls for a revival of the Tricontinental, stating "it is necessary to bring out the conditions for an alternative form of cooperation within each large region, like for example a revival of the Tricontinental, in close connection with the action of social movements."[87]

The leadership of Amin and Houtart as well as the BA's framing of the contemporary political landscape within a history of Cold War social movements has been criticized as the legacy of "the old left of the twentieth century, wrapped in the anti-globalization discourses of Seattle—as affirmations of diversity, horizontality, consensus, and the centrality of local struggles, but seeking to contain and manage these struggles according to their own blue-prints."[88] However, while the propaganda of the "old left" movement of the Tricontinental was centrally organized and its member organizations generally maintained hierarchical leadership structures, reflecting thus partially the verticality that is the subject of this critique, I have argued for the Tricontinental as a space of horizontalist relations among diverse struggles and as a platform for the representation of a variety of perspectives even within individual, local movements. In other words, I am suggesting that this largely forgotten Cold War movement has much in common with the ideals that we have come to associate with the WSF and with alter-globalization organizing in general. The suggestion that the "old" Cold War Left has nothing to offer the "anti-globalization discourses of Seattle" seems to be symptomatic of what I have identified as a general erasure of the Tricontinental's legacy within our contemporary context.[89]

However, at the same time that Tricontinental aesthetics and ideology are being revived, I would argue that one of its most significant contributions, its metonymic color politics—through which it theorized a global and nonracially deterministic resistant subjectivity through a focus on racial inequality—seem to have fallen by the wayside. In contrast, as I will explain, the contemporary global justice movement is largely complicit with neoliberalism's discourse of color-blind multiculturalism.

COLOR-BLINDNESS AND THE GLOBAL SOUTH

In contrast to the Tricontinental's global anticapitalist movement, alter-globalization movements in the Americas suffer from a rhetoric of color-blindness that undermines these movements at their core. As Jodi Melamed has convincingly argued, contemporary neoliberal globalization relies on an apparently innocuous color-blind multiculturalism to frame market ideologies of free trade, financial liberalization, and deregulation as multicultural rights. This color-blind multiculturalism implies an apparent shifting of signs regarding conventional racial categories where power in the networked society is seemingly based not necessarily on race per se but on one's value to global capital and one's access to the multicultural "rights" of the free market.[90] However, this "ethic of multiculturalism" veils "the reality that neoliberalism remains a form of racial capitalism."[91] At the same time that multiculturalism frames diversity as the spirit and benefit of neoliberal expansion, power in the capitalistic networked society continues to be upheld by the exploitation of labor from racialized bodies, by control and violence exercised over racialized populations, and by policies that ensure capital accumulation in a geographic and predominantly white North.[92] Thus, in response to the neoliberal discourse of color-blind multiculturalism, Melamed maintains, social movements have emerged at the turn of the twenty-first century to critique finance capitalism, IMF structural adjustment, and other neoliberal policies. These movements, she argues, represent a revival of the "race radicalisms" or "material antiracisms that prioritize the unevennesses of global capitalism as primary race matters" of the Cold War period.[93]

Building on but also diverging from Melamed's argument, I would argue that contemporary antineoliberal movements—in forging political networks across national, ethnic, and linguistic boundaries—have tended to emphasize the "unevenness of global capitalism" but have not necessarily emphasized that unevenness "as primary race matters."[94] Whereas a Cold War model like the Tricontinental theorized a global oppressive power structure and revolutionary subjectivity through a primary focus on racial injustice, contemporary alter-globalization organizing in the Americas tends to mirror neoliberalism's color-blind multiculturalism, producing silences around racial inequities.

Despite the international visibility of many indigenous rights groups and the impact of the 1994 Zapatista uprising, the overrepresentation of whites and overwhelming silence on racial inequality within the alter-globalization movement have been widely noted.[95] Fittingly, one of the primary critiques of the WSF has been its general silence around race. Janet Conway puts it this way: "there is a deafening silence about race vis-á-vis the anti-globalization movements as well as about the WSF as situated in national and global racial formations, about the WSF as itself a racial formation, and about the presence, marginality, or absence of movements of racialized peoples and their discourses of race and racism."[96] Similarly, in a survey of participants in the 2005 WSF, in which participants were asked to self-identify their race or ethnicity, the survey found that whites were vastly overrepresented at the forum and that many of the light-skinned participants responded to the survey by claiming that they were simply "human" or had no race or ethnicity and by rejecting the question itself as offensive and divisive.[97]

One could claim that this presence within the WSF of a color-blind discourse—which avoids discussing race and which seems unaware that many people of color are not afforded the privilege of choosing whether or not to identify with race and ethnicity—is due to the 2005 forum's location in Brazil and the influence of myths of racial democracy that predominate the region.[98] However, these problems have persisted in other forums, including even the 2007 WSF held in Kenya where African social activists and panel topics related to race were underrepresented.[99] Even the BA, which takes its cues from Tricontinentalism and which was written in the West African city of Bamako, only mentions exploitation and inequality based on race one time.

However, it is not just in the WSF where we see this problem. The politics of race in the alter-globalization movement within the United States, for example, look strikingly similar. Reportedly, only 5 percent of the U.S. participants in the 1999 World Trade Organization protests in Seattle were people of color, and this was also one of the primary critiques against the U.S. OWS movement.[100] Fordham University conducted a survey at Zuccotti Park a month after the Occupy protests began and found that, of the protestors, they were 68 percent white, 10 percent black, 10 percent Hispanic, 7 percent Asian, and 5 percent from other races.[101] As a *New York Times* writer, Alice Speri, pointed out, these numbers are radically different from the adult population of New York City, which is "36 percent white, 27 percent Hispanic, 22 percent black, 13 percent Asian and 2 percent other races."[102]

Considering the disproportionate number of African Americans and U.S. Latinos affected by unemployment and home foreclosure in the wake of the financial crisis and considering the simple fact that Wall Street itself was once the site of a slave market, the sparse representation of people of color within OWS and the limited attempts of the movement to address racialized capitalism deeply undermined the movement's message.[103] An affiliate movement called "Occupy the Hood" was even started with the sole aim of drawing people of color to Zuccotti Park.[104] Occupy the Hood did have moderate success, and the National Association for the Advancement of Colored People (NAACP) national headquarters also released a statement in support of OWS.[105] However, generally OWS has been viewed as a white middle-class movement such that the Reverend Jesse Jackson's comparison of it to the U.S. civil rights movement provoked a series of articles in news media that fiercely rejected this comparison.[106]

In the case of OWS, there have been various attempts to explain this racial disparity. Some claim, for example, that it was the movement's apparent lack of a clear message or goal that did not settle well with the targeted campaigns of recognized African American and Latinx organizations like the NAACP or the National Council of La Raza.[107] Others argue that it is a result of the digital methods of dissemination used by these movements and the way that digital spaces and digital social networks reflect the same segregations found in physical landscapes and communities.[108] While black Americans in the United States, for example, use Facebook and Twitter as much as white Americans do, the call to occupy Wall Street was initially spread through the magazine *Adbusters* and the computer-hacking collective Anonymous, venues that have traditionally reflected white involvement and white audiences.[109] Others suggest that this disparity simply reflects what Juliet Hooker calls "racialized solidarity" where political solidarities in the United States tend to be shaped by racial identification.[110] Still others maintain that it was the result of disparate experiences of interacting with the police and temerity on the part of African Americans and U.S. Latinos because of previous negative experiences, an interpretation that recent mass mobilizations of U.S. Latinos and African Americans in demonstrations against police brutality and in immigration and civil rights protests would certainly call into doubt.[111]

Of the many articles about the underrepresentation of people of color within ows, very few actually mention the discourse of the movement or the fact that a focus on racial inequities within global capitalism was hardly at the forefront of its message.[112] One article that does briefly address this issue, a *New York Times* article entitled "Occupy Wall Street Struggles to Make 'the 99%' Look Like Everybody," suggests that some protestors of color were "appalled" by what was initially going to be the first paragraph of the General Assembly's "Declaration of the Occupy of New York City."[113] The original declaration stated, "'As one people, formerly divided by the color of our skin,' . . . 'we acknowledge the reality: that there is only one race, the human race.'"[114] As a result of the objections of activists of color that this phrasing was insensitive to racial realities, the wording was changed to "as one people, united, we acknowledge the reality: that the future of the human race requires the cooperation of its members."[115]

This declaration, addressed "to the People of the World," relies—in a way similar to Tricontinentalism—on a collective subjectivity not defined by ethnicity, race, geography, or any trait-based elements.[116] However, it should be noted that the revision of the document does not necessarily resolve the problem raised by protestors of color; rather it erases race from the conversation entirely. Racial inequality is mentioned very briefly among a series of inequalities perpetuated by global capitalism. In essence, Occupy's conceptualization of the "99%" looks less like the Tricontinental's anticapitalist and transnational political subjectivity, which it forged through a metonymic color politics that foregrounded racial violence and inequity, and much more like a neoliberal discourse of color-blind multiculturalism in which discussion of race is repeatedly silenced.

Significantly, it was the influential intervention of Chicana and Triconti-nentalist activist Elizabeth "Betita" Martínez—who began her career work-ing on behalf of Robert F. Williams, attended the 1967 Organization of Latin American Solidarity meeting in Havana alongside Stokely Carmichael, and who occasionally wrote articles for *Tricontinental Bulletin* and *Tricontinental* in the 1970s—in her article "Where Was the Color in Seattle? Looking for Reasons Why the Great Battle Was So White" that sparked a series of work-shops in 2000 in the San Francisco Bay Area called "Anti-racism for Global Justice."[117] This led to the formation of the San Francisco–based Catalyst Project: Anti-racism for Collective Liberation, which specifically works to build political education on antiracism within mostly white sections of left-ist movements. Although this organization has been working over the last fifteen years to bridge alter-globalization and racial justice organizing, the alter-globalization movement continues to be dominated by white leadership and afflicted by a discourse of color-blindness that fails to fully incorporate those most affected by racial capitalism. In this sense, despite the many aes-thetic and ideological returns to Tricontinentalism in the alter-globalization movement, perhaps the Tricontinental's most significant contribution—a global anticapitalist movement organized around a struggle against antiblack racism—has failed to materialize.

RACIAL JUSTICE IN THE AMERICAS: STATE CO-OPTATION AND STATE VIOLENCE

If the movement against capitalist globalization in the American continent is largely silent on racial inequities, the contemporary racial justice movement on behalf of equality for Afro-descendant peoples in the Americas has tended to focus on either further inclusion into the state or on critiques of state vio-lence toward racialized populations, often sidelining a broader consideration of the intersection between racial violence and global capital flows. The neo-liberal multicultural turn of the late 1980s and 1990s ushered in significant changes throughout the continent in the treatment of some racialized popula-tions. For example, mostly in response to indigenous resistant organizing, the United Nations' International Labor Organization Accord 169 on Indigenous and Tribal Peoples in Independent Countries was adopted in 1989 and ratified by many Latin American countries. As a result, policy changes were initiated within the operations of multilateral banks, such as in the World Bank's Policy on Indigenous Peoples.[118] In Latin America, these policy shifts led to a wave of multicultural constitutional reforms intended to recognize indigenous cultural and economic rights, shifting from singular national identities based on assimilation discourses and toward a conceptualization of national populations as ethnically, culturally, and racially diverse.[119] While the extent of gains made has depended on individual national contexts, overall these reforms were specifically directed at indigenous groups, and peoples of African descent were nearly completely ignored.[120] The new, Latin American leftist governments that sought to extend the gains made in the early 1990s largely continued this trend. For example, constitutional reforms initiated by Hugo Chávez in Venezuela and Evo Morales in Bolivia provided strong support for indigenous rights without ever mentioning the existence of Afro-descendants.[121] With the 1990 Confederation of Indigenous Nationalities of Ecuador and the 1994 Zapatista rebellion in Mexico, as well as with more recent movements like the 2000 Cochabamba Water War in Bolivia, indigenous movements have often continued to define struggles for racial justice in Latin America and have continued to predominate in the region's conceptualizations of racial and ethnic minorities. However, through strategies like what Peter Wade has called an attempt to "indianize" claims to land rights, such as in the case of black communities' claims to territory on Colombia's Pacific coast, Afro-descendants have been able in some cases to use these multicultural reforms for their own gain.[122]

The 2001 United Nations World Conference against Racism, Racial Discrimination, Xenophobia, and Related Intolerance, held in Durban, South Africa, provided a new opportunity for Afro-descendants in Latin America to mobilize for equal rights.[123] According to Catherine Walsh, the Durban conference brought together intellectuals and activists of African descent and raised awareness especially of the struggles of Afro-Latin Americans, whose issues had long been subsumed by indigenous struggles. Through addressing the systemic and structural issues of racism and racial discrimination on a global scale, the Durban conference "established a common agenda and shared language to engage—not necessarily transform—the state."[124] The Durban conference called upon states to develop strategies to promote equal opportunity, affirmative action, and equal participation in the political process.

These state agendas that Durban helped to establish, and which were developed by new leftist Latin American governments, like Ecuador and Venezuela, have tended to focus on urban communities, contributing to the "subordination and invisibilization of rural community-based struggles" that are more intimately affected by extractivism, mining, and plantation farming.[125] In this sense, although the Durban conference helped to place racial discrimination against people of African descent on the agendas of many Latin American nations, it also resulted in a representative inclusion of Afro-Latin American urban organizations and leaders into state apparatuses in ways that do not necessarily lead to gains in racial equality on a mass scale. Rural populations are relegated to folkloric conservationism, and the real structural issues facing those populations are left undisturbed. This rural-urban divide, Walsh has suggested, is largely a product of how these new agendas are originally rooted in "the initiatives of multilateral development banks, international policy institutions, and international cooperation," such as the International Development Bank, that have helped to fund new development models for the region based on greater incorporation of minorities into the global market.[126] These strategies of incorporation and multicultural reform lead to a new status quo that allows states to make Afro-descendant populations and individuals more visible while failing to transform the income, unemployment, and education gaps that continue to disproportionately affect these populations. It is an inclusion that ultimately is more representative than transformative.[127]

Whereas broadly speaking, in Latin America, black social movements are being incorporated into the state, in recent racial justice organizing in the United States, there is a retreat from cooperation with and co-optation by the state. The Movement for Black Lives, which emerged in the wake of the 2012 shooting death of Trayvon Martin and the subsequent acquittal of his assailant, George Zimmerman, is resistant to forms of state co-optation and to discourses of color-blind multiculturalism, such as attempts to revise the hashtag #BlackLivesMatter to the color-blind #alllivesmatter. The BLM Network—which is the most visible of several racial justice organizations like Black Youth Project 100, Dream Defenders, or Hands Up United that have emerged within this broader movement—seeks to bring public attention specifically to the persistence of antiblack racism and undermine any illusion of a postracial society.[128] It has generally refused sustained cooperation with politicians or political parties, resulting at times in a generational gap between BLM organizers and some of the more long-established civil rights organizations like the NAACP.[129] However, at the same time that BLM has resisted co-optation by the state and has been criticized for its hesitance to engage in "state-centric forms of black politics," its primary critique has been focused on transforming the state, especially surrounding issues of police brutality, mass incarceration, and state racial profiling.[130]

Black Lives Matter, which began as a hashtag after the 2012 Zimmerman acquittal but quickly became emblematic for massive protests and direct action across the country, has grown significantly in response to the murders at the hands of law enforcement of African American men, women, and children like Michael Brown in Ferguson, Sandra Bland in rural Texas, Eric Garner in New York City, Korryn Gaines in Baltimore, Freddie Gray in Baltimore, Keith Scott in Charlotte, Tamir Rice in Cleveland, Alton Sterling in Baton Rouge, and Philando Castile in St. Paul, among others.[131] The original hashtag—which by March 2016 had been used almost twelve million times on Twitter—and subsequent infrastructure were created by three black queer social justice activists: Alicia Garza, an editorial writer and special projects director for the National Domestic Workers Alliance; Patrisse Khan-Cullors, a performance artist and executive director of Dignity and Power Now; and Opal Tometi, a writer and executive director of the Black Alliance for Just Immigration.[132] The central team grew significantly when Cullors and the writer Darnell L. Moore organized the BLM Freedom Ride in which six hundred activists traveled to Ferguson to join the protests in response to the murder of eighteen-year-old Michael Brown by police officer Darrell Wilson.[133] This led to the formation of BLM chapters and further protests throughout the United States.[134]

While it remains a decentered movement of diverse actors, the official BLM Network includes thirty-eight chapters (as of September 2017) and is largely led by black women.[135] Because it is a decentralized network, because the slogan has been used and sometimes misused by so many different social actors, and because it intentionally rebuffs, as Minkah Makalani writes, "any simplistic call for increased electoral participation, policy proposals, and the expansion of democratic protections as an adequate response to 'extrajudicial' killings," it can appear difficult to identify the precise discourse of BLM.[136] This aspect of BLM has frequently been criticized by the media and activists alike but, as Makalani writes, these critiques are often based on the problematic assumption that "black political movements, to be considered legitimate, must engage in reasoned, rationally ordered practices that are legible within the dominant political order."[137] However, I base my analysis of the overall goals and demands of the movement on the content contained on the official BLM website, published interviews with and articles by BLM founders, and the presentations of BLM activists in two days of panels given at the January 2015 Black Life Matters Conference.[138] The official BLM website explains the movement as an attempt to "(re)build the Black liberation movement" but in a way that foregrounds the voices of those who have been traditionally marginalized within that movement, such as women, queer, transgendered, disabled, and undocumented people.

Overall, the discourse of BLM has been directed toward critiquing state violence in its various forms. The "About Us" section of the BLM site explains, for example,

> we are broadening the conversation around state violence to include all of the ways in which Black people are intentionally left powerless at the hands of the state. We are talking about the ways in which Black lives are deprived of our basic human rights and dignity. How Black poverty and genocide is state violence. How 2.8 million Black people are locked in cages in this country is state violence. How Black women bearing the burden of a relentless assault on our children and our families is state violence. How Black queer and trans folks bear a unique burden from a hetero-patriarchal society that disposes of us like garbage and simultaneously fetishizes us and profits off of us, and that is state violence.[139]

While there is a reference here to the fetishizing of and capitalist profiteering from black bodies and black cultural forms, BLM's central discourse, as indicated in the quote, generally has focused on reforming the "state violence" that invests in incarceration and policing of black communities only to further "Black poverty and genocide." This focus on state violence keenly resists any reduction of racial inequity and racial violence to the action of individuals, calling attention to systemic issues and requiring the state to respond with systemic reform.[140] However, this platform does not necessarily venture into how nonstate capitalistic centers of power, such as multinational corporations or the finance industry, contribute to racial inequity and racial violence.

A September 2014 article by Cullors and Moore reflecting on the BLM Freedom Ride provides five practical steps to continue the movement post-Ferguson. These include working to develop a national policy to address the "systemic pattern of anti-black law enforcement violence in the US" and a call for a decrease in law-enforcement spending and reinvestment of those savings into services for black communities.[141] In August 2015, one BLM-affiliated group, Campaign Zero, released a practical policy plan for reforming police interventions in black communities. A few of the solutions proposed do allude to a larger relationship between policing and capital, such as the way local governments and police departments profit from fines and property seizures or the purchasing of military weaponry by local police from the Department of Defense. However, generally, the policy suggestions are related to community oversight, better training, independent investigations, and revisions of use-of-force policies.[142]

In August 2016, a collective of more than fifty organizations, including the BLM Network, released a detailed platform of demands and policy recommendations called "A Vision for Black Lives: Policy Demands for Black Power, Freedom, and Justice." This platform was crafted for over a year by the Movement for Black Lives Policy Table, which resulted from the July 2015 meeting of more than two thousand activists in Cleveland for the Movement for Black Lives Convening. This platform represents a marked expansion from a focus on police and criminal justice reform and shows a clear direction for the future of this political movement and collective of racial justice groups. Among its six demands (End the War on Black People, Reparations, Invest-Divest, Economic Justice, Community Control, Political Power), the recommendations for economic justice are the furthest reaching for addressing the role of global capital in racial inequity. It calls, for example, for an "end to the exploitative privatization of natural resources," the breaking up of large banks, and a "renegotiation of all trade agreements to prioritize the interests of workers." Every demand is broken down into actions that need to be taken at the federal, state, and local levels, and the platform explains "how these solutions address the specific needs of some of the most marginalized Black people."[143] The platform, which includes links to model legislation and thirty policy briefs, also demonstrates a move toward working more directly with the political process, even if many of the recommendations are quite radical within a U.S. political context. It makes clear the direction in which the movement is headed, which is that of a deeper economic analysis of the national and global forces affecting black and other poor and working-class communities.

In general, however, reforming the state security apparatus has been the predominant focus of BLM activism thus far. Whereas within Tricontinentalist discourse, the white policeman came to emblematize the entirety of global capitalistic exploitation and oppression, BLM critiques of the police and state violence have had a much narrower focus on state-policy reformation.[144] By pointing out this difference, I do not intend to devalue the work of BLM, which has inspired activists around the world, catapulted a new movement for black liberation in the United States, and offered much-needed practical solutions for decreasing antiblack violence perpetrated by the state, resulting in policy and policing reforms across the country. Rather, I aim to make clear how although alter-globalization and racial justice organizing in the Americas employ similar methods of decentered horizontalism and digital activism, there is often limited overlap between their critiques as they are currently articulated. On the one hand, the alter-globalization movement remains focused on a critique of global capitalism but falls into a color-blind multiculturalism that undercuts the movement at its core. On the other hand, the racial justice movement against antiblack racism, which resists color-blindness, is primarily directing its critique to the state, broadening out only somewhat to address other nodes of power within the contemporary capitalist networked society. However, in "A Vision for Black Lives" and in the internationalist leanings of BLM, especially in its theorization of "transformational solidarity," we are seeing a movement that—similar to Tricontinentalism—is attempting to forge these two disparate realms together.

BLACK LIVES MATTER: BUDDING INTERNATIONALISM AND TRANSFORMATIONAL SOLIDARITY

Despite little overlap with alter-globalization organizing, BLM has had significant global reach. It has one official chapter outside of the United States, and BLM protests have occurred in England, the Netherlands, France, Australia, Israel, Germany, and Russia with reports of additional solidarity actions in India and Brazil.[145] It has inspired the creation of organizations like Ferguson in Paris and other movements, like the Mothers of May in Brazil, have used the #BlackLivesMatter hashtag to address police violence against black communities in their own contexts.[146] However, perhaps because of BLM's primary focus on reforming the U.S. government and its police force, BLM has not experienced the same global reach in comparison to a movement like Occupy, whose protests took place in eighty-two countries.[147]

In some ways, however, internationalism has been present within BLM from its earliest inception, and its official website lists globalism among its key principles. It is in the internationalist impulses of BLM where, I contend, we are beginning to see links to a history of Cold War black radicalism and Tricontinentalism and where there is a potential for the formation of an anticapitalist movement articulated through a focus on black lives. For example, the BLM cofounder Opal Tometi is the executive director of the Black Alliance for Just Immigration (BAJI), which was formed as a result of the overwhelming absence of black immigrants in the 2006 immigrants' rights protests in the United States.[148] BAJI seeks to bring African Americans, black immigrants, and immigrant rights groups together in a common struggle against structural racism and discrimination.[149] Through the activism and written work of To-meti and BAJI, this organization is making a strong case for the relationship between neoliberal economics, mass migration, and antiblack racism. BAJI aims to expose a direct relationship between the massive immigration that re-sults from policies like trade liberalization, the profiteering from immigration and incarceration by private corporations through the prison industrial com-plex, and its connection with militarized policing that oppresses immigrants and African Americans alike. All of these issues, BAJI maintains, intersect in the lived experiences of black immigrants. In a way closer to Tricontinental-ism's anticapitalist discourse organized around racial justice, BAJI is making strides to address inequalities within globalization through a primary focus on fighting antiblack racism.

Tometi frames her involvement in BAJI and BLM as emerging from a belief (similar to Tricontinentalism) that black people are the vanguard of a global struggle. She writes, "Black people continuously suffer the worst by any social indicator," and thus focusing on black lives represents an effort to "uplift the issues of those community members who are most acutely impacted and are living at the margins" in order to "get closer to real justice for all of us."[150] In other words, she writes, "when black people get free, everybody gets free."[151] Similar to the way that a Tricontinentalist organization like the Young Lords Party conceived of the struggle against antiblack racism in the United States as key to addressing inequities suffered by Puerto Rican migrant and other U.S. Latinx immigrant communities, Tometi explains, "We understand that the basis of anti-immigrant sentiment is rooted in anti-Black racism and commit to the liberation of Black people as central to the liberation of all immigrants and communities of color."[152]

On behalf of both BLM and BAJI, Tometi calls for "transformational soli-darity with all oppressed people who are fighting for their liberation."[153] She defines transformational solidarity as a commitment to liberation for one-self and one's own community that is based on the knowledge that all com-munities are interrelated and that any injustice threatens liberation for all. She explains that a focus on black lives is key for transformational solidarity in general, since "we know that our destinies are intertwined and addressing anti-blackness helps us to work towards dismantling white supremacy and sys-temic racism in all forms."[154] This concept of "transformational solidarity" with "all oppressed people" that is forged precisely through an attention to black struggles is markedly similar to what I have called Tricontinentalism's model of trans-affective solidarity that binds together the Tricontinental's "exploited people of the world" in a radically open and expansive revolutionary subject formed through the crossing of national, linguistic, ethnic, racial, class, and gender boundaries.

While I would argue that Tometi's specifically internationalist interventions into BLM have not yet predominated in the overall discourse of BLM, we are beginning to see a shift within the movement toward this notion of transformational solidarity. In 2016, BLM activists traveled to Standing Rock, North Dakota, to support thousands of indigenous protestors fighting the construction of the Dakota Access Pipeline, and BLM released an official statement of solidarity with the water protectors at Standing Rock.[155] Shortly after the 2016 Olympic Games, BLM activists traveled to Rio de Janeiro to meet with activists fighting police violence there.[156] Similarly, in ways that recall the internationalist work of U.S. black activists like Stokely Carmichael and Robert F. Williams, in January 2015, BLM activists took several trips abroad—to Cuba, Palestine, and the United Kingdom—in an effort, as Cullors put it, to "build international solidarity, specifically around the global consequences of anti-black racism."[157]

In July 2015, a group of BLM activists visited Cuba with a Venceremos Brigade. Due to the monitored aspect of the Venceremos solidarity trips to Cuba, which are run through the Cuban Institute for Friendship with the Peoples, it does not appear that BLM activists came into contact with many of the more outspoken critics of the regime's racial policies. According to a blog post published on BAJI's website by three of the BLM representatives in attendance, the brigade was repeatedly told that structural racism does not exist in Cuba.[158] The writers of the blog express much skepticism regarding this claim and draw parallels between the color-blindness of Cuba's Marxist rhetoric and the multiculturalist and dismissive claim in the United States that "all lives matter." However, perhaps because of the brief and regulated nature of the trip and lack of interaction with many of the country's leading black intellectuals, the expression of solidarity with black Cubans that concludes the blog post with a celebratory "Venceremos!" (We shall overcome!) comes across as superficial and hardly approaches Tometi's "thick" notion of transformational solidarity.

However, BLM's engagement with the Palestinian struggle has been much more dialogic and thus much richer. In August 2014, Palestinian organizations and individuals in Palestine and the diaspora released a statement in solidarity with protestors in Ferguson, Missouri.[159] A few months later, in November 2014, ten Palestinian students from the Right to Education campaign in the West Bank traveled to the United States to meet with organizers in

St. Louis, Atlanta, and Detroit.[160] Then in January 2015, representatives from BLM, Dream Defenders (a Florida-based group headed by Philip Agnew that was formed in response to Trayvon Martin's death in 2012 and which often overlaps with BLM), Black Youth Project 100 (a collective of black activists, aged eighteen to thirty-five, based out of Chicago), and protestors from Ferguson all traveled for ten days to the West Bank in Palestine in order to connect with protestors there and to draw connections between state violence against Palestinians and African Americans. During a stop in Nazareth, the delegation staged a solidarity demonstration, which was filmed and distributed online.[161] Since then, the Dream Defenders have helped put together a "Black Solidarity with Palestine" statement that has been signed by nearly fifty black organizations in the United States and Europe as well as by high-profile black intellectuals like Angela Davis, Emory Douglas, Cornel West, and BLM's cofounder, Patrice Cullors.[162]

The "Black Solidarity with Palestine" statement calls for unified action against "anti-blackness, white supremacy, and Zionism," drawing connections between systems of apartheid in Israel/Palestine, the United States, and South Africa, and pointing as well to the culpability of the multinational private security company G4S in profiting from the imprisonment of Palestinian political prisoners and black and brown youth in the United States, United Kingdom, South Africa, and Australia.[163] The Palestinian statement of solidarity with Ferguson recognizes that both Ferguson and Palestine are "fighting against white supremacist regimes of oppression" and claims that "it is the moral responsibility of every Palestinian to support and foster relations with the struggles of the oppressed all over the world."[164] These statements merge racial oppression, settler colonialism, police violence, and capitalistic exploitation into a white supremacist image against which the "oppressed all over the world" are unified.[165]

In the footage of the solidarity demonstration by the delegation that traveled to Palestine, Palestinian and U.S. black activists call out repeatedly in a plaza in Nazareth, "Black lives matter!"[166] While these contemporary solidarity discourses are not an exact replica of the Tricontinental's metonymic color politics through which it defined global empire and an equally global revolutionary subjectivity, here "black lives" seem to stand in for Palestinian lives and for the "oppressed all over the world" who are subjected to a white supremacist, global enemy.[167] These transnational relationships, forged through what Tometi has called "transformational solidarity," are based around a common understanding of the racialized nature of state violence. However, as I have explained in the case of Tricontinentalism's trans-affective solidarity, the ideo-logical affinities that draw together peoples of diverse nationalities, languages, and ethnicities produce positive affect as a surplus value and are often articulated in affective terms. The statement "Black Solidarity with Palestine," for example, is accompanied by photographs of smiling members of the Dream Defenders delegation exchanging high fives with Palestinian children and standing next to graffiti that states "I love you Palistine [sic]."[168] The solidarity demonstration held in Nazareth begins with the statement "we came here to Palestine to stand in love and revolutionary struggle with our brothers and sisters," and it ends with all the demonstrators holding one another in a group hug.[169]

While the BLM official discourse calls for empathy and loving engagement with one another, this model of affective community is not forged solely through empathy or mutual identification of a history of oppression but is forged through a shared praxis of resistance. Agnew, the leader of the Dream Defenders, makes this clear in his poem "To Ferguson///Witness," in which the speaker thanks Ferguson demonstrators "for your resistance—guided by Gaza" and "For your Molotov . . . Flaming from Ferguson / To a ghetto near you."[170] Agnew's poem traces a community of resistance forged through a model of revolution exchanged between Gaza, Ferguson, and any "ghetto" in the world, a seeming riff on Che Guevara's "Message to the Tricontinental" to create "two, three, or many Vietnams."[171] This resistant community in Agnew's poem is held together by "Love: / That Deep, requited, crazy, unwavering, strong, uninhibited, full, foolish /Real LOVE,"[172] echoing thus Pedro Pietri's articulation of a resistant, political community in his statement that "to be called negrito / means to be called LOVE." Here again the resistance to the violent oppression of black people is posed as a synecdoche for a potentially global resistant community bound through the praxis of protest and love.

These moves toward transnational and transracial resistant community within some manifestations of the BLM movement may hold great potential, not because they represent a return to the Tricontinental as an organization, but because in BLM's stated goal of "working to (re)build the Black liberation movement," these moves are rescuing a significant contribution of a Tricontinentalist imaginary in which a global anticapitalist struggle is conceived through a struggle against antiblack racism. These forays into internationalism suggest a possibility for a Global South imaginary of oppressed peoples under contemporary capitalist globalization that does not engage in color-blind multiculturalism. BLM resists the color-blindness of the alter-globalization movement, yet overall its intervention thus far has generally been focused on reforming the U.S. state security apparatus. It remains to be seen what new forms this movement will take moving forward.

In conclusion, Tricontinentalism, although largely elided even in scholarship on Cold War Third World activism, is resurfacing in significant ways in contemporary social movements in the Americas. We are seeing its return aesthetically in the political posters, films, and discursive strategies employed by these movements, which are surface indicators of the ideological returns of Tricontinentalism. Tricontinentalism is being revived in theorizations of resistant political subjectivities under contemporary capitalist globalization, such as the "Global South," and in praxes of transnational horizontalist resistance.

Yet, overall, this contemporary revival of Tricontinentalism in the American region is only partial. On the one hand, protests against deregulation, integration, and corporate greed within global capitalism tend to reproduce the rhetoric of color-blind multiculturalism, generating silences around racial inequities. On the other, movements organized around racial justice tend to frame violence toward racialized populations within a context that is limited to a critique of the state. In this sense, the contemporary revival of Tricontinentalism within horizontalist politics is emptied of one of its more valuable contributions—its metonymic color politics—which framed a global anticapitalist movement through a focus on racial justice.

For this reason, studying the Tricontinental emerges as a particularly useful paradigm for recognizing the centrality of a black internationalist intellectual tradition to the phenomenon and theory of what is now being called the Global South. It calls attention to the fact that the Global South imaginary was always already a black internationalist political imaginary. In recognizing the intellectual roots of the Global South, this memory thus calls contemporary transnational solidarity politics into a renewed engagement with black internationalist thought, foregrounding the fight against racial inequities in general and the fight for justice for peoples of African descent more specifically as a prerequisite to the futurity of Global South political resistance.

CONCLUSION

Against Ferguson?

Internationalism from the
Tricontinental to the Global South

A few weeks after a grand jury exonerated Officer Darrell Wilson for the murder of an unarmed teenager named Michael Brown, and two days before Presidents Barack Obama and Raúl Castro announced the restoration of relations between Cuba and the United States, the Afro-Cuban intellectual and activist Roberto Zurbano Torres published an article online entitled "Contra Ferguson (O por qué la lucha antirracista debe ser internacionalista)" (Against Ferguson [Or Why the Antiracist Struggle Should Be Internationalist]). In this article, Zurbano explains that, despite a lifetime of antiracist work, he has chosen not to sign any of the circulating petitions that renounce the murder of Michael Brown and that protest the impunity of police violence in the United States. He is not signing, he writes, not because he does not agree with the positions expressed in these petitions, but because he believes that the emotional outcry embodied in them becomes a media spectacle that brings the public to a catharsis, eventually leading to resignation and appeasement. Zurbano is, he explains, "against Ferguson" in the sense that he is against the media's reduction of global structural racism to individual, localized incidents.

While he is against the media spectacle of Ferguson, he is, however, in favor of the protestors in Ferguson, whom he views as attempting to break the media-controlled cathartic cycle and as presenting an opportunity for a new black liberation movement in the United States. This potential, he writes, rests on the ability of such a movement to

> renounce Yankee exceptionalism and arrogance in order to incorporate other social groups . . . and to aspire to recognize itself within a context less closed than the North American one, where a counter-hegemonic discourse can be constructed from various visions, spaces, and cultures. An anti-racist discourse that is conscious of its local condition, and simultaneously, of its global condition, recognizing other formulas against racism (Dominicans, Brazilians, Colombians, Cubans, Garifunas, South Africans, and immigrants) as part of its own emancipatory struggles and not seeing them as mere copies, distant realities, or rivals in competition for protagonism or racial power.[1]

In calling for an antiracist discourse that is conscious of both its local and global conditions, he emphasizes the need to "internationalize the battle against racism, whose center is not located in a specific place, but rather in a diverse economic, ideological and cultural structure."[2] In other words, he presents structural racism as a decentered phenomenon that requires an equally geographically fluid counterstruggle.

Beyond this need for an internationalist antiracist struggle, he suggests that this movement should be articulated in the following way: "not only from and for black communities, but rather a little beyond, which makes this project of global liberation more complex, democratic, critical, and self-critical. . . . Let's not forget that, before power, all of us oppressed are an undifferentiated mass."[3] Echoed within the vision of Zurbano—widely recognized as one of the staunchest critics of racial inequity within Cuba—for a movement representing all "the oppressed" fighting for "global liberation" is a profoundly Tricontinentalist imaginary that emerges out of black internationalism and that responds to racial capitalism with a model for a global resistant subjectivity. For Zurbano, this Tricontinentalist rhetoric is not a contradiction since, as I have argued, Tricontinentalism—although disseminated by the Cuban state through its cultural products—was always rooted in a tradition of black internationalist thought.

While I have argued that current racial justice organizing in the United States, such as in the Black Lives Matter movement, is largely focused on reforming the state and thus has not yet had the same degree of internationalism seen in alter-globalization movements, I find Zurbano's characterization of it as exceptionalist, disconnected from struggles in other parts of the Americas, and wrapped up in its own protagonism, to be excessively harsh. This critique does not take into account the ongoing and expanding exchange between these newer forms of black activism in the United States and antiracist movements in other parts of the world. However, his comments may indeed be more applicable to the realm of academic scholarship, especially when we consider the limited scholarship that has been produced thus far on a movement like Tricontinentalism.

Within the abundant research on black internationalism, many studies have addressed African American activists' engagement with the Cuban Revolution. However, the general silence surrounding the organizing structure of Tricontinentalism, how it influenced U.S. intellectuals, and how it shaped anti-imperialist discourses in the Americas and around the globe speaks to an academic insularity toward the theoretical contributions of this profoundly influential movement. As I have argued, much of the erasure of the Tricontinental's legacy can be attributed to the way that the field of postcolonial studies has focused on the national contexts represented at Bandung and has employed a definition of postcoloniality that largely elides both Latin America as well as oppressed populations within wealthy countries like the United States. In response, new modes of critical analysis are emerging such that we are witnessing a shift within contemporary scholarship from the center-periphery and colonizer-colonized model of postcolonial theory to horizontalist critical approaches, like the Global South.

This shift in contemporary theory, I would suggest, is largely parallel to the discursive shift that occurred when the so-called spirit of Bandung traveled across the Atlantic to become the Tricontinental. In other words, the Tricontinental alliance joined a Bandung model of resistance to European colonialism with a more fluid theorization of imperialism, and in so doing, it forged a vision of a resistant subject position that is inherently transnational and flexible in its definition. As Bandung moved into the Americas, Tricontinentalism would take up a preexisting signifier of black anti-imperialism devised through a transatlantic and especially pan-Caribbeanist exchange, which Richard Wright expanded into a "color curtain" to include people of non-African descent, and attempt to move beyond its relationship to perceived physical difference and essentialist representations and toward an abstract use of color that traverses linguistic, geographic, and racial borders. In this way, the Tricontinental provides a framework for the "global liberation" that Zurbano describes that is based on horizontalist solidarities and decentered geographies and that is increasingly relevant to the transnational nature of contemporary social movements.

In recent years, many critical concepts like "grassroots globalization," "counterhegemonic globalization," and the "Global South" have emerged as attempts to describe how global capitalism facilitates the creation of networks among grassroots movements, yielding a transnational, resistant political imaginary. Alongside these categories, a set of horizontalist reading praxes, like "minor transnationalism" and "globalectics," has arisen that examine both contemporary and past resistant cultural production in dialogue within a global network of writers and artists.[4] This book has suggested Tricontinentalism as one of these reading praxes, framing the creation of this ideology through a transnational dialogic exchange of activists and writers and considering how its discourse appears across a global network of radical texts. However, the texts analyzed in this book represent only a small portion of cultural production that reflects Tricontinentalist influence, and it is my hope that further scholarship will trace these influences in other filmic, literary, and political movements in the Americas and in other parts of the globe.

Tricontinentalism, I have maintained, is currently reemerging both in horizontalist critical approaches and in the ideologies, discourses, and aesthetics of contemporary social movements in the American hemisphere. However, in proposing the intellectual recognition of this legacy within contemporary solidarity politics, I would like to make clear that I am in no way arguing for its triumphalist embrace. The Tricontinental is an imperfect model with inconsistencies and weaknesses that arise from, for example, an overwhelming silence on black liberation struggles within countries with leftist governments and a tendency to address itself to a heteronormative, masculinist subject. My attention to the Tricontinental is not meant to redeem it as a model for political activism, but rather to shine a light from a scholarly perspective on the insights to be gleaned from its study, which are several.

In one sense, the Tricontinental offers a long view of the Global South, a starting point from which to develop and depart, that, as I have attempted to demonstrate in this book, necessitates a close examination of foundational Cold War texts. Second, rooting the Global South in Tricontinentalism clarifies the concept not as a mere addendum to postcolonial theory but rather as an explicit divergence from postcoloniality as an organizing category in an effort to recover some of the basic tenets of Tricontinentalism. By this, I mean that the Global South as a critical model is attentive to the ideological frame—rather than the trait-based or circumstantial conditions—through which individuals imagine themselves as part of a global resistant network.

Third, recognizing a history of Tricontinentalism means explicitly acknowledging the contribution of both Latin American and African American intellectual traditions, which are often marginalized in postcolonial studies, to contemporary theories of power and resistance. This acknowledgment, which does not imply the dismissal of other intellectual traditions represented at the Tricontinental, has important implications for the U.S. and Latin American academies alike. It provides a historical platform for further comparative work in hemispheric American subaltern studies. It also implies that since postcolonial theory significantly diverged from Tricontinentalism, those Latin Americanist scholars who view postcolonialism as an overgeneralizing or foreign construction may be justified, but that Global South theory should not be labeled in quite the same way. In other words, recognizing the Tricontinentalist roots of the Global South has enormous potential for opening communication between intellectual traditions that has often been stymied under prior rubrics.

Finally, as horizontalist notions like the Global South attempt to name and theorize the present reality of transnational subaltern politics, further study of the relationship of these politics to a Cold War, Tricontinental past constitutes a key step toward a more critical engagement with our contemporary context. In confronting the current political scene, in which massive protests and transnational solidarity politics reflect a divergence between antineoliberal and racial justice discourses, remembering the Tricontinental's global movement against racial capitalism and considering its continued impact and erasure in our contemporary context could not be more valuable.

NOTES

Introduction

1 Harper, "Inside the Beltway."
2 Obama, "Statement by the President on Cuba Policy Changes."
3 On his historic visit to Cuba in March 2016, Obama remarked, "I have come to bury the last remnant of the Cold War in the Americas." Obama, "Remarks by President Obama to the People of Cuba."
4 Obama, "Remarks by President Obama to the People of Cuba."
5 Obama's March 2016 speech in Havana was much more cautious on this point, stating that the twenty-first century "depends on the free and open exchange of ideas. If you can't access information online, if you cannot be exposed to different points of view, you will not reach your full potential. And over time, the youth will lose hope." Obama, "Remarks by President Obama to the People of Cuba."
6 I use the term "alter-globalization," sometimes known as the global justice movement or the *altermundista* movement, instead of "anti-globalization," because of the way the term indicates support for internationalism while seeking to provide an alternative to neoliberal forms of globalization.
7 For discussions of Bandung as an originary moment for the field of postcolonial studies, see C. Lee, "Between a Moment and an Era," and Chakrabarty, "Legacies of Bandung." According to the Tricontinental's International Preparatory Committee, the Tricontinental originated at the 1955 Afro-Asian Bandung Conference. In reality, the Tricontinental (OSPAAAL) represented an extension of the

Afro-Asian Peoples' Solidarity Organization (AAPSO) into the Americas, and although the preparatory committee described the AAPSO, an alliance of seventy-five organizations founded in Cairo in 1957, as originating "in 1955 at the meeting of the heads of State in Bandung," the AAPSO is generally considered significantly more communist-aligned than the 1955 Bandung Conference. Still, the Bandung and Tricontinental are two major cornerstones of Cold War anticolonialism. As Gronbeck-Tedesco writes of Bandung, "The Afro-Asian Conference was the institutional and discursive predecessor to Cuba's 'Tricontinental' that became the foundation of Cuba's geopolitical strategy." Gronbeck-Tedesco, *Cuba, the United States, and Cultures of the Transnational Left*, 200–201.

8 Appadurai, "Grassroots Globalization and the Research Imagination"; Santos, *Toward a New Legal Common Sense*; Hardt and Negri, *Empire*.

9 Lionnet and Shih, *Minor Transnationalism*; Ngũgĩ wa Thiong'o, *Globalectics*; Tolliver, "Introduction." These concepts rely on earlier poststructuralist models such as Deleuze and Guattari's "rhizome" from *Capitalism and Schizophrenia* (1977: 80) and Glissant's notion of "relation" in *Poetics of Relation* (1997).

10 This usage originates in 1970s modernization and development discourses produced by organizations such as the United Nations Group of 77, which sought to facilitate economic cooperation among economically disadvantaged nation-states. Following the disintegration of the Soviet bloc in the early 1990s, "Global South" became more widely used as an alternative to "Third World," popularized by the United Nations Development Programme "Forging a Global South." See Dirlik, "Global South."

11 Through theorizing the "South" and through the comparative study of the U.S. South with other geographic and economic "Souths," new Southern studies has made a major contribution to this deterritorialized conceptualization. See Cohn, *History and Memory in the Two Souths*; Hutchinson, "Souths"; McKee and Trefzer, "Global Contexts, Local Literatures"; Milian, *Latining America*; Smith and Cohn, *Look Away!*; and Sullivan-González and Wilson, *South and the Caribbean*.

12 While there are many titles that discuss the Global South as a regional designation, key texts that use the term to refer to a critical category, body of theory, and axis for comparison include Aboul-Ela, "Global South, Local South"; Amar, *The Middle East and Brazil*; Armillas-Tiseyra, "Dislocations"; Connell, *Southern Theory*; González García, "On the Borderlands of U.S. Empire"; Klengel and Ortiz Wallner, *Sur/South*; Milian, *Latining America*; Prashad, *Poorer Nations*; Satpathy, *Southern Postcolonialisms*; Slovic, Rangarajan, and Sarveswaran, *Ecocriticism of the Global South*; and especially the many articles published in the Indiana University Press journal *The Global South* since its founding in 2007.

13 Fukuyama, *End of History and the Last Man*.

14 These studies include C. Anderson, *Eyes Off the Prize*; Arne Westad, *Global Cold War*; Borstelmann, *Cold War and the Color Line*; Dudziak, *Cold War Civil*

Rights; C. Lee, *Making a World after Empire*; Luis-Brown, *Waves of Decoloniza-tion*; Plummer, *Rising Wind*; Prashad, *Darker Nations*; and Von Eschen, *Race against Empire*. I also include here recent work on Cuban involvement in African independence struggles, such as George, *Cuban Intervention in Angola*; Gleijeses, *Conflicting Missions* and *Visions of Freedom*; Hatzky, *Cubans in Angola*; Henighan, "Cuban Fulcrum"; Millar, "Realigning Revolution"; and Peters, *Cuban Identity and the Angolan Experience*.

15 Such black internationalist studies include Daulatzai, *Black Star, Crescent Moon*; Gilroy, *Black Atlantic*; Edwards, *Practice of Diaspora*; Holcomb, *Claude McKay, Code Name Sasha*; Kelley, *Freedom Dreams*; Marable and Agard-Jones, *Transna-tional Blackness*; Robinson, *Black Marxism*; Singh, *Black Is a Country*; and Stephens, *Black Empire*. Scholarship on black-brown political solidarities is represented by, for example, Brock and Castañeda Fuertes, *Between Race and Empire*; Gronbeck-Tedesco, *Cuba, the United States, and Cultures of the Transnational Left*; Guridy, *Forging Diaspora*; J. Márquez, *Black-Brown Solidarity*; Milian, *Latining America*; Reitan, *Rise and Decline of an Alliance*; Rodriguez, "Beyond Nation"; Sawyer, *Racial Politics in Post-revolutionary Cuba*; Seidman, "Venceremos Means We Shall Over-come"; Tyson, *Radio Free Dixie*; and C. Young, *Soul Power*.

16 Laura Pulido's *Black, Brown, Yellow, and Left* also keenly describes the U.S. "Third World Left" and makes a similar argument regarding the role of the Cuban Revo-lution and the importance of print culture.

17 Pitman and Stafford concur that Tricontinentalism has received "very little aca-demic attention to date" even though its "legacy echoes, more or less explicitly, in some of the wider cultural discourses of the regions involved." Pitman and Stafford, "Introduction," 199. Beyond scholarship, however, there are several an-thologies of Tricontinental posters and writings, which include introductions that provide historical background. See *El cartel de la OSPAAAL*; Estrada Lescaille and Suárez, *Rebelión Tricontinental*; and Frick, *Tricontinental Solidarity Poster*. Tri-continental and the Cuban publishing house Editora Política have also published articles and books that commemorate anniversaries of the initial conference. See, for example, Capote, *La solidaridad Tricontinental*.

18 Pitman and Stafford, "Introduction," 197, 199. See also Barcia, " 'Locking Horns with the Northern Empire' "; Henighan, "Cuban Fulcrum"; and Stafford, "Tricon-tinentalism in Recent Moroccan Intellectual History."

19 Rodriguez, "Beyond Nation," 14.

20 Rodriguez, "Beyond Nation," vi.

21 Rodriguez, "Beyond Nation," vi. See also Rodriguez, " 'De la esclavitud yanqui a la libertad cubana' " and "Long Live Third World Unity!"

22 Seidman, "Venceremos Means We Shall Overcome," 80. See also Seidman, "Tri-continental Routes of Solidarity," in which she notes that what bound Stokely Car-michael to Cuba was a "shared Tricontinental ideology," which she describes as a particularly Cuban "political construct akin to Third Worldism" (2).

23 Seidman, "Venceremos Means We Shall Overcome," 134, 233.

24 Gronbeck-Tedesco, *Cuba, the United States, and Cultures of the Transnational Left*, 224.

25 B. Anderson, *Imagined Communities*.

26 C. Lee, "Between a Moment and an Era," 25.

27 Berlant, *Cruel Optimism*, 260.

28 For the Black Arts and Nuyorican movements, see, for example, Jackson, *Black Writers and Latin America*; Torres, *Between Melting Pot and Mosaic*. For the Cuban Revolution and Black Power, see Benson, *Antiracism in Cuba*; Gosse, *Where the Boys Are*; Guridy, *Forging Diaspora*; Latner, "Take Me to Havana!"; Marable and Agard-Jones, *Transnational Blackness*; Reitan, *Rise and Decline of an Alliance*; Rodriguez, "Beyond Nation"; Seidman, "Venceremos Means We Shall Overcome"; Tietchen, "Cubalogues"; Tyson, *Radio Free Dixie*; and C. Young, *Soul Power*. For the influence on the Third Cinema, see Guneratne, "Introduction"; and C. Young, *Soul Power*. For the "Third World Left," see Gronbeck-Tedesco, *Cuba, the United States, and Cultures of the Transnational Left*; Pulido, *Black, Brown, Yellow, and Left*; and C. Young, *Soul Power*.

29 Wright, *Colour Curtain*, 175.

30 Sawyer, *Racial Politics in Post-revolutionary Cuba*.

1. Beyond the Color Curtain

1 For a list of all delegations, invited guests, and foreign press, see U.S. Senate Committee on the Judiciary, "Tricontinental Conference," 49–69.

2 U.S. Senate Committee on the Judiciary, "Tricontinental Conference," 47.

3 Seidman, "Venceremos Means We Shall Overcome," 151–152.

4 International Preparatory Committee, "Background of Tricontinental Conference," 3. For differences between the Bandung and Cairo conferences, see Jack, "Cairo Conference." See Organization of American States (OAS), *Report of the Special Committee* V. 1, for details on the shift from the AAPSO to the OSPAAAL.

5 Gronbeck-Tedesco has made a similar point, writing that "the Afro-Asian Conference was the institutional and discursive predecessor to Cuba's 'Tricontinental' that became the foundation of Cuba's geopolitical strategy" and that "with their formulation of the Tricontinental, leaders in Havana positioned Cuba as the torchbearer of the post-Bandung world." *Cuba, the United States, and Cultures of the Transnational Left*, 200–201, 209.

6 Acharya and Seng Tan, "Introduction"; Ampiah, *Political and Moral Imperatives of the Bandung Conference of 1955*; Chakrabarty, "Legacies of Bandung"; C. Lee, "Between a Moment and an Era"; Nesadurai, "Bandung and the Political Economy of North-South Relations."

7 Robbins, "Blaming the System," 49.

8 R. Lee, "Modern World-System," 28.

9 Stern, "Feudalism, Capitalism, and the World-System," 858.

10 See the Postcolonial Studies @ Emory website, https://scholarblogs.emory.edu /postcolonialstudies.

11 See Coronil's discussion in "Elephants in the Americas?" of the many postcolonial anthologies that have elided the Latin American region.

12 For in-depth discussions of the Latin Americanist debates on postcolonial studies, see Acosta, *Thresholds of Illiteracy*; Coronil, "Elephants in the Americas?"; Lund, *Impure Imagination*. See also Seed, "Colonial and Postcolonial Discourse," and the responses to this essay in Adorno, "Reconsidering Colonial Discourse for Sixteenth- and Seventeenth-Century Spanish America"; Mignolo, "Colonial and Postcolonial Discourse"; and Vidal, "Concept of Colonial and Postcolonial Discourse."

13 Brenner, "Space of the World," 102.

14 Brenner, "Space of the World," 117.

15 Appadurai, *Modernity at Large*; Beasley-Murray, *Posthegemony*; Castells, "Network Theory of Power"; Galloway and Thacker, *Exploit*; Grewal, *Network Power*.

16 While the founding text for this intellectual movement was Quijano's "Colonialidad y modernidad/racionalidad," the project began to emerge primarily through two panels with Fernando Coronil, Quijano, and Mignolo at the 1998 International Sociological Association meeting as well as a panel with Wallerstein, Quijano, and Dussel at Binghamton University. Mignolo, "Introduction," 10. For an overview of this body of scholarship organized around a shared conceptual corpus, see Escobar, "Worlds and Knowledges Otherwise."

17 Mignolo, *Local Histories/Global Designs*, xxv.

18 Quijano, "Coloniality and Modernity/Rationality," 25. See also Escobar, "Worlds and Knowledges Otherwise," 39.

19 Mignolo, *Local Histories/Global Designs*, 45.

20 Quijano, "Coloniality and Modernity/Rationality," 17.

21 Quijano, "Coloniality and Modernity/Rationality," 23. Similarly, Quijano argues that contemporary capitalist globalization "is the culmination of a process that began with the constitution of America and colonial/modern Eurocentered capitalism." Quijano, "Coloniality of Power, Eurocentrism, and Latin America," 533.

22 The key contentions of this research program are detailed in Escobar, "Worlds and Knowledges Otherwise."

23 Hardt and Negri, *Empire*, 166.

24 Hardt and Negri, *Empire*, xii.

25 Galloway and Thacker, *Exploit*, 60.

26 Hale, "Neoliberal Multiculturalism."

27 Melamed, *Represent and Destroy*, 138.

28 Melamed, *Represent and Destroy*, 42. Similarly, Hardt and Negri write in *Empire* that the new "racist theory attacks modern anti-racism from the rear, and actually co-opts and enlists its arguments" (191).

29 See García Canclini, *Consumidores y ciudadanos*; Hale, "Neoliberal Multiculturalism"; Melamed, *Represent and Destroy*; Ong, *Neoliberalism as Exception*.

30 Hardt and Negri, *Empire*, 194.

31 Ong, *Neoliberalism as Exception*, 6.

32 Melamed, *Represent and Destroy*, 44.

33 Melamed, *Represent and Destroy*, 13.

34 The "South" as a nation-based, geopolitical formation began to emerge in the 1970s within the NAM and within development discourses produced by organizations such as the United Nations Group of 77, which sought to facilitate economic cooperation between economically disadvantaged nation-states. It was solidified and popularized with the Brandt Commission Reports, published in 1980 and 1983, which characterized global capital relations through the North-South metaphor. Dirlik, "Global South," 12–13. The Brandt Report was published by the Brandt Commission, established by former head of the World Bank Robert McNamara and named after German Chancellor Willy Brandt. It is an analysis and series of recommendations for alleviating inequity within the global economy and for apparently mutually beneficial cooperation between wealthy and poor nations in which transfers of wealth to the South would be used to buy goods from the North. Prashad, *Poorer Nations*, 69. It describes the disparity in economic power as a loose division between countries geographically located in the Northern and Southern hemispheres, with the exception of Australia and New Zealand and with a recognition of the liminal positionality of Eastern European countries and China. In this report, countries considered to be within the South generally mirror those member countries of the NAM. Brandt, *North-South*. In 1990, the South Commission—announced at the 1986 Non-Aligned Summit and chaired by Tanzanian President Julius Nyerere—published its report *The Challenge to the South: The Report of the South Commission*. This report is largely a follow-up to the Brandt Report, although it is more focused on the provision of basic needs than on a growth-first model, and frames the South as the former Third World. It critiques inequity between nations of the North and South and argues that South-South cooperation could help reduce dependence on Northern countries. Prashad, *Poorer Nations*, 82–93. Following the disintegration of the Soviet bloc and the global implementation of policies associated with the Washington Consensus, "Global" began to be affixed to "South" within these developmentalist discourses, such as the United Nations Development Program "Forging a Global South." Dirlik, "Global South," 12–13.

35 I thank Alfred J. López for pointing out to me in such clear terms how the Global South relies on Gramsci's reflection on southern Italy's relation to the North in "The Southern Question" as an alternative to an East/West economic division based around European colonialism. See also Dados and Connell, "Global South."

36 See, for example, Sheppard and Nagar's "From East-West to North-South," in which they argue that within contemporary capitalist globalization, the East-West rivalries of the Cold War, which occurred at the level of the nation-state, have been replaced with North-South relations that are supranational. The Global North, they write, "is constituted through a network of political and economic elites spanning privileged localities across the globe" and the Global South—

"whose population is disproportionately made up of 'indigenous' communities, people of color and women—is to be found everywhere: foraging the forests of South Asia, undertaking the double burden of house and paid work, toiling in sweatshops within the United States, and living in urban quasi-ghettoes worldwide." Sheppard and Nagar, "From East-West to North-South," 558. Similarly, Caroline Thomas calls for scholars "to liberate our thinking from the constraints imposed by interpretation within a territorially-based state-centric worldview, which concentrates on a North/South gap in terms of *states*." She proposes moving away from thinking the South as a referent to the states previously known as Third World and toward a conceptualization that helps us understand "the global construction of entitlement and distribution." C. Thomas, "Globalization and the South," 3. For one of the more nuanced discussions to date of the Global South, see Klengel and Ortiz Wallner, *Sur/South*.

37 Connell's *Southern Theory* is perhaps more geographically bounded in that it tends to conflate North/South with center/periphery and East/West. However, she writes, "I use the term 'Southern' not to name a sharply bounded category of states or societies, but to emphasize relations—authority, exclusion and inclusion, hegemony, partnership, sponsorship, appropriation." Connell, *Southern Theory*, viii–ix. Similarly, Comaroff and Comaroff's *Theory from the South* begins with a nationally scaled understanding of the Global South, which draws an equivalence between the Global South and the Third World. However, by the end of the introduction to the book, they nuance this definition significantly, explaining that despite the original Cold War usage of the term, now, "'the south' cannot be defined, *a priori*, in substantive terms. The label bespeaks a *relation*, not a thing in or for itself. . . . The south . . . is being recast as a spatio-temporal order made of a multitude of variously articulated flows and dimensions, at once political, juridical, cultural, material, virtual—a world that, ultimately transcends the very dualism of north and south." Comaroff and Comaroff, *Theory from the South*, 47. These works write against a tradition that has treated poorer communities as objects of study rather than as producers of knowledge. In their privileging of the South (used both geographically and relationally) as a more productive site of social theorizing, scholarship on Southern theory could be criticized for a tendency to bend toward intellectual essentialism, even as the works themselves seek to destabilize the South as a reified object.

38 Guterl, "South," 232.

39 Cassano, *Southern Thought*; Dainotto, "A South with a View"; "Does Europe Have a South?"; Gramsci, "The Southern Question."

40 Guterl, "South," 230. See, for example, Cohn, *History and Memory in the Two Souths*; Gruesz, *Ambassadors of Culture*; Mcpherson, *Reconstructing Dixie*; McKee and Trefzer, "Global Contexts, Local Literatures"; Milian, *Latining America*; Smith and Cohn, *Look Away!*

41 Brenner, "Space of the World," 103.

42 Brenner, "Space of the World," 103.

43 López, "Introduction," 1.

44 Prashad, *Poorer Nations*, 9. Similarly, Boaventura de Sousa Santos distinguishes between a geographic South (which may or may not reproduce the epistemologies of the North) and the "anti-imperial South" that should be embraced by the global Left. In this way, he proposes the South as an ideological position vis-à-vis global capitalism. Santos, *Epistemologies of the South*, 42. See also Armillas-Tiseyra, "Tales from the Corpolony."

45 Prashad, *Poorer Nations*, 9.

46 Satpathy's *Southern Postcolonialisms* argues that the Global South emerges out of postcolonial theory and responds to its limitations for addressing power relations within the global economy. Satpathy acknowledges that the "South" as a concept has the potential to obscure its own internal disparities but suggests that the Global South represents an attempt to challenge the "apparent neutrality" of a term like "globalization." Satpathy, *Southern Postcolonialisms*, 24. However, the title itself of Satpathy's volume captures a tension where, even as it attempts to move beyond the rubric of postcolonial studies, all the essays contained therein focus exclusively on the Anglophone world, a limitation that the editor openly and self-critically acknowledges. The volume thus replicates one of the primary problems within postcolonial studies to which more contemporary transnational models like the Global South intend to respond. Similarly, Klengel and Ortiz Wallner frame their South-South reading method in *Sur/South* as one that intentionally moves beyond the "postcolonial criterion of 'colonial difference' " in favor of the "entangled histories" of Indian and Latin American intellectuals and the interrelationships within globalization. Klengel and Ortiz Wallner, *Sur/South*, 12, 7.

47 The works of Robert J. C. Young and Vijay Prashad are exceptions to this elision.

48 This element of the Tricontinental's ideology is intimately tied to an exchange between the Cuban Revolution and African American intellectuals that began in the early 1960s. Besenia Rodriguez uses the term "Tricontinentalism" to refer to the "critique of global capitalism and its exploitation of the world's racialized peoples" expressed in several articles composed by African American activists who traveled to Cuba in the early 1960s through their participation in the Fair Play for Cuba Committee as well as in the writings of the Black Panther Party leader Huey Newton, who was exiled in Cuba. Rodriguez, " 'De la esclavitud yanqui a la libertad cubana,' " 63. Additionally, Sarah Seidman has written extensively on the relationship between African Americans and postrevolutionary Cuba, noting a "shared Tricontinental ideology" that connected, for example, Stokely Carmichael to Cuba. Seidman, "Tricontinental Routes of Solidarity," 2. For more on African Americans and the Cuban Revolution, see Gosse, *Where the Boys Are*; Guridy, *Forging Diaspora*; Joseph, *Waiting 'til the Midnight Hour*; Latner, "Take Me to Havana!"; Sawyer, *Racial Politics in Post-revolutionary Cuba*; Seidman, "Venceremos Means We Shall Overcome"; Tietchen, "Cubalogues"; and C. Young, *Soul Power*.

49 While I employ the terms "black Atlantic," "black internationalist," and "black transnational" interchangeably, the geography implied by Paul Gilroy's conceptu-

alization in *The Black Atlantic: Modernity and Double Consciousness* (1993) does not always map perfectly to the exchanges that I trace here because many of these intellectuals' networks and travels extend beyond the Atlantic region to the Soviet Union and beyond.

50 Price, *Object of the Atlantic*, 7.

51 Schmitt, *Nomos of the Earth*, 252.

52 Schmitt, *Nomos of the Earth*, 252.

53 I take this argument directly from Price's *Object of the Atlantic*, 18. See also Lenin, *Imperialism*.

54 Cohn, "U.S. Southern Studies and Latin American Studies," 705.

55 De la Fuente, *Nation for All*, 39–45; Kutzinski, *Sugar's Secrets*, 138.

56 Matthews, "Globalizing the U.S. South," 719.

57 Ferrer, *Freedom's Mirror*, 10.

58 Ferrer, *Freedom's Mirror*.

59 Ferrer, *Insurgent Cuba*, 49–69.

60 Ferrer, *Insurgent Cuba*, 77–89.

61 Ferrer, *Insurgent Cuba*, 95.

62 Ferrer, *Insurgent Cuba*, 4.

63 Ferrer, *Insurgent Cuba*, 126–127.

64 Ferrer, *Insurgent Cuba*, 89.

65 Ferrer, *Insurgent Cuba*, 182–191.

66 De la Fuente, *Nation for All*, 69; Helg, *Our Rightful Share*.

67 Helg, *Our Rightful Share*, 162.

68 Helg, *Our Rightful Share*, 165, 205.

69 Helg, *Our Rightful Share*, 225.

70 Cohn, "U.S. Southern Studies and Latin American Studies," 705.

71 Luis-Brown, *Waves of Decolonization*, 70. This Pan-African Conference was organized by the Trinidadian H. Sylvester Williams in London, and it included thirty delegates, mainly from England and the West Indies, and a few African Americans. According to Du Bois, this meeting "put the word 'Pan African' in the dictionaries for the first time." While the conference took place in 1900, the next conference of its kind would not be held until 1919 in Paris, which would be the official First Pan-African Congress, organized by W. E. B. Du Bois and the head of the Tuskegee Institute, Robert Morton. Padmore, *History of the Pan-African Congress*, 13.

72 Luis-Brown discusses at length Du Bois's interethnic vision of political community, which he argues is too broad to be characterized as solely Pan-Africanist. Luis-Brown, *Waves of Decolonization*, 23–24.

73 Luis-Brown, *Waves of Decolonization*, 9.

74 Quoted in Luis-Brown, *Waves of Decolonization*, 101.

75 Ayala, *American Sugar Kingdom*.

76 Gilmore, *Defying Dixie*, 22.

77 Gilmore, *Defying Dixie*, 22–24.

78 Stephens, *Black Empire*, 11.

79 In the case of the Dominican Republic, this instability was pivotal in producing the military coup that put Rafael Leónidas Trujillo Molina in power. Ayala,
American Sugar Kingdom.
80 Ayala, *American Sugar Kingdom*.
81 Luis-Brown, *Waves of Decolonization*, 193.
82 Jackson, *Black Literature and Humanism in Latin America*, 26.
83 Jackson, *Black Literature and Humanism in Latin America*, 28.
84 De la Fuente, *Nation for All*, 177–178.
85 Davis and Williams, "Pan-Africanism," 152.
86 For an overview of writers, artists, and musicians associated with negrismo, see
Luis-Brown, *Waves of Decolonization*, 192–193.
87 Kutzinski, *Sugar's Secrets*, 4–5. At the same time that much of negrista cultural
production in Cuba consisted of the "commodification and folklorization of
Afro-Cuban secular and religious culture" by white artists, formerly marginalized
Afro-diasporic music and cultural practices now had a national and international
stage. De la Fuente, *Nation for All*, 184. As Robin Moore has detailed, the broad
consumption of these cultural forms created a platform for the professional advancement of black and mixed-race artists. Beyond Afro-descendant poets from
this period, the performers Eusebia Cosme and Rita Montaner and the composer
and performer Ignacio Villa became international sensations, touring in Latin
America, Europe, and the United States, even as many of the works they performed were written by white authors who were imitating Afro-Cuban music
and speech. Through the expanding tourism industry, and as cubanidad became
increasingly identified at home and abroad with black cultural forms, working-
class Afro-Cuban musicians and cabaret performers would also gain recognition
and some economic security within Cuba. R. Moore, *Nationalizing Blackness*. For
an in-depth look at the life and work of Eusebia Cosme, see López, *Unbecoming Blackness*. The heightened valorization and influence of black cultural forms
caused discomfort for some intellectuals in the Hispanophone Caribbean, and
simultaneous artistic movements emerged as an alternative to the national narrative that negrismo provided. *Indigenismo*—which drew on *indigenista* cultural
movements that flourished in the same time period in countries with large indigenous populations, like Mexico and Peru, in which indigenous cultures were similarly appropriated for nation-building ideologies—based the cultural heritage of
the Hispanophone Caribbean in the largely constructed cultural memory of the
taíno. Indigenista composers in Cuba ascribed indigenous origins to instruments,
like the *clave* and the *marímbula*, which were developed by Afro-Caribbeans and
Hispanics, and they created work inspired by historical indigenous figures, such
as Hatuey and Anacaona. Generally eliding any discussion of the role of settler
colonialism and indigenous genocide in Cuba's national history, indigenista literature characterized figures like Chief Hatuey, a Taíno chief from the island
of Hispaniola who was burned at the stake by the Spanish for organizing militant resistance, as examples of a Cuban nationalism rooted in anticolonialism.

On a similar note, *guajiro* nationalism emerged in the same moment, upholding rural peasants (guajiros in Cuba; *jíbaros* in Puerto Rico) as the true guardians of Cuban culture and representing them not as Afro-descendants, but as Hispanic-indigenous mestizos. These nationalist cultural movements, which "were especially appealing to those uncomfortable with privileging the nation's African heritage yet desirous of establishing racial primordials as contributing factors to *cubanidad,*" however, would not have the same national or international impact as negrista works. R. Moore, *Nationalizing Blackness*, 127–31.

88 "Auto-bio-prólogo," "humana": Pedroso, *Nosotros*, 9. Translations of Pedroso's *Nosotros* are mine.

89 "Pigmentación": Pedroso, *Nosotros*, 9.

90 DeCosta-Willis, *Blacks in Hispanic Literature*, 116; Jackson, *Black Literature and Humanism in Latin America*, 26. Guillén's poetry, for example, nuances black street culture and Pedroso's and Arozarena's overtly political writings critique "bourgeois" representations of Afro-Cubans. De la Fuente, *Nation for All*, 185.

91 Ortiz, *Cuban Counterpoint*, 51.

92 Césaire, *Notebook of a Return to the Native Land*, 1.

93 For this reading of Carpentier's first novel, see Kutzinski, *Sugar's Secrets*.

94 Stephens, *Black Empire*, 50.

95 Stephens, *Black Empire*, 36–42.

96 Its first international conference, held in 1920 in Madison Square Garden, was "reputedly the largest international gathering of blacks ever witnessed in the Western world." Stephens, *Black Empire*, 47.

97 Adi, "Negro Question," 155.

98 Weiss, *Framing a Radical African Atlantic*, 57.

99 "Theses on the Negro Question."

100 "Theses on the Negro Question."

101 Huiswoud and McKay, "Speeches," 17.

102 Huiswoud and McKay, "Speeches," 17.

103 Huiswoud and McKay, "Speeches," 17.

104 He explains that black people are "a source of cheap labor for the American capitalist" and that black workers in the North, who are prevented from joining workers' unions, are brought in to replace white workers on strike. Huiswoud and McKay, "Speeches," 18.

105 Huiswoud and McKay, "Speeches," 18.

106 Huiswoud and McKay, "Speeches," 21.

107 He explains that the greatest difficulty facing the cpusa is "the fact that they have got to emancipate themselves from the ideas they entertained towards the Negroes before they can be able to reach the Negroes with any kind of radical propaganda." Huiswoud and McKay, "Speeches," 22.

108 Adi, "Negro Question," 161.

109 Weiss, *Framing a Radical African Atlantic*, 81.

110 Adi, "Negro Question," 161; Weiss, *Framing a Radical African Atlantic*, 83.

111 Becker, *Mariátegui and Latin American Marxist Theory*, 7.

112 Becker, "Mariátegui," 456.

113 Becker, "Mariátegui," 466; Communist International South American Secretariat, *El movimiento revolucionario latinoamericano*, 263–288.

114 Becker, *Mariátegui and Latin American Marxist Theory*, 22–36.

115 Becker, "Mariátegui," 471.

116 "En la América latina, en general, el problema negro no asume un acentuado aspecto racial" (translation mine). Communist International South American Secretariat, *El movimiento revolucionario latinoamericano*, 284. For the identities of the pseudonyms that are included in this document, see Jefeits and Jefeits, *América Latina en la Internacional Comunista*.

117 "El problema de las razas" (translation mine). Communist International South American Secretariat, *El movimiento revolucionario latinoamericano*, 288.

118 Communist International South American Secretariat, *El movimiento revolucionario latinoamericano*, 293.

119 Communist International South American Secretariat, *El movimiento revolucionario latinoamericano*, 302.

120 Communist International South American Secretariat, *El movimiento revolucionario latinoamericano*, 156.

121 Adi, "Negro Question," 169.

122 Adi, "Negro Question," 164; Kelley, *Hammer and Hoe*; Weiss, *Framing a Radical African Atlantic*, 120.

123 Benson, *Antiracism in Cuba*; de la Fuente, *Nation for All*, 190–193.

124 De la Fuente, *Nation for All*, 192–193. This thesis was short-lived and ultimately denounced by the Cuban Communist Party in 1935. Black Cubans continued to be closely involved in communist organizing in the 1940s. Benson, *Antiracism in Cuba*, 84–86.

125 It would continue to be debated in, for example, the "Johnson-Forest Tendency" of C. L. R. James, Raya Dunayevskaya, and Grace Lee Boggs. Joseph, *Waiting 'til the Midnight Hour*, 6; Kelley, *Hammer and Hoe*; Rodriguez, "Beyond Nation," 119; Singh, *Black Is a Country*, 109–118.

126 Joseph, *Waiting 'til the Midnight Hour*, 6.

127 For example, the Comintern's Sixth Congress created the International Trade Union Committee of Negro Workers (ITUCNW), an organization aimed at bringing black workers into trade unions, which held its first Conference of Negro Workers in 1930 in Hamburg, Germany. Adi, "Negro Question," 65. The ITUCNW published *The Negro Worker*, edited initially by the African American communist James W. Ford, who was quickly replaced by the Trinidadian afrocriollo writer George Padmore. Padmore's *The Negro Worker*, as well as the ITUCNW in general, maintained a central focus on the Caribbean. Adi, "Negro Question," 166.

128 Pujals, "'Soviet Caribbean,'" 261.

129 Pujals, "'Soviet Caribbean,'" 262–263.

130 See, for example, the salvific narrative presented in the article "Salvemos a los obreros negros en Alabama" (Let's Save Black Workers in Alabama) from the September 1931 issue of *Mundo obrero* or in "Salvemos de la muerte a los nueve jovenes negros de Scottsboro" (Let's Save the Nine Young Black Men of Scottsboro from Death) from the April 1932 issue.

131 "Hijos de obreros y campesinos, hijos de nuestra clase" (translation mine). Minor, "Salvemos a los obreros negros en Alabama," 21.

132 Pujals, "'Soviet Caribbean,'" 267.

133 For example, in Cuba, Alejo Carpentier, Nicolás Guillén, and Juan Marinello were strong supporters of the Communist Party. Benson, *Antiracism in Cuba*, 84. The Anti-imperialist League of the Americas (LADLA), which was founded in 1924 in Mexico City and backed by the Comintern, involved several Cuban writers associated with negrismo such as Rubén Martínez Villena and Alejo Carpentier. Kersffeld, "La Liga Antiimperialista de las Américas," 152, 156. For scholarship on communism and the U.S. New Negro Movement, see Holcomb, *Claude McKay*; Maxwell, *New Negro, Old Left*; Robinson, *Black Marxism*; and Stephens, *Black Empire*.

134 The Cuban Communist Party had a substantial black membership and made fighting racial discrimination a central part of its platform. For an in-depth discussion of communist organizing in Cuba in this period, and its relation to the writings of afrocubanismo, see Benson, *Antiracism in Cuba*; Gronbeck-Tedesco, *Cuba, the United States, and Cultures of the Transnational Left*.

135 See, for example, the Caribbean-born activist and journalist Cyril Briggs's organization, African Black Brotherhood, which had several thousand members in the United States and Caribbean. Adi, "Negro Question," 157; Weiss, *Framing a Radical African Atlantic*, 32–33.

136 Luis-Brown, *Waves of Decolonization*, 117.

137 Padmore, *History of the Pan-African Congress*, v.

138 Padmore, *History of the Pan-African Congress*, 9.

139 Other precursors to Bandung include the aforementioned 1927 League against Imperialism in Brussels, which was convened in response to the perceived "paternalistic imperialism" of the 1919 League of Nations, as well as the 1945 Subject Peoples' Conference in London in which Indians, Burmese, Ceylonese, Malayans, Africans, West Indians, and others took part with the intention of discussing the formation of a formal organization for the international anticolonial struggle. Prashad, *Darker Nations*, 21.

140 Branche, *Colonialism and Race in Luso-Hispanic Literature*; Jackson, *Black Literature and Humanism in Latin America*.

141 Hall, "Whites of Their Eyes," 20. Here, I am following the lead of Kutzinski, who uses Hall's term to characterize negrista writings. Kutzinski, *Sugar's Secrets*, 14.

142 Fanon, *Black Skin*, 102.

143 Fanon, *Black Skin*, 112.

144 Fanon, *Black Skin*, 112.

145 Fanon, *Black Skin*, 206.

146 Césaire, *Notebook of a Return to the Native Land*, 35.

147 Césaire, *Notebook of a Return to the Native Land*, 11–12.

148 Birkenmaier, "Jacques Roumain y el Instituto Internacional de Estudios Af-roamericanos"; Roumain, *When the Tom-Tom Beats*, 87.

149 Langston Hughes's "Lament for Dark Peoples" (1924) makes a similar move in drawing equivalences between the oppression of Afro-descendant peoples and that of indigenous peoples in the Americas. Luis-Brown, *Waves of Decolonization*, 164.

150 The translation of Pedroso's poem is from Gronbeck-Tedesco, *Cuba, the United States, and Cultures of the Transnational Left*, 153.

151 DeCosta-Willis, "Social Lyricism and the Caribbean Poet/Rebel," 118.

152 DeCosta-Willis, "Social Lyricism and the Caribbean Poet/Rebel," 118; Pedroso, *Nosotros*, 6. Significantly, much of the foundational critical literature on the trans-national exchange of negrismo, négritude, and the Harlem Renaissance emerged in the 1970s with critical works by the trailblazers of Afro-Hispanism, such as Martha Cobb, Miriam DeCosta-Willis, Richard L. Jackson, Marvin A. Lewis, and Sylvia Wynter, among others. When DeCosta-Willis writes in 1977 about Pedro-so's vision of a transnational and transethnic subaltern collectivity and compares the protest poetry of Arozarena, Guillén, and Pedroso to writers of the 1960s, she does a similar genealogical tracing of the roots of 1960s and '70s black aesthetic and Third World radicalist movements that I am attempting to do here. While she does not frame the "Third World union" that she references within Triconti-nentalism per se, we might view some of the foundational critical works of Afro-Hispanism, such as Martha Cobb's *Harlem, Haiti, and Havana*, as unearthing the roots of transnational political collectivities popularized in the 1960s and 1970s. For discussions of the development of Afro-Hispanism as a field, see DeCosta-Willis, *Blacks in Hispanic Literature*; and Tillis, "Afro-Hispanic Litera-ture in the US."

153 Edwards, *Practice of Diaspora*, 36.

154 Fanon, *Black Skin*, 112.

155 Edwards, *Practice of Diaspora*, 3.

156 Holcomb, *Claude McKay*, 37.

157 Joseph, *Waiting 'til the Midnight Hour*, 7; R. Young, "Postcolonialism," 12.

158 Kahin, *Asian-African Conference*.

159 Tan and Acharya, *Bandung Revisited*.

160 Kahin, *Asian-African Conference*, 31.

161 Guan, "Bandung Conference"; Vitalis, "Midnight Ride of Kwame Nkrumah."

162 Acharya and Tan, "Introduction"; Ampiah, *Political and Moral Imperatives of the Bandung Conference of 1955*, 214–258; C. Lee, "Between a Moment and an Era," 17; Nesadurai, "Bandung and the Political Economy"; OAS, *Report of the Special Com-mittee*, 3.

163 Nesadurai, "Bandung and the Political Economy," 80.

164 Daulatzai, *Black Star*, 45.

165 Daulatzai, *Black Star*, 28, 208.

166 Similarly, the 1958 African and Asian Writers Conference, which was held in Tashkent, Uzbekistan, and attended by Shirley Graham Du Bois and W. E. B. Du Bois, was inspired by the Bandung Conference. Rodriguez, "Beyond Nation," 51.

167 Baldwin, "Princes and Powers," 7.

168 Césaire, "Culture and Colonization," 142.

169 Césaire, "Culture and Colonization," 142.

170 Du Bois, *Souls of Black Folk*, 45.

171 Wright, *Colour Curtain*, 10.

172 Wright, *Colour Curtain*, 9.

173 Wright, *Colour Curtain*, 21, 68, 98–99.

174 Wright, *Colour Curtain*, 59.

175 Wright, *Colour Curtain*, 149–150.

176 Wright, *Colour Curtain*, 186.

177 Roberts and Foulcher, *Indonesian Notebook*, 111; Wright, "Tradition and Industrialization," 725.

178 Baldwin, "Princes and Powers," 59.

179 Gates, "Third World of Theory."

180 Kahin, *Asian-African Conference*, 39.

181 Vitalis, "Midnight Ride of Kwame Nkrumah," 270.

182 Roberts and Foulcher, *Indonesian Notebook*, 70–83.

183 Roberts and Foulcher, *Indonesian Notebook*, 10.

184 Roberts and Foulcher, *Indonesian Notebook*, 187.

185 Roberts and Foulcher, *Indonesian Notebook*, 10.

186 Roberts and Foulcher, *Indonesian Notebook*, 174.

187 Roberts and Foulcher, *Indonesian Notebook*, 174.

188 C. Lee, "Between a Moment and an Era," 26.

189 Carbonell, "Lo que Bandung significó para mí."

190 Carbonell, "Lo que Bandung significó para mí." Also, in the September 5, 1960, issue of the Cuban journal *Lunes de Revolución*, Carbonell published an article on the dangers posed to Congolese independence by European and U.S. imperialist designs alongside both an interview with Richard Wright, in which Wright discusses his experience at Bandung, as well as an excerpt from Wright's "The Ethics of Living Jim Crow" from his *Uncle Tom's Children* (1938). Carbonell, "La intervención belga y las intrigas imperialistas en la República del Congo"; "Charlado con Richard Wright"; Wright, "Una ética para vivir a lo Jim Crow."

191 C. Moore, *Castro*, 72.

192 Carbonell, "Congreso mundial de países sub-desarrollados." Translations of Carbonell's article are mine.

193 "Es hoy menos libre que el conjunto de los Estados afro-asiáticos." Carbonell, "Congreso mundial de países sub-desarrollados."

194 "El bloque de los países Americanos-afro-asiáticos ninguna potencia podrá intentar agredir, directa o indirectamente a cualquiera de los Estados Solidarios de la Comunidad de los países subdesarrollados." Carbonell, "Congreso mundial de países sub-desarrollados."

195 "El próximo Congreso de los Países Sub-desarrollados." Carbonell, "Congreso mundial de países sub-desarrollados." There was indeed an attempt to organize this Conference of Underdeveloped Countries. In January 1960, Raúl Roa traveled to Tunisia, Morocco, Egypt, and Yugoslavia to discuss this proposal. This conference, made up of representatives of nation-states, would have been more similar to the Bandung Conference in that it was intended for postcolonial governments as well as representatives from the United Nations and the Organization of American States (OAS). "La liquidación de la miseria el gran tema de esta época"; "Proyección de la reunión de los países subdesarrollados"; "Vendrán a la conferencia de la Habana países africanos"; "Ningún país se ha negado asistir la conferencia." By the time the Tricontinental Conference took place, Cuba had been dismissed from the OAS, and the conference would take on a much more radical focus.

196 "Frantz Fanon," 23.

197 "Frantz Fanon," 23.

2. In the Belly of the Beast

1 Valerio, "Foto Jacobo Rincón, 28 abril 1965."

2 "Message to the U.S. People," 31.

3 Wright, *Colour Curtain*, 175.

4 U.S. Senate Committee on the Judiciary, "Tricontinental Conference," 11.

5 Seidman, "Venceremos Means We Shall Overcome," 84; U.S. Senate Committee on the Judiciary, "Tricontinental Conference," 9–10. Further indication of these events is also evident from a series of photographs given to the author at the OSPAAAL headquarters in Havana, Cuba.

6 U.S. Senate Committee on the Judiciary, "Tricontinental Conference," 10.

7 OAS, *Report of the Special Committee*, vol. 1, 33.

8 Seidman, "Venceremos Means We Shall Overcome," 84.

9 International Preparatory Committee, "In the Country of the Conference," 9.

10 R. Young, *Postcolonialism*, 192.

11 International Preparatory Committee, "Agenda Draft," 9.

12 I will use the OSPAAAL and the Tricontinental interchangeably.

13 "General Declaration from the Tricontinental," 20.

14 "General Declaration from the Tricontinental," 18–22.

15 R. Young, "Postcolonialism," 17.

16 Vélez, *Latin American Revolutionaries and the Arab World*, 28–31. In January 1960, Raúl Roa traveled to Tunisia, Morocco, Egypt, and Yugoslavia to present the idea for a "Conferencia de Países Subdesarrollados" (Conference of Underdeveloped Countries) to be held in Havana. "La liquidación de la miseria el gran tema de

esta época." Other articles on attempts to plan this conference, which never took place, include "Proyección de la reunión de los países subdesarrollados"; "Vendrán a la conferencia de la Habana países africanos"; "Ningún país se ha negado a asistir la conferencia."

17 "Political Report Presented by the International Preparatory Committee and Approved by the Conference," 113.

18 Prashad, *Darker Nations*, 554.

19 International Preparatory Committee, "Background of Tricontinental Conference to Be Held in Havana," 4. See OAS, *Report of the Special Committee*, vol. 1, for details on the shift from the AAPSO to the OSPAAAL. The AAPSO had its own writers' bureau, the Afro-Asian Writers' Association, which published the literary magazine *Lotus*. Hala Halim argues that *Lotus* "held a promise of Global South comparatism, which it fell short of fulfilling in a sustained way," since it did not extend much beyond the geographical regions of Africa and Asia. Halim, "*Lotus*, the Afro-Asian Nexus, and Global South Comparatism," 566.

20 International Preparatory Committee, "Background of Tricontinental Conference to Be Held in Havana," 4; "Political Report Presented by the International Preparatory Committee and Approved by the Conference," 113.

21 International Preparatory Committee, "Background of Tricontinental Conference to Be Held in Havana," 3–6.

22 Chakrabarty, "Legacies of Bandung," 53–54.

23 U.S. Senate Committee on the Judiciary, "Tricontinental Conference,"14.

24 Guevara, *Message to the Tricontinental*. As the U.S. Senate's staff study on the conference would put it, the "basic goal" of the creation of the OSPAAAL was to create "more Vietnams on a tricontinental scale." U.S. Senate Committee on the Judiciary, "Tricontinental Conference," 21.

25 U.S. Senate Committee on the Judiciary, "Tricontinental Conference," 14.

26 OAS, *Report of the Special Committee*, vol. 1, 4.

27 OAS, *Report of the Special Committee*, vol. 1, 5.

28 OAS, *Report of the Special Committee*, vol. 1, 12–14. The documentation of a secret meeting is provided by the OAS report written by a special committee assigned to study the Tricontinental Conference. It should be noted, however, that the political report of the Tricontinental's International Preparatory Committee does not discuss any conflict that arose around the proposed conference, stating that the preparatory committee was nominated at the sixth meeting of the Council of Afro-Asian Solidarity in Algiers and that the meeting held in Cairo in 1964 was simply a meeting of the nominated members of the preparatory committee. "Political Report Presented by the International Preparatory Committee and Approved by the Conference," 115.

29 OAS, *Report of the Special Committee*, vol. 1, 15–18.

30 OAS, *Report of the Special Committee*, vol. 1, 16.

31 U.S. Senate Committee on the Judiciary, "Tricontinental Conference," 32, quoted in Seidman, "Venceremos Means We Shall Overcome," 87.

32 Gettig, "'Propaganda Boon for Us.'"
33 U.S. Senate Committee on the Judiciary, "Tricontinental Conference," 33–35.
34 Gettig, "'Propaganda Boon for Us.'"
35 U.S. Senate Committee on the Judiciary, "Tricontinental Conference," 37–38; OAS, *Report of the Special Committee*, vol. 1, 40; Seidman, "Venceremos Means We Shall Overcome," 86.
36 OAS, *Report of the Special Committee*, vol. 1, 61; "Reply of the Government of Uruguay to the Soviet Note," 287.
37 OAS, *Report of the Special Committee*, vol. 1, 41–43.
38 OAS, *Report of the Special Committee*, vol. 1, 19; R. Young, *White Mythologies*, 15.
39 Frick, *Tricontinental Solidarity Poster*, 73.
40 Quang Phiet, "Vietnam Struggle," 26.
41 Lenin, *Imperialism*.
42 OAS, "'First Tricontinental Conference,'" 72.
43 By claiming that the Tricontinental privileged the African American freedom movement, I do not mean to imply that other movements do not receive equal attention in Tricontinental materials. Struggles in Vietnam, the Congo, Puerto Rico, and Palestine, for example, are frequently discussed in the early years of *Tricontinental* and *Tricontinental Bulletin*. The African American cause, however, represents a unique case because, as the August–September 1966 issue of *Tricontinental Bulletin* states, "although geographically Afro-Americans do not form part of Latin America, Africa, or Asia, the special circumstances of the oppression which they suffer, to which they are subjected, and the struggle they are waging, merits special consideration and demands that the Tri-Continental organization create the necessary mechanisms so that these brothers in the struggle will, in the future, be able to participate in the great battle being fought by the peoples of the three continents." "Documents of the First Tricontinental Conference," 21. The "special consideration" that the Tricontinental offers to African Americans is, I suggest, integral to its devising of an inclusive, global revolutionary subjectivity that is geographically unbounded and that is foundational to the fluid geography of a contemporary notion like the Global South.
44 Rodriguez, "Beyond Nation," 5.
45 Rodriguez, "Beyond Nation," 63.
46 Rodriguez, "Beyond Nation," 66. See also Gosse, *Where the Boys Are*; Seidman, "Venceremos Means We Shall Overcome"; and Tietchen, "Cubalogues."
47 Joseph, *Waiting 'til the Midnight Hour*, 30; Rodriguez, "Beyond Nation," 166.
48 Other contributors to the issue include Alice Childress, John Henrik Clarke, Harold Cruse, Richard Gibson, LeRoi Jones (aka Amiri Baraka), Julian Mayfield, Lucy Smith, and Sarah E. Wright.
49 "La suerte de los veinte millones de negros americanos—aún cuando todavía algunos no lo entiendan—está muy ligado al éxito de la Revolución Cubana, como lo está el tremendo movimiento de liberación de África y Asia" (translation mine). Gibson, "El negro americano mira hacia Cuba," 6.

50 Plummer, "Castro in Harlem."

51 I am referring to William Lee Brent, Stokely Carmichael, Eldridge Cleaver, John Clytus, Angela Davis, Huey P. Newton, Assata Shakur, and Robert F. Williams.

52 OAS, "'First Tricontinental Conference,'" 68.

53 OSPAAAL, "Tasks and Objectives of the OSPAAAL," 44–45.

54 Estrada and Suárez, *Rebelión Tricontinental*, 2–3.

55 Chanan, *BFI Dossier*, 1.

56 Cushing, "One Struggle"; Santiago Feliú (editor of *Tricontinental*) in conversation with author, July 28, 2014.

57 Of the posters, 25,000 were in Spanish, 15,000 in English, and 10,000 in French. Frick, *Tricontinental Solidarity Poster*, 44.

58 The 50,000 posters using offset lithography were printed as well as 500 screen-printed editions. Frick, *Tricontinental Solidarity Poster*, 47, 81.

59 Estrada and Suárez, *Rebelión Tricontinental*, 3.

60 For example, in 1971, the French political scientist John Gerassi published a volume of writers he associated with the Tricontinental project. In response to Gerassi's invitation to contribute, the Chinese American activist Grace Lee Boggs wrote to OSPAAAL requesting all back issues of *Tricontinental* and offering to send her own articles and those by her husband, James Boggs. Gerassi, *Coming of the New International*; Rodriguez, "Beyond Nation," 124–125.

61 Hess, "Santiago Alvarez," 388; C. Young, *Soul Power*, 118–119.

62 Cushing, "Cuban Poster Art and the Spirit of Revolution"; O. Martínez, "Diseñadores," 64; Seidman, "Venceremos Means We Shall Overcome," 121, 146, 152–154, 188.

63 Cushing, "Red All Over."

64 Cushing, "Directory of San Francisco Bay Area Political Poster Workshops"; Cushing, "One Struggle"; Cushing, "Red All Over"; Dalzell, "Jane Norling."

65 Cushing, "One Struggle."

66 Cushing, "Cuban Poster Art and the Spirit of Revolution." Connections to Fairey's "Hope" poster will be discussed in depth in chapter 5.

67 Morales Campos, "Introducción," 55.

68 Chanan, *Cuban Cinema*, 35.

69 Chanan, *Cuban Cinema*, 184.

70 Charity, "Prolific Cuban Filmmaker's Inventive Newsreel Agitprop"; Hess, "Santiago Alvarez"; Rist, "Agit-prop Cuban Style"; Seidman, "Venceremos Means We Shall Overcome."

71 With the term "civil rights movement," I refer to the sector of the larger Black Liberation Movement (BLM) in the United States that practiced nonviolence and that sought "civil rights," or further incorporation into civil society. Elsewhere, I reference Black Power, by which I mean the heterogeneous section of the BLM that took a more radical approach through such ideologies as black nationalism and communism. While I recognize that the boundaries between them are often blurry and that many activists participated concurrently in organizations on both

sides, my differentiation draws from Cha-Jua and Lang's seminal article, "'Long Movement' as Vampire," which recognizes Black Power and civil rights as having differing ideologies and objectives.

72 Hess, "Santiago Alvarez," 388.

73 Chanan, BFI Dossier, 6.

74 Rascaroli, Personal Camera.

75 Hess, "Santiago Alvarez," 393.

76 Mraz, "Santiago Alvarez," 133.

77 Hess, "Santiago Alvarez," 387. The lyrics by Broadway duo Betty Comden and Adolph Green were set by the composer Jule Styne to the tune of the Hebrew folk song "Hava Nagila," thus drawing an implicit comparison between the racism suffered by Jews with that of African Americans. Buckley, Hornes, 248.

78 Later, when the SNCC came under the leadership of Stokely Carmichael, it would diverge from the reformist philosophy espoused by King.

79 For a study of King's speech, see Vail, "'Integrative' Rhetoric of Martin Luther King Jr.'s 'I Have a Dream' Speech."

80 Lena Horne, 1963 vocal performance, on 20th Century Fox Records, of "Now!," words and music by Betty Comden, Adolph Green, and Jule Styne, song © Stratford Music Corporation.

81 Castillo and Hadad, "With Santiago Álvarez."

82 Chanan, BFI Dossier, 10.

83 Álvarez's films reflect the influence of the Soviet filmmaker Sergei Eisenstein, who theorized montage as a collision of shots that, like the explosions in an internal combustion engine, drive the film and its thesis along. Mraz, "Santiago Alvarez," 133.

84 Hess, "Santiago Alvarez," 392.

85 Hodes, "Wartime Dialogues on Illicit Sex," 241.

86 Gavin, Stormy Weather, 332.

87 Castillo and Hadad, "With Santiago Álvarez."

88 Seidman, "Venceremos Means We Shall Overcome," 64.

89 Rodriguez, "Beyond Nation," 174; Tyson, Radio Free Dixie; C. Young, Soul Power, 29.

90 Seidman, "Venceremos Means We Shall Overcome," 71.

91 C. Young, Soul Power, 27.

92 "Predicar una ideología de absoluta resistencia pasiva" and "en vez de defenderse con la fuerza de la agresión de los racistas blancos" (translations mine). Gibson and Williams, "La constante lucha de los negros por su libertad," 8.

93 Hess, "Santiago Álvarez," 388–389.

94 This phrase could also be translated as "blacks and North American policeman," which would support my assertion that Álvarez seeks to dissociate the African American community from a U.S. identity.

95 Chanan, Cuban Cinema, 219.

96 "Uncle Thomas" alludes to the protagonist of Harriet Beecher Stowe's Uncle Tom's Cabin (1852).

97 Mraz, "Santiago Alvarez," 137.

98 "General Declaration from the Tricontinental," 18.

99 International Preparatory Committee, "Agenda Draft," 8.

100 Gaiter, "What Revolution Looks Like," 100; Seidman, "Venceremos Means We Shall Overcome," 153.

101 *The Black Panther* (May 18, 1968): 10. The Douglas graphic appears in *The Black Panther* directly before an article on Robert F. Williams.

102 Cushing, "One Struggle"; Gaiter, "What Revolution Looks Like," 101. Another of Douglas's mother-child drawings appears on the back cover of *Tricontinental* 10 (January–February 1969) in which a black woman sits on the edge of the bed and smiles lovingly at her toddler standing below her who is holding a gun over his right shoulder. Seidman, "Venceremos Means We Shall Overcome," 151–152.

103 Seidman, "Venceremos Means We Shall Overcome," 146–147.

104 "Black Panthers: The Afro-Americans' Challenge"; R. Brown, "Letter from Prison to My Black Brothers and Sisters," 13–14; Carmichael, "Third World—Our World," 15–22; Davis, "Angela Davis: Estados Unidos," 139–149; Davis, "De Angela Davis a los presos politicos mexicanos," 2; Featherstone, letter, 30; Forman, "United States 1967," 22–51; Hutchings, "Che Guevara and Afro-Americans," 129; Malcolm X, "U.S.A.: The Hour of Mau Mau," 23–30; Myerson, "Angela Davis habla desde la cárcel," 17–23; Newton, "Culture and Liberation," 101–104.

105 Seidman, "Tricontinental Routes of Solidarity," 3.

106 Joseph, *Waiting 'til the Midnight Hour*, 193; Seidman, "Venceremos Means We Shall Overcome," 103.

107 Joseph, *Waiting 'til the Midnight Hour*, 193; Seidman, "Tricontinental Routes of Solidarity," 6; *Tricontinental Bulletin* 1:8.

108 Carmichael, "Black Power and the Third World," 3.

109 Carmichael, "Black Power and the Third World," 3. As further evidence of the dialogic relationship between Carmichael and Tricontinental materials, footage from one of Carmichael's speeches appears in another of Santiago Álvarez's most famous newsreels, *LBJ* (1968).

110 Seidman, "Venceremos Means We Shall Overcome," 89–90. William Worthy would write about this resolution in an April 1966 article of the countercultural newsletter, *The Realist*. Rodriguez, "Beyond Nation," 140.

111 "Documents of the First Tricontinental Conference," 21.

112 Wright, *Colour Curtain*, 175.

113 Daulatzai, *Black Star*, 27; Rodriguez, "Beyond Nation," 189.

114 Daulatzai, *Black Star*, 27.

115 Rodriguez, "Beyond Nation," 190.

116 Daulatzai, *Black Star*, 26.

117 Seidman, "Venceremos Means We Shall Overcome," 90–91.

118 "Tragedy of the Blacks in Newark," 10.

119 While the authors of interviews and statements sent in by delegations are mentioned, many of the articles in *Tricontinental Bulletin* are not attributed to specific

authors. Rather, the writers are loosely defined as the executive secretariat of the OSPAAAL, which was made up of representatives from "Vietnam, Korea, Syria, Pakistan, Portuguese Guinea, Congo, United Arab Republic, Republic of Guinea, the Dominican Republic, Chile, Venezuela, Puerto Rico and Cuba," with the Cuban politician Osmany Cienfuegos acting as general secretary. *Tricontinental Bulletin* 2 (May 1966): 45; *Tricontinental Bulletin* 3 (June 1966): 3. The bulletin was initially edited by Miguel Brugueras, head of the OSPAAAL's Department of Information, but much of the information on events occurring within individual liberation struggles was provided by the delegations themselves. Estrada and Suárez, *Rebelión Tricontinental*, 1. Carlos Moore, one of many who has faced persecution in Cuba for speaking out against racism, points to Cienfuegos, the OSPAAAL general secretary, as exemplary of the racist attitudes held by some of the Cuban Revolution's prominent leaders. C. Moore, *Pichón*, 182. I mention this as one example of the disconnect between the antiracist discourse of Tricontinentalism, in which Castro's government was actively engaged, and discriminatory racial practices and rhetoric in Cuba's domestic sphere. For more on this disconnect, see chapter 4.

120 "Black Power," 5–6.

121 Carmichael, "Black Power and the Third World," 1.

122 "USA," 15.

123 "Message to the U.S. People," 31.

124 Hardt and Negri, *Empire*, xii, emphasis original.

125 "Black Power," 7.

126 Estrada and Suárez, *Revolución Tricontinental*, 2.

127 R. Young, *Postcolonialism*, 212.

128 Hardt and Negri, *Empire*, 393.

129 "Yankee Imperialism and Its Aggression," 30.

130 "United States," 32.

131 "USA," 15.

132 "USA," 15–16.

133 Rodriguez describes Williams's newsletter as "connecting local racial and economic struggles with the decolonization and nationalist efforts of the tricontinental." Rodriguez, "Beyond Nation," 162. The quotation here is from Williams, *The Crusader* (October 1964): 4.

134 Quijano, "Coloniality of Power, Eurocentrism, and Social Classification," 183.

135 Quijano, "Coloniality of Power, Eurocentrism, and Social Classification," 182.

136 Rodriguez, "'De la esclavitud yanqui a la libertad cubana,'" 75.

137 Peniel Joseph notes that in 1959, years before his shift away from black separatism, Malcolm X "ignored Castro's alabaster complexion, claiming the white skin Cubano as his own." Joseph, *Waiting 'til the Midnight Hour*, 36. Similarly, Gronbeck-Tedesco has noted that the Tricontinental inspired a "Left humanism" among radical political movements whose "associations stemmed from a racial taxonomy that made 'blackness' or 'brownness' more than a phenotypic signifier

but a racial semiotics that symbolized oppositional politics" and points out that Stokely Carmichael called Fidel Castro "one of the blackest men in America." *Cuba, the United States, and Cultures of the Transnational Left*, 231. I do not read this "coloring" of Castro as a manifestation of revolutionary Cuba's domestic racial discourse, which, as I discuss in chapter 4, has largely continued a project of national unification that celebrates nonwhite subjects while veiling the reality of racial inequalities. I emphasize rather the equivalence between the Tricontinental's frequent references to "colored peoples" and Williams's usage of the term. Color, for Williams and for the Tricontinental, is not an empty symbol of multiculturalism or of national unity that is used to deny the presence of racial inequality, but rather a political signifier that refers to a subjugated and resistant subjectivity.

138   On the other hand, it should be noted that domestically Cuba claimed to have eliminated racial inequality on the island through socialist reforms. Through internationalist forums like the Tricontinental, in which Cuba presented itself to the world as militantly antiracist, the predominantly white Cuban government externalized racial injustice to the imperialist North, denying its continued presence on the island. For a discussion of the distance between Cuba's domestic and internationalist racial discourses, see Sawyer, *Racial Politics in Post-Revolutionary Cuba*.

139   Spivak, *In Other Worlds*, 205.

140   Hess, "Santiago Alvarez," 398.

141   This is a revised quote taken from Malcolm X's memorandum, "Appeal to African Heads of State," which he submitted to the delegates of the Organization of African Unity conference, held in Cairo in July 1964. For the full text of this speech, see Malcolm X and Breitman, *Malcolm X Speaks*, 72–87. "El problema afro-norteamericano no es un problema de los negros ni un problema de los norteamericanos sino un problema de la humanidad." Translations from Álvarez's *El movimiento Panteras Negras* are mine. This quote was slightly revised from Malcolm X's memorandum, which stated that "the OAAU has in mind to internationalize the black man's problem, and make it not a Negro problem or an American problem, but a world problem, a problem for humanity." Malcolm X and Breitman, *Malcolm X Speaks*, 81.

142   Détournement (hijacking) is a technique generally associated with the cultural movement of European Marxist and avant-garde intellectuals, led by Guy Debord, called the Situationist International (1957–1972) in which an original work is appropriated to create a meaning antithetical to that original work.

143   "El mace es un novedoso producto químico para lanzar sobre los ojos de los negros amotinados. Nunca falla. Negro tocado, negro segado. Solicite una muestra gratis. Use mace y ríase de lo que pase."

144   "Económicos y eficaces contra obreros, contra estudiantes, contra negros, contra blancos, y contra todos los que perturben la paz y el orden."

145   "Año del guerrillero heróico."

146 The ICAIC produced a separate poster, with information on the director and soundtrack, to advertise Álvarez's film when it was released in 1965 in which an image of a young girl depicted in the film appears with the word "Now!" written across her face.

3. "Colored and Oppressed" in Amerikkka

1 The Lords had also submitted a letter to the church board requesting the use of the facilities but were denied. Wilson, *First Spanish United Methodist Church*, 10–11.

2 Wilson, *First Spanish United Methodist Church*, 12. For a comprehensive account of the events leading up to the church takeover, see J. Fernández, "Radicals in the Late 1960s," 118–124.

3 Guzmán, "*La Vida Pura*," 160.

4 Guzmán, "*La Vida Pura*."

5 For more information on Newsreel, see chapter 3 from Cynthia Young's *Soul Power*.

6 Dalleo and Machado Sáez, *Latino/a Canon*, 17.

7 Hess, "Santiago Alvarez," 388; C. Young, *Soul Power*, 119.

8 See, for example, M. Brown, *Gang Nation*; Dalleo and Machado Sáez, *Latino/a Canon*; J. Fernández, "Radicals in the Late 1960s"; McGill, *Constructing Black Selves*; Nöel, *In Visible Movement*; Torres, "Introduction." The most sustained discussion of the Young Lords' ideology to date can be found in Johanna Fernández's dissertation, "Radicals in the Late 1960s: A History of the Young Lords Party, 1969–1974." She describes the Lords as a "socialist organization" with a "political world-view borrowed from variants of Marxism and Third World revolutionary nationalist theories" (6). She discusses Marxist and Maoist influences on the Young Lords, as well as the inspiration of the Cuban Revolution, and she even mentions that the Tricontinental Conference gave Cuba the opportunity to "influence radicals in the United States" (140).

9 Berlant, *Cruel Optimism*, 260.

10 I take this term from Laura Pulido's *Black, Brown, Yellow, and Left* and Cynthia A. Young's *Soul Power*.

11 Abramson and Young Lords Party, *Palante*, 10.

12 J. Fernández, "Denise Oliver and the Young Lords Party," 280.

13 I have provided here a very brief version of the origins of the Young Lords. In fact, the first Young Lords members to meet Cha-Cha Jiménez were Denise Oliver and Iris Morales. The Lords' origins in New York should be located a few years earlier when, in 1964 in the Lower East Side or "Loisaida," former gang members Carlos "Chino" García, Armando Pérez, Ángelo González, and Ángelo "Papo" Giordani started a community dance hall—the "Fabulous Latin House"—in the basement of a church on Grant Avenue. The success of this endeavor encouraged these young men, hoping to find a productive outlet for their leadership skills, to

start thinking of possible ways to organize in their community. Bell, *East Harlem Remembered*, 166; Vaughan, "Real Great Society," 78–79. Despite the passage of the Economic Opportunity Act of 1964, which was part of Lyndon B. Johnson's War on Poverty and which called for the institution of community action programs that would include representatives of poor communities in administering antipoverty funds, the control of these funds had been largely usurped by white city officials. See S. Lee, *Building a Latino Civil Rights Movement*, 135–136. Johnson's "Great Society," according to these former gang members, did not reach the Lower East Side, and in response, they decided to start what they called the "Real Great Society" that would carry out the president's initiative but from a perspective of grassroots organizing. The Real Great Society (RGS) partnered with Fred Good, an artist and graduate from Georgetown University, to apply for several grants, eventually receiving funding from the Vincent Astor Foundation to start work on community programs. Bell, *East Harlem Remembered*, 166–167; Vaughan, "Real Great Society," 79. Within three years, the RGS split into three entities that included the Loisaida branch; the East Harlem branch, which started an education center for high school dropouts; and a project called University of the Streets, which aimed to create a curriculum provided for and shaped by individuals from the streets that would help these students build on their strengths and interests. Aponte-Parés, "Lessons from *El Barrio*," 405. As part of Mayor John Lindsay's Urban Task Force, college students of color were given stipends to work for the summer in poor communities in the city, bringing college students originally from El Barrio and Loisaida back into their communities, only this time as community organizers and educators. Meléndez, *We Took the Streets*, 73. These task forces included several of the founding members of the New York Young Lords, including Denise Oliver and Miguel "Mickey" Meléndez, who received much of their initial education in political activism and community organizing through working with the RGS and the University of the Streets. Fernández, "Denise Oliver and the Young Lords Party," 280; Meléndez, *We Took the Streets*, 73–74. In 1968, the RGS sent representatives to a youth conference in Denver, Colorado, organized by the Crusade for Justice. There, the future Young Lords Denise Oliver and Iris Morales met the Chicago Young Lords leader Cha-Cha Jiménez for the first time. S. Lee, *Building a Latino Civil Rights Movement*, 203. The RGS approach to community education attracted the interest of the planning committee for the newly founded State University of New York College at Old Westbury, which aimed to respond to student demand for a less Eurocentric focus in academic education, a demand that was being demonstrated in student takeovers at colleges and universities occurring across the country. Representatives from the planning committee came to the East Harlem branch of the RGS in order to recruit. Bell, *East Harlem Remembered*, 171; Meléndez, *We Took the Streets*, 75. Subsequently, several of these newly recruited undergraduates at SUNY, Old Westbury, who were interested in the history of Puerto Rican national liberation movements, formed the Albizu Campos Society (SAC). The SAC then joined with a group of politically progressive high school photography students from East Harlem led by Hiram Maristany, who would eventually become the New York Young Lords' official photographer, and a group of college and high school students from the Lower East Side, which included another of the Lords' founding members, Juan "Fi" Ortiz. Bell, *East Harlem Remembered*, 171; Guzmán, "*La Vida Pura*," 156. In this sense, when Guzmán read the article in *The Black Panther* about the Rainbow Coalition, the networks of young organizers that would form the New York Young Lords were already largely in place. For more on the history of the Young Lords, Johanna Fernández's "Radicals in the Late 1960s" is the authority on the subject.

14 Guzmán, "*La Vida Pura*," 157.

15 Bell, *East Harlem Remembered*, 173.

16 J. Fernández, "Radicals in the Late 1960s," 11; I. Morales, "¡PALANTE, SIEMPRE PALANTE!" 215.

17 I. Morales, "Power to the People," 5.

18 Abramson and the Young Lords Party, *Palante*, 12–13. The Garbage Offensive sought a solution to the trash that piled up in the streets that the city's sanitation department often failed to pick up for weeks at a time. On Sundays, the Lords and other community members began sweeping the streets. Their request for additional larger brooms from the Department of Sanitation was denied. In response, the Lords jumped the counter at the Department of Sanitation and appropriated ten brooms, which they used to form heaping piles of garbage in the street. When the sanitation trucks did a poor job picking up these piles of garbage, the following Sunday, the Lords took the trash and piled it in the middle of Second and Third Avenues and around bus stops, blocking any through traffic. They then lit the trash on fire, a decision that would call citywide attention to the problem, resulting in a visit to the Lords headquarters by the assistant to Mayor Lindsay, Arnaldo Segarra, and eventually in a change in the sanitation department's treatment of these areas. Meléndez, *We Took the Streets*, 102–109. Johanna Fernández has pointed out that the name of this highly successful endeavor contains a reference to the Tet Offensive in Vietnam and that "the juxtaposition of an issue as unremarkable as sanitation with the era's most dramatic military operation was a telltale sign of the group's ability to link international crises with local concerns." "Radicals in the Late 1960s," 88. Following this first victory, which attracted more members to the organization and legitimized the Young Lords within the community, the Lords began offering free-breakfast programs and clothing drives similar to those offered by the Black Panther Party, and in seeking a space to house these programs, they eventually occupied the First Spanish Methodist Church, notably with the support of some in the congregation. Meléndez, *We Took the Streets*, 123. In founding the People's Church, the New York Young Lords were following in the footsteps of the Chicago Young Lords, who in July 1969 occupied the Armitage People United Church, where they established their headquarters. Wilson, *First Spanish United Methodist Church*, 36–37. When the occupation ended on January 8, 1970, 106 Young Lords and supporters were arrested. Before news cameras,

they filed out of the church into police wagons, raising their fists above their heads and singing the 1968 musical homage to the Puerto Rican flag, "Qué bonita bandera" (What a beautiful flag). I. Morales, "¡PALANTE, SIEMPRE PALANTE!" 214. In October 1970, the Lords again occupied the First Spanish Methodist Church after a member, Julio Roldán, was found hanging in a prison cell in the Manhattan House of Detention shortly after his arrest over a minor incident. While the official report claimed that he had committed suicide, the Lords maintained that it was murder and marched from the funeral home to the church, placing his coffin on the altar.

19 Luciano, "Take-Over of T.B. Testing Truck," 13; Meléndez, *We Took the Streets*, 172–178.

20 I. Morales, "¡PALANTE, SIEMPRE, PALANTE!" 217.

21 Pulido, *Black, Brown, Yellow, and Left*, 91–92.

22 Pulido, *Black, Brown, Yellow, and Left*, 5; C. Young, *Soul Power*.

23 Mariscal, *Brown-Eyed Children of the Sun*, 202.

24 Mariscal, *Brown-Eyed Children of the Sun*, 71.

25 Mariscal, *Brown-Eyed Children of the Sun*, 112.

26 Martínez, "Las chicanas"; Martínez, "No son hijos de Houston."

27 Mariscal, *Brown-Eyed Children of the Sun*, 71.

28 Pulido, *Black, Brown, Yellow, and Left*, 170.

29 Shreve, *Red Power Rising*, 113.

30 Pulido, *Black, Brown, Yellow, and Left*, 116.

31 Sánchez González, *Boricua Literature*, 103. For these and other data on Puerto Rican migration, see Picó, *Historia general de Puerto Rico*.

32 The Lords viewed the conditions in El Barrio as part of a much longer history of colonial exploitation of the island of Puerto Rico and forced migration to the mainland United States, and they positioned their activism as the next phase of an anticolonial struggle at the core of Puerto Rican history. Through articles in *Palante,* including a history of Puerto Rico published in serial form, the Lords presented their readers with a version of Puerto Rican history filtered through its legacy of political resistance. This resistant narrative of Puerto Rican history sometimes required the articles' authors to make historical jumps, comparing the indigenous Taíno struggle against Spanish invaders in the 1500s to slave revolts on sugar plantations to the Grito de Lares, the first major armed revolt against Spain led by Emeterio Betances on September 23, 1868, to the nationalist struggle against the United States. Guzmán, "History of Boriken"; Guzmán, "Lucha por tu patria." In these articles, the Lords consistently remind readers how the U.S. occupation of the island on July 25, 1898, was used to impose a military regime and economic policies favorable to the U.S. economy, beginning a long history of forced migration stateside. While there were many exiled Puerto Rican and Cuban nationalists in the United States in the years leading up to the Spanish-American War, the population of Puerto Ricans in the mainland United States rapidly increased after the Foraker Law of 1900, which made Puerto Rico a U.S. territory, and the Jones Act of 1917, which named Puerto Ricans as U.S. citizens. Flores, *Divided Borders*, 144;

Luis, *Dance between Two Cultures*, xii. The Jones Act, Guzmán reminds *Palante's* readers, was passed "conveniently, four months before World War I so we could be drafted." Guzmán, "Lucha por tu patria," 3. The subsequent Great Depression would devastate the island's economy, causing an additional increase in migration as Puerto Ricans left the island in search of better opportunities on the mainland.

33 Guzmán, "Editorial," 2. The Grito de Lares refers to the first major armed revolt against Spain led by Emeterio Betances on September 23, 1868. The Ponce Massacre occurred when, during a peaceful demonstration organized on Palm Sunday, March 21, 1927, to protest the imprisonment of Albizu Campos in a federal penitentiary in Atlanta, Georgia, on sedition charges, nineteen Puerto Rican nationalists were shot and killed by police and another two hundred wounded. The Jayuya Uprising followed the passage of Public Law 600 under President Harry Truman in July 1950, which authorized Puerto Rico to draft its own constitution, thus leading to its commonwealth status. The Nationalist Party organized several revolts and held the town of Jayuya for three days, culminating on November 1, 1950, in the attempted assassination of President Truman by two Nationalists, Oscar Gollazo and Griselio Torresola, who were living in New York where the Nationalist Party had been organizing since the 1930s. Torres, "Introduction," 4. Throughout *Palante*, the Lords claim this history of nationalist resistance as their inheritance, arguing that "we are a generation of Puerto Ricans that has grown out of all this." To this history of exploitation and resistance, they also add "the shoot-out in 1954 in the house of representatives with the patriots Lolita Lebrón, Rafael Miranda, Irving Rodriguez, and Andrea Cordero," referring to the attack on U.S. Congress by four Nationalists on March 1, 1954. They conclude this lineage by claiming to have grown "out of MPI, CAL, and MIRA," or Pro-independence Movement (MPI), Armed Commandos of Liberation (CAL), and Independent Armed Revolutionary Movement (MIRA), several pro-independence organizations that formed on the island in the 1960s and that attracted a younger generation. Guzmán, "Lucha por tu patria," 3.

34 Guzmán, "Editorial," 2; G. González, "Porque Ponce," 17.

35 This photograph appears in *Caribe* 7.4, on page 29.

36 This poster also appears on the wall of a Young Lords benefit concert in a photograph taken in February 1970. Abramson and Young Lords Party, *Palante*, 128.

37 Pulido, *Black, Brown, Yellow, and Left*, 91.

38 See Stam and Shohat, *Race in Translation*, for a discussion of how "colonialism and slavery completely transformed racial, national, and cultural identities" into color categories (2).

39 Duarte, "U.S. Out of Quisquella," 18.

40 J. González, "Armed Struggle," 9.

41 "USA," 7–16.

42 Wald, "Chicanos."

43 The OSPAAAL's interest in the Young Lords stemmed not only from a focus on anticapitalist and antiracist organizations within the mainland United States

but also from a commitment to solidarity with the Puerto Rican independence struggle. In its first twelve years, the OSPAAAL designed and printed fourteen different posters calling for international solidarity with those fighting for Puerto Rican independence. Frick, *Tricontinental Solidarity Poster*. Puerto Rico's Pro-independence Movement (MPI) was represented by Narciso Rabell Martínez at the first Tricontinental Conference, and MPI members Rabell, Carlos Padilla, and Juan Mari-Brás served on the OSPAAAL's twelve-country executive secretariat. See *Tricontinental Bulletin* 4 (July 1966): 27; *Tricontinental Bulletin* 27 (June 1968): 46; *Tricontinental Bulletin* 92 (1974): 48. Padilla and Mari-Brás, the founder of MPI, which later changed its name to the Puerto Rican Socialist Party, published several articles and interviews throughout the 1970s in *Tricontinental*. Mari-Brás, "La vía decisiva"; *Tricontinental* 7 (July–August 1968): 97; Padilla, "Solidarity in the Desert." In 1968, the OSPAAAL published a book called *Puerto Rico: Analysis of a Plebiscite*, which examines the 1967 plebiscite in which Puerto Rican voters overwhelmingly affirmed the continuation of the island's commonwealth status. Additionally, the May–June 1974 and May–June 1975 issues of *Tricontinental* are dedicated to a study of Puerto Rico.

44 M. Brown, *Gang Nation*, 32.

45 J. Fernández, "Radicals in the Late 1960s," 140. Citations are from Morales, "Power to the People," 4.

46 Luciano, "Free Palestine," 20.

47 Young Lords Party Central Committee, "Young Lords Party Position," 2.

48 Young Lords Party, "Beat Is Gettin' Stronger," 2.

49 "13 Point Program," 20–21.

50 The framing of communities of color within the United States as internal colonies expanded upon the earlier "Black Belt thesis" of the 1930s Communist International, which framed African Americans in the U.S. South as an oppressed nation within the United States. This was also called the "Nation within a Nation" thesis. For a discussion of internal-colony discourse within the U.S. Third World Left more broadly, see J. Fernández, "Radicals in the Late 1960s," 259; C. Young, *Soul Power*, 156–163.

51 C. Young, *Soul Power*, 130.

52 *Palante* 2.7 (1970): 24.

53 Cosme, "Aguadilla."

54 Young Lords Party Central Committee, "Young Lords Party Position," 2. Similarly, Minister of Defense Juan González writes, "The greatest ally of Puerto Rican liberation, is the Black Nation inside the united states, the stronger the Black liberation struggle, the stronger our struggle becomes." J. González, "Armed Struggle," 8.

55 Abramson and Young Lords Party, *Palante*, 74.

56 "13 Point Program," 20.

57 I. Morales, "Racismo Borinqueño," 7.

58 I. Morales, "Racismo Borinqueño," 7.

59 I. Morales, "Racismo Borinqueño," 7.

60 Torres, "Introduction," 42.

61 Abramson and Young Lords Party, *Palante*, 68.

62 J. Márquez, *Black-Brown Solidarity*, 12.

63 J. Márquez, *Black-Brown Solidarity*, 12.

64 "13 Point Program," 21.

65 "13 Point Program," 21.

66 Benítez, "Cambodia '70," 14.

67 "Nuestros hermanos y hermanas afro-americanos, latinos, asiáticos, blancos oprimidos." G. González, "Porque Ponce," 17. While, throughout this chapter, I have used the English versions of the articles, which were all published in English and Spanish in *Palante*, the English version of this particular article has problems in the layout such that the language of the article is nonsensical. Thus, the translation of the Spanish here is mine.

68 Young Lords Party Central Committee, "Young Lords Party Position," 2.

69 Young Lords Party Central Committee, "Young Lords Party Position," 2.

70 Guzmán, "Writing a Constitution for the People," 16.

71 Guzmán, "Writing a Constitution for the People," 16.

72 Clough and Halley, *Affective Turn*, 1–2; Gregg and Seigworth, *Affect Theory Reader*, 1.

73 The "affective turn" was coined by Patricia Clough in her eponymous book. In *The Affect Theory Reader*, Gregg and Seigworth delineate eight lines of inquiry within affect theory. Here, I am most interested in the non-Cartesian traditions in political philosophy as well as what they describe as "politically engaged work— perhaps most often undertaken by feminists, queer theorists, disability activists, and subaltern peoples living under the thumb of a normativizing power—that attends to the hard and fast materialities, as well as the fleeting and flowing ephemera, of the daily and the workaday, of everyday and every-night life, and of 'experience' (understood in ways far more collective and 'external' rather than individual and interior), where persistent, repetitious practices of power can simultaneously provide a body (or better, collectivized bodies) with predicaments and potentials for realizing a world that subsists within and exceeds the horizons and boundaries of the norm." Gregg and Seigworth, *Affect Theory Reader*, 7.

74 Beasley-Murray, *Posthegemony*, 228.

75 Beasley-Murray, *Posthegemony*, 234, emphasis original. See also Dierdra Reber's in-depth discussion of what she calls the "feeling soma" in *Coming to Our Senses*.

76 Hemmings, "Affective Solidarity."

77 Hooker, *Race and the Politics of Solidarity*, 30.

78 C. Lee, "Between a Moment and an Era," 26.

79 Ideology could be said to rely, as Slavoj Žižek has argued, on that "pre-ideological kernel of enjoyment" that is at the same time "the very surplus which is the last support of ideology." Any ideology "implies, manipulates, produces a pre-ideological enjoyment structured in fantasy." Žižek, *Sublime Object of Ideology*, 124–125.

80 Berlant, *Cruel Optimism*, 260.

81 It should be noted that women had major leadership roles in several Red Power organizations, like the National Indian Youth Council and the American Indian Movement. See Josephy, Nagel, and Johnson, *Red Power*; Shreve, *Red Power Rising*.

82 J. Fernández, "Denise Oliver and the Young Lords Party," 287.

83 I. Morales, "¡PALANTE, SIEMPRE PALANTE!" 218.

84 I. Morales, "¡PALANTE, SIEMPRE PALANTE!" 218.

85 I. Morales, "¡PALANTE, SIEMPRE PALANTE!" 219.

86 "Young Lords Party Position Paper on Women," 25.

87 "Young Lords Party Position Paper on Women," 28.

88 "Young Lords Party Position Paper on Women," 26, 31.

89 Abramson and the Young Lords Party, *Palante*, 41.

90 Abramson and the Young Lords Party, *Palante*, 46. For an in-depth analysis of the gender and sexual politics of the Lords, see Enck-Wanzer, "Gender Politics."

91 Guzmán, "Writing a Constitution for the People," 16.

92 Guzmán, "*La Vida Pura*," 162.

93 For an examination of Rivera and her political organizing, see Gan, "'Still at the Back of the Bus.'"

94 Feinberg, interview with Sylvia Rivera.

95 J. Fernández, "Denise Oliver and the Young Lords Party," 277.

96 *Palante* 2.2 (1970): 17.

97 J. Fernández, "Denise Oliver and the Young Lords Party," 285.

98 "Young Lords," 18.

99 "Resolución de Solidaridad del II Congreso de la Federación de Mujeres Cubanas."

100 "Liberación nacional."

101 Davis first visited Cuba in the summer of 1969 with a delegation from the Communist Party. She then returned in 1972 on an international speaking tour. For detailed information on Davis's visits to Cuba and her celebrity there, see chapter 3 of Seidman, "Venceremos Means We Shall Overcome."

102 Myerson, "Angela Davis habla desde la cárcel," 20.

103 Fornet, "El quinquenio gris."

104 "At the Root," 129.

105 Fornet, "El quinquenio gris."

106 "Contents," 1.

107 The reasoning presented here for the loss of distributors is my own conjecture, based on the evidence available. However, this reasoning was confirmed as highly likely in an interview by the author with the current *Tricontinental* editor, Santiago Feliú, on July 28, 2014. In the case of the Feltrinelli Bookshop, the radical publisher Giangiacomo Feltrinelli went underground in 1970, which could have caused the cessation of the distribution of *Tricontinental* in 1971. However, we may also consider that Feltrinelli, on a visit to Cuba in 1965, made a note of "'Questions to Ask Fidel': His first question: 'Why is he so against homosexual intellectuals?'" See R. Young, *White Mythologies*, 26.

108 Additionally, the Young Lords leader Iris Morales visited Cuba in 1969 for the Revolution's tenth anniversary. I. Morales, "¡PALANTE, SIEMPRE PALANTE!" 212.

109 Duarte, "U.S. Out of Quisquella," 19.

110 Torres and Velásquez, *Puerto Rican Movement*.

111 The term "Nuyorican" refers to people of Puerto Rican descent who were born and raised in New York. "Neorriqueño," which combines "neoyorquino" (New Yorker) and "puertorriqueño" (Puerto Rican) and which was originally used disparagingly by island Puerto Ricans to describe New York Puerto Ricans, is often seen as the etymological origin for "Nuyorican." Jaime Carrero was the first to use the term in a literary text in his *Jet neorriqueño: Neo-Rican Jetliner* (1964), which parodies the speech patterns of New York Puerto Ricans. While the terms "Nuyorican," "Neo-Rican," "neorriqueño," "neoricano," "Neorican," and "New Yorrican" circulated in the late 1960s and early 1970s, the Nuyorican writers tended to use "Puerto Rican" in their writings. It was not until Algarín and Piñero's founding of the Nuyorican Poets Café in 1973 and the publication of their foundational *Nuyorican Poetry* that "Nuyorican" became more commonly used. Nöel, *In Visible Movement*, xxix–xxx. Although Piri Thomas was himself resistant to its categorizing impulse, claiming he wanted to be "a citizen of the world," because *Nuyorican Poetry* anthologized the generation of writers to which Piri Thomas belonged and because the Nuyorican movement generally refers in contemporary scholarship to the political and cultural outpouring of the 1960s and 1970s, I use this term to refer to Thomas and the other writers discussed in this chapter. P. Thomas, "Conversation with Piri Thomas."

112 Nöel, *In Visible Movement*, 28.

113 Guzmán, "*La Vida Pura*," 157.

114 Flores, *Divided Borders*, 134–135.

115 Nöel, *In Visible Movement*, xxvi, 19.

116 Nöel, *In Visible Movement*, xxiv.

117 Nöel, *In Visible Movement*, xxvi, xxiv.

118 Throughout this chapter, I refer to the author as Thomas and the protagonist as Piri.

119 Sánchez González, *Boricua Literature*, 105.

120 Significantly, although the narrator comes to terms with his Afro-descendancy, his father's Cuban background is silenced throughout the text. The *afrolatinidad* articulated in the text is somewhat limited, failing to address the divergences in Afro-Puerto Rican and Afro-Cuban experiences. See López, *Unbecoming Blackness*, 142–151.

121 Since the 1990s, the term "Afro-Latin@"—beyond its obvious attention to gender in the use of the at sign—has surfaced primarily in the United States to "signal racial, cultural, and socioeconomic contradictions within the overly vague idea of 'Latin@'" and to emphasize that black and Latin@ are not mutually exclusive. Flores and Jiménez Román, "Introduction," 2. While the term "Afro-Latin@," which refers to "Latin@s of visible or self-proclaimed African descent," has not traditionally been commonly used, according to Flores and Jiménez Román, "Afro-

Latin@s increasingly identify as such in recent years" (4). Drawing from W. E. B. Du Bois, they define the complexity of the experience of U.S. Afro-Latin@s as one of "triple consciousness," in which one is simultaneously "a Latin@, a Negro, an American . . . three warring ideals in one dark body" (15).

122 Flores, *Divided Borders*, 144.

123 For more on Schomburg and his writings, see Flores and Jiménez Román, *Afro-Latin@Reader*; Sánchez González, *Boricua Literature*; and Sinnette, *Arthur Alfonso Schomburg*.

124 Sánchez González, *Boricua Literature*, 20.

125 Flores, *Divided Borders*, 146–147.

126 These writings span the literary genres of theater, autobiography, poetry, and fiction, and include Carrero, *Jet neorriqueño*; Jesús Colón, *A Puerto Rican in New York, and Other Sketches* (1961); stories by José Luis González; René Marqués's *La carreta* (1953); and Pedro Juan Soto's *Spiks* (1956). Although Jesús Colón wrote poems and essays on the Puerto Rican migrant experience in newspapers, like the New York Latino Sunday newspaper *Gráfico*, as early as the 1920s, his discussion of his experience as a black Puerto Rican in his *Puerto Rican in New York* would be especially influential for later writers like Piri Thomas. Flores, *Divided Borders*, 148. For a discussion of *Gráfico* and some of Colón's work therein, see López, *Unbecoming Blackness*.

127 Flores, *Divided Borders*, 150.

128 Sánchez González, *Boricua Literature*, 55.

129 Flores, *Divided Borders*, 148.

130 Thomas, *Down These Mean Streets*, 121. Once Piri travels to the U.S. South, another array of vernaculars is represented in the text, such as Southern White Vernacular English (spoken with "a voice full of Alabama candy") and later "a soft Texas drawl," as well as an allusion to, but not a representation of, "broken Texas Spanish," spoken to Piri by a white sex worker when he pretends not to speak English so that she will believe he is African American. *Down These Mean Streets*, 186, 188, 189.

131 Many studies have discussed how Hispanic American discourses of mestizaje often emphasize indigenous and Hispanic origins, thus reflecting a dual claim to belonging and ownership of the nation, while eliding the presence and influence of African descendants. See, for example, Jackson, *Black Image in Latin American Literature*.

132 McGill, *Constructing Black Selves*; R. Pérez, "Racial Spills and Disfigured Faces"; Sánchez González, *Boricua Literature*; Sandín, *Killing Spanish*; Santiago-Díaz and Rodríguez, "Desde las fronteras raciales de dos casas letradas."

133 Caminero-Santangelo, "'Puerto Rican Negro'"; Santiago-Díaz and Rodríguez, "Desde las fronteras raciales de dos casas letradas."

134 McGill, *Constructing Black Selves*; Sandín, *Killing Spanish*.

135 Hill, "Language, Race, and White Public Space," 483.

136 Silverstein, "Monoglot 'Standard' in American," 284.

137 See Bucholz and Hall, "Language and Identity," for a concise discussion of this phenomenon.

138 Although one could argue that Thomas's italicization of Spanish terms as well as the glossary at the end of the book, which translates Spanish and slang into Standard English, serves to reestablish the ideology of the standard over the text, I would argue that the complexity of the linguistic environment of Thomas's fictionalized barrio still functions as the norm of the text.

139 For example, in the words "Pops . . . how come me and you is always on the outs? Is it something we don't know nothing about? I wonder if it's something I done, or something I am," the negative concord in "don't know nothing" and the absence of the auxiliar in "I done" are examples of the text's widespread incorporation of AAVE. Thomas, *Down These Mean Streets*, 22.

140 For studies of the linguistic interactions among African Americans and Puerto Ricans in Harlem, see Urciuoli, *Exposing Prejudice*; and Zentella, *Growing Up Bilingual*.

141 Thomas, *Down These Mean Streets*, 43.

142 Thomas, *Down These Mean Streets*, 45.

143 Thomas, *Down These Mean Streets*, 43.

144 Thomas, *Down These Mean Streets*, 67.

145 Thomas, *Down These Mean Streets*, 67.

146 Thomas, *Down These Mean Streets*, 68.

147 Thomas, *Down These Mean Streets*, 69.

148 Thomas, *Down These Mean Streets*, 120.

149 Thomas, *Down These Mean Streets*, 32.

150 Thomas, *Down These Mean Streets*, 83.

151 Thomas, *Down These Mean Streets*, 85, emphasis original.

152 Thomas, *Down These Mean Streets*, 84.

153 Thomas, *Down These Mean Streets*, 86.

154 Thomas, *Down These Mean Streets*, 121. The "dozens" is slang for the verbal dueling that has been described as a characteristic element of "black English." Mitchell-Kernan, "Signifying and Marking."

155 Thomas, *Down These Mean Streets*, 121.

156 Thomas, *Down These Mean Streets*, 123.

157 Fanon, *Black Skin*, 95.

158 Thomas, *Down These Mean Streets*, 124.

159 *Moyeto*, which is sometimes spelled *molleto*, is a slang term, used in the Spanish-speaking Caribbean, to refer to a dark-skinned, muscular man. Thomas, *Down These Mean Streets*, 143, emphasis original.

160 Thomas, *Down These Mean Streets*, 123.

161 Thomas, *Down These Mean Streets*, 191.

162 Thomas, *Down These Mean Streets*, 145.

163 Thomas, *Down These Mean Streets*, 145.

164 Thomas, *Down These Mean Streets*, 145, emphasis original.

165 Thomas, *Down These Mean Streets*, 198.

166 Thomas, *Down These Mean Streets*, 198.

167 Thomas, *Down These Mean Streets*, 198.

168 Thomas, *Down These Mean Streets*, 199.

169 López, *Unbecoming Blackness*, 150–151.

170 Thomas, *Down These Mean Streets*, 198.

171 Thomas, *Down These Mean Streets*, 199.

172 In "The African-American Speech Community," Morgan discusses perceptions of AAVE within African American communities, where, she claims, it is perceived positively by some people as an explicit rejection of the notion of Standard American English's inherent value and negatively by others because of its original formation on Southern plantations. Morgan maintains that AAVE is a dual sign of both oppression and liberation. In other words, its use reflects a power differential and simultaneously presents itself as a counterhegemonic sign.

173 Sandín, *Killing Spanish*, 112. For these prior readings, see Caminero-Santangelo " 'Puerto Rican Negro' "; R. Pérez, "Racial Spills and Disfigured Faces"; and Sandín, *Killing Spanish*.

174 Thomas, *Down These Mean Streets*, 251, emphasis original.

175 Thomas, *Down These Mean Streets*, 252.

176 R. Pérez, "Racial Spills and Disfigured Faces," 103.

177 Another moment in which Thomas plays on the association between blackness and rape occurs when Piri pretends not to speak English in order to gain entry into a brothel in Galveston, Texas. The owner of the brothel allowed "all kinds of foreigners, and Spanish people" but not African Americans because, he claims, "we got to keep these damn niggers down." After speaking in Spanish with the white sex worker, who spoke in a "broken Texas Spanish," and after having sex with her, Piri puts on his jacket to leave and, before running out of the brothel, switches into English to say, "I just want you to know . . . that you got fucked by a nigger, by *a black man*!" This moment is significant, not least because of how Piri asserts his black manhood through making an example of this woman who reacts with an apparent "look of horror" but whom Thomas never gives the chance to speak in the text. This is consistent with the ways that Piri's process of self-realization, through his relationship with Brew, is often at the expense of women where he and Brew forge their bond through their mutual objectification of them. However, this moment is also significant for how it playfully undermines the Jim Crow trope of the rape of white women by black men for which many black men have historically been falsely accused, tortured, and murdered. In Piri's view, as long as the sex worker does not know he is Afro-descendant (due to her apparent ignorance that there are Puerto Ricans of African descent), the sexual act is consensual. However, when he reveals this through performing an African American identity—which occurs at the linguistic level when he changes from Spanish to English—the sex act shifts from being consensual to a violation. In this way, Thomas makes a mockery of the colonial notions of the purity of white women and the social fear of

their violation by black men by choosing to represent these tropes through a sex worker who hardly fits within the chaste stereotype of Southern white womanhood and who, because of her ignorance of the Spanish-speaking world and her own adherence to a Jim Crow racial binary, has likely had sex with more than one Afro-descendant man without knowing it. In other words, what it means to be "a black man" and what it means to be a Southern white woman are completely destabilized in this moment. The Jim Crow racial binary, antiblack racism, and the fear of the rape of white women by black men are made farcical and used in the text as comic relief. Thomas, *Down These Mean Streets*, 188–189.

178 Thomas, *Down These Mean Streets*, 291.

179 Thomas, *Down These Mean Streets*, 323.

180 Sandín, *Killing Spanish*, 115. Similarly, Sánchez González maintains that Piri's "journey hits a dead end, when Piri capitulates his will and word to a divine and conspicuously white father figure whose omniscience is absolute and unfathomable, thus permanently deferring the text's hermeneutical crisis." Sánchez González, *Boricua Literature*, 108.

181 Thomas, *Down These Mean Streets*, 299.

182 M. Brown, *Gang Nation*, 32.

183 M. Brown, *Gang Nation*, 16–22.

184 For a reading of Pietri's poem in light of Aimé Césaire's poetry, see Nöel, *In Visible Movement*, 19.

185 Nöel, *In Visible Movement*, 17. The poem was published in *Palante* 2.19 (August 1970): 12.

186 Nöel, *In Visible Movement*, 18.

187 "Entre todo el pueblo se escribe un poema," 16; Guzmán, "apollo gig," 3.

188 Pietri, *Puerto Rican Obituary*, 1–2.

189 Pietri, *Puerto Rican Obituary*, 2.

190 Pietri, *Puerto Rican Obituary*, 4.

191 Pietri, *Puerto Rican Obituary*, 8.

192 Pietri, *Puerto Rican Obituary*, 8.

193 Pietri, *Puerto Rican Obituary*, 10–11.

194 Pietri, *Puerto Rican Obituary*, 10, emphasis original.

195 Pietri, *Puerto Rican Obituary*, 11, emphasis original.

196 Lane, *Blackface Cuba*, 3.

197 R. Moore, *Nationalizing Blackness*, 45.

198 Lane, *Blackface Cuba*, x.

199 Jill Lane's *Blackface Cuba* has made this argument for the role of the negrito in forging a nationalist discourse of *cubanía* (Cubanness). For a discussion of the negrito and Puerto Rican nationalism, see Rivero, *Tuning Out Blackness*. For a sustained discussion of the negrito figure and the role of bufo theater within Latinx communities in the United States, see the first chapter of Antonio López's *Unbecoming Blackness*.

200 Pietri, *Puerto Rican Obituary*, 10–11.

201 Pietri, *Puerto Rican Obituary*, 11.
202 Beasley-Murray, *Posthegemony*, 143.
203 Guerra, *Popular Expression and National Identity in Puerto Rico*, 78.
204 For more on the jíbaro in Puerto Rico, see Guerra, *Popular Expression and National Identity in Puerto Rico*. For a description of the very similar *guajiro* nationalism in Cuba, see R. Moore, *Nationalizing Blackness*, 131–133.
205 Luciano, "Jíbaro, My Pretty Nigger."
206 Luciano, "Jíbaro, My Pretty Nigger."
207 R. Márquez, *Puerto Rican Poetry*, 408.
208 Luciano, "Jíbaro, My Pretty Nigger."
209 Thomas, *Down These Mean Streets*, 191.
210 Thomas, *Down These Mean Streets*, 299.
211 Algarín, "Tangiers," in Algarín and Piñero, *Nuyorican Poetry*, 97.
212 Algarín, "Tangiers," 99.
213 Algarín, "Tangiers," 99.
214 Algarín, "Tangiers," 99.
215 Algarín, "Tangiers," 101.
216 For example, disagreements between the two characters are resolved by agreeing on a "nice piece of ass" who walks by. Thomas, *Down These Mean Streets*, 125.
217 *¡Presente!*
218 *¡Presente!*
219 J. Fernández, "Radicals in the Late 1960s," 290.
220 Puerto Rican Revolutionary Workers Organization, "History of the Development of the Puerto Rican Revolutionary Workers Organization."
221 I. Morales, "¡PALANTE, SIEMPRE PALANTE!" 221–223.
222 Goldstein, "Old New York Police Surveillance Is Found."
223 Stanchich, "Puerto Rico's Symbolic Power."
224 E. Morales, "Puerto Rico in Crisis."

4. "Todos los negros y todos los blancos"

1 While scholarship, written in English, on black Cubans frequently uses the term "Afro-Cuban," it is important to note that in Spanish the term "afrocubano" recalls the exoticism of the afrocubanismo movement (more broadly termed "negrismo" or "afrocriollismo") of the 1920s to 1940s, and many black Cubans do not employ the term as a community marker.
2 Zurbano Torres, "For Blacks in Cuba, the Revolution Hasn't Begun."
3 Zurbano Torres, "For Blacks in Cuba, the Revolution Hasn't Begun."
4 For an English translation of the original article, see Zurbano Torres, "The Country to Come."
5 Y. Fernández, "La revolución contra el racismo." For more on the controversy, see the special issue of *Afro-Hispanic Review* 33.1 (Spring 2014), dedicated to the so-called Zurbano Affair.

6 "Un fenómeno globalizado y la lucha contra este va más allá de cualquier frontera" (translation mine). Zurbano Torres, "Mañana será tarde."

7 In his March 2016 visit to Cuba, President Obama addressed this dichotomy by agreeing with Cuban critiques of the enduring presence of racial inequality in the United States but also emphasizing the presence of those inequities in Cuba, stating, "I'm sure we both realize we have more work to do to promote equality in our own countries—to reduce discrimination based on race in our own countries." Obama, "Remarks by President Obama to the People of Cuba." For an analysis of the racial implications of Obama's visit, see Casamayor, "Obamas and the Blacks of Cuba."

8 Chanan, *Cuban Cinema*, 203.

9 Chanan's *Cuban Cinema* organizes ICAIC's documentary production in these early years within thematic categories. These include films on the revolutionary process; didactic films on issues such as hygiene or agricultural methods; films treating cultural and artistic subjects, social history, and Cuban character; films on the revolutionary critique of capitalism and imperialism and on international solidarity and the principles of internationalism; and films on the subject of women and sports. Chanan, *Cuban Cinema*, 208. The ICAIC films that the Tricontinental claimed as part of its propaganda and many of the most well known of Álvarez's newsreels would fall into the category of films that treat international solidarity and the revolutionary critique of capitalism and imperialism. Guillén Landrián's films are better described by other categories such as discussion of the revolutionary process, didactic films, and documentaries on cultural practices, social history, and sports.

10 Scarpaci, Segre, and Coyula, *Havana*, 140.

11 According to the filmmaker, ICAIC initially praised the film and held a premiere. Guillén Landrián, "El cine postergado." The problems seem to have begun once the Havana Greenbelt campaign was unsuccessful.

12 Although diplomatic relations with the Soviet Union began in 1960, it was not until December 1961 that Castro declared that Cuba would adopt communism, cementing a relationship with the Soviets that would steadily increase throughout the 1960s. Cuban-Soviet relations continued until 1991 when Soviet subsidies to the island ended a few months before the Soviet Union's dissolution. Loss and Prieto González, *Caviar with Rum*.

13 For an in-depth study of this shift from 1959 to 1961, see Benson, *Antiracism in Cuba*.

14 Abreu, "El Black Power en la Cuba de los sesenta y setenta"; Abreu, "Subalternidad"; de la Fuente, *Nation for All*; Guerra, *Visions of Power in Cuba*; Howe, *Transgression and Conformity*, 82; Miskulin, "Las ediciones El Puente y la nueva promoción de poetas cubanos," 32; C. Moore, *Castro, the Blacks, and Africa*; Sawyer, *Racial Politics in Post-revolutionary Cuba*, 67.

15 Cleaver, *Soul on Ice*, 107–109; Clytus, *Black Man in Red Cuba*; Gates, "Cuban Experience"; C. Moore, *Castro, the Blacks, and Africa*. For scholarship on U.S.

black militants' relationship to Cuba, see Gronbeck-Tedesco, *Cuba, the United States, and Cultures of the Transnational Left*; Reitan, *Rise and Decline of an Alliance*; Sawyer, *Racial Politics in Post-revolutionary Cuba*; Seidman, "Tricontinental Routes of Solidarity"; and Tyson, *Radio Free Dixie*.

16 De la Fuente's *A Nation for All* lays out succinctly the various positions of this scholarship. See Booth, "Cuba, Color and the Revolution"; Casal, "Race Relations in Contemporary Cuba"; Domínguez, *Cuba*; Domínguez, "Racial and Ethnic Relations in the Cuban Armed Forces"; Fox, "Race and Class in Contemporary Cuba"; Masferrer and Mesa-Lago, "Gradual Integration of the Black in Cuba"; Rout, *African Experience in Spanish America*; and H. Thomas, *Cuba*.

17 Another exception is Juan René Betancourt's *El negro* (1959), which was also censored. See discussion of this text in Benson, *Antiracism in Cuba*, 113–118.

18 De la Fuente, *Nation for All*, 4.

19 Abreu, "El Black Power en la Cuba de los sesenta y setenta"; Guerra, *Visions of Power in Cuba*, 256; Ramos, "¿Un cine afrocubano?," 296. Benson also describes a 1960s movement of "Cuban black consciousness or *negrismo*." *Antiracism in Cuba*, 112.

20 Abreu, "El Black Power en la Cuba de los sesenta y setenta"; Benson, *Antiracism in Cuba*, 235; de la Fuente, *Nation for All*, 302; C. Moore, *Castro, the Blacks, and Africa*, 307–312; Sawyer, *Racial Politics in Post-revolutionary Cuba*, 66–67. Apparently because of her involvement in this document, the poet Nancy Morejón was banned from publishing poetry from 1969 to 1979. Guerra, *Visions of Power in Cuba*, 273–274. SNCC members Ralph Featherstone, Robert Fletcher, Jennifer Lawson, Chico Neblett, and Willie Ricks attended the Cultural Congress, and while discrimination against Afro-Cubans was barred from discussion, the Congress did demonstrate a continued Tricontinentalist focus on the African American struggle. Seidman, "Venceremos Means We Shall Overcome," 126–128. It should be noted that this so-called Black Manifesto Plot is a point of controversy. After Carlos Moore described this event in his book *Castro, the Blacks, and Africa*, the Afro-Cuban writer Pedro Pérez Sarduy wrote an open letter to Moore in which he criticizes the book in general for containing many falsehoods and claims that Moore overly dramatizes the occurrence and gets the names wrong of those who were involved. He writes, "It never occurred to us to be part of any manifesto. Eight or nine of us wrote a short paper for a forum prior to the congress." Pérez-Sarduy, "Open Letter to Carlos Moore."

21 For example, the Afro-Cuban filmmaker Sergio Giral had success in Cuba's film industry with a series of films dealing with the history of slavery and maroonage in Cuba. However, his film *Techo de vidrio* (Glass Roof) (1981), which dealt with contemporary themes of corruption and subtle forms of racism in employment practices, was not released for six years. Chomsky, *History of the Cuban Revolution*, 118–119. Similarly, films by the Afro-Cuban director Sara Gómez, which tended to treat issues facing black Cubans and women within society at large while not directly critiquing the government or its policies, were generally

well received. However, only one part of her 1968 trilogy about the Isle of Youth, which called attention to the overrepresentation of poor black Cubans in the Isle of Youth's detention centers and reform schools, was shown and in limited release. Guerra, *Visions of Power in Cuba*, 267–269.

22 Zayas, "Nicolás Guillén."

23 These films include *Homenaje a Picasso* (1962), *Congos reales* (1962), *Patio arenero* (1962), *El Morro* (1963), *En un barrio viejo* (1963), *Un festival* (1963), *Ociel del Toa* (1965), *Los del baile* (1965), *Rita Montaner* (1965), *Retornar a Baracoa* (1966), *Reportaje* (1966), *Coffea arábiga* (1968), *Expo Maquinaria Pabellón Cuba* (1969), *Desde La Habana, 1969* (1971), *Taller de Línea y 18* (1971), *Un reportaje sobre el Puerto Pesquero* (1972), *Nosotros en el Cuyaguateje* (1972), and *Para construir una casa* (1972). Many of these films, such as *Homenaje a Picasso*, *Congos reales*, *Patio arenero*, *El Morro*, *Rita Montaner*, and *Expo Maquinaria Pabellón Cuba*, have been lost entirely. The only ones that were exhibited publicly prior to 2002 were *En un barrio viejo* (honorary mention at the Krakow Film Festival), *Ociel del Toa* (first prize at the Valladolid International Film Festival), *Coffea arábiga*, and *Nosotros en el Cuyaguateje*. See "Nicolasito Guillén."

24 Araoz and Ramos, *Retornar a La Habana con Guillén Landrián*.

25 They were shown at the Muestra de Jóvenes Realizadores, an annual film festival funded by ICAIC for works by new Cuban filmmakers (or in this case filmmakers new to the Cuban public). Ramos, "Cine, archivo, y poder."

26 Araoz and Ramos, *Retornar a La Habana con Guillén Landrián*; Jiménez Sosa and Egusquiza Zorrilla, *Nicolás*.

27 Duarte and Ruiz, "El collage de la nostalgia"; Guerra, *Visions of Power in Cuba*; Livon-Grosman, "Nicolasito's Way"; Ramos, "Los archivos de Guillén Landrián"; Ramos, "Cine, cuerpo y trabajo"; Reyes, "Exhumaciones de Nicolás Guillén Landrián"; D. Robbins, "*Los del baile*"; D. Robbins, "On the Margins of Reality"; Stock, *On Location in Cuba*.

28 Cort, "Negrometraje"; Guerra, *Visions of Power in Cuba*, 342–343; D. Robbins, "On the Margins of Reality."

29 Cort, "Negrometraje"; Duarte and Ruiz, "El collage de la nostalgia"; Livon-Grosman, "Nicolasito's Way"; Ramos, "Cine, cuerpo y trabajo."

30 Guerra, *Visions of Power in Cuba*, 347–348.

31 Ferrer, *Insurgent Cuba*.

32 Ferrer, *Insurgent Cuba*, 95.

33 Helg, *Our Rightful Share*.

34 Helg, *Our Rightful Share*, 225.

35 See Giral's documentary on Esteban Montejo, called *Cimarrón* (1967), as well as his trilogy of films on slave resistance, *El otro Francisco* (1975), *Rancheador* (1979), and *Maluala* (1979).

36 For a discussion of how the Cuban government presented narratives of black Cubans as direct beneficiaries of Cuba's Literacy Campaign, see Benson, *Antiracism in Cuba*.

37 The term has two possible origins. The first is the name of a black Spanish officer, Juan "Eutimio" Mamby, who turned against the Spanish and joined the insurgents in Santo Domingo in the early nineteenth century. The other is an indigenous word for those who fought against the Spanish in the early colonial period. Cardona and Losada, *Weyler, nuestro hombre en La Habana*, 27–28, qtd. in López, *José Martí*, 377n7.

38 Retamar, *Caliban and Other Essays*, 16, emphasis original.

39 I thank Mark A. Sanders for making this point. Christabelle Peters has a similar reading, suggesting that "it is possible that Morejón's ambiguous usage of 'we' and 'us' without qualifying referent . . . is formulated within the discursive strategies of homogenization of difference precipitated by the Revolution and reinforced during the repressive years of the quinquenio gris: strategies that set in motion processes of standardization and uniformization to support the creation of a hegemonic national identity." Peters, *Cuban Identity and the Angolan Experience*, 29.

40 Barnet's *Biografía* was originally published by Cuba's Instituto de Etnología y Folklore; Retamar's *Calibán* was first published by Casa de las Américas; Morejón's poem "Mujer negra" was published by Casa de las Américas in commemoration of the International Year of the Woman and was later included in *Parajes de una época* (1979) published by Editorial Letras Cubanas; and films by Alea, Giral, and Solás were produced by ICAIC.

41 C. Moore, *Castro, the Blacks, and Africa*, 147.

42 C. Moore, *Castro, the Blacks, and Africa*, 145.

43 Reitan, *Rise and Decline of an Alliance*; Sawyer, *Racial Politics in Post-Revolutionary Cuba*; Seidman, "Venceremos Means We Shall Overcome."

44 C. Moore, *Pichón*, 168.

45 Sawyer, *Racial Politics in Post-Revolutionary Cuba*, 90.

46 Joseph, *Waiting 'til the Midnight Hour*, 225. For an in-depth discussion of Carmichael's relationship to Cuba, see chapter 2 of Seidman, "Venceremos Means We Shall Overcome."

47 Sawyer, *Racial Politics in Post-Revolutionary Cuba*, 95.

48 Reitan, *Rise and Decline of an Alliance*.

49 De la Fuente, *Nation for All*, 358–373.

50 Benson, *Antiracism in Cuba*; de la Fuente, *Nation for All*, 21.

51 De la Fuente, *Nation for All*, 384. Benson's *Antiracism in Cuba* provides a detailed account of the closing of black social clubs.

52 Sawyer, *Racial Politics in Post-revolutionary Cuba*, 67.

53 Miskulin, "Las ediciones El Puente y la nueva promoción de poetas cubanos," 32.

54 Luis-Brown, *Waves of Decolonization*, 94.

55 De la Fuente, *Nation for All*, 177–178.

56 De la Fuente, *Nation for All*, 184; Kutzinski, *Sugar's Secrets*, 4–7.

57 Similar to this chapter, John Gronbeck-Tedesco's *Cuba, the United States, and Cultures of the Transnational Left, 1930–75* contains a thorough discussion of how Cuba used the Tricontinental "to augment its cachet in the third world" by spreading

"the belief that its citizens lived in equal conditions, irrespective of race and without class," and he discusses the impact this had on convergences and divergences between Cuba and African American activists (211). My understanding of the internationalist and domestic discourses of the Cuban Revolution are very much in line with both Gronbeck-Tedesco and Sawyer's *Racial Politics in Post-Revolutionary Cuba*. However, while I agree that Tricontinentalism has been, as Gronbeck-Tedesco writes, "fundamental to Havana's geopolitical strategy and rhetorical leverage in the international arena," I quibble with his book's frequent conflation of Tricontinentalism with the Cuban example of revolution that inspired leftists around the globe (210, 224). That is, in my view, the example of the Cuban Revolution and Tricontinentalism are not necessarily one and the same. Tricontinentalism is at once a major aspect of the Cuban Revolution's internationalist face and a site of encounter between diverse movements across the globe. It is a multinational movement with deep roots in black internationalism. Cuba has been integral to the shaping and dissemination of Tricontinentalism, and the Cuban state has been able to use Tricontinentalism for its benefit in the international sphere, but this movement and ideology do not belong solely to Cuba or to any one nation-state. In other words, Tricontinentalism has been both a tool of Cuba's foreign policy and an ideology of a global Left that supersedes the Cuban Revolution itself.

58 Sawyer, *Racial Politics in Post-Revolutionary Cuba*, 19.
59 Sawyer, *Racial Politics in Post-Revolutionary Cuba*, 16.
60 Castro, "Angola," 94.
61 Gleijeses, *Conflicting Missions*, 8–9.
62 García Márquez, "Operation Carlota," 11.
63 Gleijeses, *Conflicting Missions*, 9.
64 Castro, "Angola," 90.
65 Castro, "Angola," 90.
66 An example of such a citation is Gronbeck-Tedesco, *Cuba, the United States, and Cultures of the Transnational Left*, 211.
67 Castro, "Shattered Myths," 15.
68 Castro, "Shattered Myths," 15.
69 Henighan, "Cuban Fulcrum," 243.
70 De la Fuente, *Nation for All*, 310.
71 De la Fuente, *Nation for All*, 311; Peters, *Cuban Identity and the Angolan Experience*, 27.
72 Henighan, "Cuban Fulcrum," 243.
73 Henighan, "Cuban Fulcrum," 238.
74 Henighan, "Cuban Fulcrum," 238.
75 See Brent, *Long Time Gone*.
76 McManus, "United States and Apartheid," 30–31.
77 "Export of Apartheid to Latin America," 36.
78 "Export of Apartheid to Latin America," 40.
79 "Export of Apartheid to Latin America," 32.

80 Bystrom and Slaughter, *Global South Atlantic*.

81 De la Fuente, *Nation for All*, 313.

82 De la Fuente, *Nation for All*, 313.

83 Henighan, "Cuban Fulcrum," 243.

84 De la Fuente, *Nation for All*, 314–315.

85 Sawyer, *Racial Politics in Post-Revolutionary Cuba*, 63.

86 *Lunes de Revolución* was the first magazine established following the Cuban Revolution. According to William Luis, since *Lunes de Revolución* had a television program and supported music events and film (in the case of *P.M.*), it was more like an arts organization than a literary magazine. It published well-known writers from Cuba and abroad, often devoting an entire issue to a specific country. Its sixty-sixth issue (July 4, 1960), "Los negros en U.S.A." (The Blacks in U.S.A.), was edited by Robert F. Williams and featured writings by the African American writers Richard Gibson, Harold Cruse, John Henrik Clarke, Langston Hughes, Julian Mayfield, Marguerite Angelos, Alice Childress, Sarah Wright, Lucy Smith, and LeRoi Jones. See Luis, *Lunes de Revolución*.

87 Cabrera Infante, "Un mes lleno de *Lunes*," 149–151.

88 The 26th of July Movement was Fidel Castro and Che Guevara's organization, named for the failed attack on the Moncada barracks on July 26, 1953, that overthrew the Batista dictatorship in 1959. In July 1961, it integrated with other organizations, such as the PSP, to become the Integrated Revolutionary Organizations (ORI). The ORI would be named the United Party of the Cuban Socialist Revolution in 1962, and in October 1965, it would become the Communist Party of Cuba.

89 Luis, *Lunes de Revolución*.

90 Luis, *Lunes de Revolución*, 47–49.

91 García Espinosa directed fourteen films between 1955 and 1998. He is most known for his film manifesto, "Por un cine imperfecto" (For an Imperfect Cinema) and for creating the Revolution's comedic hero in *Las aventuras de Juan Quín Quín* (The Adventures of Juan Quín Quín) (1967).

92 Chanan, *Cuban Cinema*, 144.

93 "Esta historia pudo suceder en Cuba en cualquier período pasado de su vida republicana. Hoy, la clase media despierta y la politiquería ha sido liquidada" (translation mine).

94 Chanan, *Cuban Cinema*, 135, 33.

95 Luis, *Lunes de Revolución*, 9.

96 For example, Guerra views Guillén Landrián's film *Los del baile* (1965), in its depiction of Afro-Cuban dancing and partying, as a direct response to the controversy and as a vindication of the censored *P.M.* Guerra, *Visions of Power in Cuba*, 342–343.

97 Navarro, "In Media Res Publicas," 198.

98 Zayas, *Café con leche*.

99 See Guerra's in-depth discussion of youth culture and ideological diversionism in chapter 7 of *Visions of Power in Cuba*.

100 Guerra, *Visions of Power in Cuba*, 343; Zayas, *Café con leche*. While this information has been corroborated by documentaries and scholarship on Guillén
Landrián, it is important to note that his mental state has served as ICAIC's
primary explanation for his expulsion and erasure. This chapter responds to this
dismissal by addressing the direct and powerful political argument that Guillén
Landrián delivered in his first film after his release from the hospital. On a similar
note, I intentionally do not employ the diminutive "Nicolasito," the nickname that
his friends and colleagues called him and that is commonly used as shorthand in
scholarship on his work. While friends, scholars, and fans of Guillén Landrián use
this nickname as a term of endearment, in other contexts, its usage can imply a
condescension that, alongside discussion of his emotional and mental state, subtly diminishes the filmmaker and emphasizes his distinction from his uncle, Poet
Laureate Nicolás Guillén Batista.

101 Guillén Landrián, "El cine postergado."

102 Scarpaci, Segre, and Coyula, *Havana*, 328.

103 Scarpaci, Segre, and Coyula, *Havana*, 206.

104 Guerra, *Visions of Power in Cuba*, 347.

105 The woman is played by Dara Kristova, Guillén Landrián's first wife. Guerra, *Visions of Power in Cuba*, 348.

106 Duarte and Ruiz, "El collage de la nostalgia."

107 The May 1959 Agrarian Reform Law nationalized landholdings in excess of 3,333
acres, redistributing it among farmers and state cooperatives. L. Pérez, *Cuba*, 243.

108 Guillén Landrián's later films often recycle images and sequences from his previously unreleased films, creating intertextual references to his own work as an au-
teur and adding yet another layer of subtle critique of ICAIC's processes of censure
and silence.

109 Guerra, *Visions of Power in Cuba*, 225.

110 This policy changed after Angela Davis's visit to Cuba in 1972 when a pro-Soviet
African American was seen wearing her hair naturally. C. Moore, *Castro, the
Blacks, and Africa*, 303. For more on Davis's visits to Cuba and her influence on
Afro-Cuban hairstyles, see chapter 3 of Seidman, "Venceremos Means We Shall
Overcome."

111 Cort, "Negrometraje," 62.

112 *Teatro bufo* is a nineteenth- and early twentieth-century satirical theater form
in which actors parodied the customs of the lower classes of Cuban society. In
addition to shaping national identity, it also helped to create many of the nation's
most entrenched racial stereotypes. See Lane, *Blackface Cuba*. Ignacio Villa (often
called "Bola de Nieve" [Snowball]) gained notoriety as a performer and composer
within the larger afrocubanismo movement. He often wrote songs that played
on the bufo trope of the *negro catedrático*, a figure used to poke fun at the black
professional class by portraying a "black professor" who "spoke with overly flow-
ery speech using a vocabulary beyond his limited education." S. Thomas, *Cuban
Zarzuela*, 84. Villa was a "classical musician who became famous for interpreting

songs of the white middle classes that depicted black street culture" and in this way, as Robin Moore has written, he "personifies all of the complexities and ironies of *afrocubanismo*." R. Moore, *Nationalizing Blackness*, 137.

113 Carbonell, *Crítica*, 19. Translations of Carbonell's text are mine.
114 "El poder ideológico de la burguesía." Carbonell, *Crítica*, 19.
115 Benítez-Rojo, *Repeating Island*, 9.
116 Benítez-Rojo, *Repeating Island*, 8, 4.
117 Benítez-Rojo, *Repeating Island*, 10.
118 Benítez-Rojo, *Repeating Island*, 24.

5. The (New) Global South

1 Fairey initially screenprinted seven hundred posters. He used the proceeds to print another four thousand to distribute at rallies and eventually posted it on his website. Arnon, "How the Obama 'Hope' Poster Reached a Tipping Point and Became a Cultural Phenomenon."
2 Schjeldahl, "Hope and Glory."
3 Schjeldahl, "Hope and Glory." See also Booth, "Obama's On-the-Wall Endorsement"; Pop, "Shepard Fairey."
4 Cushing, "Cuban Poster Art and the Spirit of Revolution."
5 Cushing, "Cuban Poster Art and the Spirit of Revolution"; Vallen, "Obey Plagiarist Shepard Fairey."
6 See, for example, posters of Lumumba and Cabral by the Cuban artists Antonio Mariño, Alfredo Rostgaard, Olivia Martínez Viera, Rafael Enríquez Vega, and Enrique Martínez Blanco in Frick, *Tricontinental Solidarity Poster*, 147, 167–173.
7 To much controversy, an illustration on the cover of the July 21, 2008, cover of the *New Yorker* satirized the far Right's representation of Barack Obama by depicting him in the Oval Office wearing a thawb and turban and exchanging a fist bump with Michelle Obama, who is wearing an afro and carrying a machine gun over her shoulder. Behind them, an American flag burns in the fireplace beneath a portrait of Osama bin Laden. Blitt, "Politics of Fear." For an example of how Fairey's "Hope" poster was used to fuel this type of alarm among the right wing, see Conservapedia, "Radical Roots of Barack Hussein Obama."
8 Fukuyama, *End of History and the Last Man*.
9 Melamed, *Represent and Destroy*, 138.
10 Exceptions to this elision include Gronbeck-Tedesco, *Cuba, the United States, and Cultures of the Transnational Left*; Prashad, *Darker Nations*; Rodriguez, "Beyond Nation"; Rodriguez, "'De la esclavitud yanqui a la libertad cubana'"; Rodriguez, "Long Live Third World Unity!"; Seidman, "Venceremos Means We Shall Overcome"; R. Young, *Postcolonialism*; R. Young, "Postcolonialism"; and Vélez, *Latin American Revolutionaries and the Arab World*.
11 "At the Root," 129.
12 Harvey, *Brief History of Neoliberalism*, 9.

13 Stahler-Sholk, Vanden, and Kuecker, "Introduction," 4–5.

14 Melamed, *Represent and Destroy*, 138.

15 Melamed, *Represent and Destroy*, 42.

16 R. Young, *White Mythologies*, 15.

17 Ashcroft, Griffiths, and Tiffin, *Empire Writes Back*, 2.

18 See Coronil's discussion of the many postcolonial anthologies that have elided the Latin American region. Coronil, "Elephants in the Americas?"

19 For in-depth discussions of the Latin Americanist debates on postcolonial studies, see Coronil, "Elephants in the Americas?"; Lund, *Impure Imagination*. See also Seed, "Colonial and Postcolonial Discourse," and the responses to this essay in Adorno, "Reconsidering Colonial Discourse for Sixteenth- and Seventeenth-Century Spanish America"; Mignolo, "Colonial and Postcolonial Discourse"; and Vidal, "Concept of Colonial and Postcolonial Discourse."

20 Beverley, "Hacia un nuevo latinoamericanismo," 25; Beverley, *Latinamericanism after 9/11*, 19–21.

21 Cohn, "US Southern and Latin American Studies"; Zamora, *Usable Past*, 119.

22 Edward Said has stated, for example, that postcolonialism does not adequately account for what he calls the "neocolonialism" of the structures of economic dependency facilitated by the International Monetary Fund and the World Bank. Said, "Conversation," 2.

23 Ashcroft, "Modernity's First Born," 14–15.

24 R. Young, "Postcolonialism."

25 See, for example, D. Thomas, *Theory and Practice of Third World Solidarity*; C. Young, *Soul Power*.

26 Rodriguez, "Beyond Nation," 14; Seidman, "Tricontinental Routes of Solidarity," 2; Seidman, "Venceremos Means We Shall Overcome," 80.

27 Hardt and Negri, *Empire*, 264.

28 Hardt and Negri, *Empire*, 6–7.

29 Grandin, "Why the Left Continues to Win in Latin America"; Hardt and Negri, *Empire*.

30 Beverley, *Latinamericanism after 9/11*, 7.

31 Rahier, "Introduction," 1–3; Walsh, "Afro In/Exclusion," 18.

32 This decline is evidenced in the November 2015 election of Mauricio Macri in Argentina, the defeat of the United Socialist Party of Venezuela in parliamentary elections in December 2015, the referendum rejection in February 2016 of a constitutional amendment allowing Bolivia's Evo Morales to run for a fourth term, and the impeachment and removal of Brazil's Dilma Rousseff in August 2016. Gulliver, "Is the 'Pink Tide' Turning in Latin America?"; Sankey, "What Happened to the Pink Tide?"; Seymour, "'Pink Tide' in Crisis."

33 Beginning in 2014, there have been widespread protests against leftist governments in Venezuela, Nicaragua, and Brazil, resulting from, for example, the corruption scandal with Brazil's state-owned Petrobras and the construction of the Nicaraguan Canal. In August 2016, striking miners of the National Federation of

Mining Cooperatives of Bolivia, who were once allies of President Evo Morales, assassinated Rodolfo Illanes, the deputy interior minister of Morales's government, shocking many who have viewed Bolivia as one of the most stable of the pink-tide states. "Bolivian Minister Rodolfo Illanes 'Killed by Miners'"; Seymour, "'Pink Tide' in Crisis."

34 Gulliver, "Is the 'Pink Tide' Turning in Latin America?"; Mitchell, "Pink Tide Recedes."

35 Essif, "How Black Lives Matter Has Spread."

36 Santiago Feliú (editor of *Tricontinental*), in discussion with the author, July 28, 2014.

37 See, for example, the exhibition *Globalize This!* by the Los Angeles–based Center for the Study of Political Graphics, which included 1987 and 2002 OSPAAAL posters.

38 "Globalizar la solidaridad," first cover.

39 "Contra la geopolítica imperialista," 3.

40 See, for example, Grau, "¿Por qué Afganistán?"

41 In an interview conducted with the OSPAAAL general secretary, Lourdes Cervantes Vásquez, by the author, it was reiterated several times that although the OSPAAAL receives funding from the Cuban state, it is considered a nongovernmental organization that attempts to represent all of the delegates within the organization.

42 Abu-Jamal, "Una democracia imperial," 36; Abu-Jamal, "Derechos humanos imperiales"; Abu-Jamal, "La raíz de la guerra es el dinero," 60; Estrada Lescaille, "La habana frente al racismo"; Marable, "Racismo, prisiones, y el futuro de los negros en los Estados Unidos."

43 Yepe, "Los latinos indignados en Estados Unidos."

44 Kuhn, "On/Off."

45 "Más de lo mismo una continuidad de la política imperial de antes, aunque aplicada con un rostro negro" (translation mine). Abascal, "Obama y el Oriente Medio," 32.

46 "Aunque sea negro, padece la misma arrogancia imperial típica de la privilegiada y mesiánica cúpula estadounidense. ¿Quién sino los cuerpos represivos de ese país molieron a palos a los integrantes de *Occupy Wall Street*" (translation mine). Cabrera, "Mandela, Obama, y Raúl," 51.

47 Sánchez, "Bienvenido, Mr. Kerry."

48 Castro, "El hermano Obama."

49 McBride, who grew up in Northern Ireland, explained in an email exchange with me that he was inspired to make the poster of Michael Brown because of his connection to "the Northern Irish Civil Rights Movement, which was inspired and based on the North American Civil Rights Movement. The situation in Northern Ireland was very similar to that of Apartheid South Africa. So, when I saw the footage of Mike Brown being shot, it reminded me of our own history. I loved reading about the Black Panthers, Malcolm X, Nelson Mandela, Fidel Castro and of course our own hero Bobby Sands and that was enough for me to become

active." McBride, who was seventeen when he made the poster (and twenty-one at the time of our email exchange), posted the image on Twitter, and it went viral. While in this email exchange, McBride never mentioned the Tricontinental, his internationalist engagement, description of his political beliefs, and artistic motivations, and even the way in which the image circulated, could not be more clearly dependent on a history of Tricontinentalism. McBride, email message to author.

50 McIntosh, "History of Subversive Remix Video."
51 B Media Collective, *Occupation Nation*.
52 For this term, see Shirky, *Here Comes Everybody*, 40–41.
53 See Martin, *New Latin American Cinema Volume 1*.
54 Getino and Solanas, "Towards a Third Cinema."
55 *Ford . . . has the better idea*, fourth cover.
56 *Man-on-the-Spot . . . in La Paz*, fourth cover.
57 *Man-on-the-Spot . . . in La Paz*, fourth cover.
58 Dery, "Merry Pranksters"; Klein, *No Logo*, 281.
59 "Adbusters About."
60 Fominaya, *Social Movements and Globalization*, 101.
61 Hardt and Negri, *Empire*, 166.
62 Hardt and Negri, *Empire*, 186.
63 Hardt and Negri, *Empire*, 393.
64 Castells, "Network Theory of Power."
65 Galloway and Thacker, *Exploit*, 30–35; Hardt and Negri, *Empire*, 23–24, 198.
66 Galloway and Thacker, *Exploit*, 60. Aihwa Ong has termed these processes of subject formation "technologies of subjection" in which individuals adhere to "health regimes, acquisition of skills, development of entrepreneurial ventures, and other techniques of self-engineering and capital accumulation" that lead to optimal productivity and the free flow of capital. Ong, *Neoliberalism as Exception*, 6.
67 Hardt and Negri, *Empire*, 189–190.
68 Hardt and Negri, *Empire*, 206.
69 Castells, "Network Theory of Power," 781; Galloway and Thacker, *Exploit*, 97. See also Castells, *Networks of Outrage and Hope*.
70 Hardt and Negri, *Empire*, 47.
71 Appadurai, "Grassroots Globalization"; Rosenberg, "Afecto y política de la cosmópolis latinoamericana"; Santos, *Toward a New Legal Common Sense*.
72 López, "Introduction," 1.
73 Prashad, *Darker Nations*, 9.
74 Conway, *Edges of Global Justice*, 41–42.
75 Conway, *Edges of Global Justice*, 18.
76 Conway, *Edges of Global Justice*, 33–34.
77 Conway, *Edges of Global Justice*, 37–38.
78 Amin, *World We Wish to See*, 107; Conway, *Edges of Global Justice*, 38.
79 Amin, *World We Wish to See*, 107.

80 Waterman, "Bamako Appeal."
81 For example, John Bellamy Foster, the editor of the *Monthly Review Press*, and Ignacio Ramonet, the former editor of *Le monde diplomatique*, are included among the signatures. Conway, *Edges of Global Justice*, 37; Waterman, "Bamako Appeal."
82 Waterman, "Bamako Appeal," emphasis original.
83 Amin, *World We Wish to See*, 111.
84 Amin, *World We Wish to See*, 111.
85 Amin, *World We Wish to See*, 111.
86 Amin, *World We Wish to See*, 79.
87 Amin, *World We Wish to See*, 115.
88 Conway, *Edges of Global Justice*, 39–40.
89 Conway, *Edges of Global Justice*, 39–40.
90 See García Canclini, *Consumidores y ciudadanos*; Hale, "Neoliberal Multiculturalism"; Melamed, *Represent and Destroy*; Ong, *Neoliberalism as Exception*.
91 Melamed, *Represent and Destroy*, 42.
92 Melamed, *Represent and Destroy*.
93 Melamed, *Represent and Destroy*, 47.
94 Melamed, *Represent and Destroy*, 47.
95 See, for example, Álvarez et al., "Contours of Color at the World Social Forum"; Conway, *Edges of Global Justice*; Martínez, "Where Was the Color in Seattle?"; Starr, "How Can Anti-imperialism Not Be Anti-racist?"
96 Conway, *Edges of Global Justice*, 20.
97 Álvarez et al., "Contours of Color at the World Social Forum," 392.
98 Álvarez et al., "Contours of Color at the World Social Forum," 393.
99 Álvarez et al., "Contours of Color at the World Social Forum," 402.
100 See, for example, Martínez, "Where Was the Color in Seattle?"; Middlebrooks, "From the Civil Rights Movement to Occupy Wall Street"; Ross, "Occupy Wall Street"; Speri, "Occupy Wall Street Struggles."
101 Speri, "Occupy Wall Street Struggles."
102 Speri, "Occupy Wall Street Struggles."
103 Ross, "Occupy Wall Street."
104 Lee and Ross, "Occupy the Hood."
105 Speri, "Occupy Wall Street Struggles."
106 Browne-Marshall, "'Occupy Wall Street' Is No Civil Rights Movement"; Gladwell, "Small Change"; Middlebrooks, "From the Civil Rights Movement to Occupy Wall Street."
107 Middlebrooks, "From the Civil Rights Movement to Occupy Wall Street"; Ross, "Occupy Wall Street."
108 Ross, "Occupy Wall Street."
109 Chen, "Truth about Anonymous's Activism"; Ross, "Occupy Wall Street."
110 Hooker, *Race and the Politics of Solidarity*, 21.
111 Farrow, "Occupy Wall Street's Race Problem"; Ross, "Occupy Wall Street."

112 One exception is the article "Occupy Wall Street's Race Problem," by Kenyon Farrow, which critiques OWS for comparing student debt to "slavery," for expressing surprise at police brutality, and for promoting a rhetoric of reclaiming America, suggesting that OWS "is actually appealing to an imagined white (re)public." See also Sen, "Race and Occupy Wall Street."

113 Speri, "Occupy Wall Street Struggles."

114 Speri, "Occupy Wall Street Struggles."

115 Occupy Wall Street New York City General Assembly, "Declaration of the Occupation of New York City."

116 Occupy Wall Street New York City General Assembly, "Declaration of the Occupation of New York City."

117 Martínez, "Las chicanas"; Martínez, "No son hijos de Houston"; Martínez, "Where Was the Color in Seattle?"

118 Chase, *Spaces of Neoliberalism*, 59; Walsh, "Afro In/Exclusion," 18.

119 Rahier, "Introduction," 2–3.

120 Walsh, "Afro In/Exclusion," 18.

121 Walsh, "Afro In/Exclusion," 19.

122 Barragan, "To End 500 Years of Great Terror," 59; Rahier, "Introduction," 5.

123 Dixon, "Transnational Black Social Movements in Latin America," 185; Walsh, "Afro In/Exclusion," 22.

124 Walsh, "Afro In/Exclusion," 22.

125 Walsh, "Afro In/Exclusion," 23. On the contrary, Law 70, known as the "Law of Black Communities" passed in 1993 in Colombia, has been focused on rural Afro-Colombians on the Pacific coast and has been criticized for eliding issues facing the urban Afro-Colombian population. Barragan, "To End 500 Years of Great Terror," 59.

126 Walsh, "Afro In/Exclusion," 26–27.

127 Walsh, "Afro In/Exclusion," 30–32.

128 Taylor, *From #BlackLivesMatter to Black Liberation*, 176.

129 Cantú and Rakia, "Fight for the Soul of the Black Lives Matter Movement"; Cooper, "Al Sharpton Does Not Have My Ear"; Oso, Tometi, and Wane, "Transformational Solidarity Webinar"; Taylor, *From #BlackLivesMatter to Black Liberation*.

130 Hesse and Hooker, "Introduction," 451. Minkah Makalani addresses the critique of this aspect of BLM that has come from other black political organizations, writing that black politics "seems capable of understanding BLM only in those terms that are on offer from dominant state apparatuses, whose protocols, procedures, and logics for redress are rooted in the same structures of liberal democratic governance that underpin the police's claim of the state's right to domestic sovereign violence." Makalani, "Black Lives Matter and the Limits of Formal Politics," 531.

131 The most comprehensive overview of the movement to date can be found in Taylor, *From #BlackLivesMatter to Black Liberation*.

132 Garza, "A #Herstory of the Black Lives Matter Movement"; Hunt, "Alicia Garza."

133 King, "#blacklivesmatter"; Oso, Tometi, and Wane, "Transformational Solidarity Webinar."

134 As of October 2015, there had been more than one thousand BLM demonstrations. "Black Lives Matter Chart of Demonstrations."

135 Taylor, *From #BlackLivesMatter to Black Liberation*, 166.

136 Makalani, "Black Lives Matter and the Limits of Formal Politics," 531; Garza, "A #Herstory of the Black Lives Matter Movement."

137 Makalani, "Black Lives Matter and the Limits of Formal Politics," 530.

138 The conference at the University of Arizona was organized by the digital publication *The Feminist Wire*.

139 "About Us."

140 Taylor, *From #BlackLivesMatter to Black Liberation*, 167.

141 Cullors and Moore, "Five Ways to Never Forget Ferguson."

142 Balko, "Black Lives Matter Policy Agenda"; *Campaign Zero*.

143 "Vision for Black Lives."

144 The same can be said of the non-state-centered black political organizations, such as the Mothers of May movement and the React or Die! campaign, that have emerged in Brazil to condemn anti-black state violence and the role of militarized police in black Brazilian communities. Mattos, "From Favelas to Ferguson"; Paschel, "From Colombia to the U.S."; Smith, "Battling Anti-Black Genocide in Brazil." Here, I am intending to point to a general tendency in contemporary black political movements in the Americas, but there are many exceptions to this tendency. For example, the November 2016 meeting of five hundred leaders of Afro-Colombian groups at the Summit of Afro-Descendant Peoples for Peace was largely focused on the role of multinational corporations in paramilitary violence and in the displacement of Afro-Colombian communities. Barragan, "To End 500 Years of Great Terror."

145 "Black Lives Matter Chart of Demonstrations."

146 Hesse and Hooker, "Introduction," 452; Paschel, "From Colombia to the U.S.," 29.

147 "Occupy Protests around the World"; "Black Lives Matter Chart of Demonstrations."

148 Oso, Tometi, and Wane, "Transformational Solidarity Webinar."

149 "About BAJI."

150 Oso, Tometi, and Wane, "Transformational Solidarity Webinar."

151 Oso, Tometi, and Wane, "Transformational Solidarity Webinar."

152 Oso, Tometi, and Wane, "Transformational Solidarity Webinar."

153 Oso, Tometi, and Wane, "Transformational Solidarity Webinar."

154 Oso, Tometi, and Wane, "Transformational Solidarity Webinar."

155 "Black Lives Matter Stands in Solidarity with Water Protectors at Standing Rock."

156 Smith, "Battling Anti-Black Genocide in Brazil," 44.

157 Hing, "'Black Lives Matter' Goes International."

158 Moore, Paye, and Shird, "Black Lives Matter Visits Cuba."

159 Baker, "Palestinians Express 'Solidarity.'"

160 Bailey, "Building Unity."

161 Dream Defenders, "Solidarity Demonstration in Nazareth."
162 "2015 Black Solidarity Statement with Palestine," www.blackforpalestine.com/read-the-statement.html, accessed February 8, 2018.
163 "2015 Black Solidarity Statement with Palestine."
164 Baker, "Palestinians Express 'Solidarity.'"
165 Baker, "Palestinians Express 'Solidarity.'"
166 Dream Defenders, "Solidarity Demonstration in Nazareth."
167 Baker, "Palestinians Express 'Solidarity.'"
168 "2015 Black Solidarity Statement with Palestine.
169 Dream Defenders, "Solidarity Demonstration in Nazareth."
170 Agnew, "To Ferguson///Witness."
171 Guevara, *Message to the Tricontinental.*
172 Agnew, "To Ferguson///Witness," emphasis original.

Conclusion

1 "Renunciar a la excepcionalidad y arrogancia yanquis para incorporar otros grupos sociales . . . y aspirar a reconocerse dentro de un contexto menos cerrado que el norteamericano, donde se pueda construir un discurso contra-hegemónico desde varias visiones, espacios y culturas. Un discurso antirracista que tome conciencia de su condición local, y, simultáneamente, de su condición global, reconociendo otras fórmulas contra el racismo (dominicanas, brasileñas, colombianas, cubanas, garífunas, sudafricanas e inmigrantes) como parte de sus propias luchas emancipatorias y no verlas como meras copias, realidades distantes o rivales en competencia por el protagonismo o el poder racial." Translations of excerpts from Zurbano's article are mine. Zurbano Torres, "Contra Ferguson."

2 "Internacionalizar la batalla contra el racismo, cuyo centro no se ubica en un lugar específico, sino en la diversa estructura económica, ideológica y cultural." Zurbano Torres, "Contra Ferguson."

3 "No solo desde y para las comunidades negras, sino un poco más allá, lo cual hace más complejo, democrático, crítico y autocrítico este proyecto de liberación global. . . . No olvidemos que, ante el poder, todos los oprimidos somos una masa indiferenciada." Zurbano Torres, "Contra Ferguson."

4 Lionnet and Shih, *Minor Transnationalism*; Ngũgĩ wa Thiong'o, *Globalectics.*

BIBLIOGRAPHY

Abascal, Ernesto Gómez. "Obama y el Oriente Medio." *Tricontinental* 168 (2010): 32–35.

Aboul-Ela, Hosam. "Global South, Local South: The New Postmodernism in U.S. Southern Studies." In "Global Contexts, Local Literatures: The New Southern Studies," ed. Katherine McKee and Annette Trefzer, special issue, *American Literature* 78.4: 847–858.

"About BAJI." Black Alliance for Just Immigration. http://www.blackalliance.org.

"About Us." Black Lives Matter. http://blacklivesmatter.com/about/.

Abramson, Michael, and Young Lords Party, eds. *Palante: Young Lords Party.* Chicago: Haymarket, 2011.

Abreu, Alberto. "El Black Power en la Cuba de los sesenta y setenta: Conversación con Juan Felipe Benemelis." *Afromodernidades.* October 20, 2012.

———. "Subalternidad: Debates teóricos y su representación en el campo cultural cubano postrevolucionario." *Argus-a* 3.10 (2013).

Abu-Jamal, Mumia. "Una democracia imperial." *Tricontinental* 152 (2002): 36.

———. "Derechos humanos imperiales." *Tricontinental* 148 (2001): 14–15.

———. "La raíz de la guerra es el dinero." *Tricontinental* 162 (2007): 60.

Acharya, Amitav, and See Seng Tan. "Introduction: The Normative Relevance of the Bandung Conference for Contemporary Asian and International Order." In *Bandung Revisited: The Legacy of the 1955 Asian-African Conference for International Order,* edited by See Seng Tan and Amitav Acharya, 1–16. Singapore: National University of Singapore Press, 2008.

Acosta, Abraham. *Thresholds of Illiteracy: Theory, Latin America, and the Crisis of Resistance*. Bronx, NY: Fordham University Press, 2014.

"Adbusters About." Adbusters. https://www.adbusters.org/about/adbusters.

Adi, Hakim. "The Negro Question: The Communist International and Black Liberation in the Interwar Years." In *From Toussaint to Tupac: The Black International since the Age of Revolution*, edited by Michael O. West, William G. Martin, and Fanon Che Wilkins, 155–175. Chapel Hill: University of North Carolina Press, 2009.

Adorno, Rolena. "Reconsidering Colonial Discourse for Sixteenth- and Seventeenth-Century Spanish America." *Latin American Research Review* 28.3 (1993): 135–145.

Afro-Hispanic Review 33.1 (Spring 2014).

Agnew, Philip. "To Ferguson///Witness." *Ebony*. September 2, 2014.

Algarín, Miguel, and Miguel Piñero, eds. *Nuyorican Poetry: An Anthology of Puerto Rican Words and Feeling*. New York: Morrow, 1975.

Álvarez, Rebecca, Erika Gutiérrez, Linda Kim, Christine Petit, and Ellen Reese. "The Contours of Color at the World Social Forum: Reflections on Racialized Politics, Representation, and the Global Justice Movement." *Critical Sociology* 34.3: 389–407.

Álvarez, Santiago, dir. *Hanoi Martes 13*. Havana: ICAIC, 1967.

———. *LBJ*. Havana: ICAIC, 1968.

———. *El movimiento Panteras Negras*. Havana: ICAIC, 1968.

———. *Now*. Havana: ICAIC, 1965.

Amar, Paul, ed. *The Middle East and Brazil: Perspectives on the New Global South*. Bloomington: Indiana University Press, 2014.

Amin, Samir. *The World We Wish to See*. New York: Monthly Review Press, 2008.

Ampiah, Kweku. *The Political and Moral Imperatives of the Bandung Conference of 1955: The Reactions of the US, UK, and Japan*. Kent, CT: Global Oriental, 2007.

Anderson, Benedict. *Imagined Communities: Reflections on the Origin and Spread of Nationalism*. London: Verso, 1983.

Anderson, Carol. *Eyes Off the Prize: The United Nations and the African American Struggle for Human Rights, 1944–1955*. New York: Cambridge University Press, 2003.

Aponte-Parés, Luis. "Lessons from El Barrio—the East Harlem Real Great Society/Urban Planning Studio: A Puerto Rican Chapter in the Fight for Urban Self-Determination." *New Political Science* 20.4 (1998): 399–420.

Appadurai, Arjun. "Grassroots Globalization and the Research Imagination." In *Globalization*, edited by Arjun Appadurai, 1–21. Durham, NC: Duke University Press, 2001.

———. *Modernity at Large: Cultural Dimensions of Globalization*. Minneapolis: University of Minnesota Press, 1996.

Araoz, Raydel, and Julio Ramos. *Retornar a La Habana con Guillén Landrián*. 2012.

Armillas-Tiseyra, Magalí, ed. "Dislocations." Special issue, *Global South* 7.2 (Fall 2014).

———. "Tales from the Corpolony: Ngũgĩ wa Thiong'o's *Wizard of the Crow* and the Dictator-Novel in the Time of Transition." *Research in African Literatures* (Forthcoming Spring 2018).

Arne Westad, Odd. *The Global Cold War: Third World Interventions and the Making of Our Times.* New York: Cambridge University Press, 2005.

Arnon, Ben. "How the Obama 'Hope' Poster Reached a Tipping Point and Became a Cultural Phenomenon: An Interview with the Artist Shepard Fairey." *Huffington Post.* August 13, 2008.

Ashcroft, Bill. "Modernity's First Born: Latin American and Post-colonial Transformation." In *El debate de la postcolonialidad en Latinoamérica: Una postmodernidad periférica o cambio de paradigma en el pensamiento latinoamericano,* edited by Alfonso de Toro and Fernando de Toro, 13–30. Madrid: Iberoamericana, 1999.

Ashcroft, Bill, Gareth Griffiths, and Helen Tiffin. *The Empire Writes Back: Theory and Practice in Post-colonial Literatures.* London: Routledge, 1989.

"At the Root." *Tricontinental* 25 (July–August 1971): 106–137.

Ayala, César J. *American Sugar Kingdom: The Plantation Economy of the Spanish Caribbean, 1898–1934.* Chapel Hill: University of North Carolina Press, 1999.

Bailey, Kristian Davis. "Building Unity, Wrecking Walls: Palestinians Come to Ferguson." *Ebony.* November 14, 2014.

Baker, Rana. "Palestinians Express 'Solidarity with the People of Ferguson' in Mike Brown Statement." *Electronic Intifada.* August 15, 2014.

Baldwin, James. "Princes and Powers." In *The Price of the Ticket: Collected Nonfiction 1948–85,* by James Baldwin, 41–63. New York: St. Martin's, 1985.

Balko, Radley. "The Black Lives Matter Policy Agenda Is Practical, Thoughtful—and Urgent." *Washington Post.* August 25, 2015.

Barcia, Manuel. "'Locking Horns with the Northern Empire': Anti-American Imperialism at the Tricontinental Conference of 1966 in Havana." *Journal of Transatlantic Studies* 7.3 (2009): 208–217.

Barnet, Miguel. *Biografía de un cimarrón.* 1966. Manchester: Manchester University Press, 2010.

Barragan, Yesenia. "To End 500 Years of Great Terror." *NACLA Report on the Americas* 49.1 (2017): 56–63.

Beasley-Murray, Jon. *Posthegemony: Political Theory and Latin America.* Minneapolis: University of Minnesota Press, 2010.

Becker, Marc. "Mariátegui, the Comintern, and the Indigenous Question in Latin America." *Science and Society* 70.4 (October 2006): 450–479.

———. *Mariátegui and Latin American Marxist Theory.* Athens: Ohio University Center for International Studies, 1993.

Bell, Christopher. *East Harlem Remembered: Oral Histories of Community and Diversity.* Jefferson, NC: McFarland, 2012.

Benítez, Iris. "Cambodia '70." *Palante* 2.2 (1970): 14.

Benítez-Rojo, Antonio. *La isla que se repite: El Caribe y la perspectiva posmoderna.* Hanover, NH: Ediciones del Norte, 1989.

———. *The Repeating Island: The Caribbean and the Postmodern Perspective.* Translated by James Maraniss. Durham, NC: Duke University Press, 1996.

Benson, Devyn Spence. *Antiracism in Cuba: The Unfinished Revolution.* Chapel Hill: University of North Carolina Press, 2016.

Berlant, Lauren. *Cruel Optimism.* Durham, NC: Duke University Press, 2011.

Betancourt, Juan René. *El negro: Ciudadano del futuro.* Havana: Cárdenas, 1959.

Beverley, John. "Hacia un nuevo latinoamericanismo (after 9/11)." *A-Contracorriente* 2.1 (2004): 21–32.

———. *Latinamericanism after 9/11.* Durham, NC: Duke University Press, 2001.

Birkenmaier, Anke. "Jacques Roumain y el Instituto Internacional de Estudios Afroamericanos: Circuitos caribeños." Paper presented at the Cuban Research Institute's Tenth Conference on Cuban and Cuban-American Studies, Miami, Florida, February 26–28, 2015.

"Black Lives Matter Chart of Demonstrations." Elephrame. https://elephrame.com /textbook/protests.

"Black Lives Matter Stands in Solidarity with Water Protectors at Standing Rock." Black Lives Matter. http://blacklivesmatter.com/solidarity-with-standing-rock/.

"Black Panthers: The Afro-Americans' Challenge." Interview with George Murray and Joudon Major Ford. *Tricontinental* 10 (January–February 1969): 96–111.

"Black Power: U.S. Version of Struggle against Colonialism." *Tricontinental Bulletin* 10 (January 1967): 5–7.

Black Solidarity with Palestine. http://www.blackforpalestine.com/.

Blitt, Barry. "The Politics of Fear." Cartoon. *New Yorker.* July 21, 2008.

B Media Collective. *Occupation Nation.* 2012. http://www.bmediacollective.org/tag /occupation-nation/.

"Bolivian Minister Rodolfo Illanes 'Killed by Miners.'" *Al Jazeera.* August 26, 2016.

Booth, David. "Cuba, Color and the Revolution." *Science and Society* 11.2 (1976): 129–172.

Booth, William. "Obama's On-the-Wall Endorsement." *Washington Post.* May 18, 2008.

Borstelmann, Thomas. *The Cold War and the Color Line: American Race Relations in the Global Arena.* Cambridge, MA: Harvard University Press, 2003.

Branche, Jerome. *Colonialism and Race in Luso-Hispanic Literature.* Columbia: University of Missouri Press, 2006.

Brandt, Willy. *North-South: A Programme for Survival: Report of the Independent Commission on International Development Issues.* Cambridge, MA: MIT Press, 1980.

Brenner, Neil. "The Space of the World: Beyond State-Centrism?" In *Immanuel Wallerstein and the Problem of the World: System, Scale, Culture*, edited by David Palumbo-Liu, Nirvana Tanoukhi, and Bruce Robbins, 101–137. Durham, NC: Duke University Press, 2011.

Brent, William Lee. *Long Time Gone.* New York: Times Books, 1996.

Brock, Lisa, and Digna Castañeda Fuertes. *Between Race and Empire: African-Americans and Cubans before the Cuban Revolution.* Philadelphia: Temple University Press, 1998.

Brown, Monica. *Gang Nation: Delinquent Citizens in Puerto Rican, Chicano, and Chicana Narratives*. Minneapolis: University of Minnesota Press, 2002.

Brown, Rap. "Letter from Prison to My Black Brothers and Sisters." *Tricontinental Bulletin* 27 (June 1968): 13–14.

Browne-Marshall, Gloria J. "'Occupy Wall Street' Is No Civil Rights Movement." *Insight News*. December 14, 2011.

Bucholz, Mary, and Kira Hall. "Language and Identity." In *A Companion to Linguistic Anthropology*, edited by Alessandro Duranti, 369–394. Malden, MA: Blackwell, 2004.

Buckley, Gail Lumet. *The Hornes: An American Family*. New York: Applause, 2002.

Bystrom, Kerry, and Joseph Slaughter, eds. *The Global South Atlantic*. Bronx, NY: Fordham University Press, 2017.

Cabrera, Ángel Guerra. "Mandela, Obama, y Raúl." *Tricontinental* 179 (2014): 51.

Cabrera Infante, Guillermo. "Un mes lleno de *Lunes*." In *Lunes de Revolución: Literatura y cultura en los primeros años de la Revolución Cubana*, by William Luis, 137–153. Madrid: Editorial Verbum, 2003.

Caminero-Santangelo, Marta. "'Puerto Rican Negro': Defining Race in Piri Thomas's *Down These Mean Streets*." *Melus* 29.2 (2004): 205–226.

Campaign Zero. http://www.joincampaignzero.org/#vision.

Cantú, Aaron Miguel, and Raven Rakia. "The Fight for the Soul of the Black Lives Matter Movement." *Gothamist*. April 7, 2015.

Capote, René Anillo. *La solidaridad Tricontinental: Mucho más que un anhelo*. Havana: Editora Política, 1996.

Carbonell, Walterio. "Congreso mundial de países sub-desarrollados." *Revolución* (December 5, 1959): 2.

———. *Crítica: Como surgió la cultural nacional*. Havana: Ediciones Yaka, 1961.

———. "La intervención belga y las intrigas imperialistas en la República del Congo." *Lunes de Revolución* 75 (September 5, 1960): 4–7.

———. "Lo que Bandung significó para mí." *Revolución* (February 4, 1960): 2.

Carmichael, Stokely. "Black Power and the Third World." Address to the Organization of Latin American Solidarity, Havana, Cuba, August 1967. Thornhill, Ontario: Third World Information Service, 1967.

———. "The Third World—Our World." *Tricontinental* 1 (July–August 1967): 15–22.

Carpentier, Alejo. *Ecué-Yamba-Ó*. Madrid: AKAL, 2010.

Carrero, Jaime. *Jet neorriqueño: Neo-Rican Jetliner*. San Juan: Universidad Interamericana, 1964.

El cartel de la OSPAAAL. Tricontinental. Varese, Italy: Il Papiro, 1997.

Casal, Lourdes. "Race Relations in Contemporary Cuba." In *The Position of Blacks in Brazil and Cuban Society*, edited by Anani Dzidzienyo and Lourdes Casal. London: Minority Rights Group, Report 7, 1979.

Casamayor, Odette. "The Obamas and the Blacks of Cuba: Some Questions of Power, Agency, and Representation." *Huffington Post*. March 28, 2016.

Cassano, Franco. *Southern Thought and Other Essays on the Mediterranean*. Edited and translated by Norma Bouchard and Valerio Ferme. New York: Fordham University Press, 2012.

Castells, Manuel. *Networks of Outrage and Hope: Social Movements in the Internet Age*. Cambridge: Polity, 2012.

———. "A Network Theory of Power." *International Journal of Communication* 5 (2011): 773–787.

Castillo, Luciano, and Manuel M. Hadad. "With Santiago Álvarez: Chronicler of the Third World." *ReVista: Harvard Review of Latin America* 8.3 (2009): https://revista.drclas.harvard.edu/book/santiago-álvarez-chronicler-third-world.

Castro, Fidel. "Angola: African Giron." Lecture, Karl Marx Theater, Havana, Cuba, April 19, 1976. In *Fidel Castro Speeches: Cuba's Internationalist Foreign Policy 1975–80*, edited by Michael Taber, 86–97. New York: Pathfinder, 1981.

———. "El hermano Obama." *Tricontinental* 182 (September 2016): 64.

———. "Shattered Myths." *Tricontinental* 48 (March–April 1976): 13–16.

Center for the Study of Political Graphics. *Globalize* THIS! *International Graphics of Resistance Exhibition Guide*. Culver City, CA: Center for the Study of Political Graphics, 2001.

Cervantes Vásquez, Lourdes. Interview by Anne Garland Mahler. Tape recording. OSPAAAL Headquarters. Havana, Cuba. July 28, 2014.

Césaire, Aimé. *Cahier d'un retour au pays natal/ Notebook of a Return to a Native Land*. 1939. Translated by Mireille Rosello and Annie Pritchard. Northumberland, UK: Bloodaxe, 1995.

———. "Culture and Colonization." Translated by Brent Hayes Edwards. *Social Text* 28.2: 127–144.

———. *Discourse on Colonialism*. Translated by Joan Pinkham. New York: Monthly Review Press, 1972.

———. *Discours sur le colonialisme*. Paris: Présence Africaine, 1955.

Cha-Jua, Sundiata Keita, and Clarence Lang. "The 'Long Movement' as Vampire: 1 Temporal and Spatial Fallacies in Recent Black Freedom Studies." *Journal of African American History* 92.2 (2007): 265–288.

Chakrabarty, Dipesh. "The Legacies of Bandung: Decolonization and the Politics of Culture." In *Making a World after Empire: The Bandung Moment and Its Political Afterlives*, edited by Christopher J. Lee, 45–68. Athens: Ohio University Press, 2010.

Chanan, Michael. *BFI Dossier, No. 2: Santiago Álvarez*. London: British Film Institute, 1980.

———. *Cuban Cinema*. Minneapolis: University of Minnesota Press, 2004.

———. *The Cuban Image: Cinema and Cultural Politics in Cuba*. London: British Film Institute, 1985.

Charity, Tom. "A Prolific Cuban Filmmaker's Inventive Newsreel Agitprop." *Village Voice*. April 5, 2005.

"Charlado con Richard Wright" [Interview with Richard Wright]. *Lunes de Revolución* 75 (September 5, 1960): 10–12.

Chase, Jacquelyn. *The Spaces of Neoliberalism: Land, Place, and Family in Latin America*. Bloomfield, CT: Kumarian, 2002.

Chen, Adrian. "The Truth about Anonymous's Activism." *Nation*. November 11, 2014.

Chomsky, Aviva. *A History of the Cuban Revolution*. West Sussex, UK: Blackwell, 2011.

Cleaver, Eldridge. *Soul on Ice*. Waco, TX: Word Books, 1978.

Clough, Patricia Tiniceto, with Jean Halley, eds. *The Affective Turn: Theorizing the Social*. Durham, NC: Duke University Press, 2007.

Clytus, John. *Black Man in Red Cuba*. Coral Gables, FL: University of Miami Press, 1970.

Cobb, Martha. *Harlem, Haiti, and Havana: A Comparative Critical Study of Langston Hughes, Jacques Roumain, Nicolás Guillén*. Washington, DC: Three Continent Press, 1979.

Cohn, Deborah. *History and Memory in the Two Souths: Recent Southern and Spanish American Fiction*. Nashville, TN: Vanderbilt University Press, 1999.

———. "US Southern and Latin American Studies: Postcolonial and Inter-American Approaches." *Global South* 1.1 (2007): 38–44.

———. "U.S. Southern Studies and Latin American Studies: Windows onto Postcolonial Studies." In "Global Contexts, Local Literatures: The New Southern Studies," ed. Katherine McKee and Annette Trefzer, special issue, *American Literature* 78.4: 704–707.

Colón, Jesús. *A Puerto Rican in New York and Other Sketches*. 1961. New York: International Publishers, 1982.

Comaroff, Jean, and John. L. Comaroff. *Theory from the South: or, How Euro-America Is Evolving toward Africa*. Boulder, CO: Paradigm, 2012.

Communist International, South American Secretariat. *El movimiento revolucionario latinoamericano: Versiones de la Primera Conferencia Comunista Latinoamericana Junio de 1929*. Buenos Aires: SSA de la IC, 1929.

Connell, Raewyn. *Southern Theory: The Global Dynamics of Knowledge in Social Science*. Cambridge: Polity, 2007.

Conservapedia. "Radical Roots of Barack Hussein Obama." Last modified February 9, 2017. http://www.conservapedia.com/Radical_roots_of_Barack_Hussein_Obama.

"Contents." *Tricontinental* 25 (July–August 1971): 1–2.

"Contra la geopolítica imperialista." *Tricontinental* 149 (2000): 3.

Conway, Janet. *Edges of Global Justice: The World Social Forum and Its "Others."* London: Routledge, 2013.

Cooper, Brittany. "Al Sharpton Does Not Have My Ear: Why We Need New Black Leadership Now." *Salon*. August 26, 2014.

Coronil, Fernando. "Elephants in the Americas? Latin American Postcolonial Studies and Global Decolonization." In *Coloniality at Large: Latin America and the Postcolonial Debate*, edited by Mabel Moraña, Enrique Dussel, and Carlos A. Jáuregui. Durham, NC: Duke University Press, 2008.

Cort, Aisha. "Negrometraje: Literature and Race in Revolutionary Cuba." PhD diss., Emory University, 2010.

Cosme, Pedro Rodríguez. "Aguadilla: Violence against the Poor Continues." *Palante* 3.20 (December–January 1971): 6.

Cullors, Patrisse, and Darnell Moore. "Five Ways to Never Forget Ferguson—and Deliver Real Justice for Michael Brown." *Guardian*. September 4, 2014.

Cushing, Lincoln. "Cuban Poster Art and the Spirit of Revolution." Lecture, Humanities Week 2014, University of Arizona, Tucson. October 15, 2014.

———. "Directory of San Francisco Bay Area Political Poster Workshops, Print Shops, and Distributors." Docs Populi. April 5, 2014. http://www.docspopuli.org /articles/BayAreaRadicalShops.html#PeoplesPress.

———. "One Struggle, Two Communities: Late 20th Century Political Posters of Havana, Cuba and the San Francisco Bay Area." Docs Populi. http://www .docspopuli.org/articles/Cuba/BACshow.html.

———. "Red All Over: The Visual Language of Dissent." *AIGA, the Professional Association for Design*. January 9, 2007. http://www.aiga.org/red-all-over/.

Dados, Nour, and Raewyn Connell. "The Global South." *Contexts* 11.1 (Winter 2012): 12–13.

Dainotto, Roberto M. "Does Europe Have a South? An Essay on Borders." In "The Global South and World Dis/Order," edited by Caroline Levander and Walter Mignolo, special issue, *Global South* 5.1 (Spring 2011): 37–50.

———. "A South with a View: Europe and Its Other." *Nepantla: Views from the South* 1.2 (2000): 375–390.

Dalleo, Raphael, and Elena Machado Sáez. *The Latino/a Canon and the Emergence of Post-Sixties Literature*. New York: Palgrave Macmillan, 2007.

Dalzell, Tom. "Jane Norling." Quirkly Berkeley: The Quirky Material Culture of Berkeley. January 28, 2014. http://quirkyberkeley.com/jane-norling/.

Daulatzai, Sohail. *Black Star, Crescent Moon: The Muslim International and Black Freedom beyond America*. Minneapolis: University of Minnesota Press, 2012.

Davis, Angela Y. "Angela Davis: Estados Unidos." *Tricontinental* 41 (November–December 1974): 139–149.

———. "De Angela Davis a los presos politicos mexicanos." *Tricontinental Bulletin* 66 (September 1971): 2.

Davis, Darién J., and Judith Michelle Williams. "Pan-Africanism, Negritude, and the Currency of Blackness: Cuba, the Francophone Caribbean, and Brazil in Comparative Perspective, 1930s–50s." In *Beyond Slavery: The Multilayered Legacy of Africans in Latin America and the Caribbean*, edited by Darién J. Davis, 143–170. Lanham, MD: Rowman and Littlefield, 2007.

DeCosta-Willis, Miriam, ed. *Blacks in Hispanic Literature*. Baltimore: Black Classic Press, 2011.

———. "Social Lyricism and the Caribbean Poet/Rebel." In *Blacks in Hispanic Literature*, edited by Miriam DeCosta-Willis, 114–122. Baltimore: Black Classic Press, 2011.

de la Fuente, Alejandro. *A Nation for All: Race, Inequality, and Politics in Twentieth-Century Cuba*. Chapel Hill: University of North Carolina Press, 2001.

Deleuze, Gilles, and Félix Guattari. *Anti-Oedipus: Capitalism and Schizophrenia*. Translated by Robert Hurley, Mark Seem, and Helen R. Lane. New York: Viking, 1977.

———. *A Thousand Plateaus: Capitalism and Schizophrenia*. Translated by Brian Massumi. London: Continuum, 2008.

Dery, Mark. "The Merry Pranksters and the Art of the Hoax." *New York Times*. December 23, 1990.

Dirlik, Arif. "Global South: Predicament and Promise." *Global South* 1.1 (2007): 12–23.

Dixon, Kwame. "Transnational Black Social Movements in Latin America: Afro Colombians and the Struggle for Human Rights." In *Latin American Social Movements in the Twenty-First Century: Resistance, Power, and Democracy*, edited by R. Stahler Sholk, H. Vanden, and G. Kuecker, 181–195. Plymouth, MD: Rowman and Littlefield, 2008.

"Documents of the First Tricontinental Conference: The Rights of Afro-Americans in the United States." *Tricontinental Bulletin* 5–6 (August–September 1966): 20–22.

Domínguez, Jorge. *Cuba: Order and Revolution*. Cambridge, MA: Belknap Press of Harvard University Press, 1978.

———. "Racial and Ethnic Relations in the Cuban Armed Forces: A Non-topic." *Armed Forces and Society* 2.2 (1982): 19–70.

Douglas, Emory, Bobby Seale, Sam Durant, and Sonia Sanchez. *Black Panther: The Revolutionary Art of Emory Douglas*. New York: Rizzoli, 2007.

Dream Defenders. "Solidarity Demonstration in Nazareth: Ferguson to Palestine." https://vimeo.com/116675694.

Duarte, Amelia, and Ariadna Ruiz. "El collage de la nostalgia: Una mirada desde la colina, Rasgos postmodernos de la obra documental de Nicolás Guillén Landrián." *Cine cubano* 20 (January–March 2011).

Duarte, Martha. "U.S. Out of Quisquella." *Palante* 2.13 (October 1970): 18–19.

Du Bois, W. E. B. *Darkwater: Voices from within the Veil*. 1920. In *The Oxford W. E. B. Du Bois Reader*, edited by Eric J. Sundquist, 481–623. New York: Oxford University Press, 1996.

———. "The Negro Problems." In *The Negro*, by W. E. B. Du Bois, 232–242. 1915. New York: Oxford University Press, 2007.

———. *The Souls of Black Folk*. Edited by David W. Blight and Robert Gooding-Williams. Boston: Bedford, 1997.

Dudziak, Mary L. *Cold War Civil Rights: Race and the Image of American Democracy*. Princeton, NJ: Princeton University Press, 2000.

Edwards, Brent Hayes. *The Practice of Diaspora: Literature, Translation, and the Rise of Black Internationalism*. Cambridge, MA: Harvard University Press, 2003.

Eisenstein, Sergei. *Film Form: Essays in Film Theory*. Translated by Jay Leyda. New York: Harcourt, 1977.

Enck-Wanzer, Darrell. "Gender Politics, Democratic Demand, and Anti-essentialism in the New York Young Lords." In *Latina/o Discourse in Vernacular Spaces: Somos de una voz?*, edited by Michelle A. Holling and Bernadette M. Calafell, 59–80. Lanham, MD: Lexington, 2011.

"Entre todo el pueblo se escribe un poema." *Palante* 3.13 (1971): 16.

Escobar, Arturo. "Worlds and Knowledges Otherwise: The Latin American Modernity/Coloniality Research Program." In *Globalization and the Decolonial Option*, edited by Walter D. Mignolo and Arturo Escobar, 33–64. New York: Routledge, 2010.

Essif, Amien. "How Black Lives Matter Has Spread into a Global Movement to End Racist Policing: The Next Baltimore Could Be Somewhere in Europe." *In These Times*. June 29, 2015.

Estrada Lescaille, Ulises. "La habana frente al racismo." *Tricontinental* 148 (2001): 3.

Estrada Lescaille, Ulises, and Luis Suárez. *Rebelión Tricontinental: Las voces de los condenados de la tierra de África, Asia y América Latina*. New York: Ocean Press, 2006.

"The Export of Apartheid to Latin America." *Tricontinental* 54 (1977): 32–40.

Fanon, Frantz. *Black Skin, White Masks*. Translated by Richard Philcox. New York: Grove, 2008.

———. *Les damnés de la terre*. Paris: François Maspero, éditeur, 1961.

———. *Peau noire, masques blancs*. Paris: Éditions du Seuil, 1952.

———. *The Wretched of the Earth*. Translated by Constance Farrington. New York: Grove, 1963.

Farrow, Kenyon. "Occupy Wall Street's Race Problem." *American Prospect*. October 24, 2011.

Featherstone, Ralph. Letter to Mr. Osmany Cienfuegos Goriarán. *Tricontinental Bulletin* 27 (June 1968): 30.

Feinberg, Leslie. Interview with Sylvia Rivera. *Workers World*. www.workers.org/ww/1998/sylvia0702.php.

Feliú, Santiago. Interview by Anne Garland Mahler. Tape recording. OSPAAAL Headquarters. Havana, Cuba. July 28, 2014.

Fernández, Johanna. "Denise Oliver and the Young Lords Party: Stretching the Political Boundaries of Struggle." In *Want to Start a Revolution? Radical Women in the Black Freedom Struggle*, edited by Dayo F. Gore, Jeanne Theoharis, and Komozi Woodard, 271–293. New York: New York University Press, 2009.

———. "Radicals in the Late 1960s: A History of the Young Lords Party, 1969–1974." PhD diss., Columbia University, 2004.

Fernández, Y. P. "La revolución contra el racismo." *La Jiribilla* 621 (March 30–April 5, 2013).

Ferrer, Ada. *Freedom's Mirror: Cuba and Haiti in the Age of Revolution*. New York: Cambridge University Press, 2014.

———. *Insurgent Cuba: Race, Nation, and Revolution, 1868–1898*. Chapel Hill: University of North Carolina Press, 1999.

"The First Afro-Asian-Latin American Peoples' Solidarity Conference." *Peking Review* 4 (January 21, 1966): 19–25.

Flores, Juan. *Divided Borders: Essays on Puerto Rican Identity*. Houston: Houston University Press, 1993.

Flores, Juan, and Miriam Jiménez Román. "Introduction." In *The Afro-Latin@ Reader: History and Culture in the United States*, edited by Juan Flores and Miriam Jiménez Román, 1–15. Durham, NC: Duke University Press, 2010.

Fominaya, Cristina Flesher. *Social Movements and Globalization: How Protests, Occupation, and Uprisings Are Changing the World*. London: Palgrave Macmillan, 2014.

Ford . . . has the better idea. Illustration. *Tricontinental* 3 (November–December 1967), fourth cover.

Forman, James. "United States 1967: High Tide of Black Resistance." *Tricontinental* 6 (May–June 1968): 22–51.

Fornet, Ambrosio. "El quinquenio gris: Revisitando el término." In *La política cultural del período revolucionario: Memoria y reflexión*. Centro Teórico-Cultural Criterios. Casa de las Américas, Havana. January 30, 2007.

Fox, Geoffrey E. "Race and Class in Contemporary Cuba." In *Cuban Communism*, 3rd ed., edited by Irving Louis Hervowitz, 421–444. New Brunswick, NJ: Transaction, 1977.

"Frantz Fanon: Man of Violence." *Tricontinental Bulletin* 23 (December 1967): 21–23.

Frick, Richard, ed. *The Tricontinental Solidarity Poster*. Bern, Switzerland: Comedia, 2003.

Fukuyama, Francis. *The End of History and the Last Man*. New York: Free Press, 1992.

Gaiter, Colette. "What Revolution Looks Like: The Work of Black Panther Artist Emory Douglas." In *Black Panther: The Revolutionary Art of Emory Douglas*, edited by Sam Durant, 93–109. New York: Rizzoli, 2007.

Galloway, Alexander R., and Eugene Thacker. *The Exploit: A Theory of Networks*. Minneapolis: University of Minnesota Press, 2007.

Gan, Jessi. "'Still at the Back of the Bus': Sylvia Rivera's Struggle." CENTRO *Journal* 19.1 (Spring 2007): 125–139.

García Canclini, Nestor. *Consumidores y ciudadanos: Conflictos multiculturales de la globalización*. Mexico: Grijalbo, 1995.

García Márquez, Gabriel. "Operation Carlota." *Tricontinental* 53 (1977): 4–25.

Garza, Alicia. "A #Herstory of the Black Lives Matter Movement." *Feminist Wire*. October 7, 2014. http://www.thefeministwire.com/2014/10/blacklivesmatter-2/.

Gates, Henry Louis, Jr. "Cuban Experience: Eldridge Cleaver on Ice." Interview with Eldridge Cleaver. *Transition* 49 (1975).

———. "Third World of Theory: Enlightenment's Esau." *Critical Inquiry* 34.S2 (2008): S191–S205.

Gavin, James. *Stormy Weather: The Life of Lena Horne*. New York: Atria, 2009.

"General Declaration from the Tricontinental." *Tricontinental Bulletin* 1 (April 1966): 18–22.

George, Edward. *The Cuban Intervention in Angola, 1965–1991: From Che Guevara to Cuito Canavale.* London: Routledge, 2012.

Gerassi, John, ed. *The Coming of the New International: A Revolutionary Anthology.* New York: World Publishing, 1971.

Getino, Octavio, and Fernando Solanas. "Towards a Third Cinema." *Tricontinental* 13 (July–August 1969): 107–132.

Gettig, Eric. "'A Propaganda Boon for Us': The Havana Tricontinental Conference and the United States Response." Paper presented at The Transnational Revolution: Tricontinentalism at Fifty symposium, Austin, Texas, April 15, 2016.

Gibson, Richard. "El negro americano mira hacia Cuba." *Lunes de Revolución* 66 (July 4, 1960): 6.

Gibson, Richard, and Robert F. Williams. "La constante lucha de los negros por su libertad." *Lunes de Revolución* 66 (July 4, 1960): 7–8.

Gilmore, Glenda. *Defying Dixie: The Radical Roots of Civil Rights, 1919–1950.* New York: W. W. Norton, 2008.

Gilroy, Paul. *The Black Atlantic: Modernity and Double Consciousness.* Cambridge, MA: Harvard University Press, 1993.

Giral, Sergio, dir. *Cimarrón.* Havana: ICAIC, 1967.

———. *Maluala.* Havana: ICAIC, 1979.

———. *El otro Francisco.* Havana: ICAIC, 1975.

———. *Rancheador.* Havana: ICAIC, 1979.

Gladwell, Malcolm. "Small Change: Why the Revolution Will Not Be Tweeted." *New Yorker.* October 4, 2010.

Gleijeses, Piero. *Conflicting Missions: Havana, Washington, and Africa (1959–1976).* Chapel Hill: University of North Carolina Press, 2002.

———. *Visions of Freedom: Havana, Washington, Pretoria, and the Struggle for Southern Africa, 1976–1991.* Chapel Hill: University of North Carolina Press, 2013.

Glissant, Édouard. *Poetics of Relation.* Translated by Betsy Wing. Ann Arbor: University of Michigan, 1997.

"Globalizar la solidaridad." *Tricontinental* 170 (2011): first cover.

Goldstein, Joseph. "Old New York Police Surveillance Is Found, Forcing Big Brother Out of Hiding." *New York Times.* June 16, 2016.

González, Gloria. "Porque Ponce." *Palante* 3.3 (February 1971): 17.

González, Juan. "Armed Struggle." *Palante* 3.13 (1971): 8–9.

González García, Monica. "On the Borderlands of U.S. Empire: The Limitations of Geography, Ideology, and Disciplinarity." In *Trans-Americanity: Subaltern Modernities, Global Coloniality, and the Cultures of Greater Mexico*, edited by José David Saldivar, 183–211. Durham, NC: Duke University Press, 2012.

Gosse, Van. *Where the Boys Are: Cuba, Cold War America, and the Making of a New Left*. London: Verso, 1993.

Gramsci, Antonio. *The Southern Question*. Translated by Pasquale Verdicchio. New York: Berdighera, 1995.

Grandin, Greg. "Why the Left Continues to Win in Latin America." *Nation*. October 27, 2014.

Grau, Lester W. "¿Por qué Afganistán?" *Tricontinental* 149 (2001): 32–39.

Gregg, Melissa, and Gregory J. Seigworth, eds. *The Affect Theory Reader*. Durham, NC: Duke University Press, 2010.

Grewal, David Singh. *Network Power: The Social Dynamics of Globalization*. New Haven, CT: Yale University Press, 2008.

Gronbeck-Tedesco, John A. *Cuba, the United States, and Cultures of the Transnational Left, 1930–75*. New York: Cambridge University Press, 2015.

Gruesz, Kirsten Silva. *Ambassadors of Culture: The Transamerican Origins of Latino Writing*. Princeton, NJ: Princeton University Press, 2002.

Guan, Ang Cheng. "The Bandung Conference and the Cold War International History of Southeast Asia." In *Bandung Revisited: The Legacy of the 1955 Asian-African Conference for International Order*, edited by See Seng Tan and Amitav Acharya, 27–47. Singapore: National University of Singapore Press, 2008.

Guerra, Lillian. *Popular Expression and National Identity in Puerto Rico: The Struggle for Self, Community, and Nation*. Gainesville: University Press of Florida, 1998.

———. *Visions of Power in Cuba: Revolution, Redemption and Resistance, 1959–1971*. Chapel Hill: University of North Carolina Press, 2012.

Guevara, Che. *Message to the Tricontinental*. Special supplement, *Tricontinental*, April 16, 1967.

Guillén, Nicolás. *West Indies, Ltd*. Havana: Imp. Ucar, García y Cía, 1934.

Guillén Landrián, Nicolás. "El cine postergado." Interview by Lara Petusky Coger, Alejandro Ríos, and Manuel Zayas. *Cubaencuentro*. September 2, 2005. arch1 .cubaencuentro.com/entrevistas/20050904/74540a9e00385c591a45bac12d946245 /1.html.

———, dir. *Coffea arábiga*. Havana: ICAIC, 1968.

Gulliver, Sophie. "Is the 'Pink Tide' Turning in Latin America?" Australian Institute of International Affairs. March 22, 2016. http://www.internationalaffairs.org.au /is-the-pink-tide-turning-in-latin-america/.

Guneratne, Anthony R. "Introduction: Rethinking Third Cinema." In *Rethinking Third Cinema*, edited by Anthony R. Guneratne and Wimal Dissanayake, 1–28. New York: Routledge, 2003.

Guridy, Frank Andre. *Forging Diaspora: Afro-Cubans and African Americans in a World of Empire and Jim Crow*. Chapel Hill: University of North Carolina Press, 2010.

Guterl, Matthew Pratt. "South." In *Keywords for American Cultural Studies*, edited by Bruce Burgett and Glenn Hendler, 230–233. New York: New York University Press, 2007.

Guzmán, Pablo "Yoruba." "apollo gig." *Palante* 2.2 (1970): 3.

———. "Editorial." *Palante* 2.12 (1970): 2.

———. "History of Boriken." *Palante* 3.3 (February 1971): 4–5.

———. "Lucha por tu patria." *Palante* 2.13 (October 1970): 2–3.

———. "*La Vida Pura*: A Lord of the Barrio." In *The Puerto Rican Movement: Voices from the Diaspora*, edited by Andrés Torres and José E. Velázquez, 155–172. Philadelphia: Temple University Press, 1998.

———. "We Are a Nation." *Palante* 2.14 (October 1970): 6.

———. "Writing a Constitution for the People." *Palante* 2.12 (1970): 16–17.

Hale, Charles. "Neoliberal Multiculturalism: The Remaking of Cultural Rights and Racial Dominance in Central America." *PoLAR: Political and Legal Anthropology Review* 28.1: 10–28.

Halim, Hala. 2012. "*Lotus*, the Afro-Asian Nexus, and Global South Comparatism." *Comparative Studies of South Asia, Africa, and the Middle East* 32.3 (2012): 563–583.

Hall, Stuart. "Whites of Their Eyes: Racist Ideologies and the Media." In *Gender, Race, and Class in Media*, edited by Gail Dines and Jean M. Humez, 18–22. Thousand Oaks, CA: Sage, 1995.

Hardt, Michael. "Militant Life." *New Left Review* 64 (July–August 2010): 151–160.

Hardt, Michael, and Antonio Negri. *Empire*. Cambridge, MA: Harvard University Press, 2000.

Harper, Jennifer. "Inside the Beltway: The Handshake Heard 'round the World." *Washington Times*. December 10, 2013.

Harvey, David. *A Brief History of Neoliberalism*. Oxford: Oxford University Press, 2005.

Hatzky, Christine. *Cubans in Angola: South-South Cooperation and Transfer of Knowledge, 1976–1991*. Madison: University of Wisconsin Press, 2015.

Helg, Aline. *Our Rightful Share: The Afro-Cuban Struggle for Equality, 1886–1912*. Chapel Hill: University of North Carolina Press, 1995.

Hemmings, Clare. "Affective Solidarity: Feminist Reflexivity and Political Transformation." *Feminist Theory* 13.2 (August 2012): 147–161.

Henighan, Stephen. "The Cuban Fulcrum and the Search for a Transatlantic Revolutionary Culture in Angola, Mozambique, and Chile, 1965–2008." *Journal of Transatlantic Studies* 7.3 (2009): 233–248.

Hess, John. "Santiago Alvarez: Cine Agitator for the Cuban Revolution and the Third World." In *Show Us Life*, edited by Thomas Waugh, 384–402. Metuchen, NJ: Scarecrow, 1984.

Hesse, Barnor, and Juliet Hooker. "Introduction: On Black Political Thought Inside Global Black Protest." In "After #Ferguson, After #Baltimore: The Challenge of Black Death and Black Life for Black Political Thought," edited by Barnor Hesse and Juliet Hooker, special issue, *South Atlantic Quarterly* 116.3 (July 2017): 443–456.

Hill, Jane H. "Language, Race, and White Public Space." In *Linguistic Anthropology: A Reader*, edited by Alessandro Duranti, 479–492. Malden, MA: Blackwell, 2001.

Hing, Julianne. "'Black Lives Matter' Goes International." *Colorlines*. January 30, 2015. http://www.colorlines.com/articles/black-lives-matter-goes-international.

Hodes, Martha. "Wartime Dialogues on Illicit Sex: White Women and Black Men." In *Divided Houses: Gender and the Civil War*, edited by Catherine Clinton and Nina Silber, 230–246. New York: Oxford University Press, 1992.

Holcomb, Gary Edward. *Claude McKay, Code Name Sasha*. Gainesville: University Press of Florida, 2007.

Hooker, Juliet. *Race and the Politics of Solidarity*. Oxford: Oxford University Press, 2009.

Howe, Linda S. *Transgression and Conformity: Cuban Writers and Artists after the Revolution*. Madison: University of Wisconsin Press, 2004.

Huiswoud, Otto, and Claude McKay. "Speeches to the 4th World Congress of the Comintern on the Negro Question." November 25, 1922. *Bulletin of the IV Congress of the Communist International* 22 (December 2, 1922): 17–23.

Hunt, Elle. "Alicia Garza on the Beauty and the Burden of Black Lives Matter." *Guardian*. September 2, 2016.

Hutchings, Phil. "Che Guevara and Afro-Americans." *Tricontinental* 8 (September–October 1968): 129.

Hutchinson, Coleman. "Souths." CR: *The New Centennial Review* 10.1 (2010): 63–64.

Ideology of the Young Lords Party. Bronx, NY: Young Lords National Headquarters, 1972.

International Preparatory Committee of the First Solidarity Conference of the Peoples of Africa, Asia and Latin America and the Cuban National Committee. "Agenda Draft." *Towards the First Tricontinental Conference* 1 (October 15, 1965): 8–9.

———. "Background of Tricontinental Conference to Be Held in Havana." *Towards the First Tricontinental Conference* 1 (October 15, 1965): 3–4.

———. "In the Country of the Conference." *Towards the First Tricontinental Conference* 2 (November 1, 1965): 9.

Jack, Homer A. "The Cairo Conference." *Africa Today* 5.2 (March–April 1958): 3–9.

Jackson, Richard L. *The Black Image in Latin American Literature*. Albuquerque: University of New Mexico Press, 1976.

———. *Black Literature and Humanism in Latin America*. Athens: University of Georgia Press, 1988.

———. *Black Writers and Latin America: Cross-Cultural Affinities*. Washington, DC: Howard University Press, 1998.

Jefeits, Lazar, and Victor Jefeits. *América Latina en la Internacional Comunista, 1919–1943, Diccionario biográfico*. Santiago: Ariadna Ediciones, 2015.

Jiménez Sosa, Victor, and Jorge Egusquiza Zorrilla. *Nicolás: El fin pero no es el fin*. Coincident Productions and Village Films, 2005.

Joseph, Peniel E. *Waiting 'til the Midnight Hour: A Narrative History of Black Power in America*. New York: Henry Holt, 2006.

Josephy, Alvin M., Joane Nagel, and Troy Johnson, eds. *Red Power: The American Indians' Fight for Freedom*. 2nd ed. Lincoln: University of Nebraska Press, 1999.

Kahin, George McTurnan. *The Asian-African Conference: Bandung, Indonesia, April 1955*. Ithaca, NY: Cornell University Press, 1956.

Kelley, Robin D. G. *Freedom Dreams: The Black Radical Imagination*. Boston: Beacon, 2003.

———. *Hammer and Hoe: Alabama Communists during the Great Depression*. Chapel Hill: University of North Carolina Press, 1990.

Kersffeld, Daniel. "La Liga Antiimperialista de las Américas: Una construcción política entre el marxismo y el latinoamericanismo." In *El comunismo: Otras miradas desde América Latina*, edited by Elvira Concheiro Bórquez, Horacio Crespo, and Massimo Modonesi, 151–166. Mexico: Universidad Nacional Autónoma de México, 2007.

King, Jamilah. "#blacklivesmatter: How Three Friends Turned a Spontaneous Facebook Post into a Global Phenomenon." *California Sunday Magazine*. March 1, 2015.

Klein, Naomi. *No Logo*. London: Macmillan, 2009.

Klengel, Susanne, and Alexandra Ortiz Wallner, eds. *Sur/South: Poetics and Politics of Thinking Latin America/India*. Madrid: Iberoamericana, 2016.

Kuhn, Leon. "On/Off." Cartoon. *Tricontinental* 167 (2009): 7.

Kutzinski, Vera M. *Sugar's Secrets: Race and the Erotics of Cuban Nationalism*. Charlottesville: University of Virginia Press, 1993.

Lane, Jill. *Blackface Cuba, 1840–1895*. Philadelphia: University of Pennsylvania Press, 2005.

Latner, Teishan. "Take Me to Havana! Airline Hijacking, U.S.-Cuba Relations, and Political Protest in Late Sixties' America." *Diplomatic History* 39.1 (January 2015): 16–44.

Lee, Christopher J. "Between a Moment and an Era: The Origins and Afterlives of Bandung." In *Making a World after Empire: The Bandung Moment and Its Political Afterlives*, edited by Christopher J. Lee, 1–42. Athens: Ohio University Press, 2010.

———, ed. *Making a World after Empire: The Bandung Moment and Its Political Afterlives*. Athens: Ohio University Press, 2010.

Lee, Richard E. "The Modern World-System: Its Structures, Its Geoculture, Its Crisis and Transformation." In *Immanuel Wallerstein and the Problem of the World: System, Scale, Culture*, edited by David Palumbo-Liu, Nirvana Tanoukhi, and Bruce Robbins, 27–40. Durham, NC: Duke University Press, 2011.

Lee, Sonia Song H. *Building a Latino Civil Rights Movement: Puerto Ricans, African Americans, and the Pursuit of Racial Justice in New York City*. Chapel Hill: University of North Carolina Press, 2014.

Lee, Trymaine, and Janelle Ross. "Occupy the Hood Aims to Draw People of Color to Occupy Wall Street." *Huffington Post*. October 14, 2011.

Lenin, Vladimir. *Imperialism: The Highest Stage of Capitalism*. London: Penguin, 2010.

"Liberación nacional: Deber impostergable de los oprimidos." *Tricontinental* 41 (November–December 1974): 131–159.

Lionnet, Françoise, and Shu-mei Shih. *Minor Transnationalism*. Durham, NC: Duke University Press, 2005.

"La liquidación de la miseria el gran tema de esta época." *Revolución* (January 4, 1960), special section.

Livón-Grosman, Ernesto. "Nicolasito's Way: Los sinuosos caminos de la estética revolucionaria." In "Especial Nicolás Guillén Landrián," ed. Julio Ramos and Dylon Robbins, special issue, *La Fuga* (Spring 2013).

Loichot, Valérie. *The Tropics Bite Back: Culinary Coups in Caribbean Literature*. Minneapolis: University of Minnesota Press, 2013.

López, Alfred J. "Introduction: The (Post)Global South." *Global South* 1.1–2 (2007): 1–11.

———. *José Martí: A Revolutionary Life*. Austin: University of Texas Press, 2014.

López, Antonio. *Unbecoming Blackness: The Diaspora Cultures of Afro-Cuban America*. New York: New York University Press, 2012.

Loss, Jacqueline, and José Manuel Prieto González, eds. *Caviar with Rum: Cuba USSR and the Post-Soviet Experience*. New York: Palgrave Macmillan, 2012.

Luciano, Felipe. "Free Palestine." *Palante* 2.7 (1970): 16–17, 20.

———. "Jíbaro, My Pretty Nigger." *Right On! Poetry on Film*, dir. Herbert Danska. New York: Leacock Pennebraker, 1968.

———. "The Take-Over of T.B. Testing Truck." In "The Young Lords Party, 1969–75," special issue, *Caribe* 7.4: 13.

Luis, William. *Dance between Two Cultures: Latino Caribbean Literature Written in the United States*. Nashville, TN: Vanderbilt University Press, 1997.

———. *Lunes de Revolución: Literatura y cultura en los primeros años de la Revolución Cubana*. Madrid: Editorial Verbum, 2003.

Luis-Brown, David. *Waves of Decolonization: Discourses of Race and Hemispheric Citizenship in Cuba, Mexico, and the United States*. Durham, NC: Duke University Press, 2008.

Lund, Joshua. *The Impure Imagination: Toward a Critical Hybridity in Latin American Writing*. Minneapolis: University of Minnesota Press, 2006.

Makalani, Minkah. "Black Lives Matter and the Limits of Formal Black Politics." In "After #Ferguson, After #Baltimore: The Challenge of Black Death and Black Life for Black Political Thought," edited by Barnor Hesse and Juliet Hooker, special issue, *South Atlantic Quarterly* 116.3 (July 2017): 529–552.

Malcolm X. "U.S.A.: The Hour of Mau Mau." *Tricontinental* 11 (March–April 1969): 23–30.

Malcolm X and George Breitman. *Malcolm X Speaks: Selected Speeches and Statements*. New York: Grove, 1965.

Man-on-the-Spot . . . in La Paz. Illustration. *Tricontinental* 8 (September–October 1968), fourth cover.

Marable, Manning. "Racismo, prisiones, y el futuro de los negros en los Estados Unidos." *Tricontinental* 146 (2001): 42–45.

Marable, Manning, and Vanessa Agard-Jones. *Transnational Blackness: Navigating the Global Color Line*. New York: Palgrave Macmillan, 2008.

Mari-Brás, Juan. "La vía decisiva." *Tricontinental* 29–30 (March–June 1972): 17.

Mariscal, George. *Brown-Eyed Children of the Sun: Lessons from the Chicano Movement, 1965–1975.* Albuquerque: University of New Mexico Press, 2005.

Márques, René. *La carreta: Drama en dos actos.* 1953. San Juan, PR: Editorial Cultural, 1983.

Márquez, John D. *Black-Brown Solidarity: Racial Politics in the New Gulf South.* Austin: University of Texas Press, 2014.

Márquez, Roberto, ed. *Puerto Rican Poetry: An Anthology from Aboriginal to Contemporary Times.* Amherst: University of Massachusetts Press, 2007.

Martí, José. *Nuestra América.* Edited by Hugo Achugar. Caracas: Biblioteca Ayacucho, 1977.

———. *Selected Writings.* Edited and translted by Hugo Esther Allen. New York: Penguin, 2002.

Martin, Michael T., ed. *New Latin American Cinema Volume 1: Theories, Practices, and Transcontinental Articulations.* Detroit: Wayne State University Press, 1997.

Martínez, Elizabeth. "Las chicanas." *Tricontinental Bulletin* 74–75 (May–June 1972): 26.

———. "No son hijos de Houston." *Tricontinental* 32 (September–October 1972): 118–134.

———. "Where Was the Color in Seattle? Looking for Reasons Why the Great Battle Was So White." *ColorLines* 3.1 (2000): 11–12.

Martínez, Olivio. "Diseñadores." In *The Tricontinental Solidarity Poster*, edited by Richard Frick, 64–65. Bern, Switzerland: Comedia, 2003.

Masferrer, Marianne, and Carmela Mesa-Lago. "The Gradual Integration of the Black in Cuba: Under the Colony, the Republic, and the Revolution." In *Slavery and Race Relations in Latin America*, edited by Robert Brent Toplin, 348–384. Westport, CT: Greenwood, 1974.

Matthews, John T. "Globalizing the U.S. South: Modernity and Modernism." In "Global Contexts, Local Literatures: The New Southern Studies," ed. Katherine McKee and Annette Trefzer, special issue, *American Literature* 78.4: 719–722.

Mattos, Geísa. "From Colombia to the U.S., Black Lives Have Always Mattered." In "A Hemispheric Approach to Contemporary Black Activism," special issue. *NACLA Report on the Americas* 49.1 (2017): 30–32.

Maxwell, William J. *New Negro, Old Left: African American Writing and Communism between the Wars.* New York: Columbia University Press, 1999.

McBride, Michael. Email message to author. September 6, 2017.

McGill, Lisa D. *Constructing Black Selves: Caribbean American Narratives and the Second Generation.* New York: New York University Press, 2005.

McIntosh, Josh. "A History of Subversive Remix Video before YouTube: Thirty Political Video Mashups Made between World War II and 2005." In "Fan/Remix Video," ed. Francesca Coppa and Julie Levin Russo, special issue, *Transformative Works and Cultures* 9 (2012). http://journal.transformativeworks.org/index.php/twc/article/view/371/299.

McKee, Katherine, and Annette Trefzer, eds. "Global Contexts, Local Literatures: The New Southern Studies." Special issue, *American Literature* 78.4 (2006).

McManus, Jane. "United States and Apartheid." *Tricontinental* 54 (1977): 24–31.

Mcpherson, Tara. *Reconstructing Dixie: Race, Gender, and Nostalgia in the Imagined South*. Durham, NC: Duke University Press, 2003.

Melamed, Jodi. *Represent and Destroy: Rationalizing Violence in the New Racial Capitalism*. Minneapolis: University of Minnesota Press, 2011.

Meléndez, Miguel "Mickey." *We Took the Streets: Fighting for Latino Rights with the Young Lords*. New York: St. Martin's, 2003.

"Message to the U.S. People." *Tricontinental Bulletin* 2 (May 1966): 29–31.

Middlebrooks, Gwendolyn. "From the Civil Rights Movement to Occupy Wall Street." *Inside Spelman*. http://www.insidespelman.com/from-the-civil-rights -movement-to-occupy-wall-street/.

Mignolo, Walter D. "Colonial and Postcolonial Discourse: Cultural Critique or Academic Colonialism?" *Latin American Research Review* 28.3 (1993): 120–134.

———. "Introduction: Coloniality of Power and De-colonial Thinking." In *Globalization and the Decolonial Option*, edited by Walter D. Mignolo and Arturo Escobar, 1–21. New York: Routledge, 2010.

———. *Local Histories/Global Designs: Coloniality, Subaltern Knowledges, and Border Thinking*. Princeton, NJ: Princeton University Press, 2012.

Milian, Claudia. *Latining America: Black-Brown Passages and the Coloring of Latino/a Studies*. Athens: University of Georgia Press, 2013.

Millar, Lanie. "Realigning Revolution: The Poetics of Disappointment in Cuban and Angolan Narrative." PhD diss., University of Texas, Austin, 2011.

Minor, Robert. "Salvemos a los obreros negros en Alabama." *Mundo Obrero* 1.2 (September 1, 1931): 20–21.

Miskulin, Silvia Cézar. "Las ediciones El Puente y la nueva promoción de poetas cubanos." In *Ediciones El Puente en La Habana de los años 60: Lecturas críticas y libros de poesía*, edited by Jesús J. Barquet. Chihuahua, Mexico: Ediciones del Azar, 2011.

Mitchell, Robie. "The Pink Tide Recedes: End of an Era?" Council on Hemispheric Affairs. January 14, 2016. http://www.coha.org/the-pink-tide-recedes-end-of -an-era/.

Mitchell-Kernan, Claudia. "Signifying and Marking: Two Afro-American Speech Acts." In *Directions in Sociolinguistics*, edited by John J, Gumperz and Dell Hymes, 161–179. New York: Holt, Rinehart, and Winston, 1972.

Moore, Anita, Amity Paye, and Shannon Shird. "Black Lives Matter Visits Cuba." Black Alliance for Just Immigration. August 17, 2015. http://www.blackalliance .org/black-lives-matter-visits-cuba/.

Moore, Carlos. *Castro, the Blacks, and Africa*. Berkeley: University of California Press, 1988.

———. *Pichón: Race and Revolution in Castro's Cuba: A Memoir*. Chicago: Lawrence Hill, 2008.

Moore, Robin. *Nationalizing Blackness: Afrocubanismo and the Artistic Revolution in Havana, 1920–40*. Pittsburgh: University of Pittsburgh Press, 1997.

Morales, Ed. "Puerto Rico in Crisis: Weighed Down by $73bn Debt as Unemployment Hits 14%." *Guardian*. June 28, 2015.

Morales, Iris. "¡PALANTE, SIEMPRE PALANTE! The Young Lords." In *The Puerto Rican Movement: Voices from the Diaspora*, edited by Andrés Torres and José E. Velázquez, 210–227. Philadelphia: Temple University Press, 1998.

————. "Power to the People." In *Palante: Young Lords Party*, edited by Michael Abramson and Young Lords Party, 4–8. Chicago: Haymarket, 2011.

————. "Racismo Borinqueño." *Palante* 2.7 (1970): 6–7.

Morales Campos, Reinaldo. "Introducción." In *The Tricontinental Solidarity Poster*, edited by Richard Frick, 52–56. Bern, Switzerland: Comedia, 2003.

Morejón, Nancy. *Antología poética*. Edited by Gerardo Fulleda León. Caracas: Monte Ávila Editores Latinoamericana, 2006.

Morgan, Marcyliena M. "The African-American Speech Community: Reality and Sociolinguists." In *Linguistic Anthropology: A Reader*, edited by Alessandro Duranti, 74–94. Malden, MA: Blackwell, 2001.

Mraz, John. "Santiago Alvarez: From Dramatic Form to Direct Cinema." In *The Social Documentary in Latin America*, edited by Julianne Barton, 131–150. Pittsburgh: University of Pittsburgh Press, 1990.

Myerson, Michael. "Angela Davis habla desde la cárcel." Interview with Angela Davis. *Tricontinental Bulletin* 63 (June 1971): 17–23.

Navarro, Desiderio. "In Media Res Publicas: On Intellectuals and Social Criticism in the Cuban Public Sphere." Translated by Alessandro Fornazzari and Desiderio Navarro. *boundary 2* 29.3 (2002): 187–203.

Nesadurai, Helen E. S. "Bandung and the Political Economy of North-South Relations." In *Bandung Revisited: The Legacy of the 1955 Asian-African Conference for International Order*, edited by See Seng Tan and Amitav Acharya, 68–101. Singapore: National University of Singapore Press, 2008.

Newton, Huey P. "Culture and Liberation." *Tricontinental* 11 (March–April 1969): 101–104.

Ngũgĩ wa Thiong'o. *Globalectics: Theory and the Politics of Knowing*. New York: Columbia University Press, 2012.

"Nicolasito Guillén." inCUBAdora: Cuban Underground Guide. http://incubadora .org/nicolasito-guillen/.

"Ningún país se ha negado a asistir a la conferencia." *Revolución* (February 5, 1960): 8.

Nöel, Urayoán. *In Visible Movement: Nuyorican Poetry from the Sixties to Slam*. Iowa City: University of Iowa Press, 2014.

Obama, Barack. "Remarks by President Obama to the People of Cuba." White House. Office of the Press Secretary. March 22, 2016.

————. "Statement by the President on Cuba Policy Changes." White House. Office of the Press Secretary. December 17, 2014.

"Occupy Protests around the World: Full List Visualised." *Guardian*. http://www
.theguardian.com/news/datablog/2011/oct/17/occupy-protests-world-list-map
?newsfeed=true.

Occupy Wall Street New York City General Assembly. "Declaration of the Occupation of New York City." Occupy Wall Street. http://occupywallstreet.net/learn.

Ong, Aihwa. *Neoliberalism as Exception: Mutations in Citizenship and Sovereignty*.
Durham, NC: Duke University Press, 2006.

Organization of American States (OAS). Council. *Report of the Special Committee to
Study Resolution II.1 and VII of the Eighth Meeting of Consultation of Ministers
of Foreign Affairs on the First Afro-Asian-Latin American Peoples' Solidarity
Conference and Its Projections ("Tricontinental Conference of Havana"): New
Instrument of Communist Intervention and Aggression*. Vol. 1. Washington, DC:
Pan American Union, 1966.

——. *Report of the Special Committee to Study Resolution II.1 and VII of the Eighth
Meeting of Consultation of Ministers of Foreign Affairs on the First Afro-Asian-
Latin American Peoples' Solidarity Conference and Its Projections ("Tricontinental
Conference of Havana"): New Instrument of Communist Intervention and Aggres-
sion*. Vol. 2. Washington, DC: Pan American Union, 1966.

Organization of American States (OAS), Special Consultative Committee on Security.
"The 'First Tricontinental Conference,' Another Threat to the Security of the
Inter- American System." Washington, DC: Pan American Union, 1966.

Ortiz, Fernando. *Contrapunteo cubano del tabaco y el azúcar*. 1940. Ed. Enrico Mario
Santí. Madrid: Cátedra, 2002.

——. *Cuban Counterpoint: Tobacco and Sugar*. Translated by Harriet de Onís. Durham, NC: Duke University Press, 1995.

Oso, Tia, Opal Tometi, and Aly Wane. "Transformational Solidarity Webinar: Why
the Migrant Rights Movement Must Show Up for Black Lives." Black Alliance
for Just Immigration. March 11, 2015. http://www.blackalliance.org/resources/tra
nsformationalsolidaritywebinar/.

Padilla, Carlos. "Solidarity in the Desert." *Tricontinental* 14 (September–
October 1969): 116.

Padmore, George, ed. *History of the Pan-African Congress*. London: Hammersmith
Bookshop, 1963.

Palés Matos, Luis. *Tuntún de pasa y grifería*. 1937. San Juan: University of Puerto Rico
Press, 1993.

Paschel, Tianna. "From Colombia to the U.S., Black Lives Have Always Mattered."
In "A Hemispheric Approach to Contemporary Black Activism," special issue.
NACLA Report on the Americas 49.1 (2017): 27–29.

Pedroso, Regino. *Nosotros*. 1933. Havana: Editorial Letras Cubanas, 1984.

Pérez, Louis A., Jr. *Cuba: Between Reform and Revolution*. 4th ed. Oxford: Oxford
University Press, 2011.

Pérez, Richard. "Racial Spills and Disfigured Faces in Piri Thomas's *Down These
Mean Streets* and Junot Díaz's 'Ysrael.'" In *Contemporary U.S. Latino/a Literary*

Criticism, edited by Lyn Di Iorio Sandín and Richard Pérez, 93–112. New York: Palgrave Macmillan, 2007.

Pérez-Sarduy, Pedro. "An Open Letter to Carlos Moore." *Cuba Update* (Summer 1990): 34–6. Reprinted in AfroCubaWeb. http://www.afrocubaweb.com /lettertocarlos.htm.

Peters, Christabelle. *Cuban Identity and the Angolan Experience.* New York: Palgrave Macmillan, 2012.

Picó, Fernando. *Historia general de Puerto Rico.* Río Piedras: Ediciones Huracán, 1988.

Pietri, Pedro. *Puerto Rican Obituary.* New York: Monthly Review Press, 1973.

Pitman, Thea, and Andy Stafford. "Introduction: Transatlanticism and Tricontinentalism." *Journal of Transatlantic Studies* 7.3 (2009): 197–207.

Plummer, Brenda Gayle. "Castro in Harlem: A Cold War Watershed." In *Rethinking the Cold War: Essays on Its Dynamics, Meaning, and Morality*, edited by Allen Hunter. Philadelphia: Temple University Press, 1997.

———. *Rising Wind: Black Americans and U.S. Foreign Affairs, 1935–1960.* Chapel Hill: University of North Carolina Press, 1996.

"Political Report Presented by the International Preparatory Committee and Approved by the Conference." In OAS Council, *Report of the Special Committee to Study Resolution II.1 and VII of the Eighth Meeting of Consultation of Ministers of Foreign Affairs on the First Afro-Asian-Latin American Peoples' Solidarity Conference and Its Projections ("Tricontinental Conference of Havana"): New Instrument of Communist Intervention and Aggression.* Vol. 2. Washington, DC: Pan American Union, 1966.

Pop, Iggy. "Shepard Fairey." *Interview.* May 4, 2010. http://www.interviewmagazine .com /art/shepard-fairey/.

Postcolonial Studies @ Emory. https://scholarblogs.emory.edu/postcolonialstudies/.

Prashad, Vijay. *The Darker Nations: A People's History of the Third World.* New York: New Press, 2007.

———. *The Poorer Nations: A Possible History of the Global South.* London: Verso, 2012.

¡Presente! The Young Lords in New York. Bronx Museum of the Arts. http://www .bronxmuseum.org/exhibitions/presente-the-young-lords-in-new-york.

Price, Rachel. *The Object of the Atlantic: Concrete Aesthetics in Cuba, Brazil, and Spain, 1868–1968.* Evanston, IL: Northwestern University Press, 2014.

"Proyección de la reunión de los países subdesarrollados." *Revolución* (January 4, 1960): 6.

El pueblo se levanta. New York: Newsreel, 1971.

Puerto Rican Revolutionary Workers Organization. "History of the Development of the Puerto Rican Revolutionary Workers Organization." In *In the U.S. Pregnant with Revisionism, the Struggle for Proletarian Revolution Moves Ahead: The Political Positions of the Puerto Rican Revolutionary Workers Organization.* New York: PRRWO, 1974. https://www.marxists.org/history/erol/ncm-1/prrwo -history.htm.

Pujals, Sandra. "A 'Soviet Caribbean': The Comintern, New York's Immigrant Community, and the Forging of Caribbean Visions, 1931–1936." *Russian History* 41 (2014): 255–268.

Pulido, Laura. *Black, Brown, Yellow, and Left: Radical Activism in Los Angeles*. Berkeley: University of California Press, 2006.

Quang Phiet, Tong. "The Vietnam Struggle Is Part of the Struggle of the Three Continents." *Tricontinental Bulletin* 26 (May 1968).

Quijano, Aníbal. "Colonialidad y modernidad/racionalidad." *Perú Indígena* 13.29 (1992): 11–20.

———. "Coloniality and Modernity/Rationality." In *Globalization and the Decolonial Option*, edited by Walter D. Mignolo and Arturo Escobar, 22–32. New York: Routledge, 2010.

———. "Coloniality of Power, Eurocentrism, and Latin America." *Nepantla: Views from the South* 1.3 (2000): 533–580.

———. "Coloniality of Power, Eurocentrism, and Social Classification." In *Coloniality at Large: Latin America and the Postcolonial Debate*, edited by Mabel Moraña, Enrique Dussel, and Carlos A. Jáuregui, 181–224. Durham, NC: Duke University Press, 2008.

Rahier, Jean Muteba. "Introduction: Black Social Movements in Latin America: From Monocultural Mestizaje and 'Invisibility' to Multiculturalism and State Corporatism/Co-optation." In *Black Social Movements in Latin America: From Monocultural Mestizaje to Multiculturalism*, edited by Jean Muteba Rahier, 1–12. New York: Palgrave Macmillan, 2012.

Ramos, Julio. "Los archivos de Guillén Landrián: Cine, poesía y disonancia." In "Especial Nicolás Guillén Landrián," ed. Julio Ramos and Dylon Robbins, special issue, *La Fuga* (Spring 2013).

———. "Cine, archivo, y poder: Entrevista a Manuel Zayas en Nueva York." In "Especial Nicolás Guillén Landrián," ed. Julio Ramos and Dylon Robbins, special issue, *La Fuga* (Spring 2013).

———. "Cine, cuerpo y trabajo: Los montajes de Guillén Landrián." *La Gaceta de Cuba* 3 (2011): 45–47.

———. "¿Un cine afrocubano? Conversación con Gloria Rolando en La Habana Vieja." *Cuadernos de Literatura* 18.35 (January–June 2014): 285–298.

Rascaroli, Laura. *The Personal Camera: Subjective Cinema and the Essay Film*. New York: Wallflower, 2009.

Reber, Dierdra. *Coming to Our Senses: Affect and the Order of Things for Global Culture*. New York: Columbia University Press, 2016.

Reitan, Ruth. *The Rise and Decline of an Alliance: Cuban and African American Leaders in the 1960s*. East Lansing: Michigan State University Press, 1999.

"Reply of the Government of Uruguay to the Soviet Note on the Tricontinental Conference and Summary of the Text of the Russian Note." In OAS Council, *Report of the Special Committee to Study Resolution II.1 and VII of the Eighth Meeting of Consultation of Ministers of Foreign Affairs on the First Afro-Asian-Latin American*

Peoples' Solidarity Conference and its Projections ("Tricontinental Conference of Havana"): New Instrument of Communist Intervention and Aggression, vol. 2, 285–288. Washington, DC: Pan American Union, 1966.

"Resolución de Solidaridad del II Congreso de la Federación de Mujeres Cubanas." *Tricontinental* 41 (November–December 1974): 124–130.

Retamar, Roberto Fernández. *Caliban and Other Essays*. Translated by Edward Baker. Minneapolis: University of Minnesota Press, 1989.

Reyes, Dean Luis. "Exhumaciones de Nicolás Guillén Landrián." In "Especial Nicolás Guillén Landrián," ed. Julio Ramos and Dylon Robbins, special issue, *La Fuga* (Spring 2013).

Rist, Peter. "Agit-prop Cuban Style: Master Montagist Santiago Álvarez." *Offscreen* 11.3 (2007). http://offscreen.com/view/agit_prop_cuban_style.

Rivero, Yeidy M. *Tuning Out Blackness: Race and Nation in the History of Puerto Rican Television*. Durham, NC: Duke University Press, 2005.

Robbins, Bruce. "Blaming the System." In *Immanuel Wallerstein and the Problem of the World: System, Scale, Culture*, edited by David Palumbo-Liu, Nirvana Tanoukhi, and Bruce Robbins, 41–63. Durham, NC: Duke University Press, 2011.

Robbins, Dylon. "*Los del baile*: Pueblo, producción, performance." In "Especial Nicolás Guillén Landrián," ed. Julio Ramos and Dylon Robbins, special issue, *La Fuga* (Spring 2013).

———. "On the Margins of Reality: Fiction, Documentary, and Marginal Subjectivity in Three Early Cuban Revolutionary Films." In *Visual Synergies in Fiction and Documentary Film from Latin America*, edited by Miriam Haddu and Joanna Page, 27–48. New York: Palgrave Macmillan, 2009.

Roberts, Brian Russell, and Keith Foulcher, eds. *Indonesian Notebook: A Sourcebook on Richard Wright and the Bandung Conference*. Durham, NC: Duke University Press, 2016.

Robinson, Cedric J. *Black Marxism: The Making of the Black Radical Tradition*. Chapel Hill: University of North Carolina Press, 1983.

Rodó, José Enrique. *Ariel*. 1900. Translated by F. J. Stimson. Cambridge, MA: Riverside, 1922.

———. *Ariel*. 1900. Madrid: Asociación de la Prensa Hispanoamericana, 2003.

Rodriguez, Besenia. "Beyond Nation: The Formation of a Tricontinental Discourse." PhD diss., Yale University, 2006.

———. "'De la esclavitud yanqui a la libertad cubana': U.S. Black Radicals, the Cuban Revolution, and the Formation of a Tricontinental Ideology." *Radical History Review* 92 (Spring 2005): 62–87.

———. "Long Live Third World Unity! Long Live Internationalism: Huey P. Newton's Revolutionary Intercommunalism." *Souls: A Critical Journal of Black Politics, Culture, and Society* 8.3 (2006): 119–141.

Romulo, Carlos P. *The Meaning of Bandung*. Chapel Hill: University of North Carolina Press, 1956.

Rosenberg, Fernando. "Afecto y política de la cosmópolis latinoamericana." *Revista Iberoamericana* 72 (215–216): 467–479.

Ross, Janelle. "Occupy Wall Street Doesn't Adequately Represent Struggling Black Population, Experts Say." *Huffington Post*. October 6, 2011.

Roumain, Jacques. *When the Tom-Tom Beats: Selected Prose and Poems*. Translated by Joanne Fungaroli and Ronald Sauer. Washington, DC: Azul Editions, 1995.

Rout, Leslie B., *The African Experience in Spanish America*. Cambridge: Cambridge University Press, 1976.

Said, Edward. "A Conversation with Neeldari Bhattacharya, Suvir Kaul, and Ania Loomba." In *Relocating Postcolonialism*, edited by Theo Goldberg and Ato Quayson, 1–14. Oxford: Blackwell, 2002.

"Salvemos de la muerte a los nueve jóvenes negros de Scottsboro." *Mundo Obrero* 2.9 (April 1932): 2.

Sánchez, Iroel. "Bienvenido Mr. Kerry." *Tricontinental*. August 26, 2015.

Sánchez González, Lisa. *Boricua Literature*. New York: New York University Press, 2001.

Sanders, Mark A. "Ricardo Batrell and the Cuban Racial Narrative: An Introduction to *A Black Soldier's Story*." In *A Black Soldier's Story: The Narrative of Ricardo Batrell and the Cuban War of Independence*, edited and translated by Mark A. Sanders, ix–lxvi. Minneapolis: University of Minnesota Press, 2010.

Sandín, Lyn Di Iorio. *Killing Spanish: Literary Essays on Ambivalent U.S. Latino/a Identity*. New York: Palgrave Macmillan, 2004.

Sankey, Kyla. "What Happened to the Pink Tide? Latin America's 'Pink Tide' Governments Challenge Neoliberalism and U.S. Hegemony, but Leave the Basic Structures of Capitalism Intact." *Jacobin: Reason in Revolt*. July 27, 2016.

Santiago-Díaz, Eleuterio, and Ilia Rodríguez. "Desde las fronteras raciales de dos casas letradas: Habla Piri Thomas." *Revista Iberoamericana* 75.229 (2009): 1199–1221.

Santos, Boaventura. *Epistemologies of the South: Justice against Epistemicide*. Boulder, CO: Paradigm, 2014.

———. *Toward a New Legal Common Sense: Law, Globalization and Emancipation*. London: Reed Elsevier, 2002.

Satpathy, Sumanyu, ed. *Southern Postcolonialisms: The Global South and the "New" Literary Representations*. London: Routledge, 2009.

Sawyer, Mark Q. *Racial Politics in Post-Revolutionary Cuba*. New York: Cambridge University Press, 2006.

Scarpaci, Joseph L. Roberto Segre, and Mario Coyula. *Havana: Two Faces of the Antillean Metropolis*. Chapel Hill: University of North Carolina Press, 2002.

Schjeldahl, Peter. "Hope and Glory: A Shepard Fairey Moment." *New Yorker*. February 23, 2009.

Schmitt, Carl. *The Nomos of the Earth in the International Law of Jus Publicum Europaeum*. Candor, NY: Telos, 2003.

Seed, Patricia. "Colonial and Postcolonial Discourse." *Latin American Research Review* 26.3 (1991): 181–200.

Seidman, Sarah. "Tricontinental Routes of Solidarity: Stokely Carmichael in Cuba." *Journal of Transnational American Studies* 4.2 (2012): 1–25.

———. "Venceremos Means We Shall Overcome: The African American Freedom Struggle and the Cuban Revolution, 1959–79." PhD diss., Brown University, 2013.

Sen, Rinku. "Race and Occupy Wall Street." *Nation.* October 26, 2011.

Seymour, Richard. "The 'Pink Tide' in Crisis: To Defend Their Social Goals, Latin American States Need to Risk Encroaching on the Profits and Rights of Investors." *Al Jazeera.* September 2, 2016.

Sheppard, Eric, and Richa Nagar. "From East-West to North-South." *Antipode* 2004: 557–563.

Shirky, Clay. *Here Comes Everybody: The Power of Organizing without Organizations.* New York: Penguin, 2008.

Shreve, Bradley G. *Red Power Rising: The National Indian Youth Council and the Origins of Native Activism.* Norman: University of Oklahoma Press, 2011.

Silverstein, Michael. "Monoglot 'Standard' in American: Standardization and Metaphors of Linguistic Hegemony." In *The Matrix of Language: Contemporary Linguistic Anthropology,* edited by Donald Brenneis and Ronald K. S. Macaulay, 284–306. Boulder, CO: Westview, 1996.

Singh, Nikhil Pal. *Black Is a Country: Race and the Unfinished Struggle for Democracy.* Cambridge, MA: Harvard University Press, 2004.

Sinnette, Elinor Des Verney. *Arthur Alfonso Schomburg: Black Bibiliophile and Collector.* Detroit: Wayne State University Press, 1989.

Slovic, Scott, Swarnalatha Rangarajan, and Vidya Sarveswaran, eds. *Ecocriticism of the Global South.* London: Lexington Books, 2015.

Smith, Christen A. "Battling Anti-Black Genocide in Brazil." NACLA *Report on the Americas* 49.1 (2017): 41–47.

Smith, Jon, and Deborah Cohn, eds. *Look Away! The U.S. South in New World Studies.* Durham, NC: Duke University Press, 2004.

Soto, Pedro Juan. *Spiks: Stories.* 1956. New York: Monthly Review Press, 1973.

The South Commission. *The Challenge to the South: The Report of the South Commission.* Oxford: Oxford University Press, 1990.

Speri, Alice. "Occupy Wall Street Struggles to Make 'the 99%' Look Like Everybody." *New York Times.* October 28, 2011.

Spivak, Gayatri. *In Other Worlds: Essays in Cultural Politics.* London: Metheun, 1987.

Stafford, Andy. "Tricontinentalism in Recent Moroccan Intellectual History: The Case of *Souffles.*" *Journal of Transatlantic Studies* 7.3 (2009): 218–232.

Stahler-Sholk, Richard, Harry E. Vanden, and Glen David Kuecker. "Introduction." In *Latin American Social Movements in the Twenty-First Century: Resistance, Power, and Democracy,* edited by R. Stahler-Sholk, H. Vanden, and G. Kuecker, 1–15. Plymouth, MD: Rowman and Littlefield, 2008.

Stam, Robert, and Ella Shohat. *Race in Translation: Culture Wars around the Postcolonial Atlantic.* New York: New York University Press, 2012.

Stanchich, Maritza. "Puerto Rico's Symbolic Power." *Huffington Post.* July 31, 2015.

Starr, Amory. "How Can Anti-imperialism Not Be Anti-racist? A Critical Impasse in the North American Anti-globalization Movement." *Journal of World Systems Research* 10.1 (2004): 119–152.

Stephens, Michelle. *Black Empire: The Masculine Global Imaginary of Caribbean Intellectuals in the United States, 1914–1962.* Durham, NC: Duke University Press, 2005.

Stern, Steve J. "Feudalism, Capitalism, and the World-System in the Perspective of Latin America and the Caribbean." *American Historical Review* 93.4 (1988): 829–872.

Stock, Ann-Marie. *On Location in Cuba: Street-Filmmaking during Times of Transition.* Chapel Hill: University of North Carolina Press, 2009.

Sullivan-González, Douglass, and Charles Reagan Wilson. *The South and the Caribbean.* Jackson: University Press of Mississippi, 2001.

Sutherland, Elizabeth. *The Youngest Revolution: A Personal Report on Cuba.* New York: Dial, 1969.

Tan, See Seng, and Amitav Acharya, eds. *Bandung Revisited: The Legacy of the 1955 Asian-African Conference for International Order.* Singapore: National University of Singapore Press, 2008.

"Tasks and Objectives of the OSPAAAL." *Tricontinental Bulletin* 37 (April 1969).

Taylor, Keeanga-Yamahtta. *From #BlackLivesMatter to Black Liberation.* Chicago: Haymarket, 2016.

"Theses on the Negro Question." *Bulletin of the IV Congress of the Communist International* 17 (December 7, 1922): 8–10.

"13 Point Program and Platform of the Young Lords Party." *Tricontinental Bulletin* 60 (March 1971): 20–23.

Thomas, Caroline. "Globalization and the South." In *Globalization and the South,* edited by Peter Wilkins and Caroline Thomas, 1–17. New York: St. Martin's, 1997.

Thomas, Darryl C. *The Theory and Practice of Third World Solidarity.* Westport, CT: Praeger, 2001.

Thomas, Hugh. *Cuba: The Pursuit of Freedom.* London: Harper and Row, 1971.

Thomas, Piri. "A Conversation with Piri Thomas." Interview by Humberto Cintrón. Edited by Suzanne Dod Thomas. http://cheverote.com/reviews/cintroninterview.html.

———. *Down These Mean Streets.* New York: Alfred A. Knopf, 1967.

Thomas, Susan. *Cuban Zarzuela: Performing Race and Gender on Havana's Lyric Stage.* Champaign: University of Illinois Press, 2009.

Tietchen, Todd F. "The Cubalogues (and after): On the Beat Literary Movement and the Early Cuban Revolution." *Arizona Quarterly* 63.4 (2007): 119–153.

Tillis, Antonio D. "Afro-Hispanic Literature in the US: Remembering the Past, Celebrating the Present, and Forging a Future." IPOTESI, *Juiz de Fora* 12.1 (2008): 21–29.

Tolliver, Cedric. "Introduction: Alternative Soldarities." In "Alternative Solidarities: Black Diasporas and Cultural Alliances during the Cold War," ed. Monica Popescu, Cedric Tolliver, and Julie Tolliver, special issue, *Journal of Postcolonial Writing* 50.4 (2014): 379–383.

Torres, Andrés. *Between Melting Pot and Mosaic: African Americans and Puerto Ricans in the New York Political Economy.* Philadelphia: Temple University Press, 1995.

———. "Introduction: Political Radicalism in the Diaspora—The Puerto Rican Experience." In *The Puerto Rican Movement: Voices from the Diaspora,* edited by Andrés Torres and José E. Velázquez, 1–24. Philadelphia: Temple University Press, 1998.

Torres, Andrés, and José E. Velázquez, eds. *The Puerto Rican Movement: Voices from the Diaspora.* Philadelphia: Temple University Press, 1998.

"The Tragedy of the Blacks in Newark." *Tricontinental Bulletin* 17 (August 1967): 9–11.

"2015 Black Solidarity Statement with Palestine." Black Solidarity with Palestine. http://www.blackforpalestine.com/read-the-statement.html.

Tyson, Timothy B. *Radio Free Dixie: Robert F. Williams and the Roots of Black Power.* Chapel Hill: University of North Carolina Press, 1999.

"United States: Armed Confrontation." *Tricontinental Bulletin* 42 (October 1969): 31–32.

Urciuoli, Bonnie. *Exposing Prejudice: Puerto Rican Experiences of Language, Race, and Class.* Boulder, CO: Westview, 1996.

"USA: From Little Rock to Urban Rebellions." *Tricontinental Bulletin* 46 (January 1970): 7–16.

U.S. Senate Committee on the Judiciary. "The Tricontinental Conference of African, Asian, and Latin American Peoples." Staff study prepared for the Subcommittee to Investigate the Administration of the Internal Security Act and Other Internal Security Laws. Washington, DC: U.S. Government Printing Office, 1966.

Vail, Mark. "The 'Integrative' Rhetoric of Martin Luther King Jr.'s 'I Have a Dream' Speech." *Rhetoric and Public Affairs* 9.1 (2006): 51–78.

Valerio, Lara. "Foto Jacobo Rincón, 28 abril 1965." Bono Cimarrón. April 28, 2012. https://bonoc.wordpress.com/ 2012/04/28/foto-jacobo-rincon-28-abril-1965/.

Vallen, Mark. "Obey Plagiarist Shepard Fairey." Art for a Change. December 2007. http://www.art-for-a-change.com/Obey/.

Vaughan, Roger. "The Real Great Society." *Life Magazine* (September 15, 1967): 76–91.

Vélez, Federico. *Latin American Revolutionaries and the Arab World: From the Suez Canal to the Arab Spring.* Burlington, VT: Ashgate, 2016.

"Vendrán a la conferencia de la Habana países africanos." *Revolución* (January 16, 1960): 1.

Vidal, Hernán. "The Concept of Colonial and Postcolonial Discourse: A Perspective from Literary Criticism." *LatinAmerican Research Review* 28.3 (1993): 113–119.

"A Vision for Black Lives: Policy Demands for Black Power, Freedom, and Justice." Movement for Black Lives. https://policy.m4bl.org.

Vitalis, Robert. "The Midnight Ride of Kwame Nkrumah and Other Fables of Bandung (Band-doong)." *Humanity: An International Journal of Human Rights, Humanitarianism, and Development* 4.2 (Summer 2013): 261–288.

Von Eschen, Penny. *Race against Empire: Black Americans and Anti-colonialism, 1937–1957.* Ithaca, NY: Cornell University Press, 1997.

Vuyk, Beb. "A Weekend with Richard Wright." 1960. Translated by Keith Foulcher. Edited by Brian Russell Roberts and Keith Foulcher. *PMLA* 126 (2011): 803–812.

Wald, Karen. "Chicanos: Identity Recovered, Corky González and Cha Cha Jiménez." *Tricontinental* 19–20 (July–October 1970): 150–165.

Walsh, Catherine. "Afro In/Exclusion, Resistance, and the 'Progressive' State: (De) Colonial Struggles, Questions, and Reflections." In *Black Social Movements in Latin America: From Monocultural Mestizaje to Multiculturalism,* edited by Jean Muteba Rahier, 15–34. New York: Palgrave Macmillan, 2012.

Waterman, Peter. "The Bamako Appeal: A Post-modern Janus?" In *A Political Programme for the World Social Forum? Democracy, Substance, and Debate in the Global Justice Movements—A Reader,* edited by Jai Sen, Madhuresh Kumar, Patrick Bond, and Peter Waterman. New Delhi, India: India Institute for Critical Action Centre in Movement; Durban: University of KwaZulu-Natal Centre for Civil Society, 2006. http://www.openspaceforum.net/twiki/tiki-read_article.php?articleId=144.

Weiss, Holger. *Framing a Radical African Atlantic: African American Agency, West African Intellectuals and the International Trade Union Committee of Negro Workers.* Leiden, Netherlands: Brill, 2013.

Williams, Robert F. *The Crusader.* Monroe, NC: Robert F. Williams, 1959–1969.

———. *Negroes with Guns.* New York: Marzani and Munsell, 1962.

Wilson, Robert L. *The First Spanish United Methodist Church and the Young Lords, 1970.* New York: National Division of the Board of Missions, United Methodist Church, 1970.

Woodward, C. Vann. *The Strange Career of Jim Crow.* 1955. Oxford: Oxford University Press, 2002.

Wright, Richard. *Black Power.* New York: Harper and Brothers, 1954.

———. *Black Power: Three Books from Exile: Black Power; The Color Curtain; and White Man, Listen!* New York: HarperCollins, 2008.

———. *The Colour Curtain: A Report on the Bandung Conference.* London: Dobson, 1956.

———. "Una ética para vivir a lo Jim Crow." *Lunes de Revolución* 75 (September 5, 1960): 7–9.

———. "Tradition and Industrialization." In *Black Power: Three Books from Exile: Black Power; The Color Curtain; and White Man, Listen!,* 699–728. New York: HarperCollins, 2008.

"Yankee Imperialism and Its Aggression." *Tricontinental Bulletin* 25 (April 1968): 28–30.

Yepe, Manuel E. "Los latinos indignados en Estados Unidos." *Tricontinental* 173 (2011): 42–43.

Young, Cynthia. *Soul Power: Culture, Radicalism, and the Making of a U.S. Third World Left.* Durham, NC: Duke University Press, 2006.

Young, Robert J. C. *Postcolonialism: An Historical Introduction*. Oxford: Blackwell, 2001.

———. "Postcolonialism: From Bandung to the Tricontinental." *Historein* 5 (2005): 11–21.

———. *White Mythologies: Writing History and the West*. London: Routledge, 2004.

"The Young Lords." *Tricontinental Bulletin* 60 (March 1971): 18–19.

Young Lords Party. "Beat Is Gettin' Stronger . . ." *Palante* 3.4 (March 1971): 2–3.

Young Lords Party Central Committee. "Young Lords Party Position on the Black Panther Party." *Palante* 3.3 (February 1971): 2–3.

"Young Lords Party Position Paper on Women." *Tricontinental Bulletin* 60 (March 1971): 25–31.

Zamora, Lois Parkinson. *The Usable Past: The Imagination of History in Recent Fiction of the Americas*. Cambridge: Cambridge University Press, 1997.

Zayas, Manuel. *Café con leche*. San Antonio de los Baños, Cuba: EICTV, 2003.

———. "Nicolás Guillén: Muerte y resurrección." Blog de Manuel Zayas. April 14, 2010. https://manuelzayas.wordpress.com/2010/04/14/nicolas-guillen-landrian -muerte-y-resurreccion/.

Zentella, Ana Celia. *Growing Up Bilingual: Puerto Rican Children in New York*. Malden, MA: Blackwell, 1997.

Žižek, Slavoj. *The Sublime Object of Ideology*. London: Verso, 1989.

Zurbano Torres, Roberto. "Contra Ferguson (O por qué la lucha antirracista debe ser internacionalista)." Negra cubana tenía que ser. December 19, 2014. http:// negracubanateniaqueser.com/2014/12/19/contra-ferguson/.

———. "The Country to Come; and My Black Cuba?" Translated by Mark A. Sanders. http://www.afrocubaweb.com/and-my-black-cuba.html.

———. "For Blacks in Cuba, the Revolution Hasn't Begun." Translated by Kristina Cordero. *New York Times*. March 24, 2013.

———. "Mañana será tarde, Eschucho, aprendo, y sigo en la pelea." *La Jiribilla* 623. April 13–19, 2013.

INDEX

Note: Page numbers followed by *f* indicate a figure.

Albizu Campos, Pedro, 111, 116, 274n33
Albizu Campos Society (SAC), 111, 270–272n13
Al Fatah, 82
Algarín, Miguel, 14, 110, 135, 137, 150
Alianza Federal de Pueblos Libres, 113
Allende, Salvador, 21, 71, 205
Almeida Bosque, Juan, 173
alter-globalization movement, 2–4, 17–18, 159, 219–222, 247n6; color-blind discourses of, 31, 201, 203–204, 225–229, 235, 240, 296n112; global reach of, 235; Latin American roots of, 208–210; transnational imaginary of, 200–201. *See also* contemporary solidarity politics; World Social Forum
Álvarez, Santiago, 15, 82, 164–165; *El movimiento Panteras Negras* of, 70, 84, 102–103; influence on New Latin American Cinema of, 214–217; *LBJ* newsreel, 267n109; on Lyndon Johnson, 91; montage style of, 185, 189–190, 192, 199, 266n83; *Now*, 82, 84–92, 101–102, 108, 192, 266n77
American Indian Movement, 112–113, 277n81
American Negro Labor Congress, 49
"Amerikkka," 14, 123, 145
Amin, Samir, 223–225
Anacaona, 256n87
Anderson, Benedict, 10
Angelou, Maya (Marguerite Angelos), 80, 289n86
Angolan Civil War, 9, 16, 73, 163, 176–179
antiapartheid movement (South Africa), 1, 3, 69f, 70, 179–183
anticolonial movements, 58–59. *See also* Angolan Civil War; Bandung movement; Congo; Guinea-Bissau; Vietnam War
Anti-imperialist League of Cuba, 54
Anti-imperialist League of the Americas (LADLA), 259n133
antiracism movements. *See* racial justice movements
Appadurai, Arjun, 5, 28
Arab Spring, 208, 209
Argentina, 31, 205, 208, 292n32
Ariel (Rodó), 206–207
Arozarena, Marcelino, 45–46, 260n152
Ashcroft, Bill, 27, 207
Asian American East Wind, 114

Attica Prison riot of 1971, 112
August 18th solidarity day, 93

Baker, Josephine, 95
Baldwin, James, 60, 62, 80
Ballagas, Emilio, 44
Bamako Appeal (BA), 17–18, 200, 223–225, 227, 295n81
Bandung movement, 9, 12, 49, 52, 58–67, 261n166; on black anti-imperialism, 59–60; Carbonell's reflection on, 65–66, 261n190, 262n195; Cold War neutrality of, 73–74; communitas of, 10, 64–65, 127–128; development discourse of, 74; essentialist representation in, 61–64; fiftieth anniversary commemoration of, 223–225; 1955 Conference of, 3, 13, 22–23, 58–60, 247n7; participants in, 59–60, 94–95; postcolonial solidarity and, 8, 63–65; precursors to, 55, 259n139; sponsors of, 59; Tricontinental's expansion of, 13, 22–23, 25, 34–35, 65–66, 243, 250n5; on U.S. civil rights struggle, 94–95
Baraka, Amiri (Leroi Jones), 80–81, 172, 264n48, 289n86
Barnet, Miguel, 170–171, 287n40
Barreiro Oliviera, Alejandro, 51
Beasley-Murray, Jon, 28, 127, 219
Becker, Marc, 51
Ben Barka, Mehdi, 75–76
Ben Bella, Ahmed, 75
Benítez, Iris, 125
Benítez-Rojo, Antonio, 54, 198–199
Beremelis, Juan Felipe, 166
Berlant, Lauren, 11, 109, 128
Betances, Emeterio, 273–274nn32–33
Betancourt, Juan René, 166, 2285n17
Bettahar, Fatiah, 132
Beverley, John, 206–207
"Beyond Nation: The Formation of a Tricontinental Discourse" (B. Rodriguez), 8–9, 291n10
Biografía de un cimarrón (Barnet), 170–171, 287n40
Birkenmaier, Anke, 57
Black Alliance for Just Immigration (BAJI), 235–237
Black Arts movement, 12
black Atlantic (as term), 254–255n49

decolonization movements, 58–59. *See also*
Angolan Civil War; Bandung movement;
Congo; Guinea-Bissau; Vietnam War
DeCosta-Willis, Miriam, 57, 260n152
*Defying Dixie: The Radical Roots of Civil
Rights, 1919–1950* (Gilmore), 43
"De la esclavitud yanqui a la libertad cubana"
(B. Rodriguez), 291n10
Deleuze, Gilles, 126, 248n9
deterritorialization, 4; in contemporary
solidarity political visions, 26, 31–33, 35–36,
163–164, 219–222, 254n44; Global South
and, 32–35; in Guillén Landrián's *Coffea
arábiga*, 199; network power theory on,
28–31; representations of the U.S. South
and, 4, 70, 105, 134; of Tricontinental's
vision of imperial power, 3–4, 12, 14, 22,
79–80, 96–99, 162–164
détournement, 102, 269n142
Discourse on Colonialism (Césaire), 57
discrimination. *See* Cuban racial politics; Jim
Crow; racial justice movements
Divided Borders (Flores), 136
Dominican Republic, 68–70, 74, 119, 134,
256n79
Douglas, Emory, 21, 93, 122, 238, 267n102
Down These Mean Streets (P. Thomas), 15,
110, 137–150; Jim Crow South in, 15, 111,
137, 140, 145; linguistic politics of, 141–147,
279nn130–131, 280nn138–139, 281n172,
281n177, 282n180; transracial/ethnic
resistant subjectivity in, 140, 145–150, 155;
vernacular multilingualism of, 139–140
Dream Defenders, 238–239
Du Bois, Shirley Graham, 8, 79, 261n166
Du Bois, W. E. B., 35, 37; on African independence movements, 55; Bandung Conference and, 94–95, 261n166; Pan-African
Congresses of, 41, 47, 54–55, 255nn71–72;
on transnational black identity, 41–42, 46,
57; on U.S. expansionism, 41
Durban World Conference Against Racism,
230–231
Dussel, Enrique, 28, 251n16

Ecuador, 208, 230–231
Ecué-Yamba-Ó (Carpentier), 47
Edwards, Brent Hayes, 57
Eisenstein, Sergei, 266n83

Ellison, Ralph, 52
El Puente publisher, 175
El Sebai, Youssef, 75
Empire (Hardt and Negri), 96–97
The Empire Writes Back (Ashcroft, Griffith,
and Tiffin), 27, 206–207
English Free Cinema, 185–187
Enríquez Vega, Rafael, 211–212, 215*f*
En un barrio viejo (Guillén Landrián), 165
Esteves, Sandra María, 135
Estrada Lescaille, Ulises, 211
"The Ethics of Living Jim Crow" (Wright),
261n190
exploitation colonialism, 78
"The Export of Apartheid to Latin America,"
180–181

Fairey, Shepard, 83, 201–202, 214, 281n1
Fair Play for Cuba Committee (FPCC), 8,
80–81, 173, 254n48
faja negra, 52
Fanon, Frantz, 55–58; on black anti-
imperialism, 60–61; on black essentialist
representation (négritude), 55–58, 61, 63,
66, 153; on overdetermination from the
outside, 145; on violence, 66
Farrow, Kenyon, 296n112
FBI (Federal Bureau of Investigation):
COINTELPRO program of, 157, 160; Most
Wanted Terrorist List of, 160–161
Featherstone, Ralph, 93, 285n20
Feliú, Santiago, 277n107
Feltrinelli, Giangiacomo, 277n107
Feltrinelli Bookshop, 133, 205
feminism, 129–135. *See also* gender and
sexual politics
Fernández, Johanna, 157, 270n8, 272–273n18
Ferrer, Ada, 38, 40
Fifth Pan-African Congress, 55
First Congress of Black Writers and Artists of
1956, 60–61, 62, 65
First Latin American Communist Confer-
ence, 50–52
First National Conference on Education and
Culture, 132–134, 205
First Pan-African Congress, 41, 255nn71–72
First Spanish Methodist Church (NYC),
106–108, 116, 117*f*, 135, 152, 272–273n18
Fitzpatrick, Jim, 201

Fletcher, Robert, 285n20
Flores, Juan, 136, 139
Fonda, Jane, 107
Fontáñez, Gloria, 157
"The Fool on the Hill" (Beatles), 165, 197
Foraker Law of 1900, 273–274n32
"For Blacks in Cuba, the Revolution Hasn't
    Begun" (Zurbano), 161
Ford, James W., 257n127
Ford, Joudon Major, 21, 93
Forjans, Jesús, 103, 104f
Forman, James, 93
Fornet, Ambrosio, 132
Foster, John Bellamy, 295n81
Franqui, Carlos, 185
Freedomways (ed. S. Du Bois), 79
"Free Palestine" (Luciano), 120
Friedman, Milton, 205
"From East-West to North-South" (Sheppard
    and Nagar), 252n36
Fuera del juego (Padilla), 132, 187–188

Gaines, Korryn, 232
Galloway, Alexander R., 28, 219
García, Carlos "Chino," 270–272n13
García Espinosa, Julio, 83, 185, 289n91
García Márquez, Gabriel, 177
Garner, Eric, 232
Garvey, Marcus, 47
Garza, Alicia, 232
Gates, Henry Louis, Jr., 62
Gay and Lesbian Caucus, 130, 134
Gay Liberation Front, 130–131
gender and sexual politics, 15, 110, 128–135,
    205, 277n81
Gerassi, John, 265n60
Getino, Octavio, 83, 85, 216–217
Gibson, Richard, 80, 264n48, 289n86
Gilmore, Glenda, 43, 97–98, 182
Gilroy, Paul, 254n49
Giordani, Ángelo "Papo," 270–272n13
Giral, Sergio, 171, 285n21
Glad Day Press, 82
"Globalization and the South" (C. Thomas),
    252–253n36
globalized capitalism. See capitalist
    globalization
global justice movement. See alter-
    globalization movement; contemporary

solidarity politics; racial justice
    movements
Global South, 4, 6–8, 12–13, 31–37, 244–245;
    black internationalist thought in, 18; color-
    blind multiculturalist discourses in, 4, 18,
    206, 225–229; contemporary revitaliza-
    tion of tricontinentalism in, 17–18, 23–26,
    31–36, 164, 200–201, 219–240; horizontalist
    solidarity in, 6–8, 24, 31, 222, 244–245,
    248n11; metaphorical deterritorialized
    South of, 26, 32–33, 163–164, 254n44; original
    usage of, 32–33, 248n10, 252–253nn34–37;
    South African apartheid and, 163–164,
    180–182; Southern Cone of Latin America
    and, 16, 164, 181–182, 205–206; as transna-
    tional political imaginary, 33–36, 200–201,
    254n46; Tricontinental's roots in, 24–25,
    254n48; World Social Forum and, 222–227.
    See also contemporary solidarity politics
Gollazo, Oscar, 274n33
Gómez, José Miguel, 41
Gómez, Juan Gualberto, 39
Gómez, Juan Vicente, 53
Gómez, Sara, 166, 285n21
González, Ángelo, 270–272n13
González, Gloria, 119, 131–132
González, José Luis, 279n126
González, Juan, 116–118, 119, 129, 275n54
González, Rodolfo "Corky," 113
Good, Fred, 270–272n13
Gramsci, Antonio, 32, 51, 252n35
La Gran Zafra campaign, 188–189
Gray, Freddie, 232
Grazini, Mario, 51
Great Recession of 2008, 209–210
Greece, 208
Gregg, Melissa, 276n73
Grenada, 205–206
Grewal, David, 28, 219
Griffith, Gareth, 27
Gronbeck-Tedesco, John A., 9, 250n5,
    268–269n137, 287–288n57, 291n10
Group of 77, 60
Grupo Minorista, 54
Gualberto Gómez, Juan, 169–170
Guattari, Félix, 126, 248n9
Guerra, Lillian, 166, 169, 190, 289n93
Guerra Cabrera, Ángel, 212
Guerra Chiquita (Cuba), 38–39, 169

Montaner, Rita, 256n87
Montejo, Esteban, 170–181
Moore, Carlos, 173–174, 267–268n119, 285n20
Moore, Darnell L., 232–233
Moore, Richard B., 49
Moore, Robin, 256n87
Morales, Evo, 208–209, 230, 292nn32–33
Morales, Iris, 123–124, 270–272n13
Morejón, Nancy, 166, 172, 285n20, 287n39
Morgan, Marcyliena M., 281n172
Morúa Delgado, Martín, 39, 41, 169–170
Mothers of May movement, 297n144
Movement for Black Lives, 234. *See also*
 Black Lives Matter
Movimiento 26 de julio, 112, 184, 193, 289n88
Movimiento Black Power, 174–175
Movimiento Liberación Nacional, 174
El movimiento Panteras Negras (Álvarez), 70, 84, 102–103
"Mujer negra" (Morejón), 172, 287n39
multiculturalist color-blind discourse, 2–4; in the alter-globalization movement, 31, 201, 203–204, 225–229, 235, 240, 296n112; of capitalist globalization, 4, 18, 29–34, 202–204, 206, 225–229, 240, 251n28; racialized privilege in, 30–31
Mundo obrero newspaper, 53–54
Murray, George, 21, 93

Nagar, Richa, 252n35
Namibia, 179
Nasser, Gamal Abdel, 59, 62, 73
National Association for the Advancement of Colored People (NAACP), 80, 89–90, 131, 227, 231
National Council of La Raza, 227
National Indian Youth Council, 114, 277n81
Nationalist Party (Puerto Rico), 274n33
National Liberation Front of Angola, 176
National Union for the Total Independence of Angola (UNITA), 176, 179
Nation of Islam, 148, 157
Navarro, Desiderio, 161–162, 188
Neblett, Chico, 285n20
Negri, Antonio: on the activism of the multitude, 5, 29, 96–97, 102, 127, 220; on a contemporary networked political imaginary, 208, 219–220; on neoliberal

color-blind multiculturalism, 251n28; on Third Worldism, 207–208
negrismo/négritude/New Negro movement, 12–13, 24–25, 35–36, 43–67, 256n87; in Cuba, 45–46, 164, 175, 256n87, 272n199, 283n1; essentialist representations in, 55–57, 153, 176, 259n141, 260n149, 260n152; internationalist visions in, 56–57; Nuyorican movement and, 137–138, 150–156, 272n199. *See also* afrocriollo movement; black internationalism and the black Atlantic
negrito figures, 151–154, 282n199
El negro: Ciudadano del futuro (Betancourt), 285n17
"El negro americano mira hacia Cuba" (Gibson), 80
Negro Commission of the Comintern, 48–49
Negroes with Guns (Williams), 89
"The Negro Problem" (Du Bois), 42
"Los Negros en U.S.A.," 80
The Negro Worker publication, 257n127
Nehru, Jawaharlal, 59, 62, 63
neocolonialism, 292n22
neoliberalism: Bamako Appeal's response to, 223–225; economic policies of, 28, 205–206, 209–210, 225–226, 236; free trade agreements of, 158, 208, 217; IMF structural readjustment programs of, 226; mass migrations and racism under, 236–237
neoliberal multiculturalism. *See* multiculturalist color-blind discourse
Neto, Agostino, 178
network power theory, 25–31, 251n16, 251n21; on lateral networks of resistance, 26, 28–29, 31, 219; on racial inequality, 29–31; on resistance from within, 26, 219–222, 294n66; on state power, 26, 28–29
New Global South, 17–18, 24, 26, 31–36, 200–201, 219–240. *See also* contemporary solidarity politics; Global South
New Latin American Cinema, 216–217. *See also* Cuban Film Institute; Third Cinema movement
New Negro movement, 12–13
Newsreel collective, 10, 81–84, 184; distribution of *Now* by, 108; *El pueblo se levanta* by, 107–108, 116, 121–122
Newton, Huey P., 8, 93, 102, 254n48, 265n51

137–150, 155, 279nn130–131, 280nn138–139, 281n172, 281n177; fame of, 137; resistance to labels of, 138, 278n111, 278n120; *Seven Long Times* of, 140

Tiffin, Helen, 27

"To Ferguson///Witness" (Agnew), 239

Tolliver, Cedric, 5

Tolliver, Julie, 5

Tometi, Opal, 232, 235–238

Torresola, Griselio, 274n33

"Towards a Third Cinema" (Getino and Solanas), 216–217

Towards the First Tricontinental, 84

trans-affective solidarity, 3–4, 10–11, 14, 109–110, 116–159; the affective turn and, 126–128, 276n73, 276n79; in contemporary solidarity politics, 128, 200–201, 235–245; forging collectivity in, 11, 109; gender and sexual politics in, 110, 128–135, 156, 277n81, 283n216; immigrants' rights activism and, 235–237; linguistic politics of, 141–150, 279nn130–131, 281n172, 281n177; in Nuyorican writings, 134–156, 278n111; in racial justice movements, 235–245; visual depictions of, 116–126; in Young Lords' political vision, 119–126, 131–134, 275n54. *See also* contemporary solidarity politics; Nuyorican movement; Young Lords Party

"Transatlanticism and Tricontinentalism" (Pitman and Stafford), 8–9, 249n17

transformational solidarity, 128, 201, 235–238

"Trayvon Martin" portrait (Fairey), 214

the Tricontinental, 1–18; anti-essentialism of, 8–9, 57–58, 63–67, 70, 99–105, 118, 176, 260n152; in the Cold War era, 1–10, 225; contemporary relevance of, 1–5, 17–18, 23, 25–36, 200–245; critical scholarship on, 8, 249n17; Cuban leadership of, 71–73; Cuba's dissonant role in, 11–12, 15–17, 24, 42, 66, 81, 110, 162–164, 176, 199, 249n22, 250n5, 269n138, 287–288n57, 293n41; cultural production of, 3–4, 7–18, 23–24, 67, 81–84, 163, 180–184, 210, 249n17, 249n22; deterritorialized notion of empire in, 4, 12, 14, 22, 35–36, 79–80, 96–99, 134, 162–164, 199, 219–222; erasure and revival of, 204–207; expansion of Bandung in, 13, 22–23, 25, 34–35, 223, 243, 247n7, 250n5; formation of, 3, 9, 21–23, 65–66, 71–77, 247n7; gender

and sexuality policies of, 129–135, 205; goals of, 72–75; horizontalism of, 225, 244–245; inclusive resistant subjectivity of, 11–12, 24–25, 206–207, 224; inconsistencies and shortcomings of, 5, 101–105; Jim Crow South as microcosm of empire in, 4, 13–15, 21–22, 23, 35, 70–71, 78–79, 97–98, 111; linking of imperialism and racial oppression in, 3, 21–25, 68–71, 77–81, 99–105, 241–245, 264n43; Maoist thought in, 77–78, 99–100; metonymic color politics of, 4, 13–14, 18, 22, 25, 35, 65, 70, 79, 99–105, 118, 201, 204, 207, 268–269n137; on militant resistance, 66, 74–75; roots of, 12–13, 24–25, 36–67, 254n48; South African apartheid and, 163–164, 179–183, 212; trans-affective solidarity vision of, 3–4, 10–11, 14, 109–110, 116–159, 235–245; transnational political imaginary of, 5–10, 34–36, 180, 200–201, 221–222, 241–245, 248nn9–11; U.S. civil rights movement and, 70–71, 78–105, 108, 116, 264n43; U.S. Third World Left and, 112–115. *See also* Havana Tricontinental Conference of 1966; Organization of Solidarity with the Peoples of Africa, Asia and Latin America

Tricontinental Bulletin, 13, 66, 81–84, 184; contents of, 82, 265n60; cover art of, 68–70, 103; editors and writers of, 267–268n119; fake advertisements in, 217; on gender and sexuality policies, 131–132; linking of imperialism and racial oppression in, 70–71, 99–101; on OSPAAAL goals, 72–73; on U.S. civil rights movement, 70–71, 93–99, 264n43; Young Lords' works in, 14–15, 110, 119–121, 131, 134, 274–275n43

Tricontinental (magazine), 13, 81–84, 183–184; on apartheid, 180; contemporary content of, 211–213; cover art of, 19–21, 133, 277n107; electronic publication of, 210; fake advertisements in, 217–218; on gender and sexuality policies, 131–133, 205; international distribution of, 133, 205, 277n107; linking of imperialism and racial oppression in, 21–22, 70–71; multilingual posters of, 81, 82, 83, 265n57; North American edition of, 83; U.S. civil rights movement in, 70–71, 93, 97, 98f, 267n102; Young Lords' works in, 119